©   Pubished by Verlag Zabert Sandmann
Munich
2nd Edition

Graphics	Georg Feigl
Food photography	Susie Eising
	(see PHOTOGRAPHY at end of INDEX for
	reference to other photography)
Recipes	Michael Koch
Editiorial	Edelgard Prinz-Korte, Martin Kintrup,
	Alexandra Schlinz, Eva-Maria Hege
Production	Karin Mayer, Peter Karg-Cordes
Lithography	MM Intec GmbH, Miesbach
Printer	Mohn media Mohndruck GmbH, Gütersloh
English	Translation Dept. and Training Kitchen, Miele UK

This book is the result of a joint project between the publisher,
Verlag Zabert Sandmann (www.zsverlag.de) and the Miele Company (www.miele.de).

BAKING, ROASTING AND COOKING

with the Miele oven

Contents

Dear Reader,

An oven that can roast, bake and cook to perfection? Why not! Miele ovens are well suited to the needs of the modern kitchen, extremely easy to use and produce perfect results. Now every household can enjoy high quality, modern appliances which offer the enthusiastic cook the opportunity of creating dishes like a true professional. And to make it all the easier, this book has over 140 recipes which not only encompass the entire spectrum of oven functions, they are also unusual and interesting, allowing you to introduce variety to every day meals. Whether you are creating light appetisers or a full roast dinner, a pasta bake for the family meal or an exotic dish for dinner guests, these recipes will turn cooking into a real pleasure. You will be amazed and enthused by these subtle and sophisticated dishes, be they influenced by the Mediterranean, a recreation of a traditional favourite, or inspired by the Orient. And most importantly, because you can rely on the oven for perfect results, you can relax and enjoy the whole cooking experience.

The multi-talented

oven

At the heart of the kitchen

Today, modern ovens can do much, much more than simply produce heat. They are so cleverly designed that for every type of food there will be just the right oven function to prepare it in the best way. For after all, the art of cooking is all about understanding the different characteristics of each type of food and knowing how to develop flavours to the full. The ideal oven will be capable of everything: baking, roasting, cooking and grilling – to perfection.

We recommend using the **Fan plus** function for baking and roasting on several levels at the same time. A lower temperature can be selected than for **Conventional** heat as the heat is distributed around the food by the fan. Select **Bottom heat** towards the end of the cooking time, for example to finish off pastry bases. **Intensive bake** is ideal for dishes which require a moist topping and a crisp base, such as pizza. Select **Economy grill** for grilling flat items and browning the tops of small dishes. The **Full grill** is more suited for browning large dishes and grilling bigger items. The **Fan grill** is excellent for mixed grills and chicken pieces. To avoid having to seal large pieces of meat on the hob, simply select **Auto roast** and at the outset select the temperature you want the meat cooked at. The oven will then do the rest. **Moisture plus** will produce optimum results when cooking not only bread and cakes, but also roasts, baked dishes and pizzas as moisture is used in addition to Fan plus. Food will be moist and tender on the inside and crispy on the outside. All recipes in this book which use the Moisture plus function are marked with the [⌀Ⅲ] symbol. On ovens without the Moisture plus function, select **Fan plus.**

The display is exceptionally easy to use and is highly intuitive.

Cooking with ease: The shelf levels are clearly marked on the front of the oven cavity.

Precise roasting: The food probe measures the core temperature.

Individually cooked for perfect enjoyment

The food probe monitors the temperature of the cooking process precisely by measuring the core temperature of meat, poultry or fish, and allows you to determine precisely how well done or rare you want your food to be cooked. For example, beef fillet and roast beef will be cooked rare at a core temperature of 60–65°C, medium at a core temperature of 70–75°C and well done at a core temperature of 80–85°C. Boned and rolled poultry, on the other hand, will require a core temperature of 85 to 90°C. It is important to ensure that the tip of the probe is not inserted into fat or bone.

The correct shelf level

The number of shelves varies from oven to oven. The recipes in this book are designed for an oven with five shelf levels. The shelf levels are counted from the bottom of the oven upwards. The table below will tell you which level to use if your oven does not have five shelf levels.

Ovens with 5 shelf levels		Ovens with 3 shelf levels
5th shelf from the bottom	‹········›	2nd or 3rd shelf from the bottom
4th shelf from the bottom	‹········›	2nd or 3rd shelf from the bottom
3rd shelf from the bottom	‹········›	1st or 2nd shelf from the bottom
2nd shelf from the bottom	‹········›	1st or 2nd shelf from the bottom
1st shelf from the bottom	‹········›	1st shelf from the bottom

Perfect results

every time

The clear display, the retractable controls with their lightrings, and the sensors controls make it easy to select the correct setting.

The Moisture plus function allows you to bake and roast using a combination of Fan plus and moisture. It is ideal for all types of bread and rolls as a crispy, glossy finish is achieved. You will be able to produce biscuits, cakes and pastries which are every bit as good as you could buy from the local baker. It is not only baked items which benefit from moisture. Fish will be tender and moist and maintain a firm consistency. When roasting meat with a high fat content, the hot steam draws out the fat and an excellent outer crust is produced.

Rolls baked in an oven containing moisture are light and cooked to perfection on the inside, with a good crust on the outside.

The filling tube is pulled forward and the quantity of water required is drawn in automatically.

Easy to use

When you select Moisture plus, you can choose between 4 different bursts of steam (Automatic burst of steam; or 1, 2 or 3 manual bursts of steam). The amount of water the oven requires will depend on the selection. For 1 burst of steam, fill a glass with approx. 80 ml of water, hold under the filling tube and allow the water to be drawn into the oven. Approx. 150 ml water is required for 2 bursts of steam and approx. 230 ml for 3 bursts of steam. If the automatic choice has been selected, the burst of steam will be injected automatically when the required temperature has been reached. With 1, 2 or 3 bursts of steam, these have to be injected manually, allowing you to individually perfect the cooking or baking process.

Bread should be exposed to steam in the first few minutes as it will rise better and will achieve a good outer crust while remaining light and soft on the inside. Meat should be roasted in an open dish or directly on the rack so that it can absorb the steam.

The great advantage of Moisture plus is that food does not dry out – it will be soft and succulent, but still with a crispy outer crust.

Starters

Gone are the days when you could dazzle your
guests with a cold starter of charcuterie, salad or
crudités. Tasty appetisers straight from the oven
require very little preparation and are guaran-
teed to be a successful culinary surprise. Earn
praise and applause with crispy tuna rolls, pizza
with fennel salami or apple tartlets with chicken
liver. These delicacies are also ideal for a light
lunch.

Carrot quiche
with lemon grass and coriander

Makes 1 quiche (26 cm Ø)

Ingredients:

For the pastry:
300 g plain flour
Salt
160 g cold butter, diced
1 medium egg

For the filling:
3 stems of lemon grass
200 ml double cream
1 kg carrots · Salt
100 g crème fraîche
4 large eggs
Ground pepper

Also:
Butter for greasing the dish
1 bunch of coriander
2 apples (Braeburn or
Cox's Orange Pippin)
2 red chillis
Salt · Ground pepper
Olive oil

1 To make the pastry, make a pile of the flour and sprinkle with 1 tsp of salt. Add the diced butter and work in well using a knife. Beat the egg lightly, add to the flour mixture and knead in. Add 2 tbsp of cold water and knead quickly to a dough. Wrap the dough in clingfilm and place in the fridge for 30 minutes.

2 For the filling, wash the lemon grass and strip off the tough outer leaves. Pat dry and chop finely. Place in a saucepan with the double cream, bring gently to the boil. Remove from the heat and leave to stand, covered, for 15 minutes. Peel the carrots, cut into thin slices and boil in salted water for 6 to 8 minutes until cooked but still firm. Pour the cream through a sieve, then stir in the crème fraîche and eggs. Season with salt and pepper.

3 Roll the pastry out to a thickness of 3 to 4 mm. Grease the quiche dish with butter. Line with the pastry, pressing it well into the edges.

4 Spread the carrots out over the pastry and pour the egg and cream mixture over. Bake the quiche at 160°C (Intensive bake) on the second shelf for 40 to 45 minutes. Remove from the oven, leave to cool slightly, then remove from the dish.

5 To make the garnish, wash the coriander, shake dry and tear off the leaves. Wash and core the apples, and either cut them into thin strips or grate them. Cut the chillis in half lengthways, remove the seeds and chop into thin strips. Mix the ingredients lightly together and season with salt, pepper and olive oil. Cut the quiche into slices and serve topped with a little of the garnish.

▶▶ Tips

For extra bite, add chopped salted peanuts to the garnish. The pastry can be prepared well in advance. Wrapped in clingfilm, it will remain fresh in the fridge for up to a week.

Savoury apple tartlets
with chicken liver and rocket

For 4 tartlets (12 cm Ø) or 1 tart (24 cm Ø)

1   To make the tartlets, defrost the puff pastry. Peel and core the apples and cut into slices. Peel the onion and garlic. Cut the onion into slices and finely chop the garlic. Wash the marjoram, shake it dry, tear off the leaves and chop them finely.

2   Heat the olive oil in a frying pan and sweat the onions until cooked but not brown. Add the lardons and garlic, and cook. Add the apple slices and continue cooking, then stir in the marjoram. Season with sea salt, pepper and sugar. Put the mixture to one side.

3   Fold the sheets of puff pastry in half and roll out thinly on a floured surface. Cut to fit the size of the tartlet tins. To make one large tart, place the sheets of pastry on top of each other and roll out to the appropriate size.

4   Divide the apple mixture between the tins and cover with the puff pastry. Chill the tarts in the fridge for 10 minutes.

Ingredients:

For the tartlets:
4 sheets of puff pastry
(approx. 75 g each; frozen)
2 sharp apples
(eg, Granny Smith, russet)
1 onion
1 clove of garlic
1/2 bunch of marjoram
1 tbsp olive oil
50 g lardons, or chopped
smoked streaky bacon
Sea salt · Ground pepper
Sugar
Also:
200 g chicken (or duck) liver
1 tbsp olive oil
Sea salt · Ground pepper
2 sprigs of rosemary
1 tbsp sugar
3 tbsp balsamic vinegar
3 tbsp apple juice
2 small bunches of rocket

5   Bake the tarts at 180°C (Moisture plus with 1 automatic burst of steam) on the second shelf for 30 to 35 minutes for the large tart or 15 to 20 minutes for the tartlets.

6   Cut the liver into walnut sized pieces. Heat the olive oil in a frying pan and fry the liver for 3 to 4 minutes. Remove from the frying pan, season with sea salt and pepper, and keep warm.

7   Wash the rosemary and shake it dry. Place the sugar, balsamic vinegar, apple juice and rosemary in the hot frying pan used to cook the liver. Bring gently to the boil and remove the rosemary.

8   Wash and dry the rocket and divide between the serving plates. Turn the tartlets out of their tins and arrange on the beds of rocket. If making one large tart, cut it into four. Top with the liver and drizzle with a little balsamic sauce.

Baked figs
with mascarpone and San Daniele ham

Serves 4–6

1 Beat together the mascarpone, honey, thyme and orange zest, and season with salt and pepper.

2 Wash the figs, and pat them dry. Cut a lid approx. 1 cm thick from the top of each fig. Scoop out about a teaspoon of the flesh from inside each fig to make room for the filling.

3 Fill the figs with the mascarpone cream, place the lids on top and press down lightly. Wrap each fig in a slice of ham.

Ingredients:

250 g mascarpone
1 tbsp honey
1 tbsp chopped thyme
1 tsp orange zest
Salt · Ground pepper
12 medium sized figs
12 slices San Daniele ham,
or prosciutto
12 slices French bread
Olive oil for greasing the dish
and drizzling

4 Spread the fig flesh on the slices of French bread. Grease a baking dish with olive oil and arrange the bread in the dish. Place a fig on each slice and press down slightly. Drizzle with olive oil and bake at 160°C (Fan plus) on the second shelf for 20 to 25 minutes.

▸▸ Tips

San Daniele ham is air dried ham from Italy. If you can't find it, use Parma ham instead. Or omit all together for a vegetarian alternative.

Grilled vegetables and mozzarella
baked in panini

For 10 panini

Ingredients:

For the dough:

500 g strong bread flour

20 g fresh yeast

1 tbsp honey

1 level tbsp sea salt

3 tbsp olive oil

For the vegetables:

1 onion

1 large eggplant/aubergine

2 zucchini/courgettes

2 red peppers

1 clove of garlic

1/2 bunch of thyme

80 ml olive oil

Sea salt

Ground pepper

Also:

2 balls of mozzarella
(125 g each)

Flour for the baking tray and
for dusting

1   To make the dough, place the flour in a bowl and make a well in the centre. Crumble the yeast and dissolve in 300 ml of lukewarm water. Stir in the honey and pour the mixture into the well in the flour. Stir the flour in from the edge to make a thin dough. Cover the bowl with a damp tea towel and leave the dough to rise for 15 minutes in a warm place. Stir in the salt and olive oil and knead the dough for 5 minutes using the kneading hook of an electric mixer until it is shiny. Cover again and leave in a warm place for 45 minutes to rise.

2   Peel the onion. Wash the aubergine and courgettes. Chop all three vegetables into 1 cm thick slices. Place in an ovenproof dish. Cut the peppers into quarters and remove the seeds. Add to the dish. Crush the garlic. Wash the thyme, shake dry and tear off the leaves. Add the garlic and thyme to the dish along with the olive oil. Season with sea salt and pepper, and leave to stand for 20 minutes.

3   Grill the vegetables at 220°C (Full grill) on the third shelf for 15 to 20 minutes, turning halfway through. Remove the skins from the red peppers. Stir the vegetables.

4   Knead the dough briefly once more and divide into 10 pieces. Roll out on a floured surface into squares 14 x 14 cm. Place the vegetables on one half of each piece. Pat the mozzarellas dry and cut into 10 slices. Place on top of the vegetables. Fold the dough over the filling and press the edges firmly together. Place the panini on the floured baking tray and leave for 15 minutes.

5   Dust the panini with flour and bake at 200°C (Moisture plus with 1 automatic burst of steam) on the second shelf for 15 to 18 minutes. Cool the panini slightly and serve with pesto (see Tips).

▶▶ Tips

The panini are delicious served with lovage pesto. In a food processor, purée the leaves of half a bunch of lovage and 1 bunch of parsley with 100 ml olive oil, 1 tbsp grated parmesan and 1 tbsp roasted pine nuts.

Braised celeriac
with ginger and prawn kebabs

Serves 4–6

1   Peel the ginger and cut into thin strips. Heat the oil in a frying pan. Fry the ginger for 2 minutes, stir in the honey and place to one side.

2   Peel and cut the celeriac into 1½ cm cubes and mix with the ginger and honey. Season with salt and pepper and place in an ovenproof dish. Drizzle with olive oil and cook at 160°C (Fan plus) on the second shelf for 40 minutes. Wash and dry the basil and tear off the leaves. Put a few to one side as garnish. 10 minutes before the end of the cooking time, stir the basil into the celeriac.

3   Peel the prawns, make a cut along the length of each one and remove the black vein. Wash the prawns and pat them dry. Bend the prawns, and place in pairs on wooden skewers.

Ingredients:

150 g ginger
1 tbsp oil
1 tbsp honey
1 bulb of celeriac
(approx. 1 kg)
Salt · Freshly ground pepper
2–3 tbsp olive oil
1 bunch of Thai or normal basil
12 jumbo prawns
1 clove of garlic
1–2 red chillis
3 shallots
Juice of 1 lime
1 tbsp palm sugar
2 unwaxed limes

4   To make the marinade, peel the garlic. Wash, deseed and finely chop the chillis. Peel and finely chop the shallots. Pound the garlic, chillis and shallots together with the lime juice and palm sugar using a pestle and mortar, or purée in a food processor. Arrange the prawns on a baking tray and brush with the marinade. Grill at 240°C (Full grill) on the third or fourth shelf for 5 to 8 minutes.

5   Wash the limes in hot water, pat dry and cut into quarters. Arrange two prawn kebabs on a bed of braised celeriac on individual serving plates, and garnish with basil leaves and lime wedges.

▸▸ Tips

The braised celeriac can be prepared a day in advance and heated up shortly before serving. If palm sugar is not available, use unrefined sugar.

Tortilla
with smoked trout and cress

Serves 4–6

1 Cut the potatoes into thin slices. Flake the smoked trout into small pieces. Beat the eggs into the crème fraîche. Stir in the horseradish and lemon zest.

2 Place the sliced potatoes and smoked trout into a large bowl and stir in the egg mixture. Season with salt and pepper. Butter an oven-proof dish, pour in the potato mixture and press down.

3 Bake the tortilla at 140°C (Moisture plus with 1 automatic burst of steam) on the second shelf for 25 to 30 minutes. Leave the tortilla to cool until lukewarm.

Ingredients:

600 g boiled waxy potatoes
(can be peeled and boiled the previous day)
200 g smoked trout fillet
(plus 1 fillet for garnish)
5 medium eggs
50 g crème fraîche
1 tbsp grated horseradish
1 tsp unwaxed lemon zest
Salt · Ground pepper
Butter for greasing the dish
1 container of mustard cress
1 bunch of watercress
1 bunch of rocket
2 tbsp white balsamic vinegar
1 tsp honey
2 tbsp olive oil

4 Wash and dry the cress and rocket, and mix together. Whisk the balsamic vinegar, honey and 2 tbsp of olive oil together and use to dress the leaves.

5 To serve, cut the tortilla into cubes and scatter over the salad. Garnish with flakes of the remaining trout fillet.

▸▸ Tips

You can make a crisp little dish on which to serve the tortilla by deep frying a piece of spring roll pastry (12 x 12 cm), pressing it down lightly with a spoon.

Crispy tuna
rolls with mango chutney

Serves 4–6

Ingredients:

For the tuna fish:

2 sheets spring roll pastry
(20 x 20 cm; defrosted if
frozen)
2 tuna steaks (each 200 g,
6 cm thick)
Coarsely ground pepper
Salt
1 tbsp oil
120 g chicken breast
150 ml double cream
1 tsp sesame oil
1/2 tsp wasabi paste
(from a tube)
40 g sesame seeds

For the chutney:

1 small red pepper
1 mango
2 spring onions
1 bunch of coriander
1 pinch ground coriander
1 pinch ground cinnamon
Salt · Ground pepper
1–2 tbsp rice vinegar or white
balsamic vinegar

Also:

Oil for frying

1 To make the chutney, halve and deseed the red pepper and roast at 160°C (Fan plus) on the second shelf for 30 to 35 minutes. Allow to cool then remove the skin and chop the pepper in small pieces.

2 Peel the mango, cut the flesh away from stone and dice it into 1/2 cm cubes. Wash the spring onions and slice finely. Wash the coriander, shake it dry and chop. Mix everything together along with the ground coriander, cinnamon, salt, pepper and vinegar.

3 To make the tuna rolls, season the tuna well with salt and coarsely ground pepper. Fry in hot oil for 1 minute.

4 Wash and dry the chicken breast and cut into small pieces. Purée in a food processor with the cream, sesame oil, wasabi and a pinch of salt. Dry roast the sesame seeds in a frying pan and stir into the purée.

5 Place the sheets of pastry side by side and spread the chicken purée thinly over two thirds of the pastry surface. Place the tuna fillets on the remaining pastry surface and fold the pastry over them, tucking the ends underneath.

6 Pour 1 cm of oil into a frying pan, heat and fry the pastry rolls for 2 to 3 minutes until crisp. Place them on an oven rack and finish cooking at 85°C (Fan plus) on the second shelf for 15 to 20 minutes.

7 Using a serrated knife, cut the pastry rolls into 1 to 2 cm thick slices and serve with the mango chutney.

▶▶ Tips

The ingredients for the chicken purée need to be very cold, as the act of puréeing them will warm them up and prevent them from binding well. For best results, place the meat in the freezer for a few minutes.

Savoury tarte
with onions and bacon

For 2 baking trays 🔥

1 To make the dough, place the flour in a large bowl and make a well in the centre. Dissolve the yeast in 90 ml of lukewarm water. Stir in the sugar and salt and pour the mixture into the well in the flour. Stir in the flour from the edges to achieve a thin dough. Stir in the liquid sour dough and cover the bowl with a damp cloth. Leave the dough to rise in a warm place for 15 minutes.

2 Knead the dough for 5 minutes using the kneading hook of an electric mixer until it is shiny and elastic. Cover once more and leave to rise in a warm place for a further 45 minutes.

3 For the topping, peel and halve the onions and cut into thin slices. Stir the soured cream and double cream together.

4 Knead the dough again and divide into two. On a floured surface, roll out to the size of the baking trays. Place the dough onto the baking trays lined with baking paper. Spread the cream mixture over the dough.

Ingredients:

For the base:
250 g strong white flour
20 g fresh yeast
$1/2$ tsp sugar
salt
75 g liquid sour dough (ready made)

For the topping:
3 onions
200 ml soured cream
100 ml double cream
50 g pine nuts
60 g pancetta or smoked streaky bacon (very thinly sliced)
Ground pepper
2–3 tbsp olive oil

For the herb salt:
25 g sea salt
$1/2$ tsp fennel seeds
$1/2$ tsp chopped rosemary
$1/2$ tsp unwaxed lemon zest

Also:
Flour for the work surface

5 Scatter over the onions and pine nuts. Place the pancetta or bacon on top. Season with ground pepper and drizzle with olive oil. Leave to rise for 10 minutes.

6 Pre-heat the oven to 220°C (Moisture plus with 1 manual burst of steam). Place one tarte into the oven on the second shelf. Activate the steam and bake for 10 to 15 minutes. Repeat with the second tarte (without pre-heating the oven).

7 To make the herb salt, grind the sea salt, fennel seeds, rosemary and lemon zest with a pestle and mortar (or in a mixer) and sprinkle over the baked tarte.

▶▶ Tips

Flammkuchen is a traditional savoury tarte made with onions, bacon and soured cream. For a delicious alternative, use roasted aubergines, courgettes or red peppers and top with mozzarella.

Pizza
with fennel salami and scamorza

For 1 baking tray

1 To make the dough, place the flour in a large bowl and make a well in the centre. Dissolve the yeast with a pinch of sugar in 125 ml of lukewarm water. Pour into the well in the flour. Stir in the flour from the edges to achieve a thin dough. Cover the bowl with a damp cloth. Leave the dough to rise in a warm place for 15 minutes.

2 Stir in the salt and olive oil and knead the dough for 10 minutes until it is shiny and elastic. Cover the dough again and leave in a warm place to rise for a further 45 minutes. Knead again, then roll out on a floured surface until 1 cm thick and the size of the baking tray. Dust the baking tray with flour and place the dough on top.

3 To make the topping, peel and finely chop the onions and garlic, then fry gently in a little olive oil. Add the passata, bring to the boil and season with salt and pepper. Wash and dry the oregano, tear off the leaves and chop finely. Stir into the passata.

Ingredients:

For the dough:
250 g strong white flour
15 g fresh yeast · Sugar
1 tsp salt
5 tbsp olive oil

For the topping:
1 onion· 1 clove of garlic
Approx. 6 tbsp olive oil
250 g passata
(ready made)
Salt · Ground pepper
1 bunch of oregano
250 g cherry tomatoes
2 scamorza (250 g;
Italian smoked cheese)
or mozzarella
50 g capers (pickled)
Sea salt
150 g fennel salami
(sliced)
Also:
Flour for the work surface and
baking tray

4 Wash the cherry tomatoes and crush with your hands. Discard the juice. Cut the scamorza in half, cut into thin slices and mix with the cherry tomatoes and capers. Season with sea salt, pepper and 3 tbsp olive oil.

5 Spread the tomato sauce over the dough and scatter the cherry tomato and cheese mixture over the top.

6 Pre-heat the oven to 220°C (Moisture plus with 1 manual burst of steam). Place the pizza on the second shelf, activate the steam and bake for 25 to 30 minutes. Spread the salami over the cooked pizza and drizzle with olive oil.

▸▸ Tips

The dough for this pizza is very thin and will serve 3 to 4 people as a starter.

Rare veal fillet
with creamed pumpkin and spinach

Serves 4–6

1 Place the filo pastry on a greased baking tray and brush with melted butter. Sprinkle with a little sea salt and chilli powder and bake at 200°C (Fan plus) on the second shelf for 5 to 8 minutes until golden. Leave to cool, then break into small pieces. Allow the oven to cool down.

2 Heat some olive oil in a frying pan. Season the veal fillet with salt and pepper, and brown all over in the olive oil. Mix the cocoa and chilli powder and coat the meat in the mixture. Roast the meat on a wire rack at 85°C (Conventional) on the third shelf for 1 hour. The core temperature should reach 60 to 65°C (using the food probe).

3 Peel the pumpkin, cut the flesh into small cubes and fry gently in butter. Add the coconut milk and simmer for 10 minutes. Purée in a food processor and season with salt, pepper and lime juice.

Ingredients:

For the pastry:
100 g filo pastry (ready made)
50 g melted butter
Sea salt · chilli powder

For the meat:
350 g fillet of veal (7 cm thick)
Salt · Ground pepper
1 tbsp olive oil
1 tsp cocoa powder
1 pinch chilli powder
1 tbsp butter

For the creamed pumpkin:
250 g pumpkin
1 tsp butter
200 ml coconut milk
Salt · Ground pepper
Juice of 1/2 lime

For the garnish:
200 g baby spinach leaves
2 tbsp olive oil
1 tbsp white balsamic vinegar
1 tsp honey

Also:
Butter to grease the baking tray

4 To make the garnish, wash and dry the spinach leaves. Mix together the olive oil, vinegar and honey, and use to dress the spinach.

5 Once the veal is cooked, toss it in foaming butter, then cut into thin slices. Spoon some of the creamed pumpkin onto individual serving plates and top with alternating layers of veal, filo pastry and spinach.

▶▶ Tips

There are several types of pumpkin. Their flesh is orange and has a sweet, nutty flavour.

Fish and seafood

If you want to serve something really special, then seafood is often the answer. But even in everyday cooking, fish is becoming more and more popular. To help it retain its wonderful flavour during cooking, try wrapping it in a salt crust, pastry, ham or baking parchment. You will never have eaten tastier, healthier fish!

Crispy prawn strudel
with tomato salad and basil aioli

Serves 4–6

Ingredients:

For the strudel:
80 g bacon (rashers) · 1 tbsp oil
400 g peeled, cooked prawns
Salt · Freshly ground pepper
2 pinches chilli powder
300 g white fish fillet
(eg. haddock, ling, perch, cod)
Ground pepper
350 ml ice-cold double cream
Lemon juice
4 sheets of filo pastry
(25 x 25 cm; ready made)
50 g melted butter

For the aioli:
1 clove of garlic · Salt
1 bunch of basil
200 ml olive oil
1 egg yolk · 1 tsp mustard
Juice of 1/2 lemon
Ground pepper

For the salad:
500 g cherry tomatoes
1 bunch of parsley
1 red onion
2 tbsp olive oil
1 tbsp caster sugar
2 tbsp white balsamic vinegar
Salt · Ground pepper

1   To make the strudel, fry the bacon in oil until crispy, then pat dry with kitchen paper. Wash and dry the prawns, and chop finely. Season with salt, pepper and chilli powder. Wash and dry the fish, and cut into small cubes. Season with salt and pepper. Briefly whiz the fish with 150 g of the ice-cold cream in a food processor, then add the rest of the cream and a squeeze of lemon, and blend to a fine purée. Pour the mixture into a bowl, crumble in the bacon and stir in the prawns. Chill the mixture in the refrigerator.

2   Spread out two sheets of filo pastry, brush with melted butter, then place the other two sheets of pastry on top. Spread the prawn filling over the pastry, fold in the edges, then roll the pastry up. Place the rolls on a baking tray lined with baking paper and brush with melted butter. Bake at 180°C (Fan plus) on the second shelf for 20 to 25 minutes.

3   For the aioli, peel and chop the garlic. Add a pinch of salt and crush using the back of a knife. Wash and dry the basil, and remove the leaves. Purée with the olive oil. Stir the egg yolk and mustard together in a bowl. Add the basil oil, a drop at a time, whisking continuously. Once the ingredients have started to blend, the oil can be added more quickly. Stir in the garlic purée and lemon juice, and season with salt and pepper.

4   To make the salad, wash and halve the cherry tomatoes. Wash, dry and chop the parsley. Peel the onions and cut into thin slices. Fry gently in olive oil. Add the tomatoes and parsley and cook gently for a further 2 to 3 minutes. Add the sugar and vinegar and transfer to a bowl. Season with salt and pepper.

5   Slice the strudels using a serrated knife and serve with the tomato salad and aioli.

Sea bream in a sea salt crust
with lime and caper butter

Serves 4

Ingredients:

For the fish:
2 cloves of garlic
1 unwaxed lemon
Coarsely ground pepper
4 tbsp olive oil
2 sea bream (700 g each;
oven ready)
4 stalks of parsley
1 bunch each of rosemary
and thyme
2.5 kg coarse sea salt
6 egg whites
80 g flour

For the vegetables:
600 g waxy potatoes
Salt
8–10 small artichokes
4 tbsp olive oil
1 clove of garlic
6 sprigs of thyme
Ground pepper

For the butter:
2–3 limes
120 g butter
1 tsp caster sugar
2 tsp small capers
Salt · Ground pepper

1 For the fish, peel and finely chop the garlic. Wash and dry the lemon, and grate the rind. Squeeze the juice from the lemon. Mix the lemon zest and juice with the garlic, 1/2 tsp of pepper and the olive oil. Wash and dry the fish. Rub inside and out with the marinade.

2 Wash and dry the parsley, rosemary and thyme. Place the parsley inside the fish. Finely chop the rosemary and thyme leaves. Mix with the salt in a bowl. Beat the egg whites until half stiff and stir into the salt. Sprinkle the flour over it and stir well.

3 Line a baking tray with baking paper and spread out approximately half of the sea salt to a depth of 1 cm. Place the fish on top and cover all over with the remaining sea salt. Press down firmly. Bake the sea bream at 180°C (Fan plus) on the second shelf for 50 to 60 minutes.

4 For the vegetables, peel the potatoes and cut in 1/2 cm cubes. Blanch in salted water for 2 to 3 minutes, then plunge into ice cold water and dry with kitchen paper. Remove the outer leaves from the artichokes and cut the artichokes into four. Heat the olive oil in a pan and fry the artichokes. Add the potato cubes and fry for a further 5 minutes. Crush the garlic, and wash and dry the thyme. Add to the vegetables and season with salt and pepper. Transfer the vegetables to an ovenproof dish.

5 Place the vegetables in the oven on the fourth shelf 15 minutes before the end of the cooking time for the fish. Once cooked, remove the thyme sprigs.

6 To make the butter, peel the limes with a knife, removing all the pith. Divide into segments. Melt the butter until foaming in a pan. Stir in the lime segments, caster sugar and capers, and season with salt and pepper.

7 Serve the sea bream in the salt crust, breaking it open at table. Garnish with lime and caper butter and the vegetables.

Fillet of salmon trout
with almond polenta and asparagus

Serves 4

1 For the fish, dry roast 60 g of the almonds in a frying pan. Bring the milk to the boil with 1 teaspoon of butter and stir in the polenta. Add the lemon zest and almonds, and leave to stand for 5 minutes. Season with salt and pepper.

2 Wash and dry the fish fillets and season with salt and pepper. Place one fish fillet skin side down and cover with the polenta. Place the other fillet on top, skin side up. Tie together in 4 or 5 places using kitchen string.

3 Grease a baking tray with oil, place the fish on it and bake at 180°C (Moisture plus with 2 bursts of steam) on the second shelf for 25 to 30 minutes. Activate the first burst of steam at the beginning, and the second 10 minutes later.

4 Snap off the tough base of the asparagus stalks, then wash and pat dry. Heat the olive oil in an oven-proof pan, and cook the asparagus for 3 to 4 minutes.

Ingredients:

For the fish:
100 g flaked almonds
175 ml milk
2–3 tbsp butter
50 g instant polenta
1 tsp unwaxed lemon zest
Salt · Freshly ground pepper
2 salmon trout fillets (450 g)
Oil for the baking tray
1 bunch of parsley

For the asparagus:
1 kg green asparagus
400 g cherry tomatoes
2 tbsp olive oil
4 sprigs of rosemary
Juice of 1/2 lemon
1 tbsp butter · Salt
Ground pepper · Sugar

5 Wash and dry the rosemary and the tomatoes. Add the rosemary, tomatoes, lemon juice and butter to the asparagus. Season with salt, pepper and sugar. Place the pan in the oven on the fourth shelf 8 minutes before the end of the cooking time for the fish.

6 Wash, dry and chop the parsley. Melt 2 tbsp of butter until foaming and fry the remaining almonds and parsley. Spread over the fish 5 minutes before the end of the cooking time.

7 Cut the fish into pieces, and serve with the asparagus.

▶▶ Tips

To decorate, cut two unwaxed lemons in half and press the flesh into some sugar. Caramilize in a frying pan, sugared side down. Cool slightly, and serve with the fish.

Stuffed trout
with Tuscan bread salad

Serves 4 [♨]

1   To gut the fish, make a 1 cm deep cut with a sharp knife from the head to the stomach. Then carefully slice open the stomach. Cut through the spine at the head and tail and remove, along with the guts. Remove the remaining bones with a pair of tweezers. Alternatively, ask your fishmonger to prepare the fish in this way.

2   Wash and dry the fish. Sprinkle with lemon juice and season with salt and pepper.

3   Cut the ciabatta into 1¹/₂ cm cubes. Wash and dry the rosemary. Crush the clove of garlic. Heat 2 tbsp of olive oil in a pan and fry the bread with the rosemary and garlic until golden brown. Remove the sprigs of rosemary.

4   Make a cross in the skin of the tomatoes and blanch in boiling water for 20 seconds. Plunge into ice cold water, then remove the skins. Quarter the tomatoes and remove the seeds. Cut into 1 cm cubes. Peel and finely slice the onions.

Ingredients:

For the fish:
4 trout (or char)
(300–400 g each;
not gutted)
Juice of 1 lemon
Salt · Ground pepper
250 g ciabatta
3 sprigs of rosemary
1 clove of garlic
8 tbsp olive oil
3 tomatoes
2 red onions
1 bunch of basil
50 g Italian salami
1 tbsp capers
2 tbsp balsamic vinegar
Oil for the baking tray

For the pesto:
1 bunch of basil
1 bunch of parsley
1 tbsp lemon thyme
40 g pine nuts
1 small clove of garlic
200 ml olive oil
40 g grated parmesan
Salt · Ground pepper

5   Place the bread cubes, tomatoes and onions in a bowl. Wash and dry the basil. Chop the salami and add to the bowl with the basil. Add the capers, 3 tbsp olive oil and the balsamic vinegar and stir well. Season with salt and pepper. Use the mixture to stuff the fish, then tie them with kitchen string.

6   Place the fish on an oiled baking tray and drizzle with the remaining olive oil. Bake at 160°C (Moisture plus with 2 bursts of steam) on the second shelf for 35 to 40 minutes. Activate the first burst of steam at the beginning, and the second 10 minutes later.

7   To make the pesto, wash and dry the herbs and tear off the leaves. Dry roast the pine nuts in a frying pan. Peel the garlic. Purée the olive oil, herbs, parmesan, pine nuts and garlic in a food processor. Season with salt and pepper.

8   Remove the fish from the oven and serve with pesto and a mixed salad.

Cod and mussels
with saffron, baked in parchment

Serves 4

1   Bring the wine and Martini to the boil in a saucepan, stir in the saffron and leave to stand for 15 minutes.

2   Make a cross in the skin of the tomatoes and blanch in boiling water for 20 seconds. Plunge into ice cold water, then remove the skins. Quarter the tomatoes and remove the seeds. Chop finely. Cut the butter into cubes. Wash and dry the basil and cut the leaves into strips.

3   Wash and dry the fish fillets, drizzle with lemon juice and season with salt and pepper. Scrub the mussels thoroughly under running cold water, remove the beards and discard any mussels that are open.

4   Take four sheets of baking parchment (30 x 24 cm) and fold them down the centre. Fold the edges up two or three times to form a bag. Divide the mussels between them. Add the tomatoes, chilli and basil. Place one fish fillet in each bag and pour in the saffron flavoured wine. Divide the cubes of butter between them and fold the opening over two or three times.

Ingredients:

For the fish:
150 ml white wine
50 ml dry Martini
1 g saffron
4 tomatoes
1 red chilli
100 g butter
1 bunch of basil
4 cod fillets (200 g each)
Juice of $1/2$ lemon
Salt · Ground pepper
600 g mussels

For the potatoes:
800 g small salad potatoes
Salt · 2 tbsp butter
2 tbsp breadcrumbs
4 sprigs of thyme
Ground pepper

5   Bake the fish at 200°C (Fan plus) on the second shelf for 20 to 25 minutes.

6   Boil the potatoes in salted water until tender, plunge into cold water, then peel.

7   Melt the butter in a frying pan until foaming and fry the breadcrumbs until golden. Wash and dry the thyme. Toss the potatoes and thyme in the buttery breadcrumbs, and season with salt and pepper.

8   Place the parchment parcels on four serving plates and serve the potatoes separately.

▶▶ Tips

The wonderful aroma of the fish will waft out deliciously as the parcels are opened at the table. Serve with rocket salad and aioli.

Monkfish roulade
with spring onions and grilled bread

Serves 4–6

Ingredients:

For the fish:
2 monkfish, ling or perch fillets
(400 g each)
10 basil leaves
6 sundried tomatoes
40 g pine nuts
4 tbsp olive oil
Ground pepper
10 slices of Parma ham or,
prosciutto
1 tbsp oil

For the onions:
3 bunches of spring onions
1 tsp caster sugar
1 tbsp butter
100 ml chicken or vegetable
stock

For the bread:
8 slices ciabatta
Olive oil
1 clove of garlic

1   Wash and dry the monkfish and basil leaves. Blend the sundried tomatoes, pine nuts, basil and olive oil to a paste in a food processor. Spread the mixture over the fish fillets and season with ground pepper. Place 2 x 5 slices of Parma ham on a plate so that the slices overlap slightly. Arrange the monkfish on the ham, and roll up.

2   Brown the monkfish roulades in a frying pan with oil for 2 to 3 minutes. Place on a baking tray and bake at 200°C (Conventional heat) on the second shelf for 15 to 20 minutes.

3   Meanwhile, wash the spring onions and cut into 6 cm long pieces. Caramelize the sugar in a frying pan. Add the spring onions, butter and stock. Cook the onions for 8 to 10 minutes until translucent.

4   Remove the monkfish roulades from the oven. Lay the slices of bread on a baking tray and drizzle with olive oil. Grill at 240°C (Full grill) on the third shelf until golden. Remove the grilled bread from the tray, allow to cool slightly, then rub all over with the clove of garlic.

5   Slice the monkfish roulades. Arrange the spring onions on the toasted bread and top with the fish slices.

▶▶ Tips

Can also be served with polenta. Stir 80 g of instant polenta into 350 ml boiling milk. Leave to swell for around 5 minutes. Stir in 50 g of grated parmesan and 1 tbsp of butter. Season with salt and ground nutmeg.

Braised octopus
with puréed potatoes

Serves 4

1   Wash and dry the octopus. Simmer for 5 minutes in lots of salted water, drain and chop into bite sized pieces. Peel and dice the carrots and onions. Cut the leaves and base from the celery stalks, remove any fibrous strings and dice.

2   Heat the olive oil in an ovenproof pan, and fry the onions. Add the carrots and celery. Stir in the tomato purée then the red wine. Bring to a fast boil and add the tomatoes.

3   Peel and chop the garlic and stir in. Wash and dry the thyme. Add the octopus and thyme to the vegetables, and season with salt and pepper. Cover and cook in the oven at 140°C (Fan plus) on the second shelf for 1$^1/_2$ to 2 hours.

4   To make the potato purée, peel the potatoes and cut into 2 cm pieces. Cook in salted water, drain, then leave to stand in the saucepan. Heat the milk and pour half over the potatoes.

Ingredients:

1 kg octopus (oven ready)
Salt
100 g each of onions, carrots, celery
2 tbsp olive oil
1 tbsp tomato purée
150 ml red wine
600 g tinned chopped tomatoes
2 cloves of garlic
1 bunch of thyme
Ground pepper
1 bunch of parsley
1 tbsp unwaxed lemon zest
1 tbsp capers

For the potato purée:
600 g floury potatoes
Salt
300 ml milk
50 ml olive oil
50 g grated parmesan
Freshly grated nutmeg

Also:
2 unwaxed lemons
2 tbsp sugar

5   Add the olive oil and parmesan, and mash with a potato masher. Gradually stir in the remaining milk to achieve a creamy purée. Do not overstir or the potatoes will become gluey. Season with salt and nutmeg.

6   Wash the lemons in hot water, pat dry and cut in half. Dip the cut surfaces in sugar. Heat a frying pan without any fat and fry the lemons cut side down to caramelize the sugar. Remove from the pan and put to one side.

7   Take the casserole out of the oven and remove the thyme. Wash, dry and chop the parsley. Stir into the sauce with the lemon zest and capers.

8   Arrange the octopus with the vegetable sauce and potato purée. Serve with the lemon halves.

Baked lobster
with celeriac cream and vanilla butter

Serves 2

1 Wash, peel and chop the vegetables and herbs. Place in a pan with 3 litres water, and bring to the boil with the caraway seeds, vinegar, bay leaf and peppercorns. Simmer for 20 minutes.

2 Hold the lobster head down for 2 to 3 minutes to numb it. Plunge it into the boiling water. Simmer for 8 to 10 minutes, then plunge into cold water. Cut in half lengthways with a large knife. Remove the claws and break open. Remove the meat from the tail. Rinse and dry the two halves of the shell.

3 To make the butter, wash and dry the basil. Purée the butter with the vanilla pulp and basil using a handheld blender. Stir in 2 pinches of sea salt and 1 pinch of chilli powder. Scoop the butter onto a piece of clingfilm and form into a log, 3 to 4 cm thick, and place in the fridge.

Ingredients:

For the lobster:
Mixed vegetables and herbs for making stock, e.g. 2 celery sticks, 2 carrots, 1 leek and some fresh parsley
1 tbsp caraway seeds
100 ml white wine vinegar
1 bay leaf
1 tbsp black peppercorns
1 lobster (700–800 g)

For the butter:
10 basil leaves
80 g soft butter
Pulp from 1/2 vanilla pod
Coarse sea salt
Chilli powder

For the cream:
250 g celeriac
1 tsp butter
150 ml double cream
Salt · Ground pepper
Freshly grated nutmeg

4 To make the cream, peel the celeriac and chop into 1/2 cm cubes. Heat the butter in a saucepan and gently fry the celeriac. Pour in the cream, cover and simmer over a low heat for 15 to 20 minutes until soft. Purée the celeriac with salt, pepper and nutmeg.

5 Fill the lobster shells with the celeriac cream. Cut the lobster meat into bite sized pieces and place on top of the cream. Put the lobster shells on a rack and cook in the oven at 200°C (Full grill) on the third shelf for 5 minutes.

6 Cut the vanilla butter into 1/2 cm thick slices, place on top of the lobster and grill for 2 to 3 minutes until the butter has melted.

▶▶ Tips

Serve with fettucine. For 2 people, cook 250 g to 300 g fresh fettucine in plenty of salted water until al dente. Heat some olive oil and toss the pasta in the oil. Sprinkle with sea salt.

Stuffed squid
with ginger and tamarind sauce

Serves 4–6

1   Wash dry and finely chop the prawns. Marinate in lime juice, fish sauce and 1 tsp of soy sauce for 30 minutes. Wash and dry the fish, and chop into small pieces. Season with salt and purée with the cream in a food processor. Stir the prawns into the fish purée.

2   Wash and dry the squid tubes and fill with the prawn and fish mixture. Seal with cocktail sticks. Place the squid in a greased ovenproof dish and drizzle with the rest of the soy sauce. Cook at 220°C (Fan plus) on the second shelf for 15 to 20 minutes.

3   Peel the ginger and cut into thin strips. Heat the oil in a frying pan and fry the ginger for 3 to 4 minutes. Drain on kitchen paper.

Ingredients:

For the fish:
300 g raw, peeled king prawns
1 tsp lime juice
1 tsp fish sauce
3 tsp light soy sauce
100 g white fish fillets
(e.g. ling, cod, haddock)
Salt
120 ml ice cold double cream
16–20 small squid tubes
Butter to grease the dish
80 g ginger
2 tbsp oil

For the sauce:
1 tbsp tamarind paste
2 tbsp plum sauce
1 tbsp fish sauce
2 tsp light soy sauce
100 ml chicken stock
1 red chilli

Also:
1 bunch of coriander
100 g salted roast peanuts

4   To make the sauce, bring the tamarind paste, plum sauce, fish sauce, soy sauce and chicken stock to the boil. Pour into a bowl. Cut the chilli in half lengthways, discard the seeds, wash and chop finely. Stir into the sauce.

5   Wash and dry the coriander, and chop along with the peanuts.

6   Sprinkle the ginger, coriander and peanuts over the squid. Serve with the sauce, garnished with lime.

▸▸ Tips

Tamarinds are the pods of the tamarind tree. Inside there are seeds embedded in soft flesh. The slightly sharp paste is used widely in Thai and Indonesian cooking.

Poultry

Take a culinary trip round the world on the wings of a chicken! When poultry is given an Asian twist or a Mediterranean flavour, then it is heaven on a plate. Those who like to watch their health will be delighted at the huge variety of ways there are to cook this tender, low fat meat.

Breast of corn fed chicken breast
with crumbed bacon and parsley

Serves 4

Ingredients:

1 clove of garlic
1 bunch of oregano
2 tbsp melted butter
1 tsp unwaxed lemon zest
Sea salt · Ground pepper
4 corn fed chicken breasts
(220 g each)
500 g wild mushrooms
(e.g. chanterelles, oyster
mushrooms, porcini)
80 ml dry white wine
1 bunch of parsley
Oil for frying
8 slices bacon
2 tbsp crème fraîche

1   Peel and finely chop the garlic. Wash and dry the oregano, and chop the leaves. Mix together the garlic, butter, oregano and lemon zest with a little sea salt and pepper in a bowl.

2   Wash and dry the chicken breasts. Turn them in the butter mixture and leave to marinate for 15 minutes. Wash, dry and chop the mushrooms.

3   Take four pieces of aluminium foil (30 x 40 cm) and fold them in half. Fold the edges over two or three times to make four bags, leaving an opening at the top. Place a chicken breast and some mushrooms in each bag. Divide the wine between the bags and fold over the top two or three times to seal the parcel. Place the parcels on a rack and cook in the oven at 200°C (Fan plus) on the second shelf for 25 to 30 minutes.

4   Wash and dry the parsley and remove the leaves. Heat a good quantity of oil in a frying pan and fry the parsley until crisp. Drain on kitchen paper and season to taste.

5   Dry fry the bacon until crispy. Crumble the bacon and parsley by hand and place in a serving bowl.

6   Remove the chicken from the oven and place the parcels on serving plates to be opened at table. Top with a blob of crème fraîche and a sprinkling of the bacon and parsley.

▶▶ Tips

Serve with new potatoes and asparagus. Cornfed chickens are fed primarily on maize which gives the skin and flesh a golden colour and an intense flavour.

Roast chicken
with chorizo and sea salt potatoes

Serves 4 [◊ﬥ]

Ingredients:

For the chicken:
1 free range chicken
(approx. 1.5 kg, oven ready)
Salt · Ground pepper
1 small bunch of marjoram
1 bunch of parsley
200 g chorizo or paprika
salami (sliced)
1 unwaxed lemon
2 bay leaves
4 tbsp olive oil

For the vegetables:
500 g baby carrots
(1$\frac{1}{2}$ cm thick; with a little
green)
1 unwaxed orange
2 cloves of garlic
1 tbsp melted butter
1 tsp sugar
Salt · Ground pepper

For the potatoes:
800 g new potatoes
1 tbsp sea salt

1 For the chicken, wash the bird inside and out, pat dry and rub with salt and pepper. Using a knife or the handle of a spoon, loosen the skin around the breast of the chicken to create a pocket. Wash and dry the marjoram and parsley and put 5 stalks of parsley to one side. Chop the remaining parsley and marjoram. Spread half the herbs and a few chorizo slices under the chicken skin.

2 Make two or three 1 cm slashes in the legs and thighs. Rub the rest of the herbs into the cuts and fill with slices of chorizo. Wash the lemon in hot water, pat dry and make two cuts in it. Then fill them with the bay leaves. Place the lemon inside the chicken, rub it with olive oil and truss it with kitchen string.

3 Put the chicken on the universal tray and roast at 160°C (Moisture plus with 2 bursts of steam) on the second shelf for 60 to 70 minutes. Activate the first burst of steam at the beginning, and the second 30 minutes later.

4 To prepare the vegetables, peel the carrots, wash the orange and cut it into eight, and crush the garlic lightly in its skin. Mix everything with the reserved 5 stalks of parsley, the melted butter, salt and pepper. Place in an ovenproof dish and cover with aluminium foil. Cook on the fourth shelf for 30 minutes.

5 Wash the potatoes and place them in a saucepan. Add 200 ml of water and the sea salt, and boil uncovered until all the water has evaporated. This will leave a layer of sea salt on the potatoes. Remove the potatoes and place in the tin with the chicken 30 minutes before the end of the cooking time for the chicken.

6 Remove the garlic, orange and parsley from the carrots, place them in a sieve and press them through onto the carrots. Serve the chicken with the potatoes and carrots.

Thai guinea fowl
with grapefruit and avocado salad

Serves 4 ⌑

1 Wash and dry the guinea fowl inside and out. Cut along the backbone with a pair of poultry shears and flatten out. Make two or three slashes in the thighs with a sharp knife

2 Remove the tough outer leaves of the lemon grass, and finely chop the soft inner core. Peel and chop the garlic. Wash, dry and chop the coriander. Using a pestle and mortar or food processor, reduce the lemon grass, garlic, coriander, fish sauce and palm sugar to a paste, then stir in the oil and pepper. Rub over the guinea fowl and leave to marinate for 2 hours.

3 Place the guinea fowl, skin side up, on the rack and roast at 160°C (Moisture plus with 2 bursts of steam) on the second shelf for 40 to 50 minutes. Place the universal tray under the rack to catch the juices. Activate the first burst of steam at the beginning, and the second 10 minutes later. If the guinea fowl are not sufficiently brown, grill them at 240°C (Full grill) on the second shelf for 5 minutes.

Ingredients:

For the guinea fowl:
2 guinea fowls
(1 kg each; oven ready)
2 stalks of lemon grass
4 cloves of garlic
12 stalks of coriander
5 tbsp fish sauce
2 tsp palm or unrefined sugar
4 tbsp peanut oil
$1/2$ tsp freshly ground pepper

For the salad:
2 ripe avocados
1 pink grapefruit
2 spring onions
1 red chilli
1 tbsp fish sauce · 1 tbsp sugar
Juice of 1 lime
1 tbsp mint (shredded)

4 To make the salad, peel and halve the avocados, remove the stones and cut into thin slices. Peel the grapefruit, removing all the pith, and separate into segments. Wash and dry the spring onions and cut into thin slices. Put everything in a bowl.

5 Cut the chilli in half lengthways, wash, deseed and chop finely. Mix with the fish sauce, sugar, lime juice and mint. Pour over the salad and toss. Serve the guinea fowl with the salad.

▶▶ Tips

A poussin or corn fed chicken can be used as an alternative to guinea fowl. Garnish with caramelized lime or lemon halves, and serve with French bread, rice or a salad.

Poussins en croûte
with lime and coriander cucumbers

Serves 4

1 To prepare the poussins, mix the flour with the salt and ¹/₂ litre warm water, and knead to a malleable dough.

2 Wash and dry the poussins inside and out. Wash the limes in hot water and pat dry. Peel the skins and cut into thin strips. Squeeze out the juice. Peel and chop the garlic. Peel the ginger and cut into thin slices. Mix the lime zest, garlic, ginger, palm sugar, salt and pepper to a paste in a food processor. Stir in the olive oil and lime juice and rub over the poussins, inside and out.

3 Divide the dough into four and roll out to a thickness of ¹/₂ cm. Wrap each poussin in a piece of dough and seal well.

4 Place on a baking tray lined with baking paper and roast at 160°C (Fan plus) on the second shelf for 55 to 60 minutes. Leave to rest, then break open the crust.

Ingredients:

For the poussins:
1 kg plain flour
100 g salt
4 poussins (350 g each)
2 unwaxed limes
2 cloves of garlic
3 cm ginger
1 tbsp palm or unrefined sugar
Salt · Freshly ground pepper
6 tbsp olive oil

For the cucumbers:
2 cucumbers
50 g sugar
40 ml rice vinegar or white
balsamic vinegar
1 bunch of coriander
Salt · Ground pepper

5 Peel the cucumbers and cut into thin slices. Lightly caramelize the sugar in a saucepan, then add the vinegar. Place the cucumbers in a bowl and marinate in the vinegar mixture. Wash and dry the coriander. Chop the leaves and scatter over the cucumbers. Season with salt and pepper.

6 Serve the poussins with the cucumber, along with fragrant rice and grilled vegetables such as spring onions or chinese cabbage.

▶▶ Tips

As an alternative, rub the poussins with a paste made of herbs such as basil and parsley, garlic and olive oil. Chicken drumsticks are also ideal for this recipe.

Baby turkey with pumpkin stuffing
and cranberry and maple vinaigrette

Serves 4–6 ⌗

1 Peel and core the apple and cut into 1/2 cm cubes. Peel the onion and chop the onion and pumpkin flesh into 1/2 cm cubes. Wash, dry and chop the sage. Peel and finely chop the ginger.

2 In a frying pan heat 2 tbsp of oil and sweat the onion for 2 to 3 minutes. Add the pumpkin and apple and cook for a further 2 to 3 minutes. Add the ginger and sage, and season with salt and pepper. Transfer the vegetables to a large bowl and wipe out the frying pan with kitchen paper.

3 Cut the bread into cubes. Heat the remaining 2 tbsp of oil and 1 tbsp of melted butter in the pan. Fry the bread cubes for 5 to 7 minutes until golden brown and add to the vegetables. Beat the eggs lightly. Sir the milk, then the eggs, then the semolina into the bread and vegetables. Season with salt, pepper and nutmeg, and leave to stand for 30 minutes.

Ingredients:

1 turkey (3–3.5 kg; oven ready)
Salt · Ground pepper
1 apple
100 g onions
400 g pumpkin or butternut squash flesh
1/2 bunch of sage or parsley
5 cm ginger
4 tbsp oil
250 g bread
100 g melted butter
200 ml warm milk
3 medium eggs
1–2 tbsp semolina
Freshly grated nutmeg
200 g bacon (sliced)
800 ml chicken stock
150 g dried cranberries
50 ml cider vinegar
2–3 tbsp maple syrup
80 ml grapeseed oil

4 Wash the turkey inside and out. Pat dry and rub with salt and pepper. Fill the turkey with the pumpkin stuffing and sew up the opening with kitchen string. Place the turkey on the universal tray and brush with the remaining melted butter. Place the slices of bacon on top. Pour over the chicken stock and cook in the oven at 150ºC (Moisture plus with 3 bursts of steam) on the second shelf for 4 1/2 to 5 hours. Baste occasionally with the stock. Activate the first burst of steam at the beginning, and the second and third at one hour intervals.

5 One hour before the end of the cooking time, remove the bacon and drain off the stock into a saucepan. Put the turkey back in the oven to finish cooking. Reduce the stock on the hob to 300 ml. Chop the cranberries. Add the vinegar, maple syrup and cranberries to the stock and leave to stand for 30 minutes. Stir in the grapeseed oil and season with pepper. Serve the turkey with the vinaigrette and the bacon, along with sweet potato purée and roasted corn on the cob.

Braised turkey drumsticks
with salsa verde and grilled vegetables

Serves 4

1 Wash and dry the turkey legs, rub with salt and pepper and place in an ovenproof dish. Wash and dry the herbs. Crush the garlic lightly in its skin. Heat the olive oil and add the herbs, garlic and lemon zest. Pour over the turkey and cook in the oven at 140°C (Fan plus) on the second shelf for 2 1/2 to 3 hours.

2 To make the salsa, wash and dry the herbs. Peel the garlic. Purée the herbs, garlic, capers, anchovies, mustard and vinegar in a food processor. Stir in the oil and season with salt and pepper.

3 To prepare the vegetables, wash and quarter the peppers and remove the seeds. Peel the onions and cut into thin rings. Wash the courgettes and aubergine and cut into thin slices. Wash, dry and chop the rosemary. Crush the garlic in its skin. Put everything into a bowl with the olive oil. Season with salt and pepper and leave to stand for 20 minutes.

Ingredients:

For the meat:
2 turkey drumsticks
(600 g each)
Salt · Ground pepper
1 bunch of mixed herbs
(e.g. rosemary, thyme, sage)
8 cloves of garlic
700 ml olive oil
Grated zest of 1 unwaxed
lemon

For the salsa:
2 bunches of parsley
2 bunches of basil
2 cloves of garlic
1 tbsp capers (pickled)
3 anchovies (salted)
1 tbsp mustard
2 tbsp white wine vinegar
80–100 ml olive oil
Salt · Ground pepper

For the vegetables:
1 red and 1 yellow pepper
1 onion
2 zucchini/courgettes
1 eggplant/aubergine
1/2 bunch of rosemary
1 clove of garlic
80 ml olive oil
Sea salt · Ground pepper
1 tsp grated unwaxed lemon
zest

4 Transfer the vegetables to a baking tray and grill at 220°C (Full grill) on the third or fourth shelf for 15 to 20 minutes until the vegetables start to brown. Stir half way through. Remove the skin from the peppers and stir the vegetables and lemon zest together in a bowl.

5 Remove the turkey legs from the oven and pat dry with kitchen paper. Place on the rack and grill at 220°C (Full grill) on the lowest shelf position for 10 to 15 minutes until well browned. Remove the turkey from the oven and serve with the vegetables and salsa verde.

▸▸ Tips

Serve with pan fried white bread or pitta bread. Cut the bread into thin slices and fry in a frying pan. While still warm, rub with a halved clove of garlic and spread with butter.

Thai curry
with pineapple and tomatoes

Serves 4–6

1 Cut away any fat and sinews from the turkey breast. Wash, dry and season with salt and pepper. Heat the oil in a casserole and brown the turkey breast for 5 minutes.

2 Heat the curry paste in a saucepan with 3 tbsp of the coconut milk and simmer for 3 to 4 minutes. Add the rest of the coconut milk and stir well. Add the lime juice, lime leaves, palm sugar and fish sauce, and bring to the boil. Pour the sauce over the turkey breast and cook in the oven at 130°C (Moisture plus with 3 bursts of steam) on the second shelf for 1 1/2 to 2 hours. Activate one burst of steam at the beginning, and the second and third at 30 minute intervals.

3 Make a slit in the skin of the tomatoes with the point of a knife and blanch in boiling water for 20 seconds. Plunge into ice cold water and remove the skins.

Ingredients:

1.2 kg turkey breast
(8–9 cm thick)
Salt
Ground pepper
2 tbsp oil
1 tbsp red curry paste
2 tins of coconut milk
(400 ml each)
Juice of 1 lime
6 kaffir lime leaves
1 1/2 tbsp palm or unrefined sugar
3 tbsp fish sauce
300 g cherry tomatoes
1/2 fresh pineapple
1 bunch of Thai basil or coriander
2 red chillis

4 Peel the pineapple, remove the core and cut the flesh into 2 cm pieces. 30 minutes before the end of the cooking time, add the tomatoes and pineapple to the sauce. Wash and dry the basil and remove the leaves. Put a few leaves to one side for decoration, and shortly before the end of the cooking time, stir the rest of the basil into the sauce.

5 Cut the chillis in half lengthways, discard the seeds, wash and chop into thin strips. Slice the turkey breast and arrange on plates. Serve with the pineapple and tomato sauce, garnished with chilli and basil.

▶▶ Tips

Serve with fragrant or basmati rice and sprinkle with ground salted peanuts. Thai basil is spicier than normal basil and has an aniseed flavour.

Duck breasts
with celeriac and raspberry dumplings

Serves 4

Ingredients:

For the dumplings:
200 ml milk
80 g butter
90 g semolina
1 medium egg
Salt · Ground pepper
Freshly grated nutmeg
100 g raspberries
1 tsp chopped thyme
Oil for frying

For the celeriac:
1/2 bunch of thyme
500 g celeriac
3 tbsp olive oil
1 tsp sugar
Salt · Ground pepper

For the duck breasts:
2 duck breasts
(350–400 g each)
Salt · Ground pepper
2 tbsp oil
50 g sugar
50 ml raspberry vinegar
1 walnut sized piece of ginger
50 ml chicken stock

1 To make the dumplings, bring the milk and the butter to the boil in a saucepan and stir in the semolina. When a white coating forms on the bottom, put the pan to one side and leave the semolina to swell for 10 minutes. Stir in the egg, and season with salt, pepper and nutmeg. Cover and leave for 1 hour to go cold.

2 For the celeriac, wash and dry the thyme. Peel the celeriac and cut into 1 1/2 cm cubes. Put into an ovenproof dish and stir in 2 tbsp olive oil and the thyme and sugar. Season with salt and pepper and cook in the oven at 160°C (Fan plus) on the second shelf for 40 minutes. Remove from the oven, and keep warm.

3 Wash and dry the duck breasts. Score the skin in a diamond pattern. Season the flesh side with salt and pepper.

4 Place the duck breasts into a cold frying pan with the oil, and heat. Fry for 5 to 6 minutes on the skin side to melt the fat. Turn and fry for 1 minute on the meat side. Transfer the duck breasts onto the rack over a baking tray to catch the juices, and roast at 120°C (Conventional heat) on the second shelf for 40 minutes.

5 Caramelize the sugar with 1 tbsp of water in a saucepan and stir in the vinegar. Peel and finely chop the ginger, and add to the pan. Pour in the stock and boil until syrupy. Brush the skin side of the duck breasts with the syrup, retaining 1 tsp of the syrup. Grill the duck at 200°C under a pre-heated grill (Full grill) on the fourth shelf position for 5 to 7 minutes.

6 For the dumplings, wash and dry the raspberries. Mix half the raspberries with the remaining syrup and the thyme. Form 8 small dumplings from the semolina, filling them with raspberries and thyme. Heat the oil and deep fry the dumplings for 5 minutes.

7 Leave the duck breasts to rest for 2 to 3 minutes, cut into slices and serve with the celeriac and dumplings. Decorate with the remaining raspberries.

Lacquered duck
with pak choi and mango and coriander salad

Serves 4 ⌂

1   Wash and dry the duck and place in a bowl into which it fits exactly. Mix the two types of salt with enough water to dissolve them completely. Pour the salt solution over the duck and add enough water to cover the duck completely. Leave in the fridge for 3 to 4 days. Remove and pat dry.

2   To make the marinade, mix the hoisin sauce, soy sauce, honey, rice vinegar, five spice powder and chilli powder, and brush over the duck. Cover the duck and leave overnight in the fridge. Put the remaining marinade to one side.

3   Place the duck on the rack. Pour the stock into the universal tray, and place it under the duck. Roast at 140°C (Moisture plus with 3 bursts of steam) on the second shelf for 2 1/2 to 3 hours. Activate the first burst of steam at the beginning, and the second and third at 1 hour intervals. Baste the duck with the marinade every 30 minutes.

4   Cut the duck in half lengthways and place it, skin side up, on the rack with the baking tray underneath to catch the drips. Grill it at 200°C (Full grill) on the third or fourth shelf for 10 to 15 minutes.

Ingredients:

For the duck:
1 duck (2.5–3 kg; oven ready)
50 g preserving salt
(from the butcher)
50 g salt
400 ml chicken stock

For the marinade:
2 tbsp hoisin sauce
2 tbsp soy sauce
2 tbsp honey
2 tbsp rice vinegar
1 tsp five spice powder
1/2 tsp chilli powder

For the salad:
1 mango (500 g)
1 bunch of coriander
2 spring onions
1 tsp caster sugar
2 tbsp rice vinegar
1 tsp sesame oil
Salt · Ground pepper

For the pak choi:
600 g pak choi or Chinese cabbage
1 tbsp oil
1 tsp caster sugar
1 tbsp soy sauce

5   Sieve the juices from the universal tray into a saucepan and drain off the fat. Reduce the juices to 200 ml.

6   To make the salad, peel the mango, cut the flesh off the stone and cut into thin strips. Wash, dry and chop the coriander. Wash the spring onions and slice thinly. Mix everything together. Stir together the sugar, rice vinegar and sesame oil, and season with salt and pepper. Pour over the mango salad and stir well.

7   Wash the pak choi and chop up if necessary. Fry in oil. Add the sugar and soy sauce and sweat for 2 minutes.

8   Carve the duck and serve with the pak choi and mango salad.

Goose legs
with pear and onion tarts

Serves 4 🔥

Ingredients:

For the meat:
4 goose legs (400 g each)
Salt · Ground pepper
200 g onions
100 g carrots
200 g celeriac
5 tbsp oil
1 tbsp caster sugar
1 tbsp tomato purée
300 ml red wine
$^1/_2$ litre goose stock
1–2 tsp cornflour
1 clove of garlic
4 sprigs of marjoram
Grated zest of $^1/_2$ unwaxed
orange

For the tart:
250 g frozen puff pastry
3 onions
2 ripe pears
1 tbsp butter
100 g crème fraîche
Salt · Ground pepper

Also:
100 g mixed herbs
(e.g. parsley, rosemary, sage)
200 ml oil for frying
Salt

1   Remove the skin from the goose legs and put to one side. Season the legs with salt and pepper. Peel and dice the onions, carrots and celeriac. Heat 2 tbsp oil in a casserole and brown the goose legs all over. Remove and fry the vegetables in the casserole with 2 tbsp oil. Add the sugar and allow to caramelize. Stir in the tomato purée and one third of the red wine. Reduce the wine, then repeat the process until all the wine is used. Replace the goose legs and add the goose stock. Cover and cook in the oven at 140°C (Fan plus) on the second shelf for 3 hours.

2   To make the tarts, defrost the pastry. Peel the onions and pears. Cut the onions into thin rings. Quarter and core the pears and cut into thin slices. Sweat both in the butter for 5 minutes. Stir in the crème fraîche, and season with salt and pepper.

3   Roll the pastry out to a thickness of $^1/_2$ cm. Cut out 4 circles (12 cm Ø). Pile the pear and onions on top and place on a baking tray.

4   Bake at 180°C (Moisture plus with 1 automatic burst of steam) on the second shelf for 15 to 20 minutes. Activate the moisture reduction system after 10 minutes.

5   Wash and dry the herbs and remove the leaves. Heat the oil and fry the herbs until crisp. Drain on kitchen paper and lightly salt. Cut the skin from the goose legs into small cubes and fry in 1 tbsp of oil. Drain on kitchen paper and lightly salt.

6   Pass the sauce from the casserole through a sieve and return the meat and vegetables to the casserole. Mix the cornflour with 2 tbsp of cold water. Bring the sauce to the boil and thicken with the cornflour. Crush the garlic in its skin. Wash and dry the marjoram. Add the garlic, marjoram and orange zest to the sauce, simmer, and season with salt and pepper. Pass the sauce through a sieve again, pour over the goose and reheat.

7   Arrange the goose on a serving dish with the sauce, topped with the herbs and crackling. Serve with the tarts.

Meat

The professionals have always known that the oven is the perfect place for cooking meat. These recipes bring variety to your meat dishes. Whether the meat is roasted with a crisp crust, braised in a tasty sauce or cooked in its own juices, every dish will be a winner.

Glazed pork fillets
with apricots and celeriac

Serves 4–6

1 Season the pork fillets with salt and pepper. Heat the oil in a frying pan and brown the fillets all over. Wash and dry the thyme. Mix with the vinegar and golden syrup, and turn the fillets in the mixture until they are evenly coated. Place the fillets on the rack with a baking tray underneath to catch the drips, and roast at 85°C (Conventional heat) on the second shelf for 50 minutes.

2 For the vegetables, peel and dice the onion, and sweat in a saucepan in 1 tbsp butter. Wash and stone the apricots, chop and add to the onions. Peel the celeriac and chop into $1/2$ cm cubes. Wash and dry the rosemary and add to the pan with the celeriac. Pour in the vegetable stock and cook for 20 minutes until the celeriac is soft. Once the liquid has almost boiled away, stir in the rest of the butter and the double cream. Season with salt, pepper and sugar. Remove the rosemary.

Ingredients:

For the pork:
2 pork fillets (380 g each;)
Salt · Ground pepper
1 tbsp oil
3 sprigs of thyme
1 tbsp balsamic vinegar
1 tbsp golden syrup

For the vegetables:
1 onion · 2 tbsp butter
4 apricots
300 g celeriac
3 sprigs of rosemary
200 ml vegetable stock
100 ml double cream
Salt · Ground pepper
Sugar

Also:
500 g salad potatoes
Sea salt

3 Clean the potatoes and boil in salted water for 20 minutes. Pour 50 ml of the cooking water into a frying pan with a large pinch of sea salt. Drain the potatoes and add to the pan. Simmer until all the water has evaporated and the potatoes are coated in little salt crystals.

4 To serve, cut the pork fillets into slices and arrange on serving plates with the celeriac, apricots and potatoes.

▶▶ Tips

You can also garnish the fillets with a sprinkling of roasted pine nuts and fried basil. When buying pork fillet, ensure that it is pink rather than pale. Organic is best.

Pork loins
with thyme flavoured dates and roast tomatoes

Serves 4–6 ⌂

1 Place the meat in a casserole, skin side down. Pour over 400 ml of stock and cook in the oven at 100°C (Fan plus) on the second shelf for 1 hour. Remove from the oven and score the rind with a sharp knife at 1 cm intervals. Lightly salt the fat. Add the stock from the dish to the rest of the stock.

2 Wipe out the casserole with kitchen paper and heat the oil in it. Fry the onions, then add the celery and carrots and fry until golden. Add the sugar and caramelize, then add the tomato purée. Pour in the red wine and reduce slightly. Add the crushed garlic and stock. Place the pork in the stock, skin side up, and cook in the oven at 160°C (Moisture plus with 2 bursts of steam) on the second shelf for 1 hour. Activate the first burst of steam at the beginning, and the second 30 minutes later.

3 Mix the dates with 2 tbsp olive oil and the thyme. Cut 8 slices of bacon in half and wrap them around the dates. Wash the tomatoes and make a cross shaped slit in the top. Wrap them in the remaining bacon. Season with salt and pepper. Heat the rest of the oil in an ovenproof frying pan, fry the dates, then add the

Ingredients:

For the pork:
2 loins of sucking pig
(500 g each; with rind and bones), or 1 kg of pork belly
800 ml chicken stock
Salt · 2 tbsp oil
200 g diced onions
80 g each diced celery and carrots
1 tsp caster sugar
1 tbsp tomato purée
1/2 litre red wine
2 clove of garlic
1 bay leaf
Grated rind of
1/2 unwaxed lemon
15 g ginger (sliced)
1 tsp Ras-el-Hanout (oriental spice mix)
Ground pepper

Also:
200 g dates
(stoned; approx. 16)
4 tbsp olive oil
1 tbsp chopped thyme
16 slices bacon
8 small tomatoes on the vine
Salt · Ground pepper

tomatoes. Place the pan in the oven 30 minutes before the end of the cooking time for the meat.

4 Take the casserole out of the oven and pass the sauce through a sieve. Remove the dates and tomatoes and keep warm. Place the pork loins on a baking tray and grill in the oven at 220°C (Full grill) on the second or third shelf for 20 minutes, until the skin is crisp. Bring the sauce to the boil in a saucepan. Add the bay leaf, lemon zest, ginger and Ras-el-Hanout. Leave to stand for 10 minutes, then pass through a sieve again. If necessary, thicken with cornflour. Season the meat with salt and pepper, and cut into slices.

5 Arrange the meat on a serving dish with the sauce, dates and tomatoes. Serve with salt potatoes that have been tossed in a little butter, lemon zest and coriander.

Pork ribs
with horseradish crust and risotto

Serves 4–6

Ingredients:

For the ribs:
2–3 kg pork ribs
1 bouquet garni
1/2 bunch of rosemary
3 tbsp honey

For the crust:
150 g bread (crusts removed)
150 g soft butter
1 clove of garlic
1/2 bunch of tarragon
1 tsp grated unwaxed lemon zest
60 g finely grated horseradish
Salt · Ground pepper

For the risotto:
1 onion
2 tbsp olive oil
150 g risotto rice
(Arborio or Carnaroli)
Juice of 1 lemon
1 tbsp butter
50 g grated Parmesan
Ground pepper

1 Divide the ribs into pairs. Barely cover with water in a casserole, cover and cook in the oven at 160°C (Fan plus) on the second shelf for 1 hour. Wash the bouquet garni herbs and rosemary. Add to the ribs along with the honey and cook for a further hour.

2 To make the crust, dice the bread. Beat the butter to soften it. Peel the garlic, and wash and dry the tarragon. Chop both finely and stir into the butter along with the lemon zest and horseradish. Stir in the bread cubes and season with salt and pepper. Scoop onto a piece of clingfilm, roll into a log and place in the fridge.

3 To make the risotto, measure out 700 ml of the stock from the ribs. Peel and dice the onion and sweat in a saucepan with the olive oil. Stir in the rice and cook briefly, then pour in 150 ml of the stock and the lemon juice. When nearly all the stock has been absorbed, add another 150 ml and continue to cook until it has nearly all been absorbed. Repeat the process until all the stock has been used. Simmer the risotto over a low heat for 20 to 30 minutes in all. Finally, remove from the heat and stir in the butter and Parmesan. Season with pepper.

4 Pre-heat the grill (Full grill) for 5 minutes to 240°C. Take the ribs out of the remaining juices and place on a baking tray with the curve uppermost. Cut the butter log into 1/2 cm thick slices and divide among the ribs. Place in the oven on the third shelf and grill until golden brown. Serve with the risotto.

▶▶ Tips

For a change, add roasted, chopped hazelnuts or almonds to the risotto. Serve the ribs with a fresh salad.

Crispy roast pork
with vegetable purée and dumplings

Serves 4–6   [◊⟨⟨⟨]

1   Place the bones on a baking tray and roast at 220°C (Fan plus) on the second shelf for 30 minutes. Drain off the fat and put the bones to one side. Reduce the oven temperature to 160°C. Place the pork belly, rind side down, in a casserole with 400 ml of stock, and cook for 45 minutes. Remove the meat and score the rind in a diamond pattern. Lightly salt the fat. Return the stock from the casserole to the remaining stock.

2   Wipe out the casserole with kitchen paper and heat the oil in it. Fry the diced onions, then add the celery and carrots and fry until golden brown. Stir in the tomato purée and the beer and reduce slightly. Add the bones, crushed garlic and stock. Place the pork in the dish, skin side up, and cook in the oven at 160°C (Moisture plus with 3 bursts of steam) on the second shelf for 1 1/2 to 2 hours. Activate one burst of steam at the beginning, and the second and third at 30 minute intervals.

Ingredients:

For the roast:

500 g chopped veal bones
1.5 kg pork belly (with rind) ·
1.4 litres chicken stock
Salt · 2 tbsp oil
200 g diced onions
80 g each diced celery and carrots
1 tbsp tomato purée
1/2 litre malt beer
2 cloves of garlic

For the purée :

400g each of carrots, celeriac and parsnips
1 bunch of parsley
1 tsp ground caraway
1 tbsp butter
Salt · Ground pepper
Freshly grated nutmeg

For the dumplings:

80 g diced onions
100 g butter
1 tbsp each chopped marjoram and parsley
200 ml milk · 3 medium eggs
Salt · Ground pepper
Freshly grated nutmeg
400 g white bread (cubed)
100 g breadcrumbs
2 tbsp melted butter

3   To make the purée, peel and chop the vegetables. Wash and dry the parsley, remove the leaves and place in a bowl with the vegetables. Stir in the caraway and butter. Season with salt, pepper and nutmeg, and transfer to an ovenproof dish. Cover and cook in the oven with the meat on the fourth shelf for 1 1/2 hours. Purée the vegetables and keep warm.

4   To make the dumplings, sweat the onions in 2 tbsp of butter. Add the herbs, remove from the hob and stir in the milk and eggs. Season with salt, pepper and nutmeg. Fry the bread in the remaining butter until golden, and transfer to a large bowl. Stir in the egg and milk and the breadcrumbs. Roll the dumpling mixture in a piece of clingfilm, wrap it in a tea towel and tie with kitchen string. Simmer in boiling water for 45 minutes. Cool slightly, cut into thin slices and brown on both sides in melted butter.

5   Remove the roast from the oven and pass the juices through a sieve. Return the meat to the oven and grill at 220°C (Full grill) on the third shelf for 15 to 20 minutes. Serve with the sauce, vegetable purée and dumplings.

Pork with soured cream
and herby bread soufflé

Serves 4–6

1 The day before, peel and dice the onions. Mix them with the pork in a large bowl. Wash and dry the thyme, and add to the pork along with the red wine, vinegar and spices. Leave to marinate for 24 hours.

2 The following day, strain the marinade through a sieve, bring it to the boil, then strain it again. Dry the meat and onions, and brown in a casserole. Stir in the tomato purée, then add the marinade. Reduce by half, then pour in the veal stock. Cover and cook in the oven at 160°C (Fan plus) on the second shelf for 2 to 2 1/2 hours.

3 To make the bread soufflé, whisk the eggs, milk and chopped herbs together. Season with salt, pepper and nutmeg. Grease an ovenproof dish and line it with the slices of bread. Pour the egg mixture over and leave to stand for 15 minutes. Dot the butter over the top and cook in the oven together with the meat on the fourth shelf for 30 or 40 minutes.

Ingredients:

For the meat:
1 kg onions
1.2 kg diced pork
1 bunch of thyme
1/2 litre red wine
1/2 litre red wine vinegar
15 black peppercorns
2 bay leaves
5 juniper berries
2 tbsp oil
1 tbsp tomato purée
1.2 litre veal stock
60 g pumpernickel bread
2 tbsp apple compote
1 tbsp golden syrup
Salt · Ground pepper
approx. 120 ml soured cream

For the bread soufflé:
4 medium eggs
400 ml milk
2 tbsp chopped mixed herbs
(e.g. rosemary, thyme, parsley)
Salt · Ground pepper
Freshly grated nutmeg
Butter to grease the dish
300 g white bread
50 g soft butter

4 Remove the meat from the sauce, pass the sauce through a sieve and reduce slightly. Crumble the pumpernickel and add to the sauce along with the apple compote and golden syrup. Boil briefly. Warm the meat in the sauce, and season with salt and lots of pepper.

5 Arrange the pork on deep serving plates, and spoon 1 tbsp soured cream over. Trim the edges of the bread soufflé and serve with the meat.

▶▶ **Tips**

Golden syrup can be used to sweeten sauces or as an accompaniment to hash browns.

Roast veal
with prawn crust and mashed potato

Serves 4

Ingredients:

For the meat:
4 slices of veal backstrap or
saddle of veal
(160 g each; 3 cm thick)
40 g smoked streaky bacon
5 peeled, cooked prawns
60 g chicken breast fillet · Salt
100 ml cold double cream
4 sprigs of thyme
Lemon juice
Ground pepper
1 tbsp olive oil

For the potatoes:
500 g floury potatoes
Salt
150 ml milk
2 tbsp butter
Ground pepper

Also:
3 bunches of spring onions
120 g butter
1 tsp caster sugar
50 ml vegetable stock
Salt · Ground pepper
Pulp from 1 vanilla pod
Sea salt

1 Take the meat out of the fridge 1 hour in advance. Chop the bacon and fry until crispy, then drain on kitchen paper. Wash, dry and dice the prawns. Place in a bowl.

2 To make the stuffing, wash, dry and finely chop the chicken breast. Purée in a food processor with the cream and some salt. Add to the prawns along with the bacon and stir thoroughly. Wash, dry and chop the thyme. Stir the thyme and lemon juice into the purée and season with salt and pepper.

3 Season the meat with salt and pepper and spread with a 1 cm thick layer of the stuffing. Fry in a frying pan with olive oil for 1 minute on the side spread with stuffing, then turn and fry for 1 minute on the other side. Place on the rack with a baking tray underneath to catch the drips, and roast at 85°C (Conventional heat) on the second shelf for 50 to 60 minutes.

4 For the potatoes, peel and boil the potatoes in salted water. Heat the butter and milk, add to the potatoes and mash with a potato masher. Season with salt and pepper.

5 Wash the spring onions and chop the white parts only. Fry in a frying pan with 2 tbsp butter. Dust with caster sugar and caramelize, then pour in the stock. Cook until the liquid has evaporated, then add salt and pepper.

6 Melt the rest of the butter in a saucepan until foaming, then stir in the vanilla pulp and a little sea salt. Arrange the veal with the mashed potatoes and spring onions, and serve with the vanilla butter.

▶▶ Tips

When meat is to be cooked at a low temperature, it should always be removed from the fridge an hour or two before cooking, depending on the size, so that it will not take so long to cook.

Roast veal
with pancetta and celeriac cannelloni

Serves 4–6

1   For the roast, slice the meat through horizontally, open out and beat flat to achieve a 2 to 3 cm thick rectangle. Season with salt and pepper. Peel the garlic, wash and dry the basil, and chop along with the pine nuts and capers. Spread over the meat. Roll the meat up. Wrap the slices of pancetta around the meat and bind with kitchen string.

2   Season with pepper, then brown in a frying pan in olive oil for 3 to 4 minutes. Place on a baking tray and roast at 160°C (Moisture plus with 2 bursts of steam) on the second shelf for 45 to 60 minutes. Activate the first burst of steam at the beginning, and the second 10 minutes later.

3   To make the cannelloni, peel the potatoes and celeriac and cut into 1¹/₂ cm cubes. Sweat in a saucepan with 1 tbsp butter, then add the vegetable stock, cover and simmer for 30 minutes. Remove the lid 5 minutes before the end so that the liquid can evaporate.

Ingredients:

For the meat:
1.5 kg roasting veal
Sea salt · Ground pepper
2 cloves of garlic
1 bunch of basil
100 g pine nuts
80 g capers (pickled)
120 g pancetta or smoked streaky bacon
3 tbsp olive oil

For the cannelloni:
200 g floury potatoes
400 g celeriac
2 tbsp butter
200 ml vegetable stock
150 g grated Parmesan
Salt · Ground pepper
Freshly grated nutmeg
500 g cannelloni
Butter to grease the dish
150 g double cream
150 g crème fraîche

4   Purée with 50 g of Parmesan. Season with salt, pepper and nutmeg. Spoon into a piping bag and fill the cannelloni.

5   Grease an ovenproof dish and arrange the cannelloni in it. Stir together the double cream, crème fraîche and the remaining Parmesan, and pour over the cannelloni. Sprinkle with salt and pepper and place in the oven on the fourth shelf 25 minutes before the end of the cooking time for the meat.

6   Slice the veal and serve with the cannelloni, garnished with basil.

▶▶ Tips

Serve with braised spring onions: Wash 2 bunches of spring onions and chop in 6 cm long pieces. Sweat in 1 tbsp butter and season with salt, pepper and a little sugar.

Rump steak
with tarragon and mustard butter

Serves 4

1 Season the rump steaks with salt and pepper. Heat the olive oil in a frying pan and brown the steaks for 1 to 2 minutes on each side. Wash and dry the thyme. Crush the garlic and add to the frying pan with the thyme. Turn the steaks in the herbs then transfer to the rack with a baking tray underneath to catch the drips, and cook in the oven at 85°C (Conventional heat) on the second shelf for 40 to 50 minutes.

2 Wash the cherry tomatoes and place them in an ovenproof dish. Season with salt, pepper and sugar. Wash and dry the thyme. Crush the garlic and add to the tomatoes along with the thyme and olive oil. Cook in the oven with the meat for 30 minutes on the 3rd or 4th shelf level.

3 Beat the butter until soft. Wash and dry the tarragon and chop finely. Stir into the butter with the mustard and honey. Season with salt and pepper, and scoop onto a piece of clingfilm. Form into a log and place in the fridge.

Ingredients:

For the steaks:
4 rump steaks
(220 g each; 3 cm thick)
Salt · Ground pepper
2 tbsp olive oil
4 sprigs of thyme
1 clove of garlic

For the tomatoes:
250 g cherry tomatoes
Salt · Ground pepper
Sugar
4 sprigs of thyme
1 clove of garlic
4 tbsp olive oil

For the butter:
140 g soft butter
1/2 bunch of tarragon
1 tbsp Dijon mustard
1 tsp honey
Salt · Ground pepper

For the purée:
400 g celeriac
1 tbsp butter
100 ml chicken stock
200 ml double cream
Salt · Ground pepper

4 For the purée, peel the celeriac and cut into 1 cm cubes. Heat the butter in a saucepan and sweat the celeriac for 2 minutes. Pour in the chicken stock and double cream, cover and simmer for 20 to 30 minutes. Season with salt and pepper, then purée.

5 Unwrap the butter and cut in 1 cm thick slices. Divide among the steaks, place them on a baking tray and heat in the oven at 85°C (Conventional heat) on the second shelf for 2 to 3 minutes to melt the butter. Arrange the celeriac purée and tomatoes on serving plates. Cut the steaks diagonally in half and place on top.

▶▶ Tips

In place of the tarragon and mustard butter, you could serve the wild garlic butter shown on p. 88. Rump steak or beef fillet should be hung for a minimum of 2 weeks and should be nicely marbled.

Rare fillet of beef
with red wine and vanilla barley

Serve 4–6

1 Remove the fillet from the fridge 1 hour in advance. Cut away any fat and sinews. Season with five spice powder, salt and pepper. Brown in the oil for 5 minutes. Place on the rack and roast at 85°C (Conventional heat) on the second shelf for 2 hours until cooked but still pink in the centre. The core temperature should be 60–65°C when measured with the food probe.

2 Simmer the pearl barley in plenty of salted water for 15 minutes, then rinse under cold water. Peel and dice the shallots and sweat in the olive oil. Add the pearl barley and cook for 1 minute. Add the red wine and port, and boil until nearly all the liquid has evaporated. Add the vanilla pulp and stock, and simmer gently for 30 minutes. Stir in the butter and remove from the heat. The barley should be creamy. Season with salt and pepper.

Ingredients:

For the fillet:
1 kg beef fillet
(approx. 7–8 cm thick)
1/2 tsp five spice powder
Salt · Ground pepper
1 tbsp oil
1/2 bunch of thyme
2 tbsp butter

For the barley:
200 g pearl barley
Salt
3 shallots
2 tbsp olive oil
150 ml red wine
100 ml port
Pulp from 2 vanilla pods
1/2 litre chicken stock
50 g cold butter, cubed
Ground pepper

Also:
300 g spring vegetables
(e.g. baby carrots, sugar snap peas, spring onions, kohlrabi)
Salt
3 tbsp butter
Ground pepper
Sugar

3 Wash and peel the spring vegetables and blanch in salted water. Plunge into ice cold water, then sweat in the butter for 2 to 3 minutes. Season with salt, pepper and a little sugar.

4 For the fillet, wash and dry the thyme. Melt the butter in a frying pan until foamy, and turn the beef and thyme in it for 1 minute.

5 Divide the barley between serving plates. Slice the meat and arrange on top, and serve with the vegetables.

▶▶ Tips

Decorate with fried herbs. Fry rosemary, parsley or thyme leaves in 1 cm of oil until crispy. Drain on kitchen paper, and season with salt.

Oxtail parcels
with porcini mushrooms and herb salad

Serves 6

1 Season the oxtail with salt and pepper. Heat the oil in a casserole and brown the meat. Add the vegetables and fry for a further 5 to 10 minutes. Sprinkle over the sugar, and caramelize. Stir in the tomato purée. Add one third of the red wine and boil until it is nearly all evaporated. Repeat until all the wine is used.

2 Wash and dry the herbs. Peel the garlic. Add the herbs, garlic, bay leaves and stock to the casserole. Cover and cook in the oven at 140°C (Fan plus) on the second shelf for 2 hours.

3 Take the meat out of the casserole, allow to cool, then remove the bones. Sieve the sauce into a saucepan and reduce to 500 ml. Mix the potato flour with a little cold water and stir into the sauce to thicken. Season with salt and pepper.

Ingredients:

1.2 kg oxtail (cut into 4 to 5 cm thick pieces)
Salt · Ground pepper
2 tbsp oil
200 g diced onions
100 g each diced celeriac and carrots
1 tbsp sugar
1 tbsp tomato purée
600 ml red wine
3 sprigs of rosemary
3 sprigs of thyme
2 cloves of garlic
2 bay leaves
1 litre beef stock
1–2 tsp potato flour
400 g fresh porcini
1 tbsp butter
200 g good quality sausage meat
1 tbsp chopped parsley
200 g pig's caul (order from the butcher)
Butter to grease the dish
2 bunches of wild or mixed herbs
Aged balsamic vinegar
Olive oil

4 Clean, but do not wash, the porcini and cut into 1 to 1 1/2 cm cubes. Heat the butter in a pan and fry the mushrooms for 1 to 2 minutes, then season with salt and pepper. Put 6 tbsp to one side for the filling, keep the rest warm.

5 Mix the oxtail with the sausage meat and parsley, and season with salt and pepper. Cut the pig's caul into 6 pieces, 25 x 25 cm. Place the sausage meat in the middle of the pieces of caul, and make a little hollow in the top of each. Fill each one with 1 tbsp of mushrooms. Fold the edges of the caul over the top and place in a greased ovenproof dish, with the join underneath. Cook in the oven at 180°C (Fan plus) on the second shelf for 20 to 25 minutes. Baste occasionally with sauce.

6 Wash and dry the herbs. Toss in balsamic vinegar and olive oil, and divide between serving plates. Arrange the meat parcels on serving plates with the mushrooms in a pool of the sauce, and serve with buttered pasta.

Lamb ossobuco
with coconut, tomatoes and coriander

Serves 4

1 For the meat, season the lamb steaks with salt. Peel and dice the onion. Heat the oil in a casserole and brown the meat all over. Add the onions, and brown. Pour in the coconut milk, add the tomatoes and boil briefly. Cut the chillis in half lengthways, discard the seeds, wash and chop finely. Peel and grate the ginger. Add to the meat along with the green peppercorns and chilli, and season with salt. Cover and cook in the oven at 140°C (Fan plus) on the second shelf for 2 hours.

2 For the vegetables, wash and dry the pak choi. Cut into 3 to 4 cm long pieces. Heat the oil in a frying pan and fry the pak choi for 1 minute. Add the soy sauce and sesame oil and cook for 3 to 4 minutes.

Ingredients:

For the meat:
4–5 lamb leg steaks
(350 g each, 3 cm thick)
Salt
1 onion
2 tbsp oil
400 ml coconut milk
600 g tinned chopped tomatoes
2 red chillis
3 cm ginger
1 tbsp green peppercorns in brine

For the vegetables:
400 g pak choi or chinese cabbage
1 tbsp oil · 2 tbsp soy sauce
1 tsp sesame oil

Also:
1 tbsp desiccated coconut
1 bunch of coriander

3 Dry fry the desiccated coconut until golden brown. Wash and dry the coriander and chop finely.

4 Place the lamb on deep serving plates with the pak choi, and sprinkle with coriander and coconut. Serve with fragrant rice or fried egg noodles.

▶▶ Tips

The classic ossobuco comes from Italy and is made from veal steaks with tomatoes, carrots, onions and stock or white wine. It is served with risotto or polenta.

Pot roasted leg of lamb
with candied garlic

Serves 4–6

1   Season the lamb with salt and pepper. Heat the olive oil in a casserole and brown the meat all over. Remove, and brown the onions. Add the celeriac and carrots, and fry. Stir in the tomato purée. Pour in the red wine and boil until nearly all the wine has evaporated.

2   Add the chicken stock and tomatoes. Wash and dry the rosemary. Add to the casserole with the bay leaves and bring to the boil. Place the lamb in the casserole and cover with the pancetta.

3   Cook the lamb in the oven at 130°C (Moisture plus with 3 bursts of steam) on the second shelf for 2 ¹/₂ to 3 hours. Activate one burst of steam at the beginning, and the second and third at hourly intervals.

4   Peel the garlic and simmer in the milk for 5 minutes. Pour off the milk and rinse the garlic in cold water. Caramelize the sugar in a small saucepan and add the garlic. Add the vinegar and chicken stock. Sweat over a gentle heat for 10 minutes, then simmer until the liquid becomes syrupy. Stir in the butter and keep the candied garlic warm.

Ingredients:

For the meat:
1 leg of lamb
(approx 1.8 kg, boned)
Salt · Ground pepper
3 tbsp olive oil
150 g diced onions
80 g each diced celeriac and carrots
1 tbsp tomato purée
400 ml red wine
450 ml chicken stock
400 g tinned tomatoes
5 sprigs of rosemary
2 bay leaves
100 g pancetta or streaky bacon
400 g flageolet beans (tinned)
1–2 tsp grated unwaxed lemon zest

For the garlic:
2 heads of young garlic
(20–24 small cloves)
200 ml milk
40 g sugar
40 ml white balsamic vinegar
50 ml chicken stock
30 g cold butter, cubed

5   Remove the meat from the casserole, place it on the rack and grill in the oven at 240°C (Full grill) on the third shelf until the pancetta is crisp. Put the sauce in the casserole on the hob. Remove the rosemary and bay leaf. Drain the flageolet beans and add to the sauce. Bring to the boil and season with salt, pepper and lemon zest.

6   Divide the beans between serving plates. Slice the lamb and place on top of the beans. Garnish with the candied garlic and a drizzle of the syrup.

Rack of lamb
with a crispy crust and balsamic vegetables

Serves 4

1 Season the lamb with salt and pepper, and brown on both sides in olive oil for 2 to 3 minutes. Place on the wire rack and roast at 85°C (Conventional heat) on the second shelf for 50 minutes. Place a baking tray underneath to catch the drips.

2 Caramelize the sugar in a frying pan until golden. Add the pine nuts, stir quickly and transfer immediately to a baking tray. Leave to cool then chop up small. Chop the olives. Beat the butter to soften and stir in the pine nuts, olives, rosemary and breadcrumbs. Season with salt and pepper. Place in a freezer bag then roll out with a rolling pin to a thickness of 7 mm. Place in the fridge.

3 Prepare the vegetables. Chop the onion, aubergine and red pepper into 2 cm pieces. Cut the courgette into 1 cm thick slices. Heat the olive oil in a frying pan and gently fry the pepper, aubergine and onion for 10 minutes. Wash and dry the rosemary. Add to the pan with the courgette and crushed garlic. Cook for a further 5 minutes, then season with salt and pepper. Remove the garlic and rosemary, and keep the vegetables warm.

Ingredients:

For the meat:
2 rack of lamb
(650 g each, on the bone)
Salt · Ground pepper
2 tbsp olive oil
1 tbsp sugar
80 g pine nuts
60 g black olives (stoned)
100 g soft butter
1 tsp chopped rosemary
1 tbsp breadcrumbs

For the vegetables:
1 onion
1 eggplant/aubergine
1 red pepper
1 medium zucchini/courgette
2 tbsp olive oil
2 sprigs of rosemary
1 clove of garlic
Salt · Ground pepper
100 ml balsamic vinegar
100 ml red grape juice or port
50 g sugar

4 Boil the vinegar, grape juice and sugar together until syrupy, and shortly before serving, pour over the vegetables.

5 Remove the lamb from the oven and pre-heat the grill to 240°C (Full grill). Cut the pine nut crust into two rectangles to fit the lamb. Place on the lamb and grill in the oven on the third shelf for 3 to 5 minutes.

▶▶ Tips

Serve with new potatoes that have been boiled, then lightly fried in olive oil and seasoned with sea salt. Make sure that the lamb is from a young animal.

Venison loin with a
white bread crust and roasted apple sauce

Serves 4

1   Heat 2 tbsp of oil in a casserole and brown the venison bones for 10 to 15 minutes. Add the onion, celeriac and carrots and cook for a further 10 minutes. Dust with sugar, and caramelize. Stir in the tomato purée, add a third of the red wine, and boil until nearly all of the wine has evaporated. Repeat the process until all the wine is used up. Add the game stock and simmer gently for 1 hour. After 45 minutes add the bay leaf, juniper berries, cranberries and orange rind. Pass the sauce through a sieve and reduce to 300 ml, thickening with cornflour if necessary. Season with salt and pepper.

2   To make the apple sauce, wash the apples and cut a 1 cm thick lid from the top of each. Use an apple corer to remove the core. Knead together the marzipan, hazelnuts and thyme and use to stuff the apples. Place the apples on a baking tray, dot with the butter, and bake in the oven at 160°C (Fan plus) on the second shelf for 30 to 40 minutes.

3   With a spoon, scoop out the insides of the apple into a saucepan. Mash with a fork and season with salt, pepper and sugar. Keep the apple sauce warm.

Ingredients:

For the meat:
3 tbsp oil
2 pieces of venison loin
(360 g each, boned, bones chopped up)
100 g diced onions
80 g each diced celeriac and carrots
1 tsp caster sugar
1 tsp tomato purée
300 ml red wine
800 ml game stock · 1 bay leaf
5 juniper berries
1 tbsp cranberries (bottled)
1 strip of unwaxed orange rind (approx. 5 cm long)
Salt · Ground pepper
180 g good quality sausage meat
1 tsp mixed herbs
1 tsp chopped parsley
8 thin slices white bread
1 tbsp butter

For the apple sauce:
3 apples (russet or Braeburn)
50 g marzipan
50 g ground hazelnuts
1 tbsp chopped thyme
1 tbsp butter · Salt
Ground pepper · Sugar

4   Cut the pieces of venison down the middle to create 4 fillets, 10 to 12 cm long. Mix the sausage meat with 1/2 tsp mixed herbs and the parsley. Season with salt and pepper. Season the venison with salt and pepper too. Brown the fillets in the rest of the oil. Remove from the pan and allow to cool slightly.

5   Trim the slices of bread and spread thinly with the sausage meat. Lay 2 slices next to each other, place a fillet on top and roll up. Repeat with the other fillets. Heat the butter in a frying pan and brown the meat rolls all over. Place on the rack and cook in the oven at 160°C (Fan plus) on the second shelf for 10 to 15 minutes. Remove from the oven and leave to rest for 5 minutes.

6   Divide the apple sauce between the serving plates. Cut the venison fillets in half, arrange on top of the apple sauce and pour the gravy over.

Vegetables and bakes

Baked dishes are often not as appreciated as they should be. Many people like them because they are easy to prepare, but few understand their full culinary potential. Whether sophisticated or rustic, discover the delights that lie hidden beneath the crisp topping. The family will want them time and again!

Baked potatoes on sea salt
with beetroot, porcini and eggplant aubergines

Serves 4

Ingredients:

12 medium potatoes
(approx. 1.2 kg)
7 tbsp olive oil
1 bunch of rosemary
1 kg coarse sea salt
1 small eggplant/aubergine
Salt
1 unwaxed lemon
400 ml soured cream
250 g crème fraîche
1 tsp grated horseradish
1 clove of garlic
1 red pepper
2 tbsp basil
(chopped)
Ground pepper
120 g beetroot
(vacuum packed)
200 g porcini mushroms
1 container cress
30 g crispy fried onions
1–2 tbsp balsamic vinegar

1 Thoroughly wash the potatoes. Dry with kitchen paper and pierce 2 or 3 times with a fork. Wash and dry the rosemary.

2 Spread the sea salt out on a baking tray and scatter the rosemary over it. Brush the potatoes with olive oil. Place the potatoes on the salt bed and bake at 160°C (Fan plus) on the second shelf for 50 to 60 minutes.

3 Wash the aubergine and cut into thin slices. Salt and leave for 15 minutes. Wash the lemon in hot water, dry, grate the rind and squeeze out the juice.

4 Stir together the soured cream and creme fraîche and divide into three bowls. Season one with a squeeze of lemon juice and the horseradish. Peel and chop the garlic and stir into the second portion of crème fraîche with 1 tsp lemon zest. For the third portion, deseed and finely chop the red pepper and stir into the cream with the basil. Season the dips with salt and pepper.

5 Pat the aubergine slices dry with kitchen paper and fry in 2 tbsp oil for 2 to 3 minutes on each side. Remove from the pan and season with pepper.

6 Slice the beetroot thinly. Cut the cress from its container. Clean and slice the mushrooms, and fry with the onions for 2 to 3 minutes in the remaining olive oil. Season with salt and pepper.

7 Cut a deep cross into the potatoes and open up. Fill 4 potatoes with each of the dips. Scatter some beetroot and cress over the potatoes filled with the horseradish cream. Spoon some mushrooms and fried onions onto the potatoes with the garlic cream. Add the aubergines to the ones with the basil cream. Drizzle with vinegar, and serve a potato containing each of the different fillings to each person.

▶▶ Tips

If fresh porcini are not available, use 40 g of dried ones. Soak for at least 30 minutes in lukewarm water, squeeze out well and fry in hot oil.

Potato bake
with chilli salmon, fennel and crispy bread topping

Serves 4–6

1   Scrub the potatoes. Cut into thin slices, cook in salted water for 5 to 6 minutes, then drain.

2   Wash and dry the fennel. Peel the garlic and onions. Finely chop the garlic. Cut the fennel and onions into thin slices, and sweat in 3 tbsp olive oil for 3 to 4 minutes. Add the garlic, wine and a pinch of saffron. Simmer for 5 minutes until the wine has evaporated. Season with salt and pepper.

3   To make the marinade, cut the chillis in half lengthways, discard the seeds, wash and chop finely. Drain and chop the anchovies. Mix the chillis and anchovies with the lemon juice. Wash and dry the salmon and cut into 2 cm thick slices. Turn in the marinade and season with salt and pepper.

Ingredients:

500 g new potatoes · Salt
400 g fennel
1 clove of garlic
2 onions
5–7 tbsp olive oil
100 ml white wine
Powdered saffron
Ground pepper
2 red chillis
2 anchovy fillets (in oil)
Juice of 1 lemon
600 g salmon fillet (skinned)
Butter to grease the dish
300 ml double cream
100 g grated Parmesan
Sea salt
100 g bread

4   Grease an ovenproof dish (approx. 30 x 25 cm) and add the fennel mixture. Stir 60 g of Parmesan into the cream and pour over the fennel. Place the fish on top and drizzle with the marinade. Cover with the slices of potato, drizzle with 1 to 2 tbsp olive oil, and season with salt and pepper. Bake at 180°C (Fan plus) on the second shelf for 20 to 25 minutes.

5   Roughly chop the bread in a food processor and mix with the remaining Parmesan. Sprinkle over the dish and drizzle with 1 to 2 tbsp olive oil. Bake for a further 10 to 15 minutes until the bread topping is golden and crispy.

> ▶▶ **Tips**
>
> *Try replacing the salmon with a firm white fish. Serve with beetroot salad topped with a dressing of sour cream, lemon juice, salt and pepper. Scatter with chopped basil.*

Pasta and broccoli bake
with red pepper crumbs

Serves 4–6

1 Cook the pasta according to the instructions on the packet until al dente. Drain, rinse in cold water and leave to dry. Wash and dry the broccoli and break into florets. Blanch for 20 seconds in salted boiling water and plunge into ice cold water. Wash and halve the cherry tomatoes. Grease an ovenproof dish (approx. 30 x 25 cm) with 2 tbsp olive oil.

2 Peel the garlic. Wash and dry the basil, and remove the leaves. Purée the tinned tomatoes, garlic, anchovies, basil and capers with a hand-held blender. Stir in 3 tbsp olive oil and season with salt and pepper.

Ingredients:

400 g pasta, e.g. orecchiette
Salt
600 g broccoli
200 g cherry tomatoes
100 ml olive oil
2 cloves of garlic
1 bunch of basil
800 g tinned tomatoes
4 anchovies (in oil)
50 g capers (pickled)
Ground pepper
100 g each Parmesan
and asiago cheese, or 200 g of
Parmesan
2 red peppers
100 g fresh white bread

3 Mix the broccoli and cherry tomatoes with the pasta and sauce, and place in the dish. Sprinkle the two cheeses on top.

4 Halve, deseed, wash and finely chop the peppers. Reduce the bread to crumbs in a food processor. Mix the pepper and breadcrumbs with the remaining olive oil and sprinkle over the pasta, along with salt and pepper. Bake at 180°C (Fan plus) on the second shelf for 30 to 35 minutes. Remove from the oven, allow to cool slightly and serve.

▸▸ Tips

Serve with and tomato and rocket salad. Asiago is an Italian hard cheese from the Venetian area. As an alternative, use Cheddar or Gouda cheese.

Macaroni bake
with tomatoes, mushrooms and taleggio

Serves 4–6

Ingredients:

400 g short macaroni · Salt
600 g tomatoes on the vine
2 cloves of garlic
1 bunch of basil
100 g Parmesan
500 ml double cream
Ground pepper
2 onions
500 g mixed mushrooms
(eg. chanterelles, porcini,
chestnut mushrooms)
5 tbsp olive oil
Freshly grated nutmeg
Butter to grease the dish
400 g taleggio cheese
1 bunch of parsley
100 g fresh white bread

1   Cook the macaroni in plenty of salted water according to the instructions on the packet until al dente. Drain, refresh under cold water and leave to stand. Make a cross shaped slit in the top of the tomatoes, blanch in boiling water for 15 seconds and then plunge into ice cold water. Remove the skins, quarter the tomatoes and remove the cores. Deseed and chop.

2   Peel the garlic. Wash and dry the basil, and remove the leaves. Purée the tomatoes, garlic and basil with a handheld blender. Grate the Parmesan finely and stir into the tomato purée along with the cream. Season with salt and pepper.

3   Peel and dice the onions. Clean and slice the mushrooms. Sweat the onions in 2 tbsp olive oil. Add the mushrooms and fry for a further 2 to 3 minutes. Season with salt, pepper and nutmeg.

4   Grease an oven dish (approx. 30 x 25 cm). Mix the pasta with the sauce and the mushrooms in the dish. Slice the cheese as thinly as possible and spread over the pasta. Cook in the oven at 180°C (Fan plus) on the second shelf for 30 to 35 minutes.

5   Wash and dry the parsley, and remove the leaves. Cut the bread into small cubes. Fry the parsley in the remaining olive oil for 2 to 3 minutes until crisp. Remove from the pan and fry the bread cubes until golden. Sprinkle the bread and parsley over the pasta, and serve.

▶▶ Tips

Taleggio is an unpasteurised cheese from the region of Bergamo. It is ripened in underground caves, is straw coloured and has a soft consistency. As an alternative, use Camembert or Brie.

Rigatoni bake
with vegetable bolognese

Serves 4–6

1 Boil the rigatoni in plenty of salted water for 5 to 6 minutes. Drain, refresh under cold water, then leave to stand. Peel the onion and 2 cloves of garlic. Wash the aubergine and courgette. Peel the peppers with a potato peeler, halve and remove the seeds. Chop the vegetables finely with a sharp knife or in a food processor.

2 Wash, dry and finely chop the oregano and thyme. Heat 2 tbsp of oil in a saucepan and fry the vegetables for 3 to 5 minutes. Add the tomato purée. Stir in the tinned tomatoes and bring to the boil. Stir in the oregano and thyme, and season with salt and pepper. Add dried chilli flakes or cayenne pepper if desired.

3 Grease an ovenproof dish (approx. 30 x 25 cm) with 2 tbsp olive oil, and stand the rigatoni upright in the dish.

Ingredients:

400 g rigatoni pasta · Salt
1 onion
4 cloves of garlic
1 eggplant/aubergine
2 small zucchini/courgettes
1 red and 1 yellow pepper
1 bunch of oregano
1 bunch of thyme
110 ml olive oil
1 tbsp tomato purée
800 g tinned chopped tomatoes
Ground pepper
150 g grated Parmesan
400 g ricotta cheese
Sea salt
1 tbsp grated unwaxed lemon zest
1 tbsp chopped parsley

4 Spread the sauce over the rigatoni so that they are almost entirely covered. Shake the dish slightly to distribute the sauce evenly. Sprinkle Parmesan over and dot with ricotta. Drizzle 2 tbsp olive oil over the ricotta and sprinkle with sea salt.

5 Bake at 180°C (Fan plus) on the second shelf for 35 to 40 minutes.

6 Peel and chop the rest of the garlic and sweat in the remaining oil. Add the lemon zest and parsley, and drizzle the herbed oil over the bake when it comes out of the oven.

▸▸ Tips

You could also flavour the herbed oil with chopped rosemary, grated unwaxed orange rind and pink peppercorns. It saves time to chop the vegetables in a food processor.

Pumpkin lasagne
with veal and pine nuts

Serves 4–6

Ingredients:

2 onions
2 cloves of garlic
50 g smoked streaky bacon
approx. 100 ml olive oil
500 g veal
1 tbsp tomato purée
300 ml chicken stock
800 g tinned chopped
tomatoes
2 dried red chillis
2 bay leaves
6 sprigs of rosemary
Sea salt
Ground pepper
Ground cinnamon
600–800 g butternut squash or
pumpkin
1 tbsp coriander seeds
4 anchovies (in oil)
400 g crème fraîche
3–4 tbsp milk
100 g grated Parmesan
400 g lasagne sheets
300 g mozzarella
60 g pine nuts

1   Peel and dice the onions and garlic. Dice the bacon and fry in a cassserole in 2 tbsp olive oil. Add the onions and garlic and cook for a further 2 minutes. Remove the casserole from the heat.

2   Chop the veal into $1/2$ cm cubes and brown in 2 tbsp olive oil for 5 minutes. Add to the casserole along with the tomato purée, stock and tinned tomatoes. Crumble in one dried chilli and add to the other ingredients along with the bay leaves and rosemary. Season with sea salt, pepper and cinnamon. Cover and cook in the oven at 140°C (Conventional heat) on the second shelf for 2 hours.

3   Peel and deseed the pumpkin or squash and cut into 1 cm thick slices. Grind the coriander and remaining chilli in a pestle and mortar. Add sea salt, pepper and a pinch of cinnamon, and stir in 3 tbsp olive oil. Place the pumpkin on a baking tray lined with baking paper and drizzle with the spiced oil. Cook in the oven with the meat on the fourth shelf for 45 minutes.

4   Finely chop the anchovies and mix with the creme fraîche, milk and Parmesan . Season with a little salt and pepper.

5   Grease an ovenproof dish (approx. 30 x 25 cm) with 2 tbsp olive oil and place a layer of lasagne in the bottom. Build up alternating layers of meat sauce, pumpkin, crème fraîche and lasagne, finishing with a layer of the crème fraîche.

6   Slice the mozzarella and distribute over the pasta. Cook in the oven at 180°C (Fan plus) on the second shelf for 35 to 40 minutes until the pasta is soft and the topping is lightly browned.

7   Dry roast the pine nuts in a frying pan, chop and sprinkle over the pasta bake.

Ricotta cannelloni
with radicchio and onion filling

Serves 4–6

1   Peel and dice the onions. Clean the radicchio and remove the stalk. Wash and dry the leaves and cut into thin strips.

2   Caramelize the icing sugar in a frying pan. Add 1 tbsp butter, the onion and radicchio, and fry for 2 to 3 minutes. Add the vinegar, thyme and grape juice, and simmer until nearly all the liquid has evaporated. Place the mixture to one side to cool. Stir in the ricotta and egg, and season with salt and pepper.

3   Grease an ovenproof dish (approx. 25 x 22 cm). Put the ricotta mixture into a piping bag and fill the cannelloni. Arrange them in the dish.

Ingredients:

4–5 red onions (approx. 200 g)
500 g radicchio
1 tbsp caster sugar
60 g butter
2 tbsp red wine vinegar
1 tbsp chopped thyme
200 ml red grape juice
250 g ricotta cheese
1 medium egg
Sea salt
Ground pepper
Butter to grease the dish
16–18 cannelloni
200 ml double cream
200 ml chicken stock
2 tbsp flour
Freshly grated nutmeg
200 g fontina or asiago cheese
50 g Parmesan
1/2 bunch of basil

4   Bring the cream and stock to the boil. Melt the remaining butter in a saucepan. Add the flour, then stir in the stock and cream and bring to the boil. Season with salt, pepper and nutmeg and put to one side.

5   Chop the fontina/asagio. Finely grate the Parmesan, and stir both cheeses into the cream mixture. Pour over the cannelloni and bake at 180°C (Fan plus) on the second shelf for 30 minutes.

6   Wash, dry and chop the basil. Remove the cannelloni from the oven and scatter over the basil before serving.

▶▶ Tips

Cannelloni are large tubes of pasta. The easiest way to fill them is to use a piping bag. Serve with a green salad dressed with balsamic vinegar and roasted nuts.

Asparagus pizza
with wild garlic leaves and cream cheese

For 1 baking tray

Ingredients:

For the dough:
250 g strong white flour
20 g fresh yeast
1/2 tsp sugar
5 tbsp olive oil · Salt

For the topping:
50 g wild garlic leaves
(or rocket)
300 g spinach
Sea salt
Ground pepper
800 g asparagus
1 tbsp butter
Sugar
1–2 red peppers
1 bunch of parsley
1 clove of garlic
100 g Parmesan
250 g mozzarella
200 g cream cheese
200 g crème fraîche
5 tbsp olive oil

1   To make the dough, place the flour in a bowl and make a well in the centre. Dissolve the yeast with the sugar in 1/8 l of lukewarm water, and pour into the well. Stir in the flour from the edges to create a thin dough. Cover with a damp cloth and leave in a warm place for 15 minutes to rise.

2   Add the olive oil and 1 tsp salt, stir in the rest of the flour and knead with the kneading hook of an electric mixer for at least 5 minutes until the dough is shiny and elastic. Cover and leave to rise again in a warm place for 45 minutes.

3   Knead again briefly, then roll out on a baking tray to a thickness of 1/2 cm. Leave to rise for another 20 minutes.

4   Wash the wild garlic and spinach, and remove any large stalks. Blanch in boiling water for 10 seconds, plunge into ice cold water and squeeze out well. Chop coarsely and season with salt and pepper.

5   Snap the woody ends off the asparagus and cut the stalks diagonally into 1/2 cm thick slices. Melt the butter in a frying pan and sweat the asparagus for 2 to 3 minutes. Season with salt, pepper and sugar.

6   Wash, halve, deseed and finely dice the peppers. Wash, dry and chop the parsley. Peel and chop the garlic. Grate the Parmesan. Cut the mozzarella into slices. Mix the cream cheese with the crème fraîche, Parmesan and 3 tbsp olive oil. Stir in the garlic, parsley and peppers. Season with sea salt and pepper.

7   Spread half of the mixture over the pizza base. Cover with the asparagus, wild garlic, spinach and mozzarella. Top with the remaining cream cheese mixture. Bake at 200°C (Moisture plus with 1 automatic burst of steam) on the second shelf for 30 to 35 minutes. Remove the pizza from the oven, drizzle with olive oil and serve.

Pumpkin pie
with orange and sesame salad

For 1 pie or tart tin (26 cm Ø)

1   To make the pastry base, pile the flour and 2 pinches of salt onto the work surface. Cut the butter into small cubes, add to the flour and work in with a knife. Beat the egg yolk and stir in. Add 1 tbsp iced water and knead quickly to a dough with cold hands. Wrap in clingfilm and put in the fridge for 30 minutes.

2   To make the filling, peel and deseed the pumpkin, and cut into 2 to 3 cm thick slices. Peel the garlic. Grind the coriander, fennel, pepper and chilli in a pestle and mortar. Add the garlic and olive oil and work in. Place the pumpkin slices in an ovenproof dish and drizzle with the spiced oil. Cook in the oven at 160°C (Fan plus) on the second shelf for 30 minutes.

3   Grease the pie dish or tart tin. Roll out the pastry for the base on a floured work surface and use to line the dish, pressing down well. Trim the edges and place in the fridge.

4   Wash, dry and chop the coriander. Crush the pumpkin flesh slightly, and mix with the crème fraîche, eggs and half the coriander. Season with sea salt.

Ingredients:

For the pastry base:
250 g plain flour · Salt
130 g cold butter
1 egg yolk
Butter to grease the dish
Flour for the work surface
300 g puff pastry, fresh or frozen
1 medium egg (beaten)

For the filling:
approx. 1.2 kg pumpkin or butternut squash
1 clove of garlic
$1/2$ tsp each coriander seeds, fennel seeds and black peppercorns
1 dried chilli
3 tbsp olive oil
1 bunch of coriander
150 g crème fraîche
2 medium eggs
Sea salt

For the salad:
3 oranges (seedless)
2 red peppers
2 tbsp olive oil
2 tbsp white wine vinegar
1 tsp honey
1 tbsp sesame seeds (toasted)
Salt · Ground pepper

5   Spread the pumpkin over the pastry. Roll the puff pastry out onto a floured surface to a thickness of $1/2$ cm. Place on top of the pumpkin, pressing the edges down well to seal the pie. Brush with the beaten egg. Make a 2 cm hole in the centre of the pastry for the steam to escape. Bake at 160°C (Intensive bake) on the second shelf for 40 to 45 minutes. Remove from the oven, cool slightly, then remove from the dish.

6   To make the salad, peel the oranges, removing all the pith. Divide into segments. Halve the peppers, remove the seeds, wash and chop finely. Mix together with the olive oil, vinegar, honey and sesame seeds. Season with salt and pepper. Stir the oranges and the remaining coriander into the dressing and leave to stand. Cut the pie into pieces and serve with the orange salad.

Sweet potato and celeriac strudel
with basil and mint pesto

Makes 2 strudels

1   To make the pastry, sieve the flour into a bowl. Beat together the egg yolk, 3 tbsp oil, 150 ml water and a pinch of salt, stir into the flour, then knead to an elastic dough using the kneading hook of an electric mixer. Divide the dough in half, form into balls, and brush with the remaining oil. Wrap in cling-flim, and leave to stand for 1 hour.

2   To make the filling, peel and grate the ginger. Peel the sweet potato and celeriac, and cut into 1 cm cubes. Fry in a casserole in 2 tbsp butter for 2 to 3 minutes. Add the chilli and ginger, and season with salt, pepper and nutmeg. Cover and cook in the oven at 160°C (Fan plus) on the second shelf for 20 minutes. Remove the chilli.

3   Purée the vegetables using a handheld blender. Stir in the crème fraîche and eggs. Fry the bread-crumbs in 80 g butter, then mix with the thyme and season with salt.

4   Roll one of the balls of pastry out thin on a floured surface and place on a floured tea towel. Oil your hands and gently stretch the pastry out to form a paper-thin rec-tangle (approx. 38 x 35 cm). Brush

Ingredients:

For the pastry:
300 g plain flour
1 egg yolk · 4 tbsp oil
Salt
Flour and oil
4 tbsp butter

For the filling:
3 cm ginger
600 g each sweet potatoes
and celeriac
100 g butter
1 dried chilli
Sea salt
Ground pepper
Freshly grated nutmeg
200 g crème fraîche
2 medium eggs
80 g breadcrumbs
1 tbsp chopped thyme

For the pesto:
1/2 bunch of mint
2 bunches of basil
1/2 clove of garlic
60 g pine nuts
40 g grated Parmesan
1 tsp grated lemon zest
150 ml olive oil
Salt · Ground pepper

immediately with melted butter, and sprinkle with half the thyme and breadcrumbs.

5   Place a 10 to 15 cm wide pile of filling along the edge of the pastry. Roll up the strudel with the help of the tea towel.

6   Place the strudel with the join underneath on a baking tray. Tuck the ends underneath. Brush with melted butter. Repeat the process to make the second strudel. Bake them in the oven at 180°C (Conventional heat) on the second shelf for 35 to 40 minutes.

7   To make the pesto, wash dry and chop the mint and basil leaves. Peel and roughly chop the garlic. Dry roast the pine nuts in a frying pan. Purée all the ingredients together with a handheld blender to make a pesto. Season with salt and pepper.

8   Remove the strudels from the oven and cool slightly. Slice and serve with the pesto.

Rabbit casserole with a
puff pastry top, sprinkled with rosemary and orange salt

Serve 4–6

Ingredients:

1 kg rabbit meat (boned)
2 leeks and 2 celery stalks
2 carrots
1 unwaxed orange
2 tbsp butter
2 level tbsp flour
200 ml dry white wine
300 ml double cream
200 ml chicken stock
2 tbsp chopped rosemary
Sea salt
Ground pepper
250 g skinned salsiccia Italian
sausages, or pork sausage
meat
1 tbsp olive oil
300 g puff pastry, fresh or
frozen
1 medium egg
4 tbsp milk

1   For the meat, remove any fat and sinews, and cut into 1 cm pieces. Wash and chop the leeks, celery and carrots into $1/2$ cm thick slices. Wash the orange in hot water, dry, grate the rind and squeeze out the juice.

2   Melt the butter in an ovenproof pan, and brown the meat for 3 to 5 minutes. Add the vegetables and fry for a further 2 to 3 minutes. Dust with the flour and fry a little more. Pour in the wine, orange juice, cream and stock. Add 1 tbsp rosemary and season with salt and pepper. Cover and cook in the oven at 160°C (Fan plus) on the second shelf for 60 minutes.

3   Form the sausage meat into little balls and fry for 1 to 2 minutes in hot olive oil. Stir the sausage balls in with the rabbit, season with salt and pepper, and transfer to an ovenproof dish.

4   Roll the puff pastry out to $1/2$ cm thick to fit the oven dish. Beat the egg yolk and milk together. Brush the edges of the oven dish with the egg mixture, place the pastry on top to form a lid, press the edges down well, and brush the top with the rest of the egg mixture. Score the pastry in a diamond pattern and bake at 190°C (Fan plus) on the second shelf for 30 to 35 minutes until golden.

5   To make the rosemary and orange salt, grind the orange rind and remaining rosemary with 1 tbsp sea salt in a pestle and mortar. Divide the rabbit pie between serving plates and sprinkle with a pinch of the orange and rosemary salt.

▸▸ Tips

Rabbit meat is generally pale and tender with a slightly sweet taste. It does not have the typical flavour of game. Serve with mashed potato or small baked potatoes.

Colourful tomato tart
with yoghurt and crunchy Parmesan

Serves 4 ⌗

1   The day before, wash, dry and chop the herbs. Peel and finely chop the garlic. Mix the herbs and garlic with the yoghurt, and season with salt and pepper. Place a sieve over a bowl, and line the sieve with a clean tea towel. Pour in the yoghurt, cover and leave to drip overnight in the fridge.

2   The next day, roll the puff pastry out to the size of a baking tray, 1/2 cm thick and trim the edges. Place the pastry on the baking tray lined with baking paper. Spread the yoghurt over the pastry, leaving a 1 cm wide band free around the edge.

3   Make a cross shaped slit in the tomatoes and blanch for 10 seconds in boiling water. Plunge into ice cold water, then remove the skins. Drizzle the tomatoes with olive oil, and season with salt, pepper and a little sugar. Distribute the tomatoes over the yoghurt. Beat together the egg yolk and cream, and brush over the edges of the pastry.

Ingredients:

1 bunch of fresh herbs
(parsley, chives, tarragon, basil)
1 clove of garlic
500 g Greek yoghurt
Sea salt
Ground pepper
300 g puff pastry, fresh or frozen
600 g red and yellow cherry tomatoes
2 tbsp olive oil
Sugar
1 egg yolk
2 tbsp double cream
Butter to grease the tin
100 g Parmesan

4   Grease a baking tray. Finely grate the Parmesan and sprinkle thinly over the tray. Press down slightly and cook under a pre-heated grill at 240°C (Full grill) on the fourth shelf for 5 minutes until golden brown and crispy. Remove from the oven and leave to cool.

5   Bake the tart in the oven at 180°C (Moisture plus with 1 automatic burst of steam) on the second shelf for 25 to 30 minutes. Remove from the oven and cool slightly. Crumble the Parmesan and sprinkle over the tart. Garnish with herbs.

▶▶ Tips

If any herbs are left over, chop them finely and freeze them in portions. An ice cube tray is ideal for this.

Stuffed onions
with ratatouille and pizza bread

Serves 4

1   To make the dough, place the flour in a bowl and make a well in the centre. Dissolve the yeast with a pinch of sugar in 65 ml lukewarm water. Pour into the well and stir in the flour from the edges to form a thin dough. Cover with a damp tea towel and leave in a warm place for 15 minutes to rise.

2   Finely chop the garlic and add to the bowl with 1/2 tsp salt, the olive oil and rosemary. Stir in the rest of the flour. Knead with the kneading hook of an electric mixer for 10 minutes to form a shiny, elastic dough. Cover and leave in a warm place for 45 minutes to rise.

3   Peel the onions and cook in salted water for 6 to 8 minutes, then leave to cool. Cut a 1 cm thick lid from the top of the onions and hollow out enough of the insides to leave room for 1 to 2 tbsp filling. Peel the garlic and chop with one third of the hollowed out onion flesh. Cut the pepper in half and deseed, and wash the eggplant/ aubergine and zucchini/courgette. Chop into 1/2 cm cubes.

Ingredients:

For the dough:
140 g plain flour
10 g fresh yeast
Sugar
1 clove of garlic
Salt
2 tbsp olive oil
1 tbsp chopped rosemary
Flour

For the onions:
4 large onions
Sea salt
1 clove of garlic
1 red pepper
1/2 eggplant/aubergine
1 small zucchini/courgette
5 tbsp olive oil
1 tbsp each chopped rosemary
and thyme
200 g tinned chopped
tomatoes
100 g grated Parmesan
Ground pepper
4 sprigs of basil

4   Fry the vegetables and onions in 3 tbsp olive oil for 4 to 5 minutes. Stir in the herbs, tinned tomatoes and garlic, and simmer for 10 to 12 minutes. Add 60 g Parmesan and season with salt and pepper. Fill the onions with the ratatouille mixture and sprinkle with the rest of the Parmesan .

5   Divide the dough into 4 pieces. Flour your hands and flatten the dough into 1 to 2 cm thick pieces. Place on a baking tray. Press the onions firmly in the centre of the dough and leave to rise for 15 minutes.

6   Brush the edges of the dough with the remaining olive oil and bake at 160°C (Moisture plus with 1 automatic burst of steam) on the second shelf for 25 to 30 minutes. Remove from the oven and allow to cool slightly.

7   Wash and dry the basil, and remove the leaves. Scatter over the pizzas and serve.

Stuffed peppers
with couscous and lemon chutney

Serves 4

1 For the peppers, dry roast the almonds in a frying pan. Place the couscous, raisins and almonds in a bowl. Bring the vegetable stock to the boil and pour over the couscous. Leave to swell for 5 minutes, then fluff up with a fork. Wash and dry the coriander. Chop and stir into the couscous with the butter. Season with sugar, salt, pepper and cumin.

2 Cut a lid from the peppers. Remove the cores and fill generously with couscous. Replace the lids.

3 To make the sauce, peel the garlic and onions. Cut the chilli in half lengthways and discard the seeds. Finely chop the chilli, onion and garlic, and sweat in olive oil. Add the tomatoes and bring to the boil. Season with salt, pepper, ground coriander and cumin.

4 Pour the sauce into an ovenproof dish. Place the peppers in the dish, cover and cook in the oven at 160°C (Fan plus) on the second shelf for 50 to 60 minutes.

Ingredients:

For the peppers:
50 g flaked almonds
260 g instant couscous
40 g raisins
600 ml vegetable stock
1 bunch of coriander
1 tbsp soft butter · 1 tsp sugar
Salt · Freshly ground pepper
Ground cumin
8 red peppers

For the sauce:
1 onion · 2 cloves of garlic
1 dried chilli
3 tbsp olive oil
800 g tinned tomatoes
Salt · Ground pepper
Ground coriander and cumin

For the cheese:
2 l milk
4 tbsp lemon juice
Salt · Ground pepper
1–2 tbsp olive oil

For the chutney:
2 unwaxed lemons
1 tbsp mustard seed
2 tbsp olive oil
30 g fresh or 50 g dried
curry leaves
1 tsp chilli powder
1 tbsp sugar
4 tbsp white balsamic vinegar

5 For the cheese, bring the milk to the boil in a large saucepan. Add the lemon juice and allow the milk to separate. Line a sieve with a clean tea towel. Pour the separated milk into the sieve. Fold the tea towel up around the curds and squeeze hard to remove the liquid. Place the cheese into a bowl and season with salt, pepper and olive oil.

6 To make the chutney, wash the lemon in hot water, dry, cut in half, remove the pips and cut into 1 cm cubes. Fry the mustard seed in olive oil. Add the curry leaves, chilli powder and sugar. Fry briefly and pour in the vinegar. Add the lemon cubes and simmer for 8 to 10 minutes until the chutney is creamy.

7 Arrange the stuffed peppers on plates. Scatter the curd cheese around them, drizzle everything with the lemon chutney and serve.

Desserts

A good dessert is "naughty but nice", and some people are even prepared to sacrifice the main course to leave room for pudding. No wonder, when there are such tempting creations as jasmine tea crème brulée, chocolate cake with raspberry meringue or crêpes au gratin. Who could resist them?

Moscato d'asti tart
with currants

For 1 cake tin (18 cm Ø)

Ingredients:

For the pastry:
120 g cold butter
250 g plain flour
100 g caster sugar · Salt
A few drops of vanilla essence
1 medium egg
50 g apricot jam

For the crème:
1/2 l Moscato d'asti
(Italian sparkling wine)
3 medium eggs · 1 egg yolk
60 g sugar
1 tbsp double cream
1 squeeze of lemon juice

Also:
Butter to grease the tin
Flour for the work surface
Dried beans (for blind baking)
300 g red and white currants
10 basil leaves
1 tbsp sugar
2 tbsp Demerara sugar

1   To make the pastry, dice the butter. Blitz in a food processor with the flour, sugar, a pinch of salt and the vanilla essence. Add the egg, wrap the pastry in clingfilm and chill in the fridge for 30 minutes.

2   Line the base of the spring form cake tin with baking paper and grease the sides. Roll the pastry out thin on a floured surface and use to line the cake tin, making an edge 3 to 4 cm high. Cover the base with baking paper and dried beans. Bake at 170°C (Fan plus) on the second shelf for 10 to 12 minutes.

3   Switch the oven off. Discard the baking paper and beans. Warm the jam and brush over the base of the pastry case.

4   Stir all the ingredients for the crème together in a saucepan. Heat to approx. 50°C (use a food thermometer to measure the temperature), stirring continuously. Pass the mixture through a sieve, and pour into the pastry case. Bake at 110°C (Fan plus) on the second shelf for 45 to 50 minutes. Remove from the oven and leave to cool.

5   Wash and drain the currants, and remove from the stalks. Wash and pat dry the basil leaves, and grind them with the sugar in a pestle and mortar.

6   Sprinkle the Demerara sugar over the tart and caramelize with a cook's blowtorch. Slice the tart with a serrated knife and decorate with the currants. Sprinkle with the basil sugar to serve.

▶▶ Tips

This tart is also good served with balsamic strawberries. Boil 100 ml balsamic vinegar, 50 g sugar and a few drops of vanilla essence until syrupy, cool then stir in 300 g of chopped strawberries.

Torrone and figs au gratin
with summer fruits

Serves 6

1 Wash, core and stone the fruit, and cut into bite sized pieces.

2 For the almonds, dissolve the caster sugar in a little water. Stir the almonds into the sugar syrup and spread out on a baking tray lined with baking paper. Cook in the oven at 180°C (Fan plus) on the second shelf for 10 to 15 minutes until the sugar has caramelized. Remove from the oven, cool, then chop the almonds coarsely.

3 To make the gratin, finely chop the chocolate, nougat and figs. Beat together the mascarpone, honey und egg yolks, and fold into the chocolate mixture. Whisk the egg whites until stiff and whisk the sugar in gradually to obtain a thick cream. Fold the egg whites into the chocolate/mascarpone mixture.

Ingredients:

For the fruit:
800 g mixed fruit
(e.g. pears, apricots,
plums and peaches)

For the almonds:
2 tbsp caster sugar
200 g peeled almonds

For the gratin:
100 g plain chocolate
100 g nougat
80 g dried figs
100 g mascarpone
2 tbsp honey
2 egg yolks
1 tbsp light sesame seeds
4 egg whites
50 g sugar

Also:
Butter to grease the tin

4 Grease an ovenproof dish and arrange the fruit in the bottom. Spread the mascarpone mixture lightly on top and bake at 180°C (Fan plus) on the second shelf for 20 to 25 minutes until the surface is golden. Remove from the oven, scatter over the almonds and serve whilst still warm.

▶▶ Tips

The gratin also tastes good with mixed berries such as raspberries, blueberries and blackberries. It can be prepared in individual dishes and baked for 10 to 15 minutes.

Vanilla quark soufflé
with blueberries and brioche

For 1 round ovenproof dish (28 cm Ø)

1 Wash the lemon in hot water, dry and grate finely. Squeeze out the juice. Beat 200 g of the sugar, the vanilla pulp, lemon zest and butter together until light and fluffy. Separate the eggs, and stir the yolks, flour and baking powder into the butter mixture. Warm the quark and milk in a saucepan to room temperature. Fold into the butter mixture. Add the lemon juice. Whisk the egg whites with a pinch of salt until stiff, and gradually whisk in the remaining sugar. Gently fold the egg whites into the butter mixture.

2 Wash and dry the blueberries. Grease an ovenproof dish and arrange the blueberries over the bottom. Pour the soufflé mixture on top and bake at 160°C (Moisture plus with 1 automatic burst of steam) on the second shelf for 40 to 45 minutes. Finish off under the grill at 240°C (Full grill) on the second shelf for 3 to 4 minutes until golden, taking care not to let it burn.

Ingredients:

2 unwaxed lemon
250 g sugar
Pulp from 2 vanilla pods
100 g soft butter
4 large eggs
100 g plain flour
1 tsp baking powder
250 g quark
300 ml milk
Salt
300 g blueberries
Butter to grease the tin
250 g brioche (sliced)

3 Remove the soufflé from the oven. Grill the slices of brioche on the rack at 240°C (Full grill) on the fourth shelf for 3 to 4 minutes on both sides.

4 To serve, arrange a slice of brioche on each plate and top with 2 large tbsp of soufflé. Alternatively, serve the brioche separately so that everyone can help themselves.

▶▶ Tips

Try replacing the blueberries with other seasonal berries such as strawberries, blackberries or blackcurrants. Serve with vanilla or yoghurt ice cream.

Filo leaves
with peaches and white chocolate mousse

Serves 4–6

1 To make the chocolate mousse, soften the gelatine in cold water. Finely chop the chocolate. Beat 220 ml double cream until stiff. Heat the milk with the rest of the cream.

2 Place the egg yolks with the sugar in a metal bowl. Gradually whisk the milk into the egg yolks. Place the bowl over a saucepan of simmering water and beat the mixture until creamy.

3 Squeeze out the gelatine and stir into the egg mixture along with the liqueur. Stir in the chocolate to melt. Beat the mixture until blood temperature and fold in the whipped cream. Transfer to a serving bowl, and place in the fridge for 1 hour.

4 For the peaches, wash and pat dry the basil leaves and cut into thin strips. Blanch the peaches in boiling water, plunge into ice cold water, remove the skins, cut into four and remove the stones.

5 Melt the butter and the Demarara sugar, and add the vanilla pulp and basil.

Ingredients:

For the chocolate mousse:
2 leaves gelatine
250 g white chocolate
280 ml double cream
60 ml milk
2 egg yolks
1 tbsp sugar
2 tbsp peach liqueur

For the peaches:
10 basil leaves
2–3 ripe peaches
2 tbsp butter
2 tbsp Demarara sugar
Pulp of 1 vanilla pod

For the filo leaves:
1 pack filo pastry (approx. 160 g)
40 g melted butter
2 tbsp icing sugar

6 Pack the peaches into an oven-proof dish and pour the flavoured butter over the top. Bake at 180°C (Fan plus) on the second shelf for 15 to 20 minutes until the peaches are soft. Remove from the oven and put to one side.

7 To make the filo leaves, cut the pastry into 6 cm pieces, or cut out with a pastry cutter, and brush with melted butter. Sieve the icing sugar over the pastry.

8 Place the pastry on a baking tray lined with baking paper and bake at 180°C (Fan plus) on the second shelf for 10 to 12 minutes until the sugar has caramelized. Allow the pastry to cool.

9 To serve, make little towers of 2 spoonfuls of mouse and 2 to 3 pieces of peach, topped with the filo leaves. Drizzle round the cooking juices from the peaches, and decorate with basil leaves and little curls of white chocolate.

Chocolate fondant
with kombucha sorbet

Serves 4–6

1 To make the sorbet, soften the gelatine in cold water. Bring the sugar to the boil in a saucepan with 100 ml water, then leave to cool slightly. Squeeze out the gelatine and dissolve in the sugar syrup.

2 Liquidize the berries with the kombucha tea. Press through a sieve into the sugar mixture. Stir well and freeze in an ice cream maker. Alternatively, place the mixture in a bowl in the freezer and whisk every 30 minutes.

3 To make the fondant, chop the chocolate and melt with the butter in a metal bowl over a saucepan of simmering water. Cool slightly. Beat the egg and the egg yolks in a bowl. Gradually add the sugar until the mixture is pale and creamy. Stir into the chocolate. Whip the egg whites until stiff and gently fold in.

Ingredients:

For the sorbet:
2 leaves gelatine
100 g sugar
100 g mixed berries
200 ml kombucha tea

For the fondant:
250 g plain chocolate
250 g soft butter
1 medium egg
3 egg yolks
250 g sugar
4–5 egg whites

Also:
Butter to grease the tin

4 Line the base of an ovenproof dish (approx. 32 x 24 cm) with baking paper and grease the sides. Fill with the chocolate mixture to a depth of 3 cm. Bake at 160°C (Fan plus) on the second shelf for 25 to 30 minutes. Remove from the oven and cool. The fondant should still be soft as it will continue to cook slightly.

5 Cut out portions of the fondant with a biscuit cutter and serve with the sorbet. Garnish with fresh berries and mint leaves.

▶▶ **Tips**

Fondant is the name for a sweet dish that melts in the mouth. Kombucha is a refreshing drink made by fermenting sweetened tea with the kombucha bacteria.

Toffee parcels
with creamy berries

Serves 4–6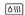

1 To make the toffee filling, grease a small dish (approx. 15 x 10 cm). Melt the butter in a saucepan. Add the condensed milk, sugar and golden syrup, bring to the boil and simmer for 6 to 8 minutes at 125°C (using a food thermometer to monitor the temperature) until the mixture is thick and releasing large bubbles. Stir in the cocoa and vanilla essence. Pour the toffee into the dish to a depth of 1 cm, and leave to cool. Once it has set, cut into 1 cm pieces.

2 To make the parcels, place the flour in a bowl and make a well in the centre. Warm the milk. Crumble the yeast into the milk and stir in a pinch of salt and the sugar. Pour into the well. Stir in the flour from the edge to create a thin dough. Cover with a damp tea towel and leave in a warm place for 15 minutes to rise.

3 Add the eggs, egg yolks, 120 g butter and the vanilla pulp. Knead with the kneading hook of an electric mixture until the dough is shiny and elastic. Cover and leave to rise for a further 30 minutes.

Ingredients:

For the toffee filling:
Butter to grease the tin
1 tbsp butter
80 ml sweetened condensed milk
125 g sugar
4 tbsp golden syrup
2 tbsp cocoa powder
A few drops of vanilla essence

For the profiteroles:
500 g strong white flour
200 ml milk
40 g fresh yeast
Salt
2 tbsp sugar
2 medium eggs
2 egg yolks
150 g soft butter
Pulp from 1 vanilla pod
Flour for the work surface
Butter to grease the tin
Icing sugar for dusting

For the creamy berries:
300 g mixed berries
80 g sugar
2 tbsp mascarpone

4 Knead again briefly, then roll out on a floured surface to approx. 1 cm thick. Cut out approx. 20 circles (4 cm Ø) and place a piece of toffee on each. Fold the dough over the toffee, seal and form into a ball shape.

5 Grease an ovenproof dish (approx. 30 x 24 cm). Pack in the parcels and dust with icing sugar to create a tasty crust when baked. Leave to rise for 20 minutes.

6 Melt the remaining butter and brush over the dumplings. Bake at 180°C (Moisture plus with 1 automatic burst of steam) on the second shelf for 25 to 30 minutes.

7 Wash the berries. Bring them to the boil with the sugar and mascarpone and transfer to a cold bowl. Dust the toffee parcels with icing sugar and serve with the creamy berries.

Jasmine tea crème brulée
with spiced oranges

Serves 4–6

Ingredients:

For the spiced oranges:

3–4 oranges (seedless)
30 g ginger
2 stalks of lemon grass
2 leaves of gelatine
400 ml apricot juice
150 ml white wine
150 g sugar
2 star anise
1 cinnamon stick
Pulp of 1 vanilla pod

For the crème brulée:

$^1/_2$ l milk · 75 g sugar
Pulp of 1 vanilla pod
3 jasmine teabags
250 ml double cream
2 medium eggs · 4 egg yolks
4–6 tbsp golden caster sugar
1 tbsp icing sugar

1 Peel the oranges, removing all the pith. Cut into $^1/_2$ cm thick slices and arrange in the bottom of an ovenproof dish.

2 Peel and slice the ginger. Remove the outer leaves of the lemon grass, wash and beat out flat with a rolling pin.

3 Soften the gelatine in cold water. Bring the apricot juice, white wine, 200 ml water and the sugar to the boil. Add the ginger, lemon grass and other spices, and simmer for 5 minutes. Leave for a short while to cool, then sieve to remove the spices. Squeeze out the gelatine and dissolve in the liquid. Pour over the oranges and chill for several hours.

4 To make the crème brulée, bring the milk, sugar and vanilla pulp to the boil and leave the teabags to steep in the milk for 5 minutes.

5 Remove the teabags and pour in the double cream. Beat the eggs and egg yolks and stir into the milk. Pour into ovenproof ramekins to a depth of 2 to 3 cm. Bake at 100°C (Fan plus) on the second shelf for 50 to 60 minutes until the crème is set. Cool to room temperature, then chill for several hours.

6 Pre-heat the grill (Full grill) for 5 minutes at 240°C. Sprinkle 1 tbsp golden caster sugar per portion over the crème and caramelize under the grill on the fourth shelf until golden.

7 Dust the crèmes with icing sugar and serve with the spiced oranges.

▶▶ **Tips**

Try flavouring the crème with other teas or spices. Do not sprinkle the caster sugar over the crème until the last minute or it will dissolve into the crème.

Chocolate cake
with raspberry meringue

For 1 round cake tin (22 cm Ø)

Ingredients:

For the cake:
200 g plain chocolate
100 g soft butter
1 tbsp instant espresso powder
Butter to grease the tin
3 medium eggs
80 g sugar
1 tbsp cornflour
120 g ground almonds
150 g pecans

For the meringue:
80 g sugar
3 egg whites
200 g raspberries

1　To make the cake, chop the chocolate and melt with the butter and espresso powder in a metal bowl over a pan of simmering water. Cool slightly.

2　Grease a cake tin or ovenproof dish (22 cm Ø). Beat the eggs with the sugar until creamy, and stir into the chocolate. Stir in the cornflour and ground almonds. Pour into the cake tin and sprinkle with the pecans.

3　Bake at 150°C (Moisture plus with 1 automatic burst of steam) on the second shelf for 15 to 20 minutes.

4　To make the meringue, boil the sugar in 40 ml of water until it releases thick bubbles. Remove from the heat and cool slightly.

5　Whisk the egg whites until half stiff. Stir in the sugar syrup, then continue to whisk until the egg whites are stiff and creamy. Clean, dry and stir in the raspberries. Spread the mixture over the chocolate base.

6　Bake at 180°C (Fan plus) on the second shelf for 5 to 10 minutes until the meringue is lightly browned. Cool and serve.

▶▶ Tips

The cakes can be baked in individual ramekin dishes (10 cm Ø). For an exotic alternative, replace the raspberries and pecans with the same quantities of mango cubes and coconut flakes.

Bavarian bread pudding
with Cointreau strawberries

Serves 6–8

Ingredients:

100 g white chocolate
$1/2$ l milk
100 ml sweetened
condensed milk
Pulp of 1 vanilla pod
5 medium eggs
3 apples
(e.g. Cox's Orange Pippins)
1 brioche or
approx. 10 brioche rolls
(400 g)
Butter to grease the tin
40 g cold butter
4 tbsp icing sugar
500 g strawberries
1 tsp orange liqueur
(e.g. Cointreau)

1 Chop the chocolate and bring to the boil with the milk, condensed milk and vanilla pulp. Cool slightly, then stir in the eggs.

2 Peel and core the apples, and cut into thin slices. Thinly slice the brioche. Grease an ovenproof dish.

3 In the dish, build up alternating layers of apple and brioche slices, moistening with the egg and milk mixture so that the brioche is evenly soaked. Pour the remaining egg and milk over the last layer of apple slices, then top with the remaining brioche. Dot with butter and bake at 180°C (Conventional heat) on the second shelf for 45 to 50 minutes.

4 Dust with 3 tbsp icing sugar, then grill at 240°C (Full grill) on the fourth shelf for 3 to 5 minutes until the sugar has caramelized. Cool slightly and cut into pieces.

5 Wash, dry and chop the strawberries. Mix with the remaining icing sugar and orange liqueur and serve with the caramel stack.

▶▶ **Tips**

Delicious served with frozen apricot yoghurt. Mix 200 g plain yoghurt with 100 g apricot jam. Stir in 200 g whipped cream and place in the freezer for at least 4 hours.

Pumpernickel soufflé
with thyme and honey cherries

Serves 4 🔲

1 For the cherries, bring the red wine, port, blackcurrant juice, grenadine syrup and honey to the boil and reduce by half.

2 To make the soufflés, grease 4 ramekins, dust with sugar and place in the fridge. Reduce the pumpernickel to crumbs in a food processor. Fry the crumbs with the icing sugar in a frying pan for 5 minutes, stirring constantly. Leave to cool.

3 Chop the chocolate, warm the milk and dissolve the chocolate in the milk. Stir in the quark, egg yolks and pumpernickel crumbs. The mixture should be lukewarm. Whisk the egg whites with the sugar until stiff, and gently fold into the pumpernickel mixture.

Ingredients:

For the cherries:
100 ml dry red wine
100 ml port
150 ml blackcurrant juice
50 ml grenadine syrup
2 tbsp honey
$1/2$ bunch of lemon thyme
300 g sweet cherries (stoned)
Arrowroot to thicken

For the soufflé:
Butter and sugar to grease the ramekins
100 g pumpernickel bread
1 tbsp icing sugar
70 g white chocolate
3 tbsp milk
100 g low fat quark
3 egg yolks
4–5 egg whites
40 g sugar

4 Fill the ramekins two thirds full with the soufflé mixture. Bake at 190°C (Moisture plus with 1 automatic burst of steam) on the second shelf for 18 to 20 minutes.

5 Wash and dry the lemon thyme and add to the wine syrup along with the cherries. Simmer for 5 minutes. Remove the thyme and thicken the syrup with a little arrowroot mixed with cold water.

6 Serve the soufflés immediately before they collapse, with the cherries alongside in little bowls.

> ▶▶ **Tips**
>
> *The soufflé goes well with chocolate crunchies. Melt 15 g butter, 150 g nougat and 60 g plain chocolate over a pan of simmering water. Stir in 60 g roughly crushed cornflakes. Spread out on baking paper, leave to cool and cut into little pieces.*

Baked bananas in filo pastry
with Creole sauce

Serves 4

1   To make the pastry parcels, squeeze the lime and mix the juice with the honey and chilli powder. Peel and thinly slice the bananas and stir into the marinade.

2   Lay out the filo pastry on the work top, brush with half the melted butter and sprinkle with the desiccated coconut. Cut out circles of brioche (8 cm Ø).

3   Place the brioche circles in the centre of the pastry sheets and cover with the banana mixture. Brush the edges of the pastry with egg white, and pinch them together to form parcels.

Ingredients:

For the pastry parcels:
1 lime
1 tbsp honey
1/2 tsp chilli powder
1–2 bananas (approx. 240 g)
4 sheets of filo pastry (40 x 40 cm; readymade)
100 g melted butter
100 g desiccated coconut
4 slices brioche or white bread (1 cm thick)
1 egg white

For the sauce:
200 ml coconut milk
Chilli powder
100 g plain chocolate
2 cl rum

4   Carefully brush the parcels with the remaining butter. Bake on a baking tray at 180°C (Fan plus) on the second shelf for 15 to 18 minutes.

5   To make the sauce, heat the coconut milk with a pinch of chilli powder. Chop the chocolate and melt in the coconut milk. Flavour with rum, cool slightly and serve with the baked parcels. Garnish with fried strips of chilli.

▶▶ Tips

Try using mango or pineapple in place of bananas.

Crêpes au gratin
with lime and quark filling

Serves 4–6

1 To make the crêpes, beat all the ingredients with a pinch of salt to a smooth paste and leave to stand for 30 minutes.

2 For the caramel, caramelize the sugar in a saucepan, pour onto a baking tray lined with baking paper and leave to cool. Break up the caramel and reduce to a powder in a food processor.

3 To make the filling, wash and dry the limes, grate the zest and squeeze out the juice. Whip the cream until stiff. Mix the remaining ingredients with the lime zest and juice, and fold in the cream.

Ingredients:

For the crêpes:
120 g plain flour
200 ml milk
200 ml double cream
A few drops of vanilla essence
4 medium eggs
2 tbsp sugar
60 g melted butter
Salt

For the caramel:
100 g sugar

For the filling:
3 unwaxed limes
150 ml double cream
220 g quark
70 g sugar
1 tbsp vanilla sugar
2 egg yolks
1–2 tbsp cornflour
A few drops of vanilla essence
2 tbsp melted butter
1–2 tbsp rum

Also:
Butter for frying
Butter to grease the tin

4 Melt a little butter in a frying pan and cook the crêpes. Spread the filling over the crêpes, roll them up and place in a breased rectangular dish.

5 Cook in the oven at 160°C (Conventional heat) on the second shelf for 30 to 35 minutes. Sprinkle the caramel powder over the top and grill at 240°C (Full grill) on the fourth shelf until caramelized.

▶▶ Tips

Serve with apricot compote. Mix 300 g stoned and quartered apricots with 100 g sugar and the pulp of 1 vanilla pod, and leave to stand for 30 minutes. Cook gently in a small saucepan for 5 to 6 minutes.

Pineapple tarte tatin
with peanut pesto

For 6 tartlet tins (12 cm Ø) order 2 tart tins (24 cm Ø)

1 To make the tarts, peel and grate the ginger. Caramelize the sugar in a saucepan and stir in the butter. Add the ginger and vanilla pulp. Pour into 6 tartlet tins (12 cm Ø) or 2 tart tins (24 cm Ø).

2 Peel and halve the pineapple and remove the core. Cut the flesh into 2 cm thick slices and place in the tart tins.

3 Roll the pastry out thinly on a floured surface. Cut out circles the size of the tins you are using.

Ingredients:

For the tarts:
450 g puff pastry
30 g root ginger
120 g sugar
120 g butter
Pulp of 1 vanilla pod
1 pineapple
Flour for the work surface

For the peanut pesto:
$1/2$ bunch of basil
40 g white chocolate
80 g roasted peanuts
50 ml grapenut oil

4 Place the pastry circles on top of the tins, press down lightly at the edges and bake at 180°C (Fan plus) on the second shelf for 20 to 25 minutes. Bake the larger tarts for 35 to 40 minutes.

5 To make the peanut pesto, wash and dry the basil leaves. Grate the chocolate and purée in a food processor with the peanuts, grapenut oil and basil leaves.

6 Remove the tarts from the oven and allow to cool slightly. Turn out onto plates, drizzle with the pesto and serve.

▸▸ **Tips**

Serve with yoghurt ice cream. Peel and slice 1 banana and purée in a food processor with 250 g yoghurt, 250 ml double cream and 120 g icing sugar. Freeze in an ice cream maker.

145

Cakes and biscuits

Peach and apricot puffs, Sachertorte with ginger, Panettone with cranberries – you'll be amazed just how creative baking can be, and those with a sweet tooth will be delighted. Our old classics with a new twist and original suggestions for all occasions will ensure that your guests will want to have the recipes ...

To make choux pastry

1 Bring water, milk, butter, sugar and salt to the boil. Tip in the flour and stir in quickly with a wooden spoon until the dough forms a ball.

2 Stir the ball of dough until it comes away from the base of the saucepan. Mix for another minute.

3 Place the ball of dough in a bowl. Stir in the eggs one at a time using the kneading hook of an electric mixer. Proceed with the pastry according to the recipe.

To make Genoese sponge

1 Whisk the egg yolks and sugar until creamy. In a separate bowl, whisk the egg whites and salt until stiff.

2 Sieve the flour into the egg yolk and sugar and stir in. Stir in melted butter if directed to by the recipe.

3 Carefully fold in one third of the egg whites. Stir in the remaining egg whites. Use immediately.

Basics
Pastries and cake mixes

Choux pastry owes its special qualities to the method of preparation. The starch in the flour is broken down to produce a tender pastry. No pores develop during baking so the gases that arise cannot escape and form large hollows inside the pastry. In this way, light, airy pastry is produced without the need for raising agents.

Genoese sponge is also made without artificial raising agents. The air trapped in the egg whites is enough to make the dough rise and increase to up to three times its original volume when baked. N.B.: Fold the egg whites in very carefully and place in a pre-heated oven immediately.

Sponge cake mix is fast and easy to make, and can be used in a huge variety of ways. The consistency depends on the order in which the ingredients are added. For a light cake, mix the egg yolks and sugar first, for a denser cake, mix the butter and sugar, and then stir in the egg yolks.

To make **sweet pastry**

1 Chill the ingredients first. Mix together flour, sugar, grated lemon zest, salt and vanilla sugar. Cut the cold butter into cubes.

2 Either place the ingredients on a work surface and cut the butter into the flour with a spatula, or use a food processor. Knead in the egg.

3 Wrap the pastry in clingfilm and chill in the fridge for at least 30 minutes. The pastry can be kept in the fridge for up to a week and can also be frozen.

To make **strudel pastry**

1 Sieve the flour into a mixing bowl and make a well in the centre. Mix the water, egg yolk, oil and salt thoroughly, and pour into the well.

2 Using the kneading hook of an electric mixer, knead to an elastic dough. Rub the dough with oil, wrap in clingfilm and leave to rest for 1 hour.

3 Roll out the dough, place it on a floured tea towel and stretch out with your hands until it is paper thin. Brush with melted butter and proceed.

Basics
Pastries and cake mixes

Sweet pastry requires cold ingredients. These need to be well mixed, cut together thoroughly and kneaded briefly with cold hands. The pastry needs to rest in the fridge before it is baked, then it will emerge from the oven dry and crisp, yet melting and tender. It is particularly light when made with icing sugar instead of caster sugar.

Strudel pasty is relatively easy to make. The important thing is to knead it thoroughly so that it doesn't tear. The art of preparing it lies in the stretching to achieve a paper thin pastry. To do this, the pastry is rolled out then placed on a floured cloth and carefully stretched until it is translucent.

Puff pastry is a little complicated to make. Many fine layers of butter between the layers of the basic dough ensure that the pastry will have a flaky consistency when baked. An easy version is shown on page 180. Luckily good quality frozen puff pastry is readily available.

Yoghurt Gugelhupf
with berries

For 1 Gugelhupf tin (22 cm Ø)

1   Grease the tin, sprinkle with biscuit crumbs and place in the fridge. To make the cake, separate the eggs. Beat the egg yolks, yoghurt, oil, vanilla pulp, orange and lemon zest with half of the sugar in a bowl until foamy. Sieve in the flour and stir in.

2   Whisk the egg whites with a pinch of salt until they stand in soft peaks. Gradually add the rest of the sugar and whisk until stiff. Fold into the cake mix a little at a time and stir in the frozen berries.

3   Transfer the dough to the cake tin, and bake at 160°C (Conventional heat) on the second shelf for 50 to 60 minutes. Allow to cool slightly in the tin, turn out and cool completely on a cake rack.

4   For the topping, caramelize the sugar in a saucepan with 50 ml water. Stir in the almonds, pour into a baking tray lined with baking paper and leave to go cold. Put the praline in a freezer bag and crush with a rolling pin.

5   Chop the chocolate and melt in a bowl over a saucepan of simmering water. Stir in the butter and oil and finally the praline. Cover the gugelhupf with the topping and leave to set.

Ingredients:

For the cake mix:
4 large eggs
250 g yoghurt
240 ml oil
Pulp from 1 vanilla pod
1 tsp each grated orange and lemon zest
200 g sugar
230 g self raising flour
Salt
400 g mixed berries (frozen)

For the topping:
100 g sugar
80 g almonds
200 g white chocolate
50 g soft butter
1 tbsp oil

Also:
Butter to grease the tin
Biscuit crumbs (e.g. sponge fingers) to line the tin

▶▶ Tips

Don't let the berries defrost before using them. If they are frozen, they will not colour the cake so much. Serve the Gugelhupf with whipped cream or vanilla ice cream.

Carrot cake
with sesame praline

For 1 springform cake tin (28 cm Ø)

1   Grease the tin, sprinkle with biscuit crumbs and place in the fridge. Peel the carrots, grate them very finely and put to one side.

2   Separate the eggs. Beat the egg yolks with the vanilla pulp, 100 g sugar, butter and lemon zest in a bowl until light and creamy. Whisk the egg whites until they stand in soft peaks, then gradually add the sugar and whisk until thick and creamy.

3   Mix together the almonds, flour, cornflour and baking powder. Stir into the egg yolk mixture along with the carrots. Fold in the egg whites a little at a time. Transfer to the springform tin and smooth the top. Bake at 180°C (Conventional heat) on the second shelf for 45 to 50 minutes.

Ingredients:

For the cake:
300 g carrots · 5 medium eggs
Pulp from 1 vanilla pod
220 g sugar
100 g soft butter
1 tsp grated lemon zest
300 g ground almonds
50 g plain flour
50 g cornflour
1 tsp baking powder

Also:
Butter to grease the tin
Biscuit crumbs to line the tin
200 g sugar
100 g sesame seeds
Oil for the palette knife
400 ml double cream
1 tbsp vanilla sugar

4   Line a baking tray with baking paper. Caramelize the sugar in a saucepan with 5 tbsp water. Stir in the sesame seeds, pour into the baking tray and spread out using an oiled palette knife. Leave to cool, then break into little pieces.

5   Remove the cake from the oven and cool in the tin on the rack, then remove from the tin. Whip the cream with the vanilla sugar and spread over the cake. Sprinkle with the sesame seed praline, and serve.

▶▶ Tips

Oil-rich sesame seeds give a sophisticated flavour to all types of cakes and biscuits. Their flavour develops more fully when they are roasted. Light coloured seeds have a milder flavour than dark ones.

Crisp almond cake
with lemon balm crème

For 1 springform cake tin (26 cm Ø)

1 Grease the tin and line the base with baking paper. To make the cake base, beat the butter, double cream and icing sugar in a bowl until light and fluffy. Chop the flaked almonds and stir into the butter mixture. Fold in the flour. Transfer the dough to the cake tin, pushing it up to form a 1 cm high edge. Bake at 190°C (Conventional heat) on the second shelf for 15 to 20 minutes. Remove the base, cool it slightly on a wire rack then brush with melted butter.

2 Bring the wine to the boil in a saucepan with 90 g sugar. Add the lemon balm leaves and allow to steep for 5 minutes. Pour through a sieve and cool. Soften the gelatine in cold water.

3 Heat 2 tbsp of the lemon balm syrup in a saucepan and dissolve 6 of the gelatine leaves in it. Measure out 400 ml of lemon balm syrup and add to the gelatine, then transfer to a large bowl. Stir over a bowl of iced water until cold.

4 Whip the double cream until it stands in soft peaks. Whisk the egg whites with a pinch of salt until half stiff, gradually add the remaining sugar and whisk until thick and creamy.

Ingredients:

For the cake:
135 g soft butter
3 tbsp double cream
135 g icing sugar
150 g flaked almonds
75 g plain flour

For the crème:
600 ml Moscato d'Asti
(Italian sparkling wine)
180 g sugar
30 g dried lemon balm leaves
8 leaves of gelatine
250 ml double cream
3 egg whites · Salt

Also:
Butter to grease the tin
50 g melted butter
500 g strawberries

5 When the lemon balm syrup begins to set, stir in the double cream then carefully fold in the egg whites. Spread over the almond base, smooth the surface and put in the fridge for 1 hour.

6 Clean and slice the strawberries and arrange on top of the cake. Squeeze out the remaining 2 leaves of gelatine and dissolve in 2 tbsp of the remaining lemon balm syrup. Add the rest of the syrup, and leave to go cold. When it begins to set, spread over the strawberries, leave to set completely, then serve.

▸▸ Tips

Lemon balm (melissa officinalis) is a member of the mint family and often grown in the herb garden. It is widely used in herbal teas where it is recognised for its calming properties.

Almond and ricotta cake
with plain chocolate

For 1 springform cake tin (24 cm Ø)

1   Grease the tin and line the base with baking paper. Place in the fridge.

2   Roast the almonds in a frying pan without fat until golden brown, then leave to cool. Beat the butter in a bowl with 80 g of sugar until light and creamy. Separate the eggs and stir the yolks into the butter mixture. Add the flour, almonds, orange zest and ricotta and stir well.

3   Whisk the egg whites with a pinch of salt until they stand in soft peaks, then gradually add the sugar and whisk until thick and creamy. Fold into the cake mixture a little at a time, transfer into the springform tin and smooth the top.

Ingredients:

Butter to grease the tin
120 g ground almonds
120 g soft butter
120 g sugar
4 large eggs (room temperature)
50 g plain flour
1 tbsp grated orange zest
125 g ricotta
Salt
80 g plain chocolate
100 g apricot jam

4   Bake at 180°C (Conventional heat) on the second shelf for 40 to 45 minutes. Take out of the oven, cool slightly, then remove the cake from the tin and cool on a cake rack.

5   Grate the chocolate. Warm the apricot jam with 50 ml water and brush over the cake. Cool, then sprinkle with the grated chocolate.

▶▶ **Tips**

You will know your cake is ready when a wooden skewer inserted into the middle of it comes out clean and dry.

Pine nut clafouti
with raspberries

For 4 tartlet tins (12 cm Ø)

1 Grease the tins, line the base with baking paper and put in the fridge. Grind the pine nuts to a fine powder in a food processor. Using a food processor or the top setting of an electric mixer, beat the sugar, butter, eggs, Amaretto, cornflour and vanilla essence for 5 minutes until foamy. Stir in the ground almonds and pine nuts. Pour into the tartlet tins.

2 Clean and drain the raspberries. Scatter over the dough, leaving 1 cm rim clear around the edge.

Ingredients

Butter to grease the tin
100 g pine nuts
125 g caster sugar
125 g soft butter
4 medium eggs
(room temperature)
2 tbsp Amaretto
2 tbsp cornflour
A few drops of vanilla essence
100 g ground almonds
300 g raspberries
150 ml soured cream
1 tbsp vanilla sugar

3 Bake at 200°C (Conventional heat) on the second shelf for 10 to 15 minutes. Remove from the oven and cool for 5 minutes. Release from the tins and cool on a wire cake rack.

4 Mix the soured cream with the vanilla sugar. Serve each clafoutis with 1 tbsp of the cream.

▶▶ Tips

Clafouti comes from Limousin in central France. It is cross between a sweet soufflé and a tart, and is traditionally made with cherries. Try other fruit such as blackberries or plums.

Creole torte
with mango and pecan nuts

For 1 springform cake tin (26 cm Ø)

1 To make the chocolate layer, chop the nougat and chocolate. Cut the butter into cubes. Melt together in a bowl over a pan of simmering water. Stir the puffed rice into the chocolate. Place a 26 cm Ø tart ring on a piece of baking paper, pour in the chocolate mixture, smooth the top and place in the fridge to set.

2 For the sponge base, whisk the egg whites to soft peaks, then gradually add 50 g sugar and whisk until thick and creamy. Sieve in the cornflour, and fold in along with the almonds, pecans and the remaining sugar. Line the springform tin with baking paper and fill with the cake mixture. Bake at 200°C (Conventional heat) on the third shelf for 10 minutes. Remove from the tin and leave to cool.

3 To make the crème, bring the sugar to the boil with 50 ml water until it is bubbling but not coloured. Whisk the egg whites until half stiff, pour in the sugar syrup, then whisk until thick and creamy.

Ingredients:

For the chocolate layer:
120 g nougat
100 g milk chocolate
50 g butter
80 g puffed rice

For the sponge base:
3 egg whites
200 g sugar
1 tbsp cornflour
75 g ground almonds
125 g chopped pecans

For the crème:
125 g sugar
2 egg whites
4 leaves of gelatine
80 g desiccated coconut
200 ml coconut milk
30 ml dark rum
125 ml double cream

Also:
1 mango
80 g flaked coconut
Sugar for roasting

4 Soften the gelatine in cold water. Roast the desiccated coconut in a frying pan without fat until golden brown. Heat the coconut milk and rum in a saucepan. Squeeze out the gelatine and dissolve in the coconut milk, then leave to cool. Whip the cream until stiff. When the coconut milk has cooled to room temperature, fold in the egg whites and cream.

5 Peel the mango, cut the flesh off the stone and cut into thin slices. Release the tart ring from around the chocolate layer and place it around the sponge base. Spread 4 tbsp of the coconut crème over the sponge and place the chocolate layer on top. Arrange the mango slices on the chocolate layer and spread the rest of the crème smoothly over the top. Place in the freezer for 1 hour.

6 Loosen the edges of the torte with the point of a knife, and remove the ring. Roast the coconut flakes in a frying pan with a little sugar, cool and scatter over the cake. Garnish with mango balls scooped out with a melon baller.

Elderflower torte
on an almond base

For 1 rectangular cake tin (20 x 30 cm)

1   Roll out the shortcrust pastry on a floured surface to a rectangle 25 x 35 cm, and place on a baking tray lined with baking paper. Bake at 160°C (Fan plus) on the second shelf for 10 to 12 minutes. While still warm cut the pastry to fit the cake tin and spread with the apple jelly.

2   To make the almond base, beat the eggs, icing sugar and almonds until creamy. Whisk the egg whites with a pinch of salt to soft peaks, then gradually add the sugar and whisk until thick and creamy. Stir the butter, 2 tbsp of the egg white mixture and the flour into the almond mixture. Fold in the rest of the egg white mixture. Spread the mixture out on a baking tray lined with baking paper Pre-heat the oven to 180°C (Conventional heat). Bake on the third shelf for 18 to 20 minutes. Remove the cake from the tin on its paper and leave to cool.

3   To make the filling, soften the gelatine in cold water. Warm 25 ml of elderflower syrup and dissolve the squeezed out gelatine in it. Stir in the remaining syrup and yoghurt, transfer to a bowl and place in the fridge.

Ingredients:

For the pastry:
250 g shortcrust pastry (readymade)
Flour for the work surface
2 tbsp apple jelly

For the almond base:
5 medium eggs
185 g icing sugar
185 g ground almonds
5 egg whites
Salt · 2 tbsp sugar
40 g very soft butter
50 g plain flour

For the filling:
7 leaves of gelatine
200 ml elderflower syrup
325 g yoghurt
400 ml double cream

Also:
100 g flaked almonds
40 g icing sugar

4   When the elderflower yoghurt has begun to set, whip the cream and fold in.

5   Peel the paper away from the almond base and cut to fit the cake tin. (Keep the trimmings for a recipe requiring cake crumbs.) Slice the base in half horizontally.

6   Place the shortcrust pastry in the cake followed by one half of the almond base and spread with half of the elderflower filling. Top with the other half of the almond base and the remaining filling. Cover and place in the fridge for 1 hour.

7   Moisten the almonds in 2 tbsp water, mix with the icing sugar and spread out on a baking tray lined with baking paper. Caramelize in the oven at 180°C (Fan plus) on the second shelf until golden brown. Cool, chop and sprinkle over the cake. Cut the cake into pieces and decorate with elderflowers.

Genoese sponge
with vanilla crème brulée

For 1 springform cake tin (26 cm Ø)

Ingredients:

For the sponge:
6 medium eggs
190 g sugar
190 g plain flour
35 g melted butter

For the crème:
2 leaves of gelatine
175 ml milk
260 g sugar
Pulp from 1 vanilla pod
3 medium egg yolks
15 g cornflour
A few drops of vanilla essence
2 tbsp Grand Marnier
3 egg whites

Also:
Butter and flour for the tin

1   Grease the springform tin, dust with flour and place in the fridge. To make the Genoese sponge, use an electric mixer to beat together the eggs and sugar in a bowl over a pan of simmering water until creamy. Remove the bowl from the heat and beat the mixture on the highest setting for 5 minutes. Beat for a further 5 minutes over cold water until the mixture has cooled. Sieve in the flour, fold in gently, then stir in the melted butter.

2   Pre-heat the oven to 180°C (Conventional heat). Pour the sponge mixture into the springform tin and smooth the surface. Bake on the third shelf for 50 to 60 minutes. Reduce the temperature to 160°C for the last 20 minutes. Remove from the oven, and leave to cool in the tin for a few minutes. Turn out onto a wire cake rack and leave to cool thoroughly. Use a knife to score a ring around the cake, 2 cm in from the edge, and hollow out the area inside the ring to a depth of 2 cm. (Keep the trimmings for a recipe requiring cake crumbs.)

3   To make the crème, soften the gelatine in cold water. Bring the milk to the boil with 40 g sugar and the pulp from the vanilla pod. Stir together the egg yolks, 40 g sugar, the cornflour and vanilla essence. Pour the boiling vanilla milk into the egg mixture, stirring continuously, and return to the saucepan. Simmer for 2 minutes. Remove from the heat and cool slightly. Squeeze out the gelatine, add to the crème along with the liqueur, and stir in. Cover with clingfilm and leave until lukewarm.

4   Boil 150 g sugar in a saucepan with 40 ml water until it is bubbling but not coloured. Whisk the egg whites to soft peaks, pour in the syrup and beat for 5 minutes until it is lukewarm.

5   Stir the egg white mixture into the vanilla crème. Transfer 5 tbsp to a piping bag and place in the fridge. Pour the rest into the hollowed out cake and spread smooth. Cover and place in the freezer for 30 minutes.

6   Sprinkle the remaining sugar over the crème and caramelize with a cook's blowtorch. Pipe the remaining vanilla crème around the edge to decorate.

Chocolate Sachertorte
with ginger

For 2 springform cake tins (22 cm Ø)

Ingredients:

For the cake:
150 g plain chocolate
150 g soft butter
1 tbsp vanilla sugar
40 g icing sugar
8 medium eggs
(room temperature)
Salt · 120 g sugar
100 g plain flour
50 g cornflour

For the syrup:
1 unwaxed lime
3 cm root ginger
60 g sugar
Pulp from 1 vanilla pod
1 cinnamon stick
50 ml orange juice
50 g apricot jam

Also:
Butter and flour for the tin
200 g apricot jam
400 g marzipan
Icing sugar for rolling out
100 g candied ginger
225 g plain chocolate
150 ml double cream
45 ml milk
75 g glucose syrup
45 g soft butter

1   Grease the tins with butter, dust with flour and place in the fridge. Chop the chocolate and melt in a bowl over a pan of simmering water. Beat the butter with the vanilla sugar and icing sugar until soft. Separate 7 eggs. Stir the egg yolks and the remaining whole egg into the butter mixture a little at a time, then stir in the chocolate. Whisk the egg whites with a pinch of salt to soft peaks, then gradually add the sugar and whisk until thick and creamy.

2   Sieve the flour and cornflour. Stir 2 tbsp of the egg white mixture into the chocolate mixture. Alternately fold in the rest of the egg white mixture and the flour mixture. Divide between the springform tins and bake, one after the other, at 160°C (Conventional heat) on the third shelf for 35 to 40 minutes. Pierce with a skewer to check if the cakes are done. Leave in the tin to cool slightly, turn out, then leave to go cold.

3   To make the syrup, wash the lime in hot water, dry, grate the zest and squeeze out the juice. Peel and slice the root ginger. In a saucepan, bring 100 ml water to the boil with the sugar, ginger, vanilla pulp, lime juice and zest and the cinnamon stick. Stir in the orange juice and jam and leave to stand for 10 minutes. Pass through a sieve and leave to cool.

4   Slice the cakes in half horizontally. Open them up and drizzle the cut sides with the syrup. Warm the jam with 5 tbsp water. Brush over the cut sides, put the cakes back together and brush all over with the remaining jam. Knead the marzipan until soft, dust it with icing sugar, and place it between 2 sheets of clingfilm. Roll out thinly. Cover the cakes and trim neatly.

5   Finely chop the candied ginger and grate the chocolate. Bring the cream, milk and glucose syrup to the boil in a saucepan. Remove from the heat and stir in the chocolate and butter until melted. Place the cakes on a cake rack and cover evenly with the chocolate cream. Sprinkle with candied ginger and place in the fridge for at least 3 hours.

Latte macchiato torte
with marzipan

For 1 springform cake tin (26 cm Ø)

Ingredients:

For the sponge:
3 large eggs
50 g honey
2 large egg whites · Salt
60 g sugar
100 g ground hazelnuts
60 g plain flour
1 tbsp instant espresso
powder

For the crème:
5 leaves of gelatine
200 ml milk
2 tbsp instant espresso
powder
150 g white chocolate
1 large egg
1 large egg yolk
2 tbsp Bailey's Irish Cream
500 ml double cream
3 large egg whites
50 g sugar

Also:
Butter and biscuit crumbs
(e.g. sponge fingers)
to line the tin
200 g white marzipan
1 tbsp cocoa powder
Icing sugar for rolling out

1   Grease the tin, sprinkle with biscuit crumbs and place in the fridge. To make the sponge, separate two of the eggs. Beat the egg yolks, the whole egg and the honey until creamy. Whisk the egg whites with a pinch of salt to soft peaks, then gradually add the sugar and whisk until thick and creamy.

2   Mix the nuts, flour and espresso powder, and stir into the honey and eggs. Fold in the egg whites a little at a time. Pour into the springform tin and smooth the top. Bake at 180°C (Conventional heat) on the third shelf for 35 to 40 minutes. Allow to cool then remove from the tin. Cool completely and slice in half horizontally.

3   To make the crème, soften the gelatine in cold water. Bring the milk to the boil with the espresso powder and leave to cool. Chop the chocolate and melt in a bowl over a pan of simmering water. Beat the egg, egg yolk and the Bailey's together in a bowl over a pan of simmering water until creamy. Squeeze out the gelatine and dissolve in the eggs. Stir in the chocolate and milk and place in the fridge.

4   Whip the cream to soft peaks. Whisk the egg whites stiffly, and gradually add the sugar. When the crème begins to set, fold in the cream then the egg whites. Put 3 tbsp of crème to one side. Put one half of the sponge in a tart ring and cover with one half of the crème. Top with the other sponge and the remaining crème and spread smooth. Place the torte in the fridge for 1 hour, then remove the ring.

5   Divide the marzipan in two, and knead the cocoa powder into one half. Roll out the light marzipan to a thickness of 1 cm. Pinch off little pieces of the dark marzipan, scatter them over the light marzipan, and press down lightly. Fold the marzipan in half, dust with icing sugar and roll out between 2 sheets of clingfilm to fit the length of the torte's circumference. Cut a strip as wide as the height of the torte. Cover the sides of the torte with the remaining crème and stick the marzipan strip around the torte. Cover the top of the torte with a thin layer of cocoa marzipan and decorate with cocoa powder and chocolate covered coffee beans.

spoonfulinto a bowl of cold water - toffee should set instantly.

Dip and enjoy

Take the pan off the heat and stir in the pecans. Dip each apple, letting any excess drip back into the pan. Place on baking tray to cool completely.

Brilliantly British

Fresh milk from UK dairy farms gives Country Life British Spreadable Butter £2.50 (500g) a lovely creamy taste.

Per serving
1397kJ/334kcals/12.3g fat/2.9g saturated fat/55.6g sugars/0.1g salt

Vanilla and caramel tartlets
with toasted almonds

For 8 tartlet tins (10–12 cm Ø)

1   The day before, place the tins of condensed milk on a sieve in a saucepan, cover with water and simmer for 3 to 4 hours. Do not allow to boil dry. Leave to cool overnight.

2   To make the pastry, cut the butter into small cubes. Mix the flour, icing sugar, lemon zest, vanilla sugar and $1/2$ tsp salt. Blitz in a food processor with the butter. Add in the egg, wrap in clingfilm and put in the fridge for 30 minutes.

3   Grease the tins. Roll the pastry out thinly on a floured surface and cut out 8 circles, each 2 cm larger than the tins. Line the tins, making a 1 cm rim that stands proud of the tin. Cover and place in the fridge for 15 minutes.

4   Cover the pastry with baking paper and fill the tins with dried beans. Blind bake at 180°C (Fan plus) on the second shelf for 10 to 15 minutes. Remove the paper and dried beans. Cool the pastry slightly, then remove from the tins.

Ingredients:

For the caramel filling:
2 tins sweetened
condensed milk (400 g each)

For the sweet pastry:
250 g cold butter
500 g plain flour
200 g icing sugar
1 tsp grated lemon zest
2 tbsp vanilla sugar
Salt · 1 medium egg

For the almonds:
200 g peeled almonds
120 g icing sugar

For the topping:
300 ml double cream
40 g sugar
Pulp from 1 vanilla pod
1 mango

Also:
Butter to grease the tins
Flour for the work surface
Dried beans for baking blind

5   Soften the almonds in a little water and mix with the icing sugar. Place on a baking tray lined with baking paper. Caramelize in the oven at 220°C (Fan plus) on the second shelf for 10 minutes. Remove from the oven and leave to cool.

6   Whip the double cream with the sugar and vanilla pod pulp until stiff. Open the tins of condensed milk and spread the caramelized contents into the pastry cases. Peel the mango, cut the flesh away from the stone and cut into small cubes. Scatter the mango over the caramel filling and cover with the vanilla cream. Scatter over the toasted almonds, and serve.

▶▶ Tips

Almonds are not the only nuts that can be toasted. Roasted and caramelized hazelnuts, peanuts and cashew nuts are all delicious and go very well with the tartlets.

Cream cheese and coconut tart
with mango

For 1 tart tin (22 cm Ø)

Ingredients:

For the sweet pastry:
120 g cold butter
250 g plain flour
100 g icing sugar
1 tsp grated lemon zest
1 tbsp vanilla sugar
Salt · 1 medium egg

For the cheese filling:
1 unwaxed lime
3 medium eggs
150 g cream cheese
60 g sugar
150 ml coconut milk
2 tbsp flour
30 g cornflour
Salt

Also:
Butter to grease the tin
Flour for the work surface
3 leaves of gelatine
250 g mango purée (tinned)
Pulp from 1 vanilla pod

1   To make the pastry, cut the butter into small cubes. Mix the flour, icing sugar, lemon zest, vanilla sugar and a pinch of salt. Blitz in a food processor with the butter. Add in the egg, wrap in clingfilm and put in the fridge for 30 minutes.

2   Grease the tin. Roll out the pastry on a floured surface and line the tart tin. Place in the fridge for 20 minutes.

3   To make the cheese filling, wash the lime in hot water, dry, grate the zest and squeeze out the juice. Separate the eggs, and mix the egg yolks with the cheese, half the sugar, the coconut milk, lime zest and juice, flour and cornflour in a bowl.

4   Whisk the egg whites with a pinch of salt to soft peaks, gradually add the sugar and whisk until thick and creamy. Fold into the cheese a little at a time.

5   Spread the filling over the pastry base and bake at 180°C (Conventional heat) on the second shelf for 20 to 25 minutes. Reduce the temperature to 140°C and cook for a further 15 minutes. Remove from the oven and allow to cool.

6   Soften the gelatine in cold water. Warm the mango purée and vanilla pulp in a saucepan, squeeze out the gelatine and dissolve in the mango. Stir over a bowl of ice cold water until cold. Spread the mango purée over the tart before it sets.

▶▶ Tips

You can make the mango purée yourself. Peel 1 or 2 mangos, depending on size. Cut the flesh away from the stone, weigh out 250 g and purée in a food processor. Add sugar to taste.

Pumpkin and pecan pie
with candied ginger

For 1 springform cake tin (28 cm Ø)

Ingredients:

For the sweet pastry:
250 g cold butter
500 g plain flour
200 g icing sugar
1 tsp grated lemon zest
2 tbsp vanilla sugar
Salt
1 medium egg

For the pumpkin filling:
300 g pumpkin or
butternut squash
60 g candied ginger
50 g butter

For the crème:
350 g ground almonds
300 g soft butter
300 g sugar
3 medium eggs
(room temperature)

Also:
Butter to grease the tin
Flour for the work surface
Dried beans for baking blind
150 g pecans
1 tbsp icing sugar

1   To make the pastry, cut the butter into small cubes. Mix the flour, icing sugar, lemon zest, vanilla sugar and a pinch of salt. Blitz in a food processor with the butter. Add in the egg, wrap in clingfilm and put in the fridge for 30 minutes.

2   Grease the springform tin. Roll the pastry out thinly on a floured surface and line the tin, creating a rim. Place in the fridge for 20 minutes.

3   Cover the pastry with baking paper and fill with dried beans. Blind bake at 180ºC (Fan plus) on the second shelf for 10 to 15 minutes. Remove the baking paper and dried beans, and put the pastry case to one side.

4   Peel and deseed the pumpkin. Chop the pumpkin and ginger into small pieces and sweat in the butter over a low heat. Purée in a food processor, return to the pan and simmer until the mixture has the consistency of jam.

5   To make the crème, roast the almonds in a non-stick frying pan without fat until golden brown, then leave to cool. Beat the butter and sugar until light and fluffy. Gradually stir the almonds and eggs into the butter crème, then leave to rest for 15 minutes.

6   Spread the pumpkin filling over the pastry base and spread the almond mixture on top. Scatter with pecans and press them down lightly. Bake at 150ºC (Fan plus) on the second shelf for 40 to 45 minutes. Remove from the oven and allow to cool for at least 30 minutes. Dust with icing sugar to serve.

▶▶ Tips

Instead of pumpkin, try using apricots. Gently stew the same quantity of stoned apricots until the liquid has almost all evaporated, then proceed according to the recipe.

Passion fruit rice pudding tart
with caramelized Demerara sugar

For 1 tart tin (24 cm Ø) | *A new way with an old favourite*

1   To make the pastry, cut the butter into small cubes. Mix together the flour, icing sugar, lemon zest, vanilla sugar and a pinch of salt. Blitz in a food processor with the butter. Add in the egg, wrap in clingfilm and put in the fridge for 30 minutes.

2   Roll the pastry out thinly on a floured surface and line the tart tin. Place in the fridge for 15 minutes.

3   Cover the pastry with baking paper and fill with dried beans. Blind bake at 180ºC (Fan plus) on the second shelf for 15 to 20 minutes. Remove the paper and dried beans. Warm the jam. Brush over the pastry base and put to one side.

4   To make the filling, heat the butter in a pan and sweat the rice. Stir together the passion fruit and coconut milk. Add one third to the rice and boil a little, stirring continuously.

For the sweet pastry:

120 g cold butter
250 g plain flour
100 g icing sugar
1 tsp grated lemon zest
1 tbsp vanilla sugar
Salt
1 medium egg

For the filling:

1 tbsp butter
150 g pudding rice
200 g passion fruit pulp or
200 ml passion fruit juice
200 ml coconut milk
120 g sugar
Pulp from 1 vanilla pod
200 g cream cheese
2 medium eggs
2 tbsp Demerara sugar

Also:

Flour for the work surface
Dried beans for baking blind
50 g apricot jam

5   Add the sugar and vanilla pulp. Add the rest of the liquid a little at a time, and simmer the rice for around 20 minutes. Remove from the heat and allow to cool.

6   Stir the cream cheese and eggs into the rice. Spread into the pastry case and smooth the top. Bake at 150ºC (Fan plus) on the second shelf for 20 to 25 minutes.

7   Remove the tart from the oven. Sprinkle the Demerara sugar evenly over the top, and caramelize with a cook's blowtorch. Cool slightly, slice with a serrated knife and serve.

▶▶ Tips

Passion fruit have a sweet/sour flavour and a strong aroma. When buying them, select fruit that is slightly wrinkled as these are the ripe ones that have the best flavours.

Mini panettone
with cranberries

For 8 ramekins (à 8 cm Ø)

1 Put the flour into a bowl and make a well in the centre. Crumble the yeast and dissolve in the milk with the sugar. Pour into the well. Stir in the flour from the edge to create a thin dough. Cover the bowl with a damp tea towel and leave in a warm place to rise for 15 minutes.

2 Add the eggs, butter and a pinch of salt and stir in with the rest of the flour. Knead with the kneading hook of an electric mixer until the dough is shiny and elastic. If the dough is too soft, add more flour. Cover and leave to rise for a further 30 minutes.

3 Chop the chocolate, nougat, nuts and cranberries, and knead them into the dough. Grease the ramekins and line them with strips of baking paper so that the paper stands 3 cm above the top of the ramekins.

Ingredients:

250 g strong white bread flour
20 g fresh yeast
50 g sugar
80 ml lukewarm milk
2 medium eggs
50 g soft butter
Salt
60 g plain chocolate
60 g nougat
50 g macadamia nuts
50 g dried cranberries
Butter to grease the tins

4 Divide the dough into 8 pieces and form into balls. Place in the ramekins and allow to rise for another 15 minutes.

5 Bake at 180°C (Moisture plus with 1 automatic burst of steam) on the second shelf for 10 to 15 minutes. Remove from the oven, cool on a wire cake rack, then remove the panettone from the ramekins.

▶▶ Tips

The panettone can be varied by adding chopped pistachios, raisins, mixed peel or candied cherries. They will keep for a while in a cake tin.

Rosemary "Bienenstich"
with candied lemon

For 1 springform cake tin (28 cm Ø)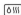

1   Put the flour into a bowl and make a well in the centre. Crumble the yeast and dissolve in the milk with the two types of sugar. Pour into the well. Stir in the flour from the edge to create a thin dough. Cover the bowl with a damp tea towel and leave in a warm place to rise for 15 minutes.

2   Add the egg, lemon zest, butter and a pinch of salt and stir in, along with the rest of the flour. Knead with the kneading hook of an electric mixer until the dough is shiny and elastic. Cover and leave to rise for another 45 minutes.

3   To make the topping, melt the butter in a saucepan and dissolve the sugar in it. Stir in the honey, cream, almonds and rosemary. Simmer briefly, then leave to cool.

4   Grease the springform tin and line the base with baking paper. Roll out the dough and line the tin. Prick the dough several times with a fork. Spread the almond mixture on top and leave to rise for 30 minutes.

Ingredients:

For the yeast dough:
250 g strong white flour
20 g fresh yeast
1 heaped tbsp sugar
1 tbsp vanilla sugar
80 ml lukewarm milk
1 medium egg
1 tsp grated lemon zest
50 g soft butter
Salt

For the topping:
75 g butter
50 g sugar
1 1/2 tbsp honey
75 ml double cream
100 g flaked almonds
1 tsp chopped rosemary

For the crème:
3 leaves of gelatine
100 g candied lemon peel
250 ml double cream
1/4 l milk
60 g sugar
Pulp from 1 vanilla pod
1 tbsp cornflour
A few drops of vanilla essence
3 medium egg yolks

Also:
Butter to grease the tin

5   Bake at 180°C (Moisture plus with 1 automatic burst of steam) on the second shelf for 30 to 35 minutes. If the almond mixture starts to brown too much, reduce the heat to 160°C. Remove from the oven, take out of the cake tin and cool on a wire cake rack.

6   To make the crème, soften the gelatine in cold water. Chop the candied lemon peel. Whip the cream until stiff. Heat 200 ml milk with the sugar and vanilla pulp. Stir the rest of the milk with the cornflour and egg yolks until smooth, and stir into the vanilla milk. Bring to the boil, remove from the heat, cool slightly, then stir in the squeezed out gelatine to dissolve. Add the lemon peel and beat the crème over a bowl of iced water until cold. As soon as it starts to set, fold in the double cream.

7   Cut the cake in half horizontally and slice the top half into 16 pieces with a serrated knife. Spread the crème over the bottom half and put the cake back together. Leave to stand for 1 hour.

Rhubarb puffs
with frangipane

Makes 10 ⌂

1 To make the frangipane, beat the butter and icing sugar until soft. Add the almonds and flour, and stir in the eggs one at a time. Stir in the peach liqueur and put to one side.

2 To make the filling, cut the rhubarb into 1 cm slices. Bring the wine and sugar to the boil, stir in the vanilla pulp, grenadine and rhubarb and simmer, uncovered, for 30 minutes until it has the consistency of marmalade. Leave to cool.

3 Wash and dry the basil leaves and cut into thin strips. Stir into the cooled filling.

4 Roll the pastry out on a floured surface to a rectangle measuring 55 x 30 cm. Cut in half along the length, then into four times across the width to make 10 small rectangles 11 x 15 cm. Spread the frangipane over half of each slice, leaving a 1 cm wide band free at the edge. Top with 2 to 3 tsp of the rhubarb filling.

Ingredients:

For the frangipane:
125 g butter
125 g icing sugar
125 g ground almonds
50 g plain flour
2 large eggs
4 cl peach liqueur

For the rhubarb filling:
600 g rhubarb
200 ml sweet white wine
150 g sugar
Pulp from 1 vanilla pod
3 tbsp grenadine syrup
10 basil leaves

Also:
750 g puff pastry
Flour for the work surface
2 egg yolks
4 tbsp milk
50 g icing sugar

5 Mix the egg yolks and milk and brush over the edges of the pastry. Fold the pastry over the filling and press the edges together firmly to seal. Line a baking tray with baking paper and place the puffs on the tray.

6 Bake at 180°C (Moisture plus with 1 automatic burst of steam) on the second shelf for 15 to 17 minutes. Pre-heat the grill (Full grill) to 240°C. Dust the puffs thickly with icing sugar and caramelize under the grill for 3 to 4 minutes. Remove from the oven and cool on a wire rack. Dust again with icing sugar before serving.

▶▶ Tips

The puffs can also be filled with shop-bought fruit compote or jam. Check that the jam has a low sugar content as the frangipane is already very sweet.

Peach and apricot puffs
with a white chocolate filling

Makes 1 tart (26 cm Ø) ⌂ﬀ

1   For the fruit, wash, dry and stone the peaches and apricots and cut them into pieces. Mix together with the sugar, vanilla pulp, cinnamon and star anise and leave to stand for 30 minutes.

2   Cook in a saucepan over a gentle heat until the fruit is soft. Mix the cornflour with 1 tbsp cold water and stir until smooth, then use to thicken the fruit. Remove the cinnamon stick and star anise and leave to cool.

3   To make the crème, warm the double cream with the vanilla sugar. Chop the chocolate and dissolve it in the cream. Pour into a bowl and leave to cool.

4   On a floured surface, roll the pastry out into 2 circles (26 cm Ø). Lay each on a sheet of baking paper. Mix the egg yolk and milk and brush over the pastry. Coarsely chop the macadamia nuts and sprinkle over the pastry.

Ingredients:

For the fruit:
2 peaches
4 apricots
80 g sugar
Pulp from 1 vanilla pod
1 cinnamon stick
1 star anise
1 tsp cornflour

For the crème:
220 ml double cream
1 tbsp vanilla sugar
400 g white chocolate

Also:
500 g puff pastry
Flour for the work surface
1 medium egg yolk
2 tbsp milk
125 g salted macadamia nuts
50 g icing sugar

5   Bake the pastry circles one at a time on a baking tray in the oven at 180°C (Moisture plus with 1 automatic burst of steam) on the second shelf for 20 minutes. Pre-heat the grill (Full grill) to 240°C. Dust the pastry thickly with icing sugar and grill for 3 to 4 minutes each to caramelize the sugar. Remove from the oven and cool.

6   Beat the cooled chocolate and cream mixture with an electric mixer for 5 to 7 minutes to produce a light, fluffy chocolate crème.

7   Place one circle of pastry on a serving plate and cover with chocolate crème. Top with the apricots and peaches. Cut the second circle of pastry into 12 slices with a serrated knife and arrange on top of the fruit (or leave the pastry whole). Place in the fridge for 30 minutes before serving.

Apple strudel
with butter biscuits and almonds

Makes 2 strudels

Ingredients:

For the strudel pastry:
300 g plain flour
1 egg yolk
5 tbsp oil · Salt

For the filling:
50 g raisins
3 cl dark rum
1.2 kg cooking apples
(e.g. Granny Smiths/Bramleys)
1 tsp ground cinnamon
120 g sugar
Juice of 1 lemon
120 g petit beurre biscuits
200 ml sour cream
100 g flaked almonds

Also:
Flour and oil for working the
pastry
60 g melted butter
Butter for the tin
60 g icing sugar

1   Sieve the flour into a bowl. Beat together the egg yolk, 3 tbsp oil, 150 ml lukewarm water and a pinch of salt. Pour into the flour and knead with the kneading hook of an electric mixer until the dough is elastic. Divide the dough in 2 and form into balls. Rub each one with oil, wrap in clingfilm and leave to stand for 1 hour.

2   To make the filling, soak the raisins in the rum. Peel, quarter and core the apples, and cut into thin slices. Mix the apples, rum, raisins, cinnamon, 50 g sugar and the lemon juice in a bowl. Crumble the biscuits and stir into the apple mixture along with the soured cream.

3   Caramelize the remaining sugar in a frying pan. Stir in the almonds and pour immediately onto a baking tray lined with baking paper. Leave to cool then chop finely.

4   Roll out one ball of strudel pastry on a floured surface to a square 40 x 40 cm. Place the pastry on a floured tea towel and, with oiled hands, stretch out until paper thin.

5   Brush with melted butter and sprinkle with half the almond praline. Place half the apple filling along one side in a 10 to 15 cm wide band. Roll up the strudel with the help of the tea towel. Prepare the second strudel in the same way.

6   Grease a baking tray. Place the strudels close together on the tray with the join underneath and tuck the ends under. Brush with the remaining melted butter.

7   Bake at 190°C (Conventional heat) on the second shelf for 30 to 35 minutes. Remove from the oven and cool slightly. Dust thickly with icing sugar and serve in slices. Vanilla ice cream goes well.

Rhubarb quark strudel
with an elderflower cream filling

Makes 2 strudels

1   Sieve the flour into a bowl. Mix together the egg yolk, 3 tbsp oil, 150 ml lukewarm water and a pinch of salt. Pour into the flour and knead with the kneading hook of an electric mixer until the dough is elastic. Divide the dough in 2 and form into balls. Rub each one with oil, wrap in clingfilm and leave to stand for 1 hour.

2   To make the filling, cut the rhubarb into small pieces. Mix with 100 g sugar and leave for a few minutes to draw out the juice. Roast the almonds in a dry frying pan.

3   Beat the butter, vanilla pulp, lemon zest and icing sugar until soft. Stir in the egg and quark. Whip 120 ml double cream until stiff and stir into the quark mixture along with the elderflower syrup.

4   Roll out one ball of strudel pastry on a floured surface to a square 40 x 40 cm. Place the pastry on a floured tea towel and, with oiled hands, stretch out until paper thin. Brush with melted butter and sprinkle with half the almonds.

Ingredients:

For the strudel pastry:
300 g plain flour
1 egg yolk
5 tbsp oil · Salt

For the filling:
400 g rhubarb
140 g sugar
60 g ground almonds
60 g soft butter
Pulp from 1 vanilla pod
1 tsp grated lemon zest
60 g icing sugar
2 large eggs
(room temperature)
500 g low fat quark
320 ml double cream
100 ml elderflower syrup

Also:
Flour and oil for working the pastry
60 g melted butter
Butter for the tin

5   Spread half the quark filling along one side in a 10 to 15 cm wide band. Drain the rhubarb, retaining the juices, and spread half over the quark. Roll up the strudel with the help of the tea towel. Prepare the second strudel in the same way.

6   Grease a baking tray. Place the strudels close together on the tray with the join underneath and tuck the ends under. Brush with the remaining melted butter and sprinkle with the rest of the sugar.

7   Bake at 190°C (Conventional heat) on the second shelf for 20 minutes. Mix the remaining double cream with the rhubarb juice and pour over the strudels. Bake for a further 20 to 25 minutes. Remove from the oven and cool slightly. Dust thickly with icing sugar and serve in slices.

Cherry and rice pudding strudel
with nougat

Makes 2 strudels

Ingredients:

For the strudel pastry:
300 g plain flour
1 egg yolk
5 tbsp oil · Salt

For the filling:
120 g risotto or pudding rice
400 ml milk
50 g sugar
Pulp from 1 vanilla pod
500 g cherries
60 g soft butter
60 g icing sugar
Grated zest of 1 orange and
1 lemon
2 medium eggs
(room temperature)
200 g crème fraîche
(room temperature)
200 g nougat

Also:
Flour and oil for working the
pastry
60 g melted butter
Butter for the tin
Icing sugar

1 Sieve the flour in a bowl. Mix together the egg yolk, 3 tbsp oil, 150 ml lukewarm water and a pinch of salt. Pour into the flour and knead with the kneading hook of an electric mixer until the dough is elastic. Divide the dough in 2 and form into balls. Rub each one with oil, wrap in clingfilm and leave to stand for 1 hour.

2 Bring the rice to the boil with the milk, sugar and vanilla pulp, and simmer for 15 to 20 minutes. Pour into a bowl and leave to cool. Wash and stone the cherries.

3 Beat the butter with the icing sugar and orange and lemon zest until soft. Stir in the eggs one at a time. Stir in the crème fraîche, and mix into the rice. Cut the nougat into 1¹/₂ cm thick pieces.

4 Roll out one ball of strudel pastry on a floured surface to a square 40 x 40 cm. Place the pastry on a floured tea towel and, with oiled hands, stretch out until paper thin. Brush with melted butter.

5 Spread half the rice pudding filling along one side in a 10 to 15 cm wide band. Top with half the cherries and pile half of the nougat pieces down the centre. Roll up the strudel with the help of the tea towel. Prepare the second strudel in the same way.

6 Grease a baking tray. Place the strudels close together on the tray with the join underneath and tuck the ends under. Brush with the remaining melted butter.

7 Bake at 190°C (Conventional heat) on the second shelf for 30 to 35 minutes. Pre-heat the grill (Full grill) to 240°C. Dust the strudels generously with icing sugar and grill for 2 to 3 minutes to caramelize the sugar. Remove from the oven and cool slightly.

Éclairs
with spiced coffee mousse

Makes 30

1 To make the mousse, chop the chocolate and melt in a bowl over a pan of simmering water along with the spices and the coffee powder. Soften the gelatine in cold water. Beat the egg, egg yolk, sugar and liqueur in a bowl over a pan of simmering water until creamy, then stir in the chocolate. Squeeze out the gelatine and dissolve in the egg mixture. Cool the mixture to 30 to 35°C, then whip the cream and fold in gently. Place the mousse in the fridge for 2 hours.

2 To make the choux pastry, bring 1/8 l water, the milk, butter, sugar and a pinch of salt to the boil. Tip in the flour. Stir with a wooden spoon until the dough comes away from the base of the saucepan. Stir for at least 1 minute longer. Transfer the dough to a bowl and mix in the eggs one at a time, using the kneading hook of an electric mixer. Stir until the dough is smooth and shiny.

3 Grease a baking tray and dust with flour. Put half the dough into a piping bag with an 8 mm Ø nozzle, and pipe 5 cm long strips onto the baking tray, leaving a 4 cm gap between each one. Mix the egg yolk and milk and brush over the pastry.

Ingredients:

For the mousse:
250 g white chocolate
1 pinch each of ground coriander, cinnamon and cloves
1 tbsp instant espresso powder
2 leaves of gelatine
1 egg · 1 egg yolk
2 tbsp sugar
2 tbsp coffee liqueur (e.g. Kahlúa)
500 ml double cream

For the choux pastry:
1/8 l milk
100 g soft butter
1 tsp sugar · Salt
150 g plain flour
4 medium eggs

Also:
Butter and flour for the tin
1 egg yolk · 1 tbsp milk
Cocoa powder to dust

4 Bake at 190°C (Moisture plus with 1 automatic burst of steam) on the second shelf for 15 to 17 minutes. Remove from the oven. Repeat the process with the remaining dough.

5 While the éclairs are still hot, split them lengthways and leave to cool. Put the coffee mousse in a piping bag with a star shaped nozzle and pipe into the bottom half of each éclair. Replace the top halves, dust with cocoa powder, and if desired, decorate with a little mousse and chocolate coated coffee beans.

▶▶ Tips

Kahlúa is a coffee liqueur from Mexico which has been popular in Europe for many years. It is an important ingredient in cocktails such as a White Russian and is indispensable in any cocktail bar.

Passion fruit sponges
with vanilla syrup

Fills 8–10 shot glasses (200 ml each)

1 Separate the eggs. Beat the egg yolks in a bowl with the vanilla sugar and 70 g icing sugar until creamy. Mix the almonds, flour and a pinch of salt. Slightly warm the passion fruit juice and alternately stir the juice and the almond and flour mixture into the eggs.

2 Whisk the egg whites with a pinch of salt to soft peaks, then gradually, add the remaining icing sugar and whisk until thick and creamy. Fold into the passion fruit mixture a little at a time.

3 Grease the glasses and two thirds fill with the passion fruit mixture. Bake at 160°C (Conventional heat) on the second shelf for 15 to 20 minutes.

Ingredients:

4 medium eggs
1 tbsp vanilla sugar
120 g icing sugar
120 g ground almonds
60 g plain flour
Salt
100 ml passion fruit juice
Butter for the glasses
1 lime
2 cm stem ginger
Pulp from 2 vanilla pods
80 g sugar

4 Meanwhile, squeeze the juice from the lime. Peel and thinly slice the ginger. In a saucepan, boil 120 ml water with the lime juice, vanilla pulp, sugar and ginger. Remove the the syrup from the heat, leave to stand briefly, then remove the ginger.

5 Take the sponges out of the oven and cool slightly on a cake rack. Drizzle each one with 2 tbsp of the vanilla syrup. If desired, cut 1 passion fruit in half and spoon a little of the pulp over the sponges to garnish.

▶▶ Tips

You can make your own vanilla sugar by placing one or two vanilla pods in a jar of caster sugar and leaving for a week or so to absorb the flavour.

Pine nut
and apricot biscotti

Makes 40–50

1   Lightly roast the pine nuts in a frying pan without fat and leave to cool. Mix the flour with the baking powder. Finely chop the dried apricots.

2   Beat the butter with the icing sugar until soft. Add the eggs one at a time, then stir in the cinnamon, a pinch of salt and the orange zest. Add the flour mixture, stir well and knead to a smooth dough. Knead in the apricots and pine nuts.

3   Divide the dough into four. Flour your hands and roll the dough into 30 cm long logs. Line the baking tray with baking paper. Place the rolls of dough on the tray, well spaced out. Flatten them evenly so that they are 4 cm wide and 1 1/2 cm thick.

Ingredients:

150 g pine nuts
280 g plain flour
1/2 tsp baking powder
100 g dried apricots
125 g soft butter
185 g icing sugar
2 medium eggs
(room temperature)
1/2 tsp ground cinnamon
Salt
1 tsp grated orange zest
Flour for rolling out

4   Bake at 180°C (Conventional heat) on the second shelf for 30 to 35 minutes. Remove from the oven and cool on a cake rack. Do not switch off the oven. Cut the rolls into 2 cm thick slices and put the slices back on the baking tray. Bake for a further 5 to 10 minutes until golden. Remove from the oven and cool completely. Dust thickly with icing sugar.

▶▶ Tips

These biscotti are delicious dunked in syrup. Bring the juice of 2 lemons to the boil with 120 g sugar, 1 bunch of basil and 400 ml water. Leave to stand for 5 minutes, pass through a sieve and leave to cool.

Shortbread
with walnut nougat

For one rectangular tin (20 x 30 cm)

1 Line the tin with baking paper. Beat the butter with the icing sugar, vanilla sugar and a pinch of salt until soft. Stir in the flour. Press the dough evenly into the tin. Bake at 160°C (Conventional heat) on the second shelf for 25 to 30 minutes. Remove from the oven and cool slightly.

2 To make the topping, finely chop the walnuts and heat in a saucepan with the muscovado sugar, condensed milk and butter, but do not boil. When the sugar has dissolved, spread the mixture over the shortbread and place in the fridge for 20 minutes.

Ingredients:

For the shortbread:
250 g soft butter
120 g icing sugar
1 tbsp vanilla sugar
Salt
300 g plain flour

For the topping:
150 g walnuts
120 g muscovado sugar or brown sugar
120 ml condensed milk
120 g butter
200 g nougat
60 ml double cream

3 Chop the nougat into small pieces. Bring the cream to the boil in a saucepan and add the nougat. Melt gently, then carefully spread over the shortbread and put back in the fridge.

4 Remove the shortbread from the tin. Cut in half lengthways, then cut into 2 cm wide fingers and serve with tea or coffee.

▶▶ **Tips**

Muscovado sugar is a soft, unrefined cane sugar with fine crystals, a caramel aroma and slightly liquorice flavour.

Bread
and rolls

Making bread yourself is quicker and easier than many people believe. Whether sweet or savoury, home made bread not only tastes great, it also gives you free rein to experiment with flavours. And there is nothing nicer than the smell of freshly baked rolls wafting through the house on a Sunday morning.

To make **yeast dough**

1 Put the flour in a bowl and make a well in the centre. Dissolve the fresh yeast and sugar in lukewarm water, pour into the well and work a little flour in from the edge.

2 Cover and leave to rise for 15 minutes. Knead thoroughly with the kneading hook of an electric mixer. Cover and leave to rise for 30 minutes.

3 Knead the dough again briefly and roll out on a floured surface. Proceed according to the recipe and allow to rise for a further 15 minutes before baking.

To make **sour dough**

1 Stir rye flour and lukewarm water together to create a thick porridge. Cover and leave for several days until the dough is grey and produces bubbles.

2 Stir in the rest of the flour and the salt and knead thoroughly with the kneading hook of an electric mixer until the dough is elastic.

3 Place the dough in a bowl lined with a floured cloth and fold the ends of the cloth over the dough. Cover the bowl with clingfilm. Leave the dough to rise overnight.

Basics
Doughs

Yeast dough is prepared with the help of baker's yeast. When the micro organisms of the yeast encounter favourable conditions, their ability to metabolise accelerates quickly. This produces carbon dioxide which causes the dough to rise and become lighter. Sugar is added as well as flour as additional nutrition for the yeast. Sufficient liquid and temperatures between 30 and 40°C create the perfect conditions for the yeast to grow.

Sour dough, like yeast dough, is used as a natural leavening agent for dough, especially for rye bread. The principle is similar to yeast dough, making use of the natural occurence of yeast and lactic acid bacteria. A starter dough is prepared which will produce the desired micro organisms. This starter dough is sometimes available ready made.

To make mixed flour bread

1 Put the rye kernels in a bowl and cover with water. Leave at room temperature for a day to swell. Drain through a sieve.

2 Put the rye and wheat flour in a large bowl and mix thoroughly, eg. with a whisk, and make a well in the centre.

3 Crumble the yeast. Stir together with the sour dough starter, sugar and water until the yeast has dissolved. Pour into the well in the flour.

4 Stir in some of the flour from around the edge to create a thin dough. Cover with a tea towel and leave in a warm place for 30 minutes to rise.

5 Add the rye kernels, salt and spices and stir in the rest of the flour. Knead thoroughly on a floured surface until the dough is elastic.

6 Cover and leave to rise for 1 hour. Form one or more loaves from the dough. Place on a floured baking tray and leave to rise for another hour.

Basics
Doughs

Wheat flour is the standard flour for baking, and forms the basis of numerous breads, cakes and biscuits. Characteristic of wheat flour are the glutens which swell considerably and create a strong structure – which is why wheat flour is so favourable for baking.

Rye flour has a protein structure that means it cannot be used on its own with yeast to make bread. Acidifying the dough with the help of sour dough strongly improves its baking qualities and nutritional physiology. Wheat and rye flour are generally mixed together, and both yeast and sour dough are used to combine the benefits of both leavening methods and to produce a tasty bread with a good consistency.

Rustic sour dough bread
with rye flour

Makes 1 loaf (2 kg) ⌂

Ingredients:

750 g rye flour
750 g strong white flour
Salt
Flour for the work surface

1 To make the sour dough starter, place 500 g of rye flour in a bowl with 700 ml lukewarm water, stir to a thick porridge and cover with clingfilm. Leave in a warm place for at least 3 or 4 days until the starter is producing bubbles and has turned grey.

2 Mix the sour dough starter with the remaining rye flour and the wheat flour plus 1 tbsp salt. Knead with the kneading hook of an electric mixer until the dough is elastic. Line a bowl with a floured tea towel. Place the dough in the tea towel and fold the cloth over it. Cover the bowl with clingfilm so that it doesn't dry out and leave the dough to rise overnight for 12 to 14 hours.

3 Place the dough on a floured surface and form into a round loaf. Place the loaf on a baking tray, dust with flour and cut a cross into the surface, 1 cm deep. Bake the bread at 180°C (Moisture plus with 1 automatic burst of steam) on the second shelf for 1 hour. The bread is ready when it sounds hollow if tapped. Remove from the oven and cool on a wire rack.

▶▶ Tips

To make a loaf using a ready made sour dough starter, use 500 g rye flour, 350 g strong wholemeal bread flour, 40 g fresh yeast, 150 g sour dough, 1 tbsp sugar, 450 ml warm water and 3 tsp salt. Prepare as for yeast dough and bake as above for 50 to 60 minutes.

Beer rolls
with aniseed

For 1 springform tin (28 cm Ø)

1 Caramelize the sugar in a saucepan until golden brown. Pour in the beer and boil quickly until the sugar has dissolved. Remove from the heat and cool until lukewarm.

2 Sieve the flours into a bowl and make a well in the centre. Crumble the yeast and dissolve in the caramel beer, then pour into the well. Stir in some of the flour from around the edge to create a thin dough. Cover the bowl with a tea towel and leave in a warm place to rise for 15 minutes.

3 Add the salt and aniseed and stir in the rest of the flour. Knead with the kneading hook of an electric mixer for at least 5 minutes until the dough is shiny and elastic. Cover with a damp tea towel and leave in a warm place to rise for a further 45 minutes.

Ingredients:

100 g sugar
625 ml dark beer (bitter)
500 g strong white flour
500 g plain flour
40 g fresh yeast
1 tbsp fine sea salt
1 tsp aniseed
Butter for the tin
Flour for the work surface

4 Grease the springform tin. Divide the dough into 6 pieces and roll into balls. Place one ball in the centre of the tin and place the other balls around it. Dust with flour and leave to rise again for 30 minutes.

5 Bake at 190°C (Moisture plus with 1 automatic burst of steam) on the second shelf for 30 to 35 minutes. Remove from the oven and cool on a wire rack. Turn out of the tin and divide into individual rolls.

▶▶ Tips

If you are baking for children, try using malt beer instead of bitter. Reduce the amount of sugar to 80g, though, because malt beer is already quite sweet.

Mixed flour rye bread
with five spices

Makes 1 loaf (1.4 kg) ⌂≋

1   Put the rye kernels in a bowl and cover with water. Leave for 1 ½ days to swell. Drain through a sieve.

2   Crumble the yeast and dissolve in 350 ml lukewarm water with the sour dough and sugar. Put both types of flour in a bowl, mix well and make a well in the centre. Pour the yeast mixture into the well. Stir in some of the flour from around the edge to create a thin paste. Cover the bowl with a tea towel and leave in a warm place to rise for 30 minutes.

3   Add the rye kernels, five spice powder and salt, and stir in the rest of the flour. Knead with the kneading hook of an electric mixer for at least 5 minutes until the dough is shiny and elastic. Cover with a damp tea towel and leave in a warm place to rise for an hour.

Ingredients:

200 g rye kernels
20 g fresh yeast
125 g liquid sour dough
(ready made)
1 tbsp sugar
300 g rye flour
300 g strong white flour
1½ tbsp five spice powder
1 level tbsp fine sea salt
1 tbsp fennel seeds
1 tbsp coriander seeds
Flour for dusting

4   Form the dough into a long loaf and place on a baking tray. Sprinkle with fennel and coriander seeds and press them in lightly. Cover with a cloth and leave in a warm place to rise for 1 hour.

5   Dust the loaf with flour. Bake at 190°C (Moisture plus with 1 automatic burst of steam) on the second shelf for 50 to 60 minutes. Remove from the oven and cool on a wire rack.

▸▸ Tips

You can create your own five spice powder by mixing ½ tablespoon each of ground caraway and coriander with ½ teaspoon each of ground aniseed, fennel and cardomom.

Baguettes
with assorted fillings

For 2 baguettes (400 g)

Ingredients:

For the dough:
300 ml lukewarm milk
1 tsp sugar
20 g fresh yeast
500 g strong white flour
1 level tbsp fine sea salt

For the eggplant/aubergine filling:
1 red pepper
1 eggplant/aubergine
(approx. 350 g)
2 tbsp olive oil
Salt · Ground pepper

For the nut filling:
200 g hazlenuts (chopped)

Also:
Flour for the work surface
2 tbsp milk to glaze

1   For the dough, dissolve the yeast in the milk and 150 ml lukewarm water, and stir in the sugar. Put the flour in a bowl and make a well in the centre. Pour the yeast mixture into the well. Stir in some of the flour from around the edge to create a sticky paste. Cover the bowl with a tea towel and leave in a warm place to rise for 30 minutes.

2   Add the salt and stir in the rest of the flour. Knead with the kneading hook of an electric mixer for at least 5 minutes until the dough is shiny and elastic. Cover with a damp tea towel and leave in a warm place to rise for a further 45 minutes.

3   To make the eggplant filling, cut the pepper in half, remove the seeds and chop coarsely. Wash the eggplant and cut into small cubes. Sweat in olive oil over a medium heat for 3 to 4 minutes. Add the pepper and cook until the eggplant is soft. Season with salt and pepper. For the nut filling, roast the hazelnuts in a frying pan without fat.

4   Knead the dough again briefly, divide in half and knead the nuts into one piece. Roll each half into a 40 cm long loaf, and flatten the second one slightly. Distribute half the aubergines over the centre of the flattened dough, then fold the dough around the filling. Place the loaves on a baking tray, well spaced apart. Slash several times with a knife. Cover with a floured tea towel and leave to rise for 30 minutes.

5   Brush the dough with milk. Top the eggplant baguette with the remaining eggplant. Bake at 180°C (Moisture plus with 1 automatic burst of steam) on the second shelf for 30 minutes. They are done when they sound hollow if tapped. Cool on a wire rack.

6   Try using onions or feta cheese as an alternative. For an onion baguette, knead 2 tbsp chopped thyme and 150 g fried onions into one portion of dough. For a feta baguette, knead in 200 g crumbled feta and 1 tbsp honey, then bake as above.

Walnut bread
with maple syrup

Makes 2 loaves (500 g each)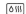

1 Put the flour in a bowl and make a well in the centre. Crumble the yeast and dissolve in the maple syrup with 300 ml lukewarm water. Pour into the well. Stir in some of the flour from around the edge to create a sticky paste. Cover the bowl with a tea towel and leave in a warm place to rise for 30 minutes.

2 Grind half the walnuts finely in a food processor, and chop the other half coarsely. Add the butter, walnuts, walnut oil and salt to the dough and knead with the kneading hook of an electric mixer for at least 5 minutes until the dough is shiny and elastic. Cover with a damp tea towel and leave in a warm place to rise for a further 45 minutes.

Ingredients:

250 g strong white flour
250 g plain flour
20 g fresh yeast
1 tbsp maple syrup
200 g walnuts
50 g soft butter
2 tbsp walnut oil
1 tsp fine sea salt
Flour for the work surface

3 Knead the dough again briefly and divide in half. Form into long loaves and place on a baking tray, well spaced apart. Cover with a floured cloth and leave to rise for 30 minutes.

4 Carefully remove the cloth. Dust the loaves with flour. Bake at 200°C (Moisture plus with 1 automatic burst of steam) on the second shelf for 35 to 40 minutes. For a darker crust, raise the temperature towards the end of the cooking time. Cool the loaves on a wire rack for approx. 30 minutes.

▶▶ Tips

To make hazelnut bread, replace the walnuts and walnut oil with the same quantities of hazelnuts and hazelnut oil. Or try using unsalted macadamia nuts and oil.

Potato bread
with caraway

Makes 1 loaf (1 kg) | *Crisp and crusty*

1 Put the flour in a bowl and make a well in the centre. Crumble the yeast and dissolve in the milk. Pour into the well with the caraway and the malt extract. Stir in some of the flour from around the edge to create a sticky paste. Cover the bowl with a tea towel and leave in a warm place to rise for 15 minutes.

2 Peel the cooked potatoes and grate into the bowl. Add the egg and salt and stir in with the rest of the flour. Knead well with floured hands until the dough is elastic. Cover and leave to rise in a warm place for 30 minutes.

Ingredients:

400 g strong white flour
40 g fresh yeast
100 ml lukewarm milk
1 tbsp ground caraway
1 tbsp malt extract
400 g boiled floury potatoes
(cooked the previous day)
1 medium egg
1 tsp salt
Flour for the work surface
Sea salt to sprinkle

3 Knead the dough again briefly, form into a long loaf and place on a baking tray. Sprinkle with sea salt, cover and leave to rise for a further 30 minutes.

4 Remove the cloth carefully and dust the dough with flour. Bake at 190°C (Moisture plus with 1 automatic burst of steam) on the second shelf for 45 to 50 minutes. Remove the bread from the oven and cool on a wire rack.

▶▶ Tips

Malt extract is a malt sugar syrup that is produced by a special process. It improves the flavour of bread when baking. It can be replaced by golden syrup or treacle if preferred.

Focaccia
with goat's cheese and almonds

For 1 baking tray

Ingredients:

750 g strong white flour
40 g fresh yeast
1 tbsp honey
1 tbsp grated lemon zest
1 tbsp fine sea salt
8 tbsp olive oil
Flour for the work surface
1/2 bunch of thyme
70 g sugar
150 g almonds (skins removed)
200 g goats cheese

1 Put the flour in a bowl and make a well in the centre. Crumble the yeast and dissolve with the honey in 350 ml lukewarm water. Pour into the well and stir in some of the flour from around the edge to create a thin paste. Cover the bowl with a tea towel and leave in a warm place to rise for 15 minutes.

2 Add the lemon zest, sea salt and 5 tbsp olive oil to the dough, stir in the rest of the flour and knead with the kneading hook of an electric mixer for at least 5 minutes until the dough is shiny and elastic. Cover with a damp tea towel and leave in a warm place to rise for a further 45 minutes.

3 Knead the dough again briefly and roll out on a floured surface to a rectangle to fit the baking tray (approx. 40 x 30 cm). Place the dough on the tray. Cover with a cloth and leave in a warm place for 30 minutes to rise.

4 Wash and dry the thyme and remove the leaves. Caramelize the sugar in a frying pan. Stir in the almonds, pour onto a baking tray and leave to cool. When cold, chop the almonds coarsely.

5 Remove the cloth carefully. Break the cheese into small pieces and scatter over the dough with the almonds. Press down slightly, sprinkle with thyme and drizzle with the remaining olive oil.

6 Bake at 170°C (Moisture plus with 1 automatic burst of steam) on the second shelf for 25 to 30 minutes. Take out of the oven and cool on a wire rack until lukewarm. Cut into pieces and serve.

Filled ciabatta
with tomatoes and Parma ham

For 1 oval ring loaf (40 x 30 cm)

1 Put the flour in a bowl and make a well in the centre. Crumble the yeast and dissolve with the honey in 600 ml lukewarm water. Pour into the well and stir in some of the flour from around the edge to create a thin paste. Cover the bowl with a tea towel and leave in a warm place to rise for 15 minutes.

2 Add the salt and olive oil to the dough, stir in the rest of the flour and knead with the kneading hook of an electric mixer for at least 5 minutes until the dough is shiny and elastic. Cover with a damp tea towel and leave in a warm place to rise for a further 45 minutes.

3 To make the filling, wash, dry and chop the basil leaves. Dice the sundried tomatoes into pieces and cut the ham into strips. Finely grate the Parmesan.

Ingredients:

For the dough:
1 kg strong white flour
30 g fresh yeast
2 tbsp honey
2 level tbsp fine sea salt
6 tbsp olive oil

For the filling:
2 bunches of basil
200 g sundried tomatoes (in oil, drained)
12 slices Parma ham or prosciutto
200 g Parmesan
100 g capers (pickled)

Also:
Flour for dusting

4 Knead the dough again briefly and roll out 1 cm thick to a rectangle measuring 80 x 20 cm. Place the filling ingredients along the centre. Fold the dough over from both sides and press firmly together to seal.

5 Form the dough into an oval and press the ends together well. Place on a baking tray with the join underneath. Dust with flour and leave in a warm place for 30 minutes to rise.

6 Bake at 180°C (Moisture plus with 1 automatic burst of steam) on the second shelf for 40 to 50 minutes. Remove from the oven, cool on a cake rack and serve lukewarm.

▶▶ Tips

Experiment with other Mediterranean products for the filling. For example, try roasted zucchini or peppers, and replace the Parmesan and basil with other types of cheese and herbs.

Mediterranean country bread
with coarse sea salt

Makes 2 loaves (700 g each)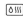

1   Put the flour in a bowl and make a well in the centre. Crumble the yeast and dissolve with the honey in 550 ml lukewarm water. Pour into the well and stir in some of the flour from around the edge to create a sticky paste. Cover the bowl with a tea towel and leave in a warm place to rise for 15 minutes.

2   Add the sour dough, salt and olive oil to the dough, stir in the rest of the flour and knead with the kneading hook of an electric mixer for at least 5 minutes until the dough is shiny and elastic. Cover with a damp tea towel and leave in a warm place to rise for a further 45 minutes.

Ingredients:

500 g strong white flour
500 g plain flour
30 g fresh yeast
1 tbsp honey
150 g liquid sour dough
(ready made)
75 ml extra virgin olive oil
1 tbsp coarse sea salt
Flour for dusting

3   Knead the dough again briefly and divide in half. Form into two round loaves and place on a baking tray. Cover with a cloth and leave to rise for 30 minutes.

4   Remove the cloth carefully and dust the loaves with flour. Bake at 180°C (Moisture plus with 1 automatic burst of steam) on the second shelf for 40 to 50 minutes. The loaves are done when they sound hollow if tapped. Remove from the oven and cool on a wire rack.

▶▶ Tips

The basic recipe can be enhanced by adding other ingredients e.g. 2 tbsp capers, chopped sundried tomatoes, fresh herbs or sliced olives.

Bread rolls
with parsley pesto and aubergines

Makes 10-12 rolls

1   Put the flour in a bowl and make a well in the centre. Crumble the yeast and dissolve with the sugar in 625 ml lukewarm water. Pour into the well and stir in some of the flour from around the edge to create a thin paste. Cover the bowl with a tea towel and leave in a warm place to rise for 15 minutes.

2   Add the salt, stir in the rest of the flour and knead with the kneading hook of an electric mixer for at least 5 minutes until the dough is shiny and elastic. Cover with a damp tea towel and leave in a warm place to rise for a further 45 minutes.

3   To make the pesto, wash and dry the herbs. Chop the leaves and purée with the olive oil, Parmesan and pine nuts. Season with salt and pepper.

4   Cut the aubergines in half lengthways then cut into $1/2$ thick slices. Salt and pepper the slices then leave to drain for 10 minutes. Pat dry with kitchen paper and fry in olive oil for 2 minutes on each side.

Ingredients:

For the dough:
1 kg strong white flour
40 g fresh yeast
2 tbsp sugar
1 tbsp sea salt

For the pesto:
1 bunch of parsley
$1/2$ bunch of lovage
100 ml olive oil
50 g grated Parmesan
50 g pine nuts (roasted)
Salt · Ground pepper

For the eggplant:
3 aubergines/eggplants
(900–1000 g)
Salt · Ground pepper
60 ml olive oil

Also:
Flour for the work surface

5   Knead the dough again briefly and divide in half. Roll each piece out on a floured surface to a square 40 x 40 cm and 1 cm thick. Spread evenly with pesto. Scatter the eggplant on top and roll the dough up. Cut into 5 cm thick slices. Place close together on a baking tray with the cut side up, cover and leave to rise for 30 minutes.

6   Bake at 180°C (Moisture plus with 1 automatic burst of steam) on the second shelf for 20 to 25 minutes. Remove from the oven, carefully separate the rolls and cool on a cake rack.

▶▶ Tips

You could use slices of pumpkin in place of the eggplant. Cook them in the oven at 180°C (Fan heat) for 25 minutes until soft. The pine nuts should then be replaced by toasted pumpkin seeds.

Rosemary and fig rolls
in a cup

For 8–10 cups (150 ml each)

Ingredients:

500 g strong white flour
20 g fresh yeast
1 tbsp honey
$^1/_4$ l lukewarm milk
40 g soft butter
1 tsp fine sea salt
200 ml port
2 tbsp sugar
10 fresh figs
1 tbsp chopped rosemary
Butter to grease the cups

1   Put the flour in a bowl and make a well in the centre. Crumble the yeast and dissolve with the honey in the milk. Pour into the well and stir in some of the flour from around the edge to create a thin paste. Cover the bowl with a tea towel and leave in a warm place to rise for 15 minutes.

2   Add the butter and sea salt to the dough, stir in the rest of the flour and knead with the kneading hook of an electric mixer for at least 5 minutes until the dough is shiny and elastic. Cover with a damp tea towel and leave in a warm place to rise for a further 45 minutes.

3   Meanwhile, reduce the port with the sugar in a frying pan until the liquid is syrupy. Wash the figs, cut a cross in the top and place in the port syrup with the rosemary. Simmer briefly and transfer to a bowl so that the figs do not become too soft.

4   Cut a sheet of baking paper into 10 small squares and dampen them with water. Grease the cups and line with the paper. Knead the dough again briefly and form into 10 evenly sized balls. Place the balls in the cups and press a hollow into the centre with your thumb. Place 1 fig and little syrup in each hollow, and leave to rise for 15 minutes.

5   Bake at 180°C (Moisture plus with 1 automatic burst of steam) on the second shelf for 15 to 20 minutes. Remove from the oven and cool slightly. Tip out of the cups and cool on a wire rack.

▶▶ Tips

For an alternative filling, rapidly fry 100 g dried apricots with 2 tsp chopped chervil and 100 g diced bacon, cool and knead into the dough.

Savoury bread rolls
with onions and marjoram

Makes 8 rolls

1 Put the flour in a bowl and make a well in the centre. Crumble the yeast and dissolve with the honey in 625 ml lukewarm water. Pour into the well and stir in some of the flour from around the edge to create a thin paste. Cover the bowl with a tea towel and leave in a warm place to rise for 15 minutes.

2 Add salt, stir in the rest of the flour and knead with the kneading hook of an electric mixer for at least 5 minutes until the dough is shiny and elastic. Cover with a damp tea towel and leave in a warm place to rise for a further 45 minutes.

3 To make the filling, wash and dry the marjoram, and remove the leaves. Peel and finely slice the onions. Brown the onions in the oil over a medium heat until crisp. Stir in the marjoram, add the sugar and caramelize. Season with a pinch of sea salt. Put one third of the mixture to one side and knead the rest into the dough.

Ingredients:

For the dough:
1 kg strong white flour
30 g fresh yeast
2 tbsp honey
2 level tbsp sea salt

For the filling:
1 bunch of marjoram
300 g onions
2 tbsp oil
1/2 tbsp sugar
Sea salt
1 red pepper
200 g scamorza
(smoked mozzarella)

Also:
Butter for the tins
Flour for the work surface

4 Grease 8 individual bread tins (400 ml capacity) and line with baking paper.

5 Halve and deseed the pepper and chop finely. Cut the scamoza into 8 cubes. Flour your hands and form the dough into 8 evenly sized discs. Place a piece of scamorza and some chopped pepper on each. Seal the dough around the filling and roll into balls. Place the balls in the baking tins and scatter the remaining onions on top. Leave to rise for 30 minutes.

6 Bake at 170°C (Moisture plus with 1 automatic burst of steam) on the second shelf for 20 minutes. Remove from the oven and cool slightly. Tip out of the tins and leave on a wire rack until lukewarm.

Banana bread rolls
with macadamia nuts

For 1 springform tin (28 cm Ø)

Ingredients:

500 g strong white flour
20 g fresh yeast
100 ml maple syrup
50 ml lukewarm milk
1 lime
2–3 bananas
Salt
Butter for the tin
200 g roasted, salted
macadamia nuts

1   Put the flour in a bowl and make a well in the centre. Crumble the yeast and dissolve with 60 ml maple syrup in the milk. Pour into the well and stir in some of the flour from around the edge to create a thin paste. Cover the bowl with a tea towel and leave in a warm place to rise for 15 minutes.

2   Squeeze the lime. Peel the bananas and purée with the lime juice. Weigh out 300 g of purée, and if there is not enough, make up the difference with water. Add the purée and a pinch of salt to the dough, stir in the rest of the flour and knead with the kneading hook of an electric mixer for at least 5 minutes until the dough is shiny and elastic. Cover with a damp tea towel and leave in a warm place to rise for a further 30 minutes.

3   Knead the dough again briefly then form into golf ball sized balls. Pack together in the springform tin, cover and leave to rise for 30 minutes.

4   Brush the dough with the remaining maple syrup. Chop the nuts finely and sprinkle on top.

5   Bake at 180°C (Moisture plus with 1 automatic burst of steam) on the second shelf for 25 to 30 minutes. Remove from the oven and cool slightly. Remove from the tin and cool on a cake rack.

▶▶ Tips

Macadamia nuts are harvested from an evergreen tree native to Australia that can live for over 100 years. The nuts are extremely hard to extract making them very expensive. Their creamy texture and crunchy bite make them the perfect ingredient in baking.

Chocolate plait
with chilli

Makes 2 loaves

1   Heat the milk in a saucepan. Chop the chocolate and stir into the milk to melt. Leave until lukewarm.

2   Put the flour in a bowl and make a well in the centre. Add the sugar, chilli powder and finely crumbled yeast and pour the chocolate milk into the well. Stir in some of the flour from around the edge to create a thin paste. Cover the bowl with a tea towel and leave in a warm place to rise for 15 minutes.

3   Add the egg, butter and a pinch of salt to the dough, stir in the rest of the flour and knead with the kneading hook of an electric mixer for at least 2 minutes until the dough is shiny and elastic. If the dough is too soft, add more flour. Cover with a damp tea towel and leave in a warm place to rise for a further 30 minutes.

Ingredients:

150 ml milk
150 g plain chocolate
600 g strong white flour
1 tbsp sugar
$1/2$ tsp chilli powder
40 g fresh yeast
1 medium egg
120 g soft butter
Salt
Flour for the work surface
1 medium egg yolk
50 ml double cream

4   Knead the dough again briefly and divide in half. Divide each half into three and roll out on a floured surface into 25 cm long pieces. Use three to make a plait and fold the ends in underneath. Repeat with the other three pieces.

5   Place the plaits on a baking tray. Mix the egg yolk and cream and brush over the dough. Leave to rise for 30 minutes.

6   Bake at 180°C (Moisture plus with 1 automatic burst of steam) on the second shelf for 25 to 30 minutes. Remove from the oven and cool on a wire rack.

▶▶ Tips

The chocolate plait goes well with ice cream such as vanilla, walnut or chocolate. Slice the plait and serve with ice cream and roasted almond flakes.

Sweet espresso rolls
with vanilla butter

Makes 10 rolls

Ingredients:

For the vanilla butter:
100 g soft butter
Pulp of 1 vanilla pod
2 tbsp icing sugar

For the dough:
500 g strong white flour
100 ml sweetened condensed milk
200 ml lukewarm strong espresso
20 g fresh yeast
Salt
80 g Amarettini
(Italian almond biscuits)

1 To make the vanilla butter, beat the butter with the vanilla pulp and icing sugar until soft. Put in a little bowl and place in the fridge.

2 For the dough, put the flour in a bowl and make a well in the centre. Crumble the yeast and dissolve in the condensed milk and espresso. Pour into the well and stir in some of the flour from around the edge to create a thin paste. Cover the bowl with a tea towel and leave in a warm place to rise for 15 minutes.

3 Work in the rest of the flour and the salt and knead with the kneading hook of an electric mixer for at least 5 minutes until the dough is shiny and elastic. Cover with a damp tea towel and leave in a warm place to rise for a further 30 minutes.

4 Chop the amarettini coarsely and knead into the dough. Divide into 10 evenly sized pieces and roll into balls.

5 Cut a sheet of baking paper into 10 strips 6 x 30 cm. Roll the balls up in the paper and tie loosely with kitchen string. Place on a baking tray and leave to rise for 30 minutes.

6 Bake at 180°C (Moisture plus with 1 automatic burst of steam) on the second shelf for 20 to 25 minutes. Remove from the oven and cool slightly. Remove the baking paper and cool on a wire rack. Spread with vanilla butter while still warm and serve.

> **▶▶ Tips**
>
> *Amarettini are light, crunchy Italian almond biscuits. They take their name and characteristic flavour from the addition of amaretto liqueur and go very well with coffee.*

223

Cherry focaccia
with rosemary

Makes 10 small rolls

1   Put the flour and rosemary in a bowl and make a well in the centre. Crumble the yeast and dissolve in the milk with the sugar. Pour into the well and stir in some of the flour from around the edge to create a thin paste. Cover the bowl with a tea towel and leave in a warm place to rise for 15 minutes.

2   Wash, dry and stone the cherries. Stir with the sugar and put to one side. Work the rest of the flour and a pinch of salt into the dough and knead with the kneading hook of an electric mixer for at least 5 minutes until the dough is shiny and elastic. Cover with a damp tea towel and leave in a warm place to rise for a further 30 minutes.

3   Knead the dough again briefly, divide into 10 evenly sized pieces and roll out on a floured surface into 1 cm thick discs. Place on a baking tray.

Ingredients:

For the dough:
500 g strong white flour
1 tbsp chopped rosemary
20 g fresh yeast
2 tbsp sugar
300 ml lukewarm milk
Salt

Also:
400 g cherries
2 tbsp sugar
Flour for the work surface
2 tbsp icing sugar
100 g white chocolate

4   Distribute the cherries evenly over the dough, and press down lightly. Dust with icing sugar and leave to rise for 30 minutes.

5   Bake at 180°C (Moisture plus with 1 automatic burst of steam) on the second shelf for 25 to 30 minutes. Remove from the oven and cool on a wire rack. Grate the chocolate coarsely and scatter over the cooled focaccia.

▶▶ Tips

Sweet focaccia tastes equally good with other fruit. Try raspberries, blackberries or blueberries. Sliced apricots and apples could also be baked on top.

THE EUROPEAN UNION SERIES

General Editors: Neill Nugent, William E. Paterson, Vincent Wright

The European Union series is designed to provide an authoritative library
on the European Union, ranging from general introductory texts to
definitive assessments of key institutions and actors, policies and policy
processes, and the role of member-states.

Books in the series are written by leading scholars in their fields and reflect
the most up-to-date research and debate. Particular attention is paid to
accessibility and clear presentation for a wide audience of students, practitioners
and interested general readers.

The series consists of four major strands:

- General textbooks
- The major institutions and actors
- The main areas of policy
- The member-states and the Union

General textbooks

Published

Desmond Dinan **Ever Closer Union: An
Introduction to European Integration**
(2nd edn)

Simon Hix **The Political System of the
European Union**

John McCormick **Understanding the
European Union: A Concise
Introduction**

Neill Nugent **The Government and
Politics of the European Union**
(4th edn)

John Peterson and Elizabeth Bomberg
**Decision-Making in the European
Union**

Ben Rosamond **Theories of European
Integration**

Forthcoming

Simon Bulmer and Andrew Scott
**European Union: Economics, Policy
and Politics**

Andrew Scott **The Political Economy of
the European Union**

Richard Sinnott **Understanding
European Integration**

In preparation

The History of the European Union

The European Union Source Book

The European Union Reader

The major institutions and actors

Published

Renaud Dehousse **The European Court
of Justice**

Justin Greenwood **Representing
Interests in the European Union**

Fiona Hayes-Renshaw and
Helen Wallace **The Council of
Ministers**

Simon Hix and Christopher Lord
Political Parties in the European Union

Forthcoming

Simon Bulmer and Wolfgang Wessels
The European Council

David Earnshaw and David Judge
The European Parliament

Neill Nugent **The European
Commission**

Anne Stevens **The Administration of the
European Union**

(continued overleaf)

The main areas of policy

Published

Michelle Cini and Lee McGowan
Competition Policy in the European Union

Wyn Grant **The Common Agricultural Policy**

Brigid Laffan **The Finances of the European Union**

Malcolm Levitt and Christopher Lord
The Political Economy of Monetary Union

Janne Haaland Matláry **Energy Policy in the European Union**

John Peterson and Margaret Sharp
Technology Policy in the European Union

Forthcoming

David Allen and Geoffrey Edwards
The External Economic Relations of the European Union

Laura Cram **Social Policy in the European Union**

Martin Holland **The European Union and the Third World**

Sonia Mazey **Women and the European Union**

Anand Menon **Defence Policy and the European Union**

James Mitchell and Paul McAleavey
Regionalism and Regional Policy in the European Union

Jörg Monar **Justice and Home Affairs in the European Union**

John Redmond and Lee Miles **Enlarging the European Union**

Hazel Smith **The Foreign Policy of the European Union**

Mark Thatcher **The Politics of European High Technology**

Rüdiger Wurzel **Environmental Policy in the European Union**

In preparation

Political Union

The USA and the European Union

The member-states and the Union

Published

Alain Guyomarch, Howard Machin and Ella Ritchie **France in the European Union**

Forthcoming

Simon Bulmer and William E. Paterson
Germany and the European Union

Carlos Closa and Paul Heywood **Spain and the European Union**

Phil Daniels and Ella Ritchie **Britain and the European Union**

Brigid Laffan **The European Union and its Member States**

In preparation

Reshaping the States of the Union

Italy and the European Union

European Union Series
Series Standing Order
ISBN 0–333–71695–7 hardcover
ISBN 0–333–69352–3 paperback
(*outside North America only*)

You can receive future titles in this series as they are published by placing a standing order. Please contact your bookseller or, in the case of difficulty, write to us at the address below with your name and address, the title of the series and one or both of the ISBNs quoted above.

Customer Services Department, Macmillan Distribution Ltd, Houndmills, Basingstoke, Hampshire RG21 6XS, England

Theories of
European Integration

Ben Rosamond

First published 2000 by
MACMILLAN PRESS LTD
Houndmills, Basingstoke, Hampshire RG21 2XS
and London
Companies and representatives
throughout the world

ISBN 0–333–64716–5 hardcover
ISBN 0–333–64717–3 paperback

A catalogue record for this book is available
from the British Library.

Copy-edited and typeset by Povey–Edmondson
Tavistock and Rochdale, England

10   9   8   7   6   5   4   3   2   1
09   08   07   06   05   04   03   02   01   00

Printed and bound in Great Britain by
Creative Print & Design (Wales), Ebbw Vale

 Published in the United States of America by
ST. MARTIN'S PRESS, INC.,
Scholarly and Reference Division
175 Fifth Avenue, New York, N.Y. 10010

ISBN 0–312–23119–9 (cloth)
ISBN 0–312–23120–2 (paper)

To Jane

'Each man begins the world afresh. Only institutions grow wiser; they store up the collective experience; and, from this experience and wisdom, men subject to the same laws will gradually find, not that their natures change but that their experience does.'

Henri Frédéric Amiel

Contents

List of Tables and Figures

Tables

Figure

List of Abbreviations

APEC	Asia Pacific Economic Co-operation
ASEAN	Association of South East Asian Nations
ASEM	Asia Europe Meeting
CAP	Common Agricultural Policy
CFSP	Common Foreign and Security Policy
CP	Comparative Politics
DG	Directorate General (of the European Commission)
EC	European Communities
ECJ	European Court of Justice
ECSC	European Coal and Steel Community
EEC	European Economic Community
EMU	European Monetary Union
EPC	European Political Co-operation
EPU	European Payments Union
EU	European Union
Euratom	European Atomic Energy Community
GATT	General Agreement on Tariffs and Trade
IO	International Organization
IPE	International Political Economy
IR	International Relations
LAFTA	Latin American Free Trade Area
LI	Liberal Intergovernmentalism
MEP	Member of the European Parliament
Mercusor	Mercado Común del Sur (Common Market of the South)
MIT	Massachusetts Institute of Technology
MLG	Multi-Level Governance
NAFTA	North American Free Trade Agreement
OEEC	Organization for European Economic Co-operation
QMV	Qualified Majority Voting
SADC	Southern African Development Co-operation
SEA	Single European Act
TEU	Treaty on European Union
UK	United Kingdom
WTO	World Trade Organization

Preface and Acknowledgements

The writing of this book has seemed at times – to use an old neofunctionalist phrase – like an 'inherently expansive task'. This is partly because of the sheer range and vibrancy of theoretically informed work touching on the European Union and European integration, much of which has appeared during the time of writing. It also has something to do with my interest in the intellectual environments within which theories emerge and develop. Theoretical work on European integration is obviously bound up in complex ways with the unfolding story of the EU. But it also needs to be thought about in terms of the broader context provided by the social and political sciences. To tell the story of 'integration theory' properly requires a sense of the intellectual games and academic norms within which theoreticians themselves work. In some ways, an understanding of the development of EU studies as an academic subdiscipline is best developed through the exploration of theoretical work past and present. But we are not all sociologists of knowledge and an understanding of the work covered in this book is generally acknowledged to be central to a thorough initiation in the mysteries of studying the EU.

With the foregoing in mind, the book tries to accomplish at least four things. The first is to offer a concise critical analysis of the main theoretical perspectives that have grown up and been applied to the scholarly analysis of European integration and the European Union. The second aim is to make an argument about the centrality of theoretical reflection to the study of these (and indeed any phenomena). The third is to raise issues about the broad contexts within which theories arise and develop and the fourth is to made selective interventions in ongoing theoretical discussions. The book's somewhat murky origins reside in some personal discomfort with the state of theoretical play in 'EU studies' circles in the early to mid-1990s. I would now have to say that theoretical work on integration is in a rugged state of theoretical health – with the rider that not all scholars and students of the EU are as reflective as they might be about their core concepts and the theoretical roots of their work. So, to an extent, the agenda of the book has shifted slightly, but its central plea for theory to be more than an optional add-on remains firmly intact. Beyond that, I would also want to make the point that the bigger debates about theory can be caricatured as neither 'to theorize or not to theorize?' nor 'which theory to choose?' Rather, theoretical endeavour operates within the boundaries of context-bound social scientific norms and so any proper evaluation of theories has to attend to broader 'sociology of knowledge' questions. It seems to me that such an approach drives a coach and horses through current debates about the appropriate disciplinary homeland for 'EU studies' (crudely, International Relations versus Comparative Politics). The dismissal of International Relations carries with it another danger. The rush to embrace 'new' theoretical work means that we might lose sight of a number of questions posed by early integration theorists that remain unresolved. Put crudely, these consist of a series of puzzles about political economy, and this book starts from the premise that the thoroughgoing contemplation of the so-called 'pre-theories' of integration still has considerable merit. In any case, such work is certainly what most have in mind when 'integration theory' is mentioned. However, it should be noted that there are interesting alternative theoretical pathways developing within EU studies that cannot be covered to any great extent here. These include the socio-legal literature and those strands of normative theory that seek to connect the study of the EU to issues of citizenship, democracy and ethics.

The completion of this book has taken rather longer than first imagined. The fact that it has appeared at all owes much to my publisher Steven Kennedy's considerable talents with the carrot and the stick. His own intellectual engagement with my work has been highly constructive. Thanks are also due to Willie Paterson and two anonymous readers for their thorough, encouraging and thoughtful comments on the draft manuscript. Many others have read and commented on my work, acted as interlocutors or simply offered encouragement or help. They include (in alphabetical order) Barrie Axford, Dave Baker, Brigitte Boyce, Gary Browning, Walter Carlsnaes, Thomas Christiansen, Dimitris Chryssochoou, Clive Church, Raymond Duvall, Andrew Gamble, Andrew Geddes, Stephen George, Wyn Grant, Morten Greve, Richard Higgott, Knud-Erik Jørgensen, Kristoffer Klebak, Rey Koslowski, Christian Lequesne, Duncan Matthews, Neill Nugent, Tony Payne, John Peterson, Claudio Radaelli, Glenda Rosenthal, Tim Sinclair, Helen Wallace, Alex Warleigh and Daniel Wincott. Students taking my various MA classes at the University of Warwick, Columbia University and New York University have been the unwitting recipients of many of the ideas in this book (usually in the rather roughshod verbal first draft form!). I have also learned much from them over the years. Charlie Dannreuther, Rohit Lekhi and Peter Newell have been exemplary colleagues and great friends over the past few years. Without them this would have been a lot harder to accomplish.

Milly and Alice saw rather less of me than they should have done in the final stages of writing this book. They are two very special people who serve as a constant reminder of what really matters in life. Most of all, Jane Booth's support and intellectual input has been constant. For that and for her unbelievable courage and humanity in the face of all sorts of adversity, this book is dedicated to her as modest reparation for my sociopathic sessions at the PC.

Leamington Spa   BEN ROSAMOND

Chapter 1

Introduction

This is a book about 'integration theory'. This term carries particular connotations amongst scholars of the European Union (EU). Integration theory is – or perhaps, more accurately, was – the theoretical wing of the EU studies movement. The emergence and development of the institutions of economic integration in Western Europe after the Second World War provided a valuable site for both the application of existing theories and the development of new perspectives. The clutch of theoretical accounts that emerged in the 1950s and 1960s offered rival narratives of how and why regimes of supranational governance developed and how closer cooperation in relatively narrow, technical, economic spheres of life could generate wider political integration among countries. There were two big political science issues here: the relationship between economics and politics and the future of the nation-state as a viable and desirable method of organizing human affairs in advanced societies. While the nascent European Communities offered the ideal empirical laboratory for the pursuit of these issues, the ambitions of most of these theorists stretched well beyond Europe. Perhaps the experiment of the six original member-states could be shown to be part of a trend that would come to affect other parts of the world. Perhaps, therefore, universal dynamics of regional integration could be revealed. Perhaps theorists could lead creative policy-makers into the design of rational institutions to secure better forms of governance in a modern, interdependent world.

More often than not, integration theorists traded in the vocabulary of the discipline of International Relations (IR). What seemed to be at stake in Western Europe were not just the Westphalian nation-state, but also the interstate system that grew outwards from this territorial way of organizing government. The great rows that developed within early IR were about the alleged relationships between the states system and war or, conversely, between 'post-national' forms of organization and peace. For many intellectuals and politicians of the first part of the twentieth century, the civilized mind needed to turn itself to the avoidance of war. So, federalists contemplated the ways in which states could engineer some sort of mutual constitutional settlement that involved the delegation of power upwards to a higher form of government, thereby securing peace. Functionalists, on the other hand, chastised the nation-state as an irrational and value-laden concept. For them, the task was to secure the most efficient method of administering to the real material needs of people. Often – perhaps predominantly – human welfare could be best served on a post-national, post-territorial basis. In the meantime, social scientists were developing new investigative techniques as their disciplines became increasingly professionalized. Armed with new ideas, scholars began to speculate about the mechanisms by which communities form. Interesting analogies were drawn between the processes of communication that helped historically to solidify national communities and the growth of cross-border, international transactions as the century developed. The earliest theories of European integration grew out of this intellectual context. Neofunctionalism grew out of the efforts of a small cluster of American political scientists to apply functionalist thinking to a delimited international region. Using the experiences of the European Coal and Steel Community (ECSC) and the European Economic Community (EEC) as their starting point, neofunctionalists set about the task of describing how the deliberate merger of economic activity in particular economic sectors across borders could generate wider economic integration. They also sought to explain how this economic integration would produce political integration and how the creation of supranational institutions could accelerate these processes.

These claims came under serious scrutiny from writers eager to point out, à la Mark Twain, that reports of the death of the nation-state had been somewhat exaggerated. Indeed, the evidence of West European politics in the 1960s illustrated some rather profound truths about the persistence and continued dominance of national interests and international exchange. The resultant conversation between neofunctionalists and intergovernmentalists is usually presented as the main ongoing schism in the integration theory literature since the mid-1960s. In many ways they present stark alternatives. In terms of identifying key actors, intergovernmentalists emphasize the centrality of national executives whereas neofunctionalists point to supranational institutions such as the Commission as well as national and transnational interest organizations. Neofunctionalism is a theory of change and transformation, whereas intergovernmentalists emphasize international politics as usual, albeit under novel conditions. While there is still much mileage in this particular joust, other writers have begun to think about the EU in different ways. The fate of the nation-state or the issue of 'more versus less integration' was not the only issue at stake. For many, the Communities constitute a polity – a venue where interested actors pursue their goals and where authoritative actors deliver policy outputs. This may be a radically new form of political system or simply a polity like any other, but from this perspective the most appropriate theoretical tools may not be those calibrated to predict the supposed destination of the integration project. Indeed 'integration theory' could be perceived as moribund; an interesting, but ultimately futile intellectual experiment.

This book does not set out to advance a revisionist account of the above story. But it does seek to add nuance and critical rigour to this conventional narrative. The tale of integration theory and the growth of theoretical work on EU governance provides a valuable case study of all sorts of things. Students of regional integration, and for that matter students of any aspect of social scientific endeavour, can learn much about the genesis, development, fusion and critique of theoretical perspectives as applied to the experience of regional institution-building in Europe. There is much to be grasped in this story about the means by which theories should be evaluated and perhaps even more about the relationship between academic mindsets and the 'reality' of the social world. Moreover, there are specific issues about the appropriate disciplinary homeland of 'EU studies' – an increasingly self-contained intellectual pursuit. Perhaps the book's main message is that there are serious problems involved in cordoning off 'theory' in EU studies. An always latent danger is that EU studies becomes populated by sub-specialisms such as the Common Agricultural Policy and the relationship between German domestic politics and EU decision-making.

In that regard, this book does represent a reminder that theory has to be taken seriously in the study of European integration. But at the same time it is not conceived with a view to studying theory for theory's sake. The book is written from a perspective that treats theory and theorizing as integral (and indeed *inescapable*) facets of human inquiry. Therefore, it recommends theoretical literacy as a fundamental prerequisite for the proper study of any aspect of the social world. This is not to say that we should all be exposed to some sort of theoretical initiation ceremony before being let loose into the empirical world of European integration. Rather, it is to suggest that we should be constantly theoretically self-aware, conscious that theoretical perspectives – wittingly or unwittingly – inform our approach to the world that we observe. The book begins from the premise that we write better analyses of the CAP or the role of German domestic politics if we are theoretically reflexive.

Consequently, the first task of this chapter is to make a few general comments about both the inescapability and the value of theoretical work. Turning to the specific subject matter of the book, it goes on to consider the thorny question of the meaning of (European) integration and tries to show that it has been a concept of considerable elasticity. It continues with some thoughts about the nature of integration theory and the applicability of concepts elaborated in the light of the European experience to the wider world in general and other instances of regional international cooperation in particular. It concludes by elaborating the structure of the rest of the book.

Theory

An observer enters a room and begins to take note of what he or she sees. Five things are noted: brown carpets on the floor, plain white walls, steps, inset spotlights in the ceiling and 61 people. A second observer of the same scene also notes five things. One individual is standing at the front of the room doing most, if not all, of the talking. This person is standing by a device projecting images and text onto a white screen on the wall. The other 60 are best described as being variously engaged with what the person at the front is saying. The room is tiered. The event lasts about 50 minutes. Our two observers have seen the same event, but they have chosen to observe different aspects of that event. The first observer has the sense that s/he has observed 61 people in a room with particular physical features, whereas the second has clearly seen a lecture.

Our first observer has no framework for ordering or making sense of what s/he sees. Unlike the second observer, s/he has no sense of which data might matter most; this person has no tools available to make sense of the event that is being witnessed, or at least to attribute *meaning* to that event. The second person fits what s/he sees into a predefined conceptual category ('lecture'). So, in many ways, the relevance of theory to inquiry in the social sciences is easily stated. Theories are necessary if we are to produce ordered observations of social phenomena. Theory, as Gerry Stoker puts it,

> helps us to see the wood for the trees. Good theories select out certain factors as the most important or relevant if one is interested in providing an explanation of an event. Without such a sifting process no effective observation can take place. The observer would be buried under a pile of detail and be unable to weigh the influence of different factors in explaining an event. Theories are of value precisely because they structure all observations.
>
> (Stoker, 1995: 16–17)

This fundamental point is often made to demonstrate that theory is important; that to 'do' social science properly, researchers need to conduct their inquiries under the auspices of a particular theoretical perspective. But it suggests something else: that it is impossible to make *any* statement about social phenomena in a theoretical vacuum. Like it or not, we are all informed by theoretical perspectives, even if we adopt an avowedly non-theoretical posture (Axford *et al.*, 1997). Thus, what is written about European integration – by academics, students and journalists alike – is always grounded in a particular set of assumptions about the way in which the world operates. It is always instructive to tease these assumptions out of texts such as newspaper accounts of EU events or largely descriptive surveys of EU politics. To take a concrete example, it is often argued that a major turning point in the history of European integration came with the signing of the Single European Act (1986) (SEA), and that this was achieved thanks to a convergence of policies among the most powerful member-states around a broadly neoliberal, free market economic policy agenda. Yet this account is not an unproblematic and objective statement of truth. It relies upon a set of propositions that proclaim the centrality of state and intergovernmental interaction to the conduct of European integration. It also possesses a sense of what constitutes a *significant event* in European integration. The SEA and other 'history-making moments' are often treated as the key nodal points in the unravelling story of post-war European unity. Others suggest that these treaty revisions amount to nothing more than the formal consolidation of emergent practices and that the 'everyday politics' of the EU and the private actions of economic actors are equally, if not more, important to gaining a full understanding of the integration process. These are not just issues of empirical disagreement; they reflect differing assumptions about key actors, the environment within which action takes place and the relationship between structure and action. The fact that an issue such as the origins of the SEA is so hotly debated is indicative of the importance of teasing out the diversity of theoretical starting points (see for example Agnelli, 1989; Cameron, 1992; Moravcsik, 1991, 1993; Sandholtz and Zysman, 1989; Wincott, 1995b). Disagreement might also reflect alternative disciplinary starting points. To understand these deeper-lying questions is to acquire a more nuanced understanding of the debate and, therefore, of the core subject matter of 'EU studies'. Put another way, it is not just theories about the world that differ and generate disagreement. It is also important to recognize the disciplinary and historical context within which work arises. Knowledge is not neutral. We gather it according to agreed rules that change over time and which, in turn, influence the sorts of question we ask. In other words, knowledge has its own sociology and any attempt to recreate intellectual sequences needs to be aware of this.

Theorizing intellectualizes perceptions. It is not just that theory helps us to identify that which is significant. Any event may involve multiple happenings that appear to be meaningful. To return to an educational theme, Andrew Sayer's example of an undergraduate seminar is instructive:

It involves far more than a discussion of some issues by a group of people: there is usually an economic relationship (the tutor is earning a living); students are also there to get a degree; the educational institution gets reproduced through the enactment of such events; relations of status, gender, age and perhaps race are confirmed or challenged in the way people talk, interrupt and defer to one another; and the participants are usually also engaged in 'self-presentation', trying to win respect or at least not to look stupid in the eyes of others.

(Sayer, 1992: 3)

Events are multidimensional and theorists have to decide what they plan to explain from the array of multiple games embedded in any single situation. Theorists have to generate speculations or hypotheses about which of the games is to take precedence. But they also need to arrive at a view of the nature of the relationship between the different dimensions identified. Another example from the EU might help to reinforce the point. On the face of it, a meeting of the Council of Ministers is the primary forum for bargaining between governments in the EU system. The representatives of the national governments are there to elaborate and defend their national interests and to negotiate from the basis of these positions in a particular policy or issue area. But there is a lot else going on besides. Ministers have to attend to the problems of coordinating their position with those of their colleagues who sit in other Councils. Also, ministers have to engage in calculus about the appropriate way to present significant policy outputs to domestic constituencies from the point of view of their positions both as members of a government and as politicians in particular domestic contexts. Meetings of Councils are not without their institutional memories. Many Councils have evolved distinctive working practices and bargaining styles over time (Hayes-Renshaw and Wallace, 1996) and others such as the Council of Agricultural Ministers have a peculiar longevity of membership plus the common perception among members that agricultural ministries face similarly distinctive sorts of problems in relation to other government departments (Grant, 1997). Moreover, the member-state holding the presidency of the Council has issues of agenda management and brokerage to contend with as well as the conventional representation of national preferences. In short, the sociology – perhaps the anthropology – of the Council of Ministers is a feature of its operation. Theorists may find orthodox intergovernmental approaches appropriate, but it may also be the case that the multidimensionality of such events opens the space for alternative concepts and theories, perhaps involving refined notions of supranationality or drawing on policy analysis literature or even theories of social psychology. This leads to the increasingly popular conclusion that the EU and the processes of European integration are just too complex to be captured by a single theoretical prospectus. The debate generated by that observation is a central preoccupation of this book.

Theoretical debate could be construed as disputes about different ways of obtaining or producing knowledge. This is important because *different theoretical perspectives produce and reproduce different types of knowledge*. As Susan Strange put it in her discussion of the main perspectives used to study International Political Economy (IPE):

> Each begins their analysis from a particular assumption that determines the kind of question that they ask, and therefore the answer they find. They are like ... toy trains on separate tracks, travelling from different starting points and ending at different (predetermined) destinations, and never crossing each other's path.
>
> (Strange, 1994: 16)

The extent to which this is (a) a problem and (b) solvable is a matter for debate rather beyond the scope of this book (but no less interesting for that). The sense of dissatisfaction implicit in Strange's statement owes much to what she perceived as the rather stagnant nature of theories of IPE, rather than to the unsatisfactoriness of coexistent and largely self-contained paradigms *per se*. Indeed, there are strong and much-rehearsed arguments for the pursuit of academic work within a confined set of theoretical assumptions as the most efficient way to advance knowledge. Each distinct theoretical perspective has its own 'home domain' of description and explanation, which influences the level at which data is analysed (Alford and Friedland, 1985). Or, put another way, each theory begins with a 'basic image' of social reality (an *ontology*) upon which is built a theoretical superstructure including established ways of gathering knowledge (*epistemology*). This allows like-minded scholars with shared assumptions to advance knowledge significantly within the lingua franca provided by a particular theoretical discourse. While good theories are on the whole internally coherent, they run into conflict with one another over a range of issues such as which actors are significant, what is the 'dependent variable' (i.e. what is it that the theory is trying to explain?), which processes are important, and so on (Banks, 1985). The consequence of this depiction of theories as internally consistent paradigms may, of course, be viewed in a positive sense – as a way of advancing knowledge with efficiency and rigour. Moreover, any friction between perspectives can be understood as a zone of 'essentially contested concepts' (Gallie, 1956) where fundamentals, such as the nature of 'power', come under sustained philosophical scrutiny. In any case, there are always likely to be trans-paradigm mavericks in the social sciences who look to establish constructive dialogues and to accomplish theoretical syntheses. The key point is that there is clearly a relationship between theoretical assumptions and the way in which the processes and outcomes of something like European integration are depicted.

If theory is inescapable, then it might appear that the traditional arguments for theory are not worth stating. Not so. The rehearsal of the case is useful since, while theory may be inevitable, not all analysts appear to be conscious of this important point. So, for the purposes of theoretical self-consciousness it is worth reminding ourselves what theory is for. However, here again we begin to run into ambiguity. There are clearly different types of theory, all of which have alternative purposes. Theory is sometimes thought to be about the generation of law-like statements. Others conceive of theory as the instrument with which investigators can test hypotheses or propositions about social phenomena. For some, theorizing is an activity with normative (value-laden) consequences; for others, it is a political act: the way in which we criticize the present with a view to maximizing the prospects for human freedom in the future. Finally, theory may also involve the contemplation of the process of theorizing itself (Burchill, 1996: 8). Most − if not all − of these purposes have found their way into the broad field of integration theory. To take an example, the neofunctionalist perspective, which is discussed at length in Chapter 3, was the creation of writers operating in the behaviouralist *zeitgeist* of post-war American political science (Eulau, 1963). Their approach was largely consistent with the attempt to connect natural scientific methods to the study of social reality. The study of the European experience was thought likely to yield law-like generalizations about regional integration that might be applied to other instances elsewhere. It was thought to have failed, by its practitioners as much as anyone, because of its empirically dubious depiction of the events of European integration through the 1960s and early 1970s. Neofunctionalists have also come under sustained criticism for their supposed normative purposes. One pair accuse the neofunctionalists of acting as a kind of theoretical 'Trojan horse' for the aspirations of US foreign policy in the 1940s and 1950s (Milward and Sørenson, 1993). This view sees neofunctionalist integration theory as a vehicle for lending legitimacy to the project of creating a federal Europe via the integration of national economies. Less aggressively, neofunctionalism is often thought of as the formal intellectual depiction of the political strategies of a group of post-war European politicians such as Jean Monnet and Robert Schuman.

So, how do we judge theories? What might be the basis for preferring one over another? As this book progresses, it will become obvious that these questions have been central to the enterprise of integration theory. These issues are explored in greater depth in Chapter 8, but for now it is worth reiterating that the alleged failings of neofunctionalism, as documented by intergovernmentalists like Stanley Hoffmann (1966) and neo-functionalists themselves (notably Haas, 1975a), concerned its failure to correspond to the observed 'reality' of the integration experience as exemplified by the EC. Such reasoning may seem commonsensical, but it is worth remembering that this is only one way in which theories might be evaluated. Indeed, it could be argued that the selection of this particular evaluative criterion reflects deep assumptions about both the nature of the social world and the processes/purposes of theorizing. More 'constitutive' (Burchill, 1996) or 'critical' (Cox, 1981) approaches to theory would approach the issue in rather different ways (see Chapter 8). In his discussion of International Relations theory, Scott Burchill presents six criteria against which theories might be evaluated:

1. a theory's *understanding* of an issue or process;
2. a theory's *explanatory power* of the theory;
3. the theory's success at *predicting* events;
4. the theory's intellectual *consistency* and *coherence*;
5. the *scope* of the theory;
6. the theory's capacity for *critical self-reflection* and intellectual *engagement* with contending theories.

(Burchill, 1996: 24, emphasis in original)

In other words, theories may stand or fall according to rather more than whether they can successfully describe a phenomenon or predict the consequences of that phenomenon. One particular concern of this book is to think about theories of European integration both in terms of the criteria they appear to set themselves and, in a critical sense, as manifestations of particular forms of knowledge production located in particular contexts. Therefore, the book also seeks to think about theories in the light of the context – in terms of the social sciences as well as the 'real world' of integration practice – in which they arose and in terms of the relationship between *theories* of European integration and the *practice* of integration and EU governance.

The meaning of 'integration'

So, the process of theorizing is, to a very large extent, a mechanism for the generation and organization of disagreement. Put more positively, being theoretically conscious sharpens the sense in which analysts are aware of their own assumptions about the way in which the world works. For students of European integration, this is a particularly poignant lesson. As suggested at the beginning of this chapter, the unfolding events in Europe after 1945 offered a generation of social scientists an alluring set of events to describe, categorize, explain and predict. During the 1950s, the quite extraordinary processes of international cooperation and the subsequent institutionalization manifested initially in the European Coal and Steel Community (ECSC) and later in the European Economic Community (EEC) and Euratom were genuinely novel. Here, at the very least, was an instance of quite intensive international cooperation among a group of states. Moreover, this was *perceived* as a radical experiment, especially from the vantage point of 1950s social science (Caporaso, 1998). The heavy institutionalization associated with the early communities suggested something yet more profound (the Treaty of Paris of 1951 which established the ECSC set in place an institutional pattern, involving clear elements of supranationality, which has endured until today). Thus, an immediate theoretical controversy was to develop around the question of whether the communities constituted a new 'post-national' political system in which the authority of national governments was destined to recede. To accept this proposition led to two sorts of conclusion. Firstly, Western Europe was undergoing a quite profound period of transformation in which the established patterns of political authority were being radically reordered. Secondly, it was possible to see an unfolding logic to this transformation, where a new sort of state form *above* the nation-state would be the outcome. To deny the proposition would be associated with the assertion that the nation-state possessed historical durability. States controlled the integration process and any outcome would be fundamentally intergovernmental or at least would reflect the preferences of the most powerful states in the game.

These events provided an important stimulus for theoretical work in their own right. For example neofunctionalism (see Chapter 3) can be read at one level as a theory provoked entirely by the integrative activity among the original six member-states. The study of European integration became a major site for debates in the academic discipline of International Relations which, by the 1950s, had spawned the sub-field of International Organization. Practitioners here were concerned with collective international and transnational institutions and the emergence of significant non-state actors in the world polity. Integration theory emerged in this context, tapping into pre- existing concerns, and generated new debates. In some ways, integration theory became a pioneering site for the development of non-state-centred forms of International Relations scholarship, and many sub-fields of present-day IR and International Political Economy are rooted in the endeavours of functionalists, neofunctionalists and transactionalists. Also, as academic work on the Communities grew throughout the 1960s and 1970s, so rival integration theories became the 'pet theories' of an emerging sub-discipline – EC (and later EU) studies. Greater attention to the EC, along with developments in the Communities themselves, began to open up the questions of (a) whether the EC had acquired systemic properties and, therefore, (b) whether theories derived from IR any longer offered the best frameworks for analysis.

So, the attractions for social scientists were and, no doubt, still are obvious. But what was it that they were trying to explain? Writing in 1971 and reflecting on no less than a decade and a half of intensive theoretical work on integration in Europe, Ernst Haas argued that '[a] giant step on the road toward an integrated theory of regional integration ... would be taken if we could clarify the matter of what we propose to explain and/or predict' (Haas, 1971: 26). This was a succinct statement of the so-called 'dependent variable problem' in integration theory – what is it that theorists are trying to explain when they contemplate the processes of institution-building and integration that have characterized the post-war European Communities? As Haas put it:

> the task of selecting and justifying variables and explaining their hypothesized interdependence cannot be accomplished without an agreement as to possible conditions to which the process is expected to lead. In short, we need a dependent variable.
>
> (Haas, 1971: 18)

At one level this is a matter of definition. Is integration an economic or a political phenomenon? If it is an economic phenomenon, what levels of interdependence need to be achieved among a group of national economies for them to be described as 'integrated'? Is the achievement of a free trade area the appropriate condition? Or is the end point of economic integration a customs union, or a common market, or full economic and monetary union? Does economic integration imply political integration? Or, at least, what levels of common institutionalization are associated with an integrated economic space? Do all customs unions/common markets/ monetary unions have similar levels of institutionalization? Does economic integration *generate* the momentum for political integration? Or, to turn the issue on its head, does political integration create the space for economic integration to flourish? Turning to political questions, does integration amount to the dissolution of national authority within a given geographical region? If this is so, does integration consist of the replacement of traditional structures of governance with new types of institution and new forms of authority? Or is integration accomplished when a group of geographically-adjacent states reach an accommodation – perhaps in terms of a federal union or a system of common security, or in terms of a widespread sharing of core values among elites and masses across nations? In short, what does it mean to say that Europe is integrated or is in the process of integrating? Posed this way, the issue also becomes a matter of whether we should understand integration as a *process* or as an *outcome*.

Both Leon Lindberg's elaboration of the definition of regional integration (1963: 4–5) and Haas's look backwards at the early 'pretheorizing' of integration identified this particular ambiguity (1971: 6–7; see also Pentland, 1973 for an extended discussion). Indeed, all of the possibilities canvassed in the previous paragraph were represented in the integration theory of the 1950s and 1960s. One problem was that integration theorists, while focusing on a common set of events, evidently had different conceptions of process and outcome in mind. Karl Deutsch's work (for example, Deutsch *et al.*, 1957; see also Chapter 2) clearly understood integration as the creation of security communities (or zones of peace) among states in a region. This did not require the transcendence of formal statehood. Alternatively, many writers define integration precisely in terms of the radical reordering of both the conventional international order and of the existing authoritative structures of governance. Haas defined integration as 'the voluntary creation of larger political units involving the self conscious eschewal of force in relations between participating institutions' (1971: 4) and elsewhere as

> the process whereby political actors in several distinct national settings are persuaded to shift their loyalties, expectations and political activities toward a new center, whose institutions possess or demand jurisdiction over pre-existing national states. The end result of a process of political integration is a new political community, superimposed over the pre-existing ones

(Haas, 1968: 16)

Others, notably the authors of previous texts on integration theory, put it more starkly. Michael Hodges offered integration as 'the formation of new political systems out of hitherto separate political systems' (1972: 13). Reginald Harrison, like Haas, pointed to the importance of central institutions: '[t]he integration process may be defined as the attainment within an area of the bonds of political community, of central institutions with binding decision-making powers and methods of control determining the allocation of values at the regional level and also of adequate consensus-formation mechanisms' (Harrison, 1974: 14). The difficulties of definition were memorably summed up by Donald Puchala (1972) who compared the quest for a definition of integration to blind men being confronted with the task of defining an elephant. This recalls the argument, introduced earlier in this chapter, about different starting points leading to different destinations. Different theoretical conventions have spawned differing methodologies in pursuit of independent variables (those factors that do the explaining). Thus, the transactionalist school relied heavily on the accumulation of aggregate survey data, whereas the neofunctionalist method often amounted to the theoretically-focused case study. Consequently, the understanding of different theoretical approaches to integration is vital to a developed understanding of 'integration' itself. As Haas puts it: 'it is they [the approaches] rather than the nature of things which lead students to postulate the relationships between variables; it is they, not the nature of things, which lead us to the specification of what is an independent and a dependent variable' (1971: 19).

Where definitions have been advanced in more recent literature, they have tended to be rather more broad-ranging. To take an example, William Wallace defines integration as 'the creation and maintenance of intense and diversified patterns of interaction among previously autonomous units' (Wallace, 1990: 9). It should be clear that the classical phase of what is normally understood as integration theory was concerned with *political* integration. This is not to say that economic change was excluded from the analysis. Nonetheless, Wallace's discussion alerts the student of the EU to the relationship between economic and political integration. In particular, he makes a distinction between 'formal' and 'informal' integration. The former consists of outcomes (institutions, policies, legislative change) that have occurred as a consequence of deliberate political sanction. The latter are processes that have effective consequences without formal, authoritative intervention (see Wallace, 1990: 8–12). This connects to Richard Higgott's distinction between *de facto* structural regionalization on the one hand and *de jure* institutional economic cooperation on the other (Higgott, 1997). In both cases, the issue at stake is one of *political economy*: the relationship between political and economic processes in shaping change. Several permutations are possible here. For example, it could be argued that changes in the informal economic domain such as heightened capital mobility, increasing volumes of cross-border trade, alterations in the production process and shifting corporate strategies decisively structure and constrain the agenda of authoritative political actors. Faced with no alternative, governments seek closer cooperation through the construction of political institutions designed to 'capture' and control these economic processes. Here regional political integration is a consequence of regional economic integration. Of course, an alternative way of thinking would invert this argument to suggest that informal changes are, at the very least, facilitated by the deliberate sanction of government authority. Here economic integration can only happen because states produce policies that enable the flourishing of informal transborder economic activity. This debate also latches onto the question of whether the factors that initiate integration can be used to explain its maintenance. Do different periods of integration require different theoretical perspectives?

These issues are covered further in Chapters 7 and 8. The parts of this book that analyse the established schools of integration theory focus for the most part on political integration broadly defined, largely in response to and in the terms set by the literatures under discussion. However, it is worth noting that a large literature on economic integration has grown up in the field of International Economics. While the connections between the political and the economic are central to this book, a detailed analysis of the body of work on economic integration is rather beyond the scope of this volume (but see for example Balassa, 1962; El-Agraa, 1997; El-Agraa and Jones, 1981; Robson, 1998).

Theory and European integration

As we have seen, anyone seeking to engage academically with a subject must be conscious not only of their theoretical predispositions, but also of the nature of their subject matter. Combining these two aspects of theoretical awareness, it can be argued that the type of theoretical approach adopted will be related to the subject matter. In this sense 'subject matter' is not simply the events or phenomena to be interpreted, but the sorts of generalizations which intellectual inquiry aspires to make. Here James Rosenau's guiding question – 'of what is this an instance?' – becomes a vital prerequisite for any work with theoretical aspirations (Rosenau and Durfee, 1995). To answer the question requires an exercise in abstraction, and when faced with any phenomenon the question can induce multiple responses. The argument here is that (a) the study of European integration has to be theoretically-informed and (b) we need to be theoretically reflexive. To be blunt, we need to know what we want to get out of studying European integration, not in terms of what we want/ expect our answers to be, but in terms of where we seek to locate our investigations. The study of the EU/European integration seems to have at least four such locations.

The first of these approaches would be to understand the European Union as an international organization. The literature on international organizations (IOs) is substantial and ever developing (Kratochwil, 1995), but IOs are traditionally thought of as intergovernmental bodies designed in the explicit context of converging state preferences or common interests. For traditional liberal theorists of international relations, IOs constitute one of the principal means through which interstate harmony and, therefore, lasting peace can be secured. Quite a lot of the theoretical work reviewed in this book draws on this tradition, but the EU is evidently rather more than a straightforward instance of an intergovernmental organization. Whether it is dominated by state preferences is a moot point (see Chapter 6), but the EU is peculiarly institutionalized and the configuration of forces thereby created rather militates against the discussion of European integration in terms of established IO debates.

The second treats European integration – to coin the contemporary vocabulary – as an instance of 'regionalism' in the global political economy. The ultimate aim of such work is to offer reflections upon and possibly generalizations about the tendency of groups of territorially-adjacent states to cluster together into blocs. Inquiry of this sort can be motivated by a number of guiding questions. Most obviously, is it possible to make meaningful comparisons between the EU and other regional groupings such as the North American Free Trade Agreement (NAFTA), Asia Pacific Economic Cooperation (APEC) or Mercusor in South America? Do instances of regionalism arise in similar sorts of circumstances regardless of time or place? Do global economic and political pressures *force* or *enable* the creation of such organizations? How do variations in levels of institutionalization in regional blocs affect the interests and preferences of actors? Does the emergence of regional forms have implications for the construction of new identities and the deconstruction of established identities (at both elite and mass level)? Does regionalism accelerate or retard free trade and multilateral exchanges between states? Do regional agreements and institutions form a uniform threat to the nation-state and the international system of states? The pursuit of questions like these explains why many specialists in International Relations and International Political Economy regard the EU as worth studying.

The third broad approach aims to treat the EU as useful location for the study of policy-making dynamics. Here the EU is an instance of a complex policy system in which perspectives on policy-making developed largely in the context of national polities can be put to the test and perhaps developed. So, attention is turned to the interaction of interested actors and the processes of agenda setting, policy formulation, legislation, interest intermediation and policy implementation. The analysis of these processes raises questions about the location of power and the relationship between formal and informal policy processes. From this vantage point, the development of the EU affords an exciting opportunity to consider policy networks and the role of institutions in conditions where (old) national and (new) supranational politics overlap.

The final approach is less inclined to treat the EU and European integration as an instance of anything other than itself. Such an approach would regard the EU as a *sui generis* phenomenon. That is to say, there is only one EU and, therefore, European integration cannot be a theoretical testing site for the elaboration of broader generalizations. The inclination rather would be to treat the EU as an historically-rooted phenomenon, arising in utterly specific conditions and therefore without meaningful historical precedent or contemporary parallel.

Each of these broad approaches is open to work from many theoretical perspectives and one of the purposes of this book is to investigate these perspectives in greater depth. (For instance one theme which emerges in this volume is the current debate about the relative merits of 'International Relations' versus 'Comparative Politics/Policy Studies' approaches to the EU. In particular, Chapters 5 and 7 discuss this matter which could be seen as a debate between the second and third of the approaches sketched above.) Having said that, it might be argued that work in the fourth category inclines towards crude empiricism with its tendency to chronicle the intricacies of the EU system. It is, therefore, less able to offer insight into broader theoretical issues (Rosamond, 1995) or indeed into more normative questions about the 'real' problems facing Europe and its citizens (Hix, 1996).

One response to this criticism – from the fourth position perhaps – would be to argue that it is folly to attempt draw generalizations from the study of the EU because it is such a unique organization that emerged out of a unique set of historical circumstances. It possesses an institutional and legal architecture quite unlike both national political systems and other international organizations. Such sentiments latch onto the fundamental problem of what integration theory might achieve and especially whether it could do anything more than make systematic generalizations about *European* integration.

For reasons which will be discussed in later chapters, this has been a particular problem for approaches drawing their ammunition from International Relations scholarship. The founders of integration theory imagined that generalizations would emerge from their intensive case study of the European Communities. The results could then generate hypotheses for the study of regional integration in a more general sense. Such aspirations are made explicit in the work of the early theorists of European integration, such as Karl Deutsch (1957), Ernst Haas (1961; 1968), Phillippe Schmitter (1971) and Joseph Nye (1971), and were more or less integral to the foundation of the *Journal of Common Market Studies* in 1962. For those with an interest in treating the EU as an instance of regionalism the same applies. The comparability of, say, the Association of South East Asian Nations (ASEAN) and NAFTA with the EU is thrown into doubt if it can be established that the EU is fundamentally different in a number of respects.

This begs the question of whether the EU represents an *n* of 1, as James Caporaso puts it (Caporaso, 1997). For some the answer is clearly 'yes'.

For example, William Wallace has drawn attention to the specificities of the historical experience in Western Europe:

> The experience of deep integration within Western Europe does not ... provide a model for others to follow. Its historical development was rooted in a stage of economic development and a security framework that have now both disappeared. The institutional structures that west European governments agreed to under those past circumstances have managed to respond to the very different challenges posed by economic and industrial transformation in the 1970s and 1980s. Political, economic, and security motivations have been entangled in the evolution of West European regional integration from the 1940s to the 1990s.
>
> (Wallace, 1994: 9)

Indeed, it is reasonably clear that the initiators of some of the newer regional blocs – for example in the Asia–Pacific – have explicitly identified the EU as an example of 'bad practice' which should not be emulated (Kohler, 1995). So, perhaps practitioners of regionalism elsewhere in the world are ill-advised to seek to emulate the EU. But what about theoreticians? If the EU is unique, and is nothing other than an instance of itself, then we have a dilemma. Findings cannot be generalized to other cases because of this uniqueness and as a consequence general theories of integration are not attainable. Moreover, it has been argued that the uniqueness of the EU is also a barrier to theorizing the EU in general terms. As one analyst has put it, 'We do not have a general theory of American or German politics so why should there be a general theory of the EU?' (Hix, 1996: 804).

The question is penetrating and raises all kinds of issues about disciplinary segmentation as well as the particular matter of how to study and theorize the EU. It is not just that the EU arose and evolved in historically specific circumstances. It is also the case that 'EU studies' has become a narrow specialism – largely a sub-domain of Political Science and International Relations. Simon Hix's objection is grounded in the view that bridges need to be (re)built between theories of comparative politics and EU studies and that the appropriate way to view the EU is as a polity rather than as an International Relations phenomenon. As Gary Marks notes, work drawing on this position has become commonplace in EU studies and generates comparative possibilities by 'slicing polities into subsystemic parts' such as interest groups, policy networks and so on (Marks, 1997: 2). This kind of work is presented by Mark Pollack (1997b) as following the guidelines for 'good' comparative social science (see King, Keohane and Verba, 1994). If the object of the exercise is to explain 'integration', then the EU is indeed the only available case. If other dependent variables are selected in conjunction with appropriate deductive theories then the $n = 1$ problem vanishes. This, of course, favours the depiction of European integration in terms of the third approach outlined above. Having said that, Gary Marks (1997) suggests that comparison can go well beyond internal analyses of the EU system. Other organizations, he argues, exercise limited degrees of supranational authority and the fact that the EU is peculiarly supranational would not prevent the construction of a continuum. Also, as Alberta Sbragia (1992) has argued, the polity-like qualities of the EU beg comparison with other federal and quasi-federal systems. Germany and the United States can both be understood as 'federal' systems, but there are significant differences in the type of federalism that prevails. Clearly, two phenomena do not have to be identical in order to be compared effectively. Finally, Marks suggests that the radical processes of institutional change represented by the EU might be usefully compared to previous reorderings of authority such as the break-up of the Carthaginian Empire.

The pursuit of a general theory of European integration/the EU may indeed be misplaced. But, as Hix would no doubt acknowledge, the potential for EU studies to be a fertile site of social scientific theorizing is immense. Both US and German politics have been important venues for the development of particular branches of theory-driven political science, around ideas about pluralism, federalism, interest group liberalism, community power structures and the regulatory state (to name but a few). 'Integration theory' – defined here very broadly indeed – matters not just because of what it can tell us about the development of the EU or processes of regionalization, but also because of what it can tell us about the use of a fertile empirical location for the conceptual and theoretical development of the political sciences – again broadly defined.

The plan of the book

This book aims to do a number of things. The first is to provide an up-to-date cartography of theoretical work on European integration. This involves revisiting the classical 'pretheories' of integration, charting their development and their engagements with one another, and it involves a critical analysis of contemporary theoretical work. A second aim, perhaps more modestly realized, is to offer a 'sociology of knowledge' approach to this intellectual history. Rather too many accounts of integration theory fail to contextualize their material. Writers often succumb to the temptation of dismissing the theoretical work of several decades ago as 'wrong' or misguided. The point here, as stated above, is to set debates within their historical and intellectual contexts. Theorists obviously have one eye on the 'real world' as they see it. But – perhaps more importantly – theorists operate within particular academic contexts and particular notions of what is (or isn't) good social science. A third and connected aim is to reflect upon the disciplinary questions about the social science of European integration. If the book has an argument to advance here, then it is that 'international theory' has been too readily written off by contemporary writers seeking to offer theoretical treatments of the EU. To detach 'EU studies' from International Relations (again broadly defined) is to misunderstand and misread some very important developments in IR and IPE. It does not automatically necessitate a futile search for a general theory of European integration, but can open up important avenues of inquiry to complement the more public policy-oriented work on EU governance that has opened up in recent years.

The book is organized as follows. Chapter 2 explores the genesis of contemporary theoretical analyses of European integration. It examines the premises and claims of three early 'schools' of thought – federalism, functionalism and transactionalism – which found themselves attached in various ways to the unravelling experience of states in post-war Western Europe and to the growing formalization of the social sciences. Chapter 3 provides an extensive examination of the neofunctionalist perspective, perhaps the quintessential theory of integration, while the following chapter explores the way in which neofunctionalism and other self-conscious theories of integration were criticized by adherents and un-sympathetic critics alike. Chapter 5 begins a survey of contemporary theoretical approaches to integration. The emphasis here is on two things: the attempt to resuscitate old 'paradigms' in the face of an apparently more receptive empirical 'reality' and the appearance of alternative ways of conceptualizing the EC/EU as a 'political system' in preference to an 'international experiment'. Chapter 6 offers a critical analysis of the predominantly state-centric character of much contemporary theoretical work on European unity, while Chapter 7 – in slightly more speculative mode – considers the broad canvas of contemporary international theory and suggests some productive linkages that might be made with the study of European integration. Chapter 8 takes time to consider some of the deeper questions about the 'sociology of knowledge' of integration theory its relationship to social scientific trends, the interplay between the theory and practice of integration and the knotty problem of the evaluation of theoretical work.

Chapter 2

Federalism, Functionalism and Transactionalism

For as long as there have been states, intelligent people have been trying to think of ways in which conflict between them might be averted. A venerable tradition of writers, stretching back well beyond the pivotal figure of Immanuel Kant in the eighteenth century, has sought to devise schemes for the eradication of conflict or systems for perpetual peace (Luard, 1992: 400–23). Less normatively, others have sought to theorize the conditions for peace by seeking to establish the mixture of environmental factors and/or institutions that would need to be in place for the risk of war to be lessened. The concern to end war has been an intellectual and political 'holy grail' for most of the twentieth century – for understandable reasons – and such sentiments lay at the heart of the new academic discipline of International Relations as it emerged in the wake of the carnage of the First World War. While the idealist idea that conflict could be ameliorated through constitutional engineering was contested vigorously by the tradition of realist International Relations, the experience of global conflict over the course of the century has set a compelling agenda for both politicians and social scientists alike.

Europe was a particular focal point for such discussions. For many, the experiences of 1914–1918 demonstrated the terminal decline of the European states system and the demise of its supposed self-correcting tendencies through balance of power mechanisms. According to theorists of the balance of power, for much of the nineteenth century European order had been founded upon a relatively fluid system of shifting alliances which, due to a process of systemic self-adjustment, disallowed the accumulation of excessive power by any one state. The balance of power idea has become very important, particularly to realist and neorealist International Relations scholars, although the potential elasticity of the concept has been noted (Wight, 1966). It is also true to say that the idea had a significant presence in elite political discourse, notably through political figures such as Viscount Palmerston in nineteenth-century Britain. The consolidation of the German nation in the second half of the nineteenth century provided a direct challenge to this balancing mechanism and had spilled over into major conflicts on the continent, notably the Franco–Prussian War of 1870–1871 and the Great War of 1914–1918. Even thinkers with an inclination to conceptualize the world in largely state-

20

centric terms were driven to argue that a reordering of the European states system was necessary. Others versed in a liberal–idealist suspicion of the nation-state as the ultimate form of human governance, were minded to treat the experiences of major European conflict as proof of the inherently unsatisfactory nature of the states system. For the liberal founders of modern International Relations, conflict was not endemic to international politics. Nor was it an inevitable consequence of human nature. The optimistic liberal prospectus concluded that the imperfections of international politics could be engineered away. Systemic 'anarchy' (the absence of any form of authority above the nation-state) could be replaced. The alternative, 'collective security', would be achieved in part by the progressive spread of liberal values (such as democracy and justice) and liberal processes (notably commerce), but also by the establishment of international organizations and bodies of international law. Spurred on by the gradual formalization of the study of International Relations, the intellectual climate of the inter-war period was ripe for creative thinking about the future of Europe. The gauntlet was taken up by a mixture of politicians and intellectuals, and in their hands the so-called 'European idea' began to take shape. Having said that, many historians correctly point out that the construction of grand schemes to unify 'Europe', or at least substantial parts of what we now refer to as the European continent, has not simply been a twentieth-century preoccupation. For instance, Heater (1992) conducts a thorough review of a number of such projects beginning as far back as the fourteenth century.

Nonetheless, the inter-war period was notable for significant activism on behalf of a putative 'united Europe'. Much of this activism took place on the boundary between the intellectual and the 'political'. Perhaps the most important single intellectual intervention was Richard Coudenhove-Kalergi's book *Pan-Europa*, which was first published in 1923 (Coudenhove-Kalergi, 1926). The vision here was of a united Europe underwritten by a federal constitution. This was motivated by two core perceptions. On the positive side, it was felt that 'Europe' was in many ways a natural entity that could become a significant global force. Rather more negative was the assertion that unless substantial changes were to occur to the political organization of Europe, the continent would tear itself apart in nationalistic internecine conflict. The post-Versailles order might have eradicated empires with aggrandizing tendencies, but had replaced this system with potentially problematic national units that were often internally incoherent. The book and its associated movement were demonstrable influences on many of the leading politicians of the period, notably the French foreign minister Aristide Briand. On behalf of the French government, Briand issued in 1930 his famous 'Memorandum on the Organization of a Regime of European Federal Union' (Weigall and Stirk, 1992:

11–15). Although it was received with some scepticism and became quickly overwhelmed by events, the memorandum remains important because it amounted to the first twentieth-century proposal by a European government for European unity.

Writers like Coudenhove-Kalergi are difficult to read as theorists in the modern social scientific sense of the term. Nonetheless, there are clear thematic connections with inter-war idealist international relations thinking (Long and Wilson, 1995), a category in which writers such as David Mitrany (see below) are normally placed. The fact that books like *Pan Europa* and the host of other schemes to unify Europe did not present themselves as formal academic texts does not mean that they were somehow atheoretical or non-theoretical. In any case, it is probably fair to say that the formalization of disciplines such as Political Science and International Relations was far from complete in the inter-war period, especially in Europe. Such books were written in the context of a rather more pamphleteering culture than our own, with a perceived audience consisting of intelligent but essentially lay people, not professional peers versed in the conventions and vocabularies of particular social scientific discourses.

What is most interesting is the fact that the theme of European unity had moved squarely onto the intellectual and political agendas of post-First World War politicians (particularly in the late 1920s). Indeed, there appeared to be some sort of relationship between these emerging intellectual schemes and the actions of certain politicians. Aside from the interesting question of the intellectual influences upon would-be history-makers, there is also the matter of the status of theories and ideas more generally as structures and agents in the 'real world'

Not surprisingly, such intellectual efforts emerged from the Second World War with enhanced legitimacy. Again, arguments raged about the extent to which the rise of Nazism in Germany could be attributed to the states system and to the attendant problem of the relationship between nationalist sentiments and international conflict. At the level of hard-nosed *realpolitik*, West European elites were faced with a series of overlapping and immediate concerns. Most obviously, the resolution of the now perennial 'German question' lay at the heart of the new European calculus. In particular, there was a perceived need to attend to the historic tensions between France and Germany. Was it possible to secure an alliance between these two powers? Were there ways in which they could be rendered interdependent? Were there ways to ensure that militarism did not recur as the central feature of foreign policy in the new Germany? In addition, the unravelling of the new cold war game across Europe created imperatives among policy elites to ensure Germany's future with the Western alliance. Furthermore, Alan Milward (1992) has argued that policy-makers in Western European democracies were searching for ways to ensure the successful implementation of policy programmes. This was a time of strategic thinking, to say the least.

This story is told (and debated) elsewhere. For the purposes of this chapter, it is useful to understand the political climate in which the early manifestations of integration theory arose, not least because different theoretical perspectives privilege certain elements of the account over others. Milward, for instance, has been a consistent and forceful critic of neofunctionalist integration theory as well as a historian with his eye on empirical details. It is also probably true to say that the immediate post-war period in Western Europe represents a moment when theory and practice not so much blurred as merged. Two of the early perspectives considered in this chapter – federalism and functionalism – offer excellent examples of this overlap. The third, transactionalism, grew out of a conscious effort by social scientists to bring about the formal separation of theory from practice. However, together these three perspectives offer variations on a similar theme. All seek to theorize the conditions for the eradication of international conflict and all have been used as tools for the analysis of post-war Western Europe.

Federalism

Given the diversity among European states, the attractions of federalism for the study of European integration are more than obvious. Unlike the other theories discussed here and in Chapter 3, there is no clear-cut academic school of European federalism and certainly no leading lights to compare with the likes of Karl Deutsch, David Mitrany and Ernst Haas. In part this is because federalism has tended to be a political project, with particular goals in mind. As one long-standing member of the European federalist movement put it:

> [Federalists] plan to form a small nuclei [sic] of nonconformists seeking to point out that the national states have lost their proper rights since they cannot guarantee the political and economic safety of their citizens. They also insist that European union should be brought about by the European populations, and not by diplomats, by directly electing a European constituent assembly, and by the approval through a referendum, of the constitution that this assembly would prepare.
>
> (Spinelli, 1972: 68)

Nonetheless, federalism has been described as 'a very convenient, increasingly popular, always ambiguous, and sometimes dangerous concept' (Bulpitt, 1996: 179). This conceptual elasticity does not make for easy definition, although when they speak of federalism, most people tend to have in mind an idea of a constitutional settlement, where authority is dispersed into two or more levels of government. In particular, federalism most commonly describes political systems in which there is a division of authority between central and regional or state government: '[t]he Federalist integration process requires the establishing of two levels of government – separate but coordinate – being the government of the whole, the federal level, and the government of the parts, the state or local level' (Taylor, 1993: 90). Federal systems are usually understood as resting on historic compromises involving the permanent compact between territorial units. These territorial units yield a measure of authority to common, centralized institutions, but remain largely intact as units, retaining at least a measure of autonomy. The 'magic formula' for federal systems involves the optimum mixture of unity and diversity. Proponents of federal forms of government argue that this formula allows the constituent units to perform common tasks with maximum efficiency while maximizing decentralization and autonomy (Wheare, 1963). It is a way of ensuring constitutional government in *plural* liberal democratic societies. So, one way of defining federation is as 'a distinctive organizational form or institutional fact which exists to accommodate the constituent units of a union in the decision-making procedure of the central government by means of constitutional entrenchment' (Burgess, 1986: 19).

Scholars have tended make an important analytical distinction between federalism and federation. Federalism is used to describe an ideology whereas federation depicts the derivative organizational principle (King, 1982; Burgess, 1986, 1993). Consequently, a further distinction is often made between normative or 'ideological' approaches to developing regional federations and the analytical mapping of federalism as a form of governance. Preston King identifies three tendencies in the ideology of federalism: centralist, de-centralist and balanced, indicating that federalism is a very broad church indeed, ranging from calls for world government at one end of the continuum to near anarchism at the other. This also explains why federalism has become such an elastic and controversial concept in the politics of European integration. To take an example, observers have often drawn attention to the very different understandings of federalism held by the British government and some of its continental counterparts. In the deliberations leading up to the Maastricht European Council of 1991, British representatives negotiated ferociously for the removal of the word 'federal' from the early sentences of the (then) putative Treaty on European Union (TEU). However, the preferred replacement of the British, 'ever closer union', was thought by some to be more centralist than the original formulation. Similarly, the doctrine of 'subsidiarity', enshrined in article 3b of the TEU, and so frequently cited by the British government as a justification for the retention of national sovereignty within the EU, has – for some at least – a decidedly federalist look about it. (Church and Phinnemore, 1994). The key part of Article 3b reads:

> The Community shall act within the limits of the powers conferred upon it by this Treaty and of the objectives assigned to it therein. In areas which do not fall within its exclusive competence, the Community shall take action, in accordance with the principle of subsidiarity, only if and in so far as the objectives of the proposed action cannot be sufficiently achieved by the Member States and an therefore, by reason of the scale or effects of the proposed action, be better achieved by the Community (Council of the European Communities/Commission of the European Communities, 1992: 13–14).

In practical terms too, federal solutions have inherent ambiguities. As Michael Burgess suggests, the confusion over the principle of federation is explained by the fact that there is no core prescription about the division of powers. Rather, federation suggests that 'it is constitutional autonomy which matters' (Burgess, 1986: 18), but what this actually means may be congruent with a whole range of organizational outcomes.

The historical lineage of federalist approaches to European integration is long and complex (Bosco, 1991; Forsyth, 1981; Friedrich, 1968; Spinelli, 1972). The federalist legacy amounts to a mixture of governing schemes devised by political philosophers and committed proponents of European unity in various guises (Heater, 1992) plus lesson-drawing from the experiences of 'federal' states such as the USA. The latter demonstrates – on the face of it at least – the practical possibilities for the application of federal principles to systems composed of diverse units. Murray Forsyth picks out three strands of federalist theory that have fed directly into deliberations about European integration (Forsyth, 1996: 33–35). The first draws on the legacy of ideas associated with Immanuel Kant, who advocated an expanding federation as the most appropriate constitutional safeguard against the threat of war. The second draws on those elements of democratic theory concerned with devising ways of ensuring efficient governance within a democratic framework so that authority is supplied as closely as possible to the people. The third strand is the scholarly contemplation of federalising tendencies and processes. This involves the analysis of the background conditions and the social movements that induce federal outcomes. Federal approaches can have different points of departure. Charles Pentland (1973: 147) picks out two key starting points: one 'sociological', the other 'constitutional' and from these flow a number of strands in the integration theory literature. The former envisages progress and peace emerging from the interaction of peoples. The latter sees harmony and stability flowing from enlightened constitutional design, thereby tempering the more atavistic tendencies of states. In federalist terms, the journeys from both starting points will lead to the same destination: a clearly defined supranational state. Reginald Harrison gives a succinct exposition of the logic that leads to this preference, which in turn also helps to distinguish federalism from other approaches discussed in this chapter:

> The federalist position is, clearly, the position of maximum scepticism about human nature and about the potential for good will and co-operation among states. it leads, therefore, in its most radical form, to a profound distrust of more confederal solutions, international functional organisation, and economic integration as instruments of integration.
>
> (Harrison, 1974: 44)

The expectation of a federal state-like entity as the end point of the federalist project suggests that federalist writers see statehood as either a desirable or inevitable mode of governance (Pentland, 1973: 149). This distinguishes federalism from other approaches discussed in this chapter that advocate or foresee processes that culminate in the transcendence of the nation-state and the replacement of the states system with an alternative mode of world order. For federalists, the supranational state generates efficiencies of scale through a degree of centralization and upward devolution of policy competence. This helps to distinguish a federation from a *confederation* where policy competence in key areas affecting sovereignty remains largely in the hands of the component member-states. This centralization is to be balanced by the nurturing of democratic impulses produced by the constitutional allowance of multiple sovereignties achieved through the devolution of authority in selected policy domains. The federalist project involves achieving appropriate balances between different, rival levels of authority on the one hand and between efficiency and democracy on the other. Federalists think that it is possible to engineer a happy coincidence of unit autonomy and overarching harmony in pursuit of common objectives. The pursuit of these objectives *must* be constitutionalized rather than left to traditional diplomatic devices (Spinelli, 1972). A federalist axiom is that the long-run realization of common aims cannot be achieved through either individual unit action or the construction of international alliances (Riker, 1996).

The federalist formula has, in the eyes of its advocates, two decisive advantages. The first is the prevention of the capture of a system by any one group. Federalism disallows domination and, therefore, particular modes of aggrandizing or totalitarian politics. The second advantage is that the federated state becomes a stronger unit in the face of external threat. This presents a potential dilemma for proponents of a federalist variant of European integration in that their logic is potentially two-faced. The rationale behind the advocacy of federalist solutions is the hope that the conflictual tendencies inherent in the (European) states system might be overcome. Yet, the normal outcome of federalist engineering is the reproduction of a state-like entity, replicating the format of the nation-state, albeit in supranational form. The extent to which such an outcome could successfully dissolve the existing modalities of international order is questionable. If part of the impulse behind federalist thinking is to render actors more capable of dealing with existing states of affairs, then the root cause of international conflict has not been addressed; it may even have been exacerbated, especially since the culmination of federalist logic might be the emergence of a global system of superstates.

The method of achieving this constitutional endpoint has been a key point of disagreement among federalist thinkers and accounted for the several splits that blighted the 'federalist movement' in Western Europe from its emergence after the First World War (Harrison, 1974: 46–54). One view was that federation should be an act of constitutional immediacy; a once and for all revolutionary settlement (Héraud, 1968). The other view might be described as gradualist (Brugmans, 1948, 1969). From this second viewpoint, federalism had to be cultivated as a popular movement to create the impetus for a federal pact among political elites. Thus, federalists had a place as activists on behalf of their cause, as consciousness-raisers among mass publics and as persuaders of key industrial and commercial actors. But the securing of federal institutions would emerge from the creation of a popularly elected constituent assembly to draft a federal constitution for ratification in national parliaments. None of this could be accomplished without popular will and several champions of the cause argued for the exploitation of crisis situations as moments for the widespread propagation of federalist ideas. Federal discourses would not advance through the forward march of rational argument as some democratic theorists might believe. Opportunities needed to be taken when they arose. Of special importance was the development of tactics and strategic openings to bypass the inevitable resistance of national governments who, needless to say, had a vested interest in the preservation of the old order. The strategic dexterity exhibited by this kind of gradualist federal thinking drew some writers into noting a resemblance to neofunctionalism (Haas, 1971: 21; Harrison, 1974: 49; see also Chapter 3 on neofunctionalism).

The tactical deliberations of federalists fed into some of the more avowedly academic treatments of the subject in the European context. Carl Friedrich (1968) argued for a shift in the conventional focus of scholars of federalism away from the manufacture of cast-iron constitutional principles to the investigation of federalizing tendencies. Federalism should be seen as a process; as 'an evolving pattern of changing relationships, rather than a static design regulated by firm and unalterable rules' (Friedrich, 1968: 21). Rules certainly mattered but in many ways they were secondary to the broad historic shifts that they represented. Tellingly, Friedrich commented that 'the main question is: What *function* does a federal relationship have? – rather than what *structure*' (1968: 21, emphasis added). The major work by Amatai Etzioni, *Political Unification* (Etzioni, 1965), tended to defy categorization in terms of the main schools of integration theory discussed in this book. Yet it seemed both to exhibit a federalist set of working assumptions and to confirm some of the insights of gradualist federalism (Pentland, 1973: 148). Etzioni's work treated integration very much as an outcome or as a terminal condition (Haas, 1971: 6), and an extremely federalist one at that:

> A *political community* is a community that possesses three kinds of integration: (a) it has an effective control over the means of violence (though it may 'delegate' some of this control to member units); (b) it has a center of decision-making that is able to affect significantly the allocation of resources and rewards throughout the community; and (c) it is the dominant focus of political identification for the large majority of politically aware citizens.
>
> (Etzioni, 1965: 4, emphasis in original)

The emphasis in Etzioni's work on the processes by which this end point could be attained displayed parallels with contemporaneous integration theories such as transactionalism and neofunctionalism, but, as one critic notes, really offered a rigorous attempt to operationalize classic federalist ideas with a view to understanding how federalizing processes work (Pentland, 1973: 162–3). This amounted to asking a series of crucial questions and generating numerous hypotheses about the nature of relations between states prior to the initiation of the unification process; about the powers allocated to the component units once unification begins; about whether unification is an uneven process and whether certain actors are more heavily implicated than others in the early stage; and about the functions of a system once unification has been accomplished or has been interrupted (Etzioni, 1965: Ch. 2).

In spite of differing emphases and different approaches, federalist analyses are united by the assumption of the primacy of the 'political' (Hodges, 1972: 12; Pentland, 1973: 149). Political problems require political solutions, and the means to attain those desirable outcomes are political. This puts federalism very much at odds with the varieties of functionalism discussed in this book. These lay stress on the *political economy* of integration where economic forces and processes are thought to generate political transformation and, in some accounts, where the guiding logic of human action ceases to be political and becomes altogether more technocratic. Unlike the transactionalist approach discussed later in this chapter, federalism does not regard sociological change as a sufficient condition for the attainment of integration. Institutions matter, either as human creations to inaugurate a transnational federalist legal order, or as advocates shaping mass ideational change in favour of federation as a preferred structure of governance.

Evaluation and critique

Any discussion of federalism applied to European unification demonstrates clearly how blurred the boundary between theoretical analysis and policy practice can be. It is not uncommon to argue that the discourse of federalism has been integral to the practice of European integration since the Second World War (Forsyth, 1996). The European federalist movement grew up around key works written in the inter-war period and many of the architects of the European Communities were prepared to articulate avowedly federalist goals (Burgess, 1989: 43–64), even though they may have been prepared to use functionalist means to attain them. American political scientists with an interest in federalism were ready dispensers of policy advice to the designers of post-war European federalist solutions (Friedrich and Bowie, 1954). So, it is very difficult to separate federalist theorizing from federalist advocacy and, by the same token, it is difficult to find a single, coherent body of European federalist theory. The purpose for many federalists of contemplating the structures and processes of federalism and federation was to ascertain the most appropriate tactics and legal formulae for the implementation of their normative agendas. Moreover, the ongoing influence of the concept of federalism in the day-to-day workings of the EU and particularly in the debates about 'Europe' within the member-states makes it difficult to accept the view that 'the federalist prospectus barely dented the European political establishment' (O'Neill, 1996: 25). Federalist organizations may, in retrospect, appear to have been marginal shaping influences in the history of the Communities, but federalist sentiments and ideas 'have permeated the Community and help to define both its problems and its responses' (Pentland, 1973: 186).

Some of the more obvious criticisms of federalist approaches to Europe arose as thinking in this tradition developed. Most notable was the 'evolutionary' federalist critique of the earlier supposition that integration (in a federalist sense) could be accomplished rapidly after careful and rational constitutional design – a kind of 'big bang' approach. Elements of evolutionary federalist work managed a partial separation between theory and advocacy. In some ways this was not just a conscious attempt to render federalism less 'ideological'. It probably had more to do with the increasing 'professionalization' of the social sciences in the 1950s and 1960s so that writers such as Etzioni (1965) were effectively conditioned to write quasi-scientific treatises about sociological processes rather than normative pleas for constitutional reordering.

The federalist concern with politics directs attention to the creation of a state-like institutional order at the European level. This leads to the fear that federalist theory misunderstands the nature of the problems it seeks to solve or, at least, that it devises a wholly inappropriate solution. Other schools of thought build on the notion that 'the state' – understood in terms of the organizational form that governs bounded territories – either is an irrational capsule for human governance or is possessed with inherent warlike propensities. The federalist mistake, therefore, is to advocate the reproduction of this organizational form at a European level. This has two basic dangers. The first is that the concentration of significant elements of governing capacity at the European level creates a dangerous distance between the governors and the governed. The advantage of nation-states, it is argued, is that they have a very powerful claim on the loyalties of peoples and in many respects constitute viable political communities in ways that powerfully federated entities cannot (Miller, 1994). The second danger follows from an external projection of federalist logic. This leads, in some eyes, to an Orwellian nightmare of interregional rivalries as 'superstates' reproduce the flaws of a nation-state-based international system – but on a bigger scale.

These concerns connect to the particular concern of federalist writers with the terminal condition of European integration. The main issue here is whether a federated EU would be a desirable outcome for the promotion of both efficient and democratic government (Lord, 1998). But what a federal Europe would look like is, as noted above, highly ambiguous. For some, it would mean transforming the existing member-states into entities analogous to US states, Canadian provinces or German Länder. It might mean accepting the apparent logic of 'differentiated integration' (Stubb, 1996) where the future EU is characterized by variegated patterns of integration and where the depth to which member-states are integrated may vary considerably from case to case. A federal Europe might resemble 'Europe of the regions' where the rigidity of national territorial barriers begins to wither away and the two primary levels of governance are regional (i.e. subnational) and European. Alternatively, a federal Europe might amount to a serious delimitation of the powers of central European-level institutions, with carefully designed constitutional principles in place to protect the rights of member-states. This brings us back to a core problem of federalism: its conceptual elasticity. This means that it is potentially useful to a variety of political projects and is, therefore, incredibly difficult to specify in academic terms.

Additionally, the claim that federal constitutions are the best means to protect individual freedom are, at best, unproven. Research published in the 1960s hinted that federalist systems were accomplished at protecting minority rights (Riker, 1964), but it followed that such protection could often be granted to movements whose entire *raison d'être* would be the *subversion* of democratic tendencies. The so-called 'states rights' movement in the United States used the language of constitutional federalism as a device to keep institutionalized racism entrenched and operative in certain southern states against the express concerns of central legislators. The late establishment of full female suffrage in Switzerland could also be attributed to the ability of federal constitutions to prevent the realization of key liberties.

The intellectual and political efforts of European federalists should not be underestimated. As Chapter 5 indicates, some recent writers have tried to employ a more analytically detached variant of federalism to the study of institution building at the EC/EU level (for example, Sbragia, 1992). Nonetheless, perhaps the most significant thing to be said about federalism is that it continues to be a powerful discourse of some of the possibilities inherent in the European integration process; an idea deployed less by theorists and more by politicians often fearful of the federalist 'other' to their preferred Europe of states (Thatcher, 1993).

Functionalism

Functionalist approaches have been central to the study of international integration. They also form a core element of the study of International Relations more generally. Paul Taylor (1994a: 125) identifies functionalism as the 'intellectual ancestor' of not only neofunctionalist integration theory (see Chapter 3), but also of diverse recent approaches to the study of international order such as interdependence theory, world society approaches, linkage politics and regime theory. Looking backwards, most students of functionalism would recognize its place within the liberal–idealist tradition of International Relations stretching from Kant through Woodrow Wilson and beyond. The foundations of functionalism tend to reside in a positive view of human possibilities and, to some extent, of human nature. Rational, peaceful progress is possible; conflict and disharmony are not endemic to the human condition. Functionalism is a central component of the study of international and non-governmental organizations; its assumptions form the basis for perhaps the most sustained challenge to state-centric 'power politics' views of world affairs.

By some distance, the key figure of functionalist theory is David Mitrany (1888–1975). Mitrany was Romanian by birth, but spent his formative intellectual years as a student at the LSE and wrote most of his key works in England. These are more than mere biographical details. Mitrany operated in a distinct and important intellectual circle. His autobiographical memoir (Mitrany, 1975a) identifies his influences as the politics of the international peace movement, social democracy and the anti-dogmatic political science built around English pluralism that emerged at the London School of Economics in the inter-war period (Navari, 1995). So, while much of what Mitrany wrote has direct relevance for the structuring of *international* society, his ideas bear the distinctive fingerprints of a radical–rationalist sentiment that found political expression in the UK via movements such as Fabianism, Guild Socialism and even syndicalism (Taylor, 1968). Mitrany's functionalism, as represented by works such as *A Working Peace System* (1943) (Mitrany, 1966), is underscored with an optimism for enlightened social engineering. It is not stretching the point too far to suggest that Mitrany's key ideas emerged in the same intellectual moment as John Maynard Keynes's *General Theory of Employment, Interest and Money* (1936) and William Beveridge's famous report on lifelong schemes of social insurance (1942). It is also important to understand another aspect of the context of functionalist work. The fact that the first edition of *A Working Peace System* appeared towards the end of the Second World War is important. Like federalism, functionalism was a branch of the broad movement that sought to theorize the conditions for ending human conflict and which found intellectual space in the turbulent political climate of the 1940s. Nonetheless, throughout his work Mitrany declared himself to be an adamant social scientist and thought his purpose to be the avoidance of normative dogma in the production of prescriptions for future human governance. He was concerned to recommend strategies for achieving systems of lasting peace, but his aim was to build arguments carefully and to reject the rigidities associated with inter-war idealism. For Mitrany, the starting point should not be a question about the 'ideal' *form* of international society, but about what its essential *functions* should be (Mitrany, 1933: 103). To illustrate the point, some significance should be attached to the fact that Mitrany's supposed natural intellectual foe, Hans J. Morgenthau, was able to write a sympathetic introduction to the second edition of *A Working Peace System* (Mitrany, 1966: 7–12; see also Taylor, 1975). While the work of inter-war idealists such as Norman Angell (1938) and Leonard Woolf (1917, 1933) was relatively easily dismissed by realists, Mitrany's cautious, rational 'social scientific' elaboration of functionalism was an altogether more obdurate opponent.

Functionalism, as Taylor and Groom note, is 'an approach rather than a tightly knit theory' (1975: 1). It does not begin from a rigid set of foundational propositions that are shared by all functionalists. However, functionalist approaches to world politics – and therefore to European integration – have tended to coalesce around a distinct, if somewhat broad-ranging, agenda. At the core of this agenda is the prioritization of human needs or public welfare, as opposed to, say, the sanctity of the nation-state or the celebration of any particular ideological credo. Indeed, functionalists tend to express considerable nervousness about the capabilities of nation-states to fulfil human needs. This is not simply because some needs have a transnational aspect, but also because the very existence of nation-states tends to uphold certain sorts of dogma which distract policy away from the maximization of public welfare. It follows that human beings need to be both rational about what their needs are and creative with respect to the construction of authoritative institutions that can perform the *function* assigned to them (hence the term 'functionalism').

Mitrany's functionalism offers a largely *technocratic* vision of human governance. On the whole, government by politicians implies that the prevailing motive of politics is the acquisition and retention of power rather than the pursuit of the common good. Ernst Haas has alluded to the idea that functionalism bears some resemblance to the Marxist–Leninist aspiration of replacing the 'government of men' with the 'administration of things' (Haas, 1964: 9). Perhaps, but it is also true that Mitrany was heavily critical of aspects of Marxism and socialist theory more generally. In particular, he found himself at odds with the way in which most writers in the English Fabian tradition came to accentuate the role of the state as the most plausible agent of social change (Navari, 1995: 219–20). So, Mitrany's technocratic anti-dogmatism was extended to the state. It was not just that the organization of the world into states generated damaging dogmatic tendencies. It also invested too heavily in the state for the sake of the state. To regard the state as a given, was to impose an unnecessary inflexibility when it came to thinking about how the requirements of human beings could best be served. Thus, it followed that some needs would be best served by ignoring the conventions of national territory. It might be that transnational institutions would be better and more efficient providers of welfare than national governments. Furthermore, the creation of such bodies would have two likely effects. The first was that the efficient performance of tasks by inter- or transnational institutions would result in a process of popular loyalty transference away from the nation-state. The second – a considerable bonus – was that the chances of international conflict would be reduced. The application of a technocratic and rationalistic approach to human governance was the basis of a working peace system. So, functionalism had two sides, one technocratic and rationalistic, the other highly normative. The two aspects came together most evidently in Mitrany's work. It might be overstating it a little to describe national sovereignty as Mitrany's 'basic enemy' (Harrison, 1974: 28), but there is no doubt that the search for clear-headed forms of governance to maximize human welfare was grounded in a revulsion of the sort of formal political arrangements that induced the two great wars of the twentieth century.

The functionalist *mantra* has tended to be 'form follows function'. Human needs change over time and vary across space. This means that the design of institutional solutions has to be an open-minded and flexible process. Herein, argue its followers, lies the great strength of functionalism. It is not hooked on any particular blueprint of international organization. The prioritization of human needs is the central concern, not the accomplishment of a particular integrated end state (Mitrany, 1966; Taylor 1968). Flexibility is the watchword. Needs emerge and alter; others vanish. The rigid nomination of certain sorts of institutional outcome over others is a fatal mistake. To some extent, therefore, functionalism is not really a theory of integration at all because the term 'integration' is suggestive of a particular institutional end stage.

Mitrany's early work, exemplified by his Yale lecture series published as *The Progress of International Government* (Mitrany, 1933), laid out some of the key principles that later became formalized into functional theory. A central concern for Mitrany in this period was an attempt to debunk the 'state fixation' which characterized so much 'first principles' thinking about international politics. For Mitrany, the state – essentially a means to human fulfilment – had become an end in itself. This critique emerged from three central observations. Firstly, it was a mistake to regard the world in terms of the conventional legal imagery of formally separate sovereign entities. Indeed, Mitrany preferred to speak of states in terms of their 'material interdependence' (1933: 101), a term that only really entered the International Relations mainstream some forty years later. Secondly, state fixation tended to constrain the possibilities for innovative thinking by assuming that the only available replacement for the states system was a state-like entity dispensing governance to the whole world. This was an argument not dissimilar to that presented against rigid forms of state-centrism by Ruggie (1998) sixty years later. Mitrany's work can be read as an attempt to develop a kind of 'third way' between this rigid dichotomous logic and its associated 'conceptual stagnation'. Indeed, Mitrany was highly critical of contemporary thinkers who sought to present schemes for world government. In the lecture 'The Communal Origin of World Affairs', he castigated the likes of H. G. Wells and Bertrand Russell for the assumption that a 'world state' would produce stable order. Such schemes were read by Mitrany as analogous to empire building and, therefore, would be likely to induce the sorts of antagonisms that weakened and eventually dissolved imperial orders (Mitrany, 1933: 135). The third difficulty with state fixation emerged in the light of internal challenges to the capability of states that posed problems to established techniques of government. For Mitrany, the state in the 1930s was becoming 'hybridized'. The relatively new welfare systems of the time confronted the old image of the state as essentially a guardian of peace and order. The imperatives of creative thinking in the context of domestic polities were also present in the international sphere because (a) the dissolution and/or reorganization of governance for domestic purposes might in itself reorder the international system and (b) the 'material interdependence' of states meant that the necessary innovative thinking ought to yield at least a measure of transnational creativity to solve problems of public management, distribution, welfare and communication. In some ways these processes were beginning to emerge informally with the growth of interstate contacts in the sphere of technology that were projected to replace traditional modes of diplomacy (1933: 127).

Herein lay a tension in functionalist thinking. Much of Mitrany's output consisted of the development of a specific manifesto, advocating purposeful manipulation of the structures of national and international governance. The implication is that the realization of his ideas was contingent upon the exercise of deliberate acts of human agency. Yet, there was also a quasi-Darwinian, evolutionary strand in much of his argumentation. A telling passage in *A Working Peace System* used the language of natural selection to describe how and why functional international organizations 'would merely rationalize and develop what is already there' (Mitrany, 1966: 81). Indeed: 'because of the legalistic structure of the state and of our political outlook, which treats national and international society as two different worlds, *social nature*, so to speak, *has not had a chance to take its course*' (1966: 82, emphasis added). Of course, in the terms set out by functionalist arguments this was not a difficulty. After all, functionalists viewed themselves as thoughtful interpreters of social change and identified rigid constitutionalism as a barrier to such enlightenment, but there was a continuing question about the relationship between the shifting pattern of human needs and the necessity of human action to realize the institutional logic of such shifts.

Functionalists like Mitrany foresaw a proliferation of flexible task-oriented international organizations as the means to address the priorities dictated by human need. They were to be flexible in that 'activities would be selected specifically and organised separately – each according to its nature, to the conditions under which it has to operate, and to the needs of the moment' (Mitrany, 1966: 70). The upshot of this 'essential principle' would be a cobweb of diverse and overlapping institutions of governance, differing in form as functions varied. After running through a number of varying forms of candidate functional organizations (railway systems to be administered on a continental basis, the intercontinental organization of shipping and the universal management of aviation and broadcasting),

Mitrany developed the argument that form would be more or less self-selecting:

> Here we discover a cardinal virtue of the functional method – what one might call the virtue of technical self-determination. The functional *dimensions* ... determine themselves. In a like manner the function determines its appropriate *organs*. It also reveals through practice the nature of the action required under the given conditions, and in that way the *powers* needed by the respective authority.
>
> (Mitrany, 1966: 72–3, emphasis in original)

The matter of how these functional organizations might be linked and whether an overarching authority would be needed was raised, but again questions of appropriate levels of agency remained open. The issue of the connection between the organizations and the realization of an 'international society' was also presented in largely evolutionary language, albeit in terms that appeared to anticipate the neofunctionalist conception of 'spillover' (Taylor, 1994: 131). The establishment and profusion of task-oriented agencies was expected to induce substantial attitudinal change among those directly affected by their operation. The functionalist expectation was for the practical experience of functionalism in action to produce the conditions for the expansion and reproduction of such agencies. The fact that functional organizations were founded on the basis of rational engagement with real human needs meant that their operation would deliver discernible benefits which in turn would encourage wider participation within these bodies and unravel previously stubborn cases of 'state fixation'. In addition, the complex web of organizations would help to cement processes of growing interdependence among states and societies. The high tariff associated with dismantling this informal enmeshment would in itself be an incentive to maintain the functionalist logic, but would also bind groups together in ways unlikely to produce conflict.

Functionalism and European integration

One of the most interesting facets of Mitrany's work, at least from the point of view of this book, was his powerful and consistent rebuttal of *regional* integration arrangements. This critique set functionalism aside from some of the other major contributions to the debate about establishing the conditions for peace. Mitrany's distaste for West European integration was apparent in his critique of the Briand Plan (see above). The latter was dismissed as statist and exclusionary (Navari, 1995: 229). The argument, using functionalist reasoning, was emergent in *The Progress of International Government*, found expression in *A Working Peace System* and was most forcefully stated in an essay originally published in the *Journal of Common Market Studies* in 1965. The functionalist argument evidently objected to the territorial closure implicit in schemes of regional integration. In a lively engagement with Coudenhove-Kalergi's notion of pan Europe (Mitrany, 1933: 111–18; see also Mitrany, 1975b: 151–9), Mitrany posed some fairly fundamental questions about the definition of 'Europe' in terms of its boundaries and, therefore, about the impact upon the world outside. Those advocating European union in the 1930s might think that they were recapturing the spirit of Penn, Saint-Pierre and Kant (see Luard, 1992: 400–23), but the schemes of the eighteenth century were thought of as universal; it just so happened that Europe was the known universe. More seriously, schemes of continental unification were castigated by Mitrany for their statism:

> Between the conception of continental unions and that of a universal league there is a difference not merely of degree but of essence. The one would proceed in the old way by a definition of territory, the other by definition of functions; and while the unions would define their *territory* as a means of *differentiating* between members and outsiders, a league would select and define *functions* for the contrary purpose of *integrating* with regard to the interests of all.
>
> (Mitrany, 1933: 116, emphasis in original)

In other words, regionalism was a recipe for reproducing the faults of the states system writ large. The continued deployment of territorial logic (as opposed to functional logic) created the potential for interregional antagonisms. This point was made most clearly in the 1965 essay 'The Prospect of Integration: Federal or Functional' (Mitrany: 1975c: 53–78) which applied functionalist analysis to the maturing project of regional integration represented by the European Communities. Mitrany attacked what he termed the federal and regional fallacies, both of which were finding expression in the EC. The regional fallacy described the tendency to draw boundaries and to impose limits upon membership within entities such as the Communities. The federal fallacy referred to the tendency to construct such arrangements for political purposes – a 'United States of Europe' in the context of the EC:

> a political union must be nationalistic; and ... as such it must impede and it may defeat, the great historic quest for a general system of peace and development. Under the pressures of a planned and radical social transformation it is bound to shape towards a centralised system –

closed, exclusive, competitive; and whatever else it may do, such a system would hardly be suited to mediate between the new ideological divisions, or temper the raw nationalism of the new states to steer them towards the new greener pastures of a mutual international community.

(Mitrany, 1975c: 72)

Moreover, regional schemes – as understood by their proponents – would not only reproduce territorial state-like functions at the supranational level, but would also keep intact the decision- making structures of the component states. This would, in Mitrany's view, lead to domination by the most powerful states (1966: 45–6). Regional unions are constructed in a manner analogous to the processes of state-building, but they lack the 'natural cohesiveness' of nations. In terms of more recent academic debates about nationalism, they are difficult to construct as 'imagined communities' (Anderson, 1991). In short, regional integration projects offended some of the basic tenets of functionalism. They were atavistic because they generated antagonism and were recidivist because they took governance back to the anachronistic foundations of statehood and territory.

Having said that, Mitrany did harbour considerable respect for the European Coal and Steel Community (ECSC) and the European Atomic Energy Community (Euratom). In both he saw elements of clear functional logic, notably in the technocratic consultative mechanisms that linked officials to producer groups and in the inherent possibilities for cooperative contacts with non-member countries (Mitrany, 1975c: 69–70). The ECSC was attractive to Mitrany because it seemed to be an appropriate functional solution to a particular set of sectoral needs that arose in post-war Europe. It represented an instance where problems actually had a defined geographical scope (Taylor, 1993: 20–1). The problem with European integration was that – by the mid-1960s at least – it had come to be dominated by the formal processes associated with the European Economic Community (EEC). This was a much wider-ranging body that grew out of pre-existing functional schemes. There was no reason why issues beyond the spheres of atomic energy and coal and steel should be slotted into regionally defined institutions. European integration represented the application of territorial rather than functionalist logic.

Evaluation and critique

The most obvious claim about the importance of functionalism is that it laid the foundations for neofunctionalist integration theory – the branch of international theory most closely associated with the development of the European Communities. Indeed, many neofunctionalists appeared to claim Mitrany as a direct intellectual ancestor. In many ways, the emphasis on the technocratic fulfilment of needs as the basis for more profound and lasting systems of peace, along with the evolutionary logic anticipating later arguments about spillover (see Chapter 3) certainly points to a close linkage. However, the evidence suggests that Mitrany was rather uncomfortable with this association, not least because he perceived there to be a linkage between neofunctionalist integration theory and the quasi-federalist strategies of the founders of the EC. As Cornelia Navari makes clear, Mitrany objected to the associations between neofunctionalism and the construction of new political communities. The latter, in his view, was anathema to the functionalist project (Navari, 1995: 233).

More generally, functionalism is usually thought to have provided an innovative and distinctive approach to the study of international politics and international organization that opened up decided possibilities for thinking beyond conventional categories (Imber, 1984). Most obviously, as Paul Taylor points out, functionalism offered a distinctive alternative to normal ways of thinking about a post-Westphalian international order. With the recent renewal of interest in 'regionalism' in world politics and the international political economy (Fawcett and Hurrell, 1997; Gamble and Payne, 1996; Mansfield and Milner, 1997), the functionalist alternative, 'sectoralism', becomes all the more apparent and striking (Taylor, 1993: 40). This is especially important since – in a normative sense at least – functionalism applies such a thoroughgoing critique of post-national regionalism. For those working beyond the state-centric universe of realist International Relations, Mitrany provided an early example of how to avoid some of the traps of idealist thinking while still pursuing an explicitly post-statist agenda. In addition, it was an alternative to realism that, for some, allowed the generation of testable hypotheses (Harrison, 1975; Pentland, 1975). Affinities with neofunctionalist integration theory aside, Mitrany's work can be read as an anticipation of work on interdependence (Keohane and Nye, 1977), transnationalism and governance without government (Rosenau and Czempiel, 1992). Paradoxically, although many current scholars of integration would deny an affiliation to functionalism, recent work on EU governance certainly shares the imagery of complex, overlapping, multi-level authorities that we find in the functionalist repertoire. One recent contribution has even suggested that functionalism offers 'perhaps the best theoretical framework ... for understanding [the EC's] technical nature' and that 'it is possible to see in ... [Mitrany's] doctrine of the functional organisation of international relations a particularly apposite summary of the assumptions behind the integration process' (Forsyth, 1996: 29).

Criticisms of functionalism fall into four main categories. The first criticism emerges from the functionalist assumption that the determination of needs is an objective and technocratic exercise. It is difficult not to see this as a fundamentally political, and thus an inherently conflictual, task. A rather telling example from *A Working Peace System* reveals the problem. Mitrany had little problem in ascertaining the appropriate form for the administration of railways, shipping and aviation, but admitted that coordination in spheres such as production, trade and distribution would be inherently more complex because of their competitive nature (1966: 71). It is difficult to see how functionalist logic would work in the normal conditions of a market economy, either domestically or internationally, given the imperatives of competition and the associated propensity to create winners and losers. Much of the impetus behind Mitrany's work was a revulsion for *laissez-faire* capitalism, but the application of a functionalist template to systems of production, finance and trade would be a task requiring fundamental alterations to the behavioural logic of firms, markets and financiers.

This leads directly to the second criticism: that Mitranian functionalism is hopelessly naïve and rests upon unreasonable assumptions about the ability of peoples and governments to move in rational directions. To some extent, functionalism was blinded by its own rationality, which was a rationality premised upon the primacy of human needs. It is a way of thinking that is rooted in the tradition of Benthamite utilitarianism, where the goal of government should be the pursuit of maximum human happiness (Imber, 1984: 103). Other rationalities flow from alternative premises (such as the normative propriety of nationhood and the assumption that national governments are the most effective capsules for efficient and representative governance – both of which lay at the heart of well-argued intellectual positions). The rational–technocratic foundations of functionalist International Relations may have been present in the minds of functionalists, but they were by no means rife among mass publics and political elites. The technocratic emphasis of functionalists led to an underestimation of the continuing salience of politics. In part, this was because of the perception of politics as behaviour premised upon dogma, whereas the administration of things also involves groups of people making collective decisions (i.e. is inherently political by most under-standings). The functionalist idea that integration was 'the gradual triumph of the rational and the technocratic over the political' (Pentland, 1981: 551) presents a false dichotomy. Technocracy is deeply political and it is difficult to maintain that certain matters are inherently and *only* technical (Navari, 1995: 234). Thus, drawing on sympathetic critics such as Claude, Sewell and Engle, Ernst Haas criticized Mitranian functionalism for assuming a separation between power and welfare (1964: 23). This connects to a further related flaw. Functionalist reasoning contained deep assumptions about the capacities and probabilities for cognitive change. The argument seems to be that the objective fulfilment of needs will almost automatically generate support for the institutional form being used to address those needs. Indeed, the mechanisms through which needs are identified in the first place are also underspecified. This type of argument faces similar problems to those confronted by neofunctionalist assumptions about spillover (these are addressed in Chapter 3), and what functionalism lacked was a theory of communicative action: how actors come to (or would come to) believe certain things about the world. The functionalist recourse to an objective rationality is not enough, certainly in terms of current social science.

A third common criticism of functionalism is that it has a poor record of prediction (Haas, 1975a; Thompson, 1980: 204). In essence, things have not turned out the way Mitrany envisaged. There may be a case for saying that this is an invalid criticism. Mitrany's work was about advocacy rather than prediction and, therefore, to judge functionalism on this basis is to use a form of theoretical evaluation that is not appropriate to the theory in question. As Haas noted, 'prescriptive intent is central to Functionalist theory' (1964: 7). It is certainly true that Mitrany continued to advocate a functionalist world order until his death and in so doing was highly critical of what he saw as the erroneous regionalist tendencies in the global political economy. So, at one level, Mitrany's work was theory as political intervention rather than theory as the production of law-like generalization. Having said that, there was a predictive element in functionalism. The emphasis on the progress and nature of social change meant that the recommendations for international organization produced by Mitrany reflected assumptions about the evolution of human need and the tendency of forms of governance to adapt. Haas again clarified the position of functionalists who 'claim to possess a theoretical apparatus capable of analysing existing society and of pinpointing the causes of its undesirable aspects; they claim, further, to know the way in which a normatively superior state of affairs can be created' (Haas, 1964: 7).

Relatedly and fourthly, functionalism has been criticized for a lack of scientific rigour (Thompson, 1980). For some, the theory suffers from sloppy construction and is methodologically naïve. It is true that there is no foundational theoretical statement of functionalism. But this requires some qualification. It is not so much that Mitrany's functionalism emerged out of the inter-war idealist debates where, as Navari points out, methodological precision was uncommon (Navari, 1995: 234). Indeed, Mitrany continued to reflect upon functionalist themes for thirty years after the publication of *A Working Peace System*. Moreover, Hans Morgenthau's attempt to lay the scientific foundations of realist international thought dates from 1948. Rather, Mitrany's position as a public figure: part journalist, part corporate consultant, part foreign affairs analyst, meant that his intended audience was not always an academic one. Perhaps the surprisingly wide influence of Mitrany's ideas can be put down to this fact. In saying that, it might be tempting to dismiss any claims of functionalism to be 'scientific'. Perhaps (in the current understanding of social scientific propriety), but in terms of the inter-war debates, Mitrany was a self-conscious political scientist who sought to develop arguments through an appropriation of how things actually were, rather than through idealist impulses. It is also true that Mitrany's flexible functionalism represented a direct eschewal of 'grand theory' (Taylor, 1994: 126). For Mitrany, theoretical rigour (in the modern sense) was problematic because it denoted practical rigidity and creative closure.

Transactionalism

Federalism and functionalism both culminate in the transcendence or at least the containment of the nation-state. Other approaches have sought to theorize the conditions for the stabilization of the nation-state system. From this vantage point, if higher authority or international organizations have a place, then it is to provide the conditions for the creation and maintenance of this equilibrium. Such comity results from international interaction through all manner of economic, social and cultural processes. The guiding puzzle is endemic to International Relations: the problem of war. Integration becomes the achievement of a sense of security within a region, so that war is ruled out as the way of resolving international differences, but nation-states are not necessarily dissolved.

The transactionalist (or communications, or pluralist) approach to international integration, associated most forthrightly with the work of Karl Deutsch, is the best representative of this broad perspective. Deutsch was a formidable scholar of both international politics and nation-building. In many ways, these two branches of his work converged in Deutsch's analysis of integration. In the introduction to the second edition of his seminal *Nationalism and Social Communication*, originally published in 1953, Deutsch made it clear that the study of nationalism and the integration of national communities shared much with the emerging study of supranational integration (Deutsch, 1966a: 7–14). His work on nationalism underscored the importance of communication as the key mechanism of the social mobilization of communities that in turn was responsible for historical processes of national development (1966a: Ch. 8). Similar processes were thought to characterize the international sphere in circumstances where states build security communities among themselves. Thus, international integration is defined as being about the achievement of security within a region or among a group of states. Successful integration is about the radical reduction in the likelihood of states using violent means to resolve their differences.

Deutsch was the lead researcher on the project that formed the basis of *Political Community and the North Atlantic Area* (Deutsch *et al.*, 1957). The book is usually taken as the primary statement of the transactionalist perspective. The guiding puzzle of this project was the 'the study of possible ways in which men might some day abolish war' (1957: 3). The focus was on the operation of security communities – political communities within which the expectation of war was minimized. The definition of 'security community' was bound up with the conception of integration advanced by Deutsch and his colleagues. Security communities were groups of people that had become 'integrated'. Further, integration was defined as 'the attainment, within a territory, of a "sense of community" and of institutions and practices strong enough and widespread enough to assure for a "long" time, dependable expectations of "peaceful change" among its population' (Deutsch *et al.*, 1957: 5). This definition was elaborated with the presentation of two distinct sorts of security community. The first, *amalgamated* security communities, involved the formal merger of separate units (for example states) into a larger unit through some sort of institutional fusion. In the international sphere, this appeared to be what writers from other schools, notably federalism and neofunctionalism, had in mind when they spoke of 'integration' (Pentland, 1981). The second, *pluralistic* security communities, were defined as entities where the component governments retain their separate legal identities and, thus, where integration occurs without institutional merger or the creation of a supreme overarching authority (see also Deutsch, 1968: 193–5). The second form appeared to be Deutsch's favoured model on the grounds that it was both more likely to arise in practice and potentially more durable than amalgamated security communities. Amalgamated communities were vulnerable to a number of potential destabilizing factors. These included increased military burdens (on the whole or the component units), very rapid increases in social mobilization and political participation within component units, relatively swift shifts in social differentiation, a decline in administrative capabilities, a closure of political elites and a dissonance between government action and societal expectations (Deutsch, 1968: 195–6). Pluralistic communities required only three conditions to exist: compatibility of major values among the units, a capacity for politically relevant groups to respond to each other's stimuli without violence and a 'mutual predictability of the relevant aspects of one another's political, economic and social behaviour' (1968: 195).

Important to this view of international politics is the famous distinction, made by the German sociologist Ferdinand Tönnies, between *Gemeinschaft* and *Gesellschaft*. *Gemeinschaft* (community) denotes a situation when people are held together by common sentiments and common loyalties. Relationships with non-members of the group are considerably less significant than the sense of kinship that develops within the group. *Gesellschaft* (society) is a condition binding people less through trust and more through a mixture of self-interest, division of labour and contract. The distinction is often thought of as equivalent to that between non-contractual allegiance and quasi-contractual obligation (Scruton, 1983: 186). Deutsch was interested in *Gemeinschaft* as a condition of integration. The end point of integration, from this perspective, is a sense of community – a qualitative leap from pacts, treaties and alliances among states. Deutsch's task was to investigate the conditions and processes through which this emerged.

The guiding hypothesis of transactionalist work on integration was that a sense of community *among* states would be a function of the level of communication *between* states. The route to international *Gemeinschaft* was the establishment of a network of mutual transactions. The more interaction that existed between state *a* and state *b*, so the greater the reciprocal importance (or 'mutual relevance') of *a* and *b* to one another. Perceptions that the interaction is beneficial will promote feelings of trust between *a* and *b*. With trust would come further interaction (Deutsch, 1964: 54). The empirical task becomes the measurement of both the rate of change of transaction flows and the degree of mutual responsiveness within the system. The potential – but only the *potential* – for integration (in Deutsch's sense) would occur in situations of high international transaction. The actuality of integration would be secured where *mutual responsiveness* also prevailed. Responsiveness, in this sense, was defined as 'the probability of getting an adequate response within an acceptable limit of time' (Deutsch, 1964: 69). Responsiveness was not simply a consequence of willingness to interact on the part of actors. It also had a lot to do with the actual capabilities of actors to interact. The availability of communication-facilitating technology was obviously important here, but capabilities were also affected – in a potentially negative sense – by the demands being placed on the system of interaction at any given time. Demands were a function of needs occasioned by 'industrial, economic and technological change; migrations; changes in consumer tastes; long range secular dynamics of culture; and international challenges' (Deutsch, 1964: 71). So, for integration to be accomplished, capabilities needed in fact to remain ahead of the development of needs.

The emphasis on needs is suggestive of a connection with functionalism. However, Deutsch was critical of specific aspects of functionalist logic. In particular, he regarded the levels of communication undertaken by functional international organizations as insufficient to generate the necessary loyalties among mass publics and thus to secure a lasting peace.

International civil servants (i.e. those staffing functional organizations), out of a mixture of habit and necessity, tended to communicate with governments rather than with the people for whom they were directly responsible. So '[t]hey are hampered in receiving and answering direct communications from the public, and even more in doing anything about them. Under these conditions, popular loyalties to international agencies and symbols are unlikely to grow, and the appeal of nationalist images and symbols is unlikely to weaken' (Deutsch, 1968: 167). Functionalist methods of integration would not fulfil the conditions necessary – in Deutschian terms – for the widespread cognitive shifts necessary to make a lasting difference to world order. Having said that, Deutsch was in alliance with functionalists against federalists, whom he accused of advocating 'premature overall amalgamation' (1968: 198).

In his work on integration Deutsch showed signs of operating under the (then fashionable) influence of systems theory. Some of his ideas about communications and international integration/amalgamation were at least implicit in some of his later work which tried to connect the study of cybernetics to political science. Cybernetics was concerned with the operation of communications and control within systems. The research agenda developed by Deutsch, notably in *The Nerves of Government* (Deutsch, 1963), concentrated attention on the flows of information through political systems and on how systems accepted, mediated or rejected these communication flows.

Evaluation and Critique

Deutsch is often cited as one of the pivotal political scientists of the century (Merritt and Russett, 1981). Deutsch's work spanned the discipline, was theoretically innovative, opened up the potential for the application of new techniques to the study of political phenomena and was devoted to the pursuit of rigour in explanation and to the generation of hugely influential large-scale research programmes. His doctoral students included figures such as Arend Lijphart and Peter Katzenstein. In International Relations alone, he is thought of as a key contributor to the development of a serious non-realist strand of scholarship. In particular, he is credited with offering a plausible redefinition of the discipline that guided scholars away from the narrow domain of inter*state* interaction to the study of the relations between *societies and peoples* more generally. His contribution to the discipline has been identified as the groundbreaking investigation of the 'sentimental relations among peoples' (Puchala, 1981: 151), their causes and their consequences. Deutsch relied on the analytical separation of the legal state from the sociological nation. This constituted a direct challenge to orthodox realist conceptions that tended to conflate the ideas of nationhood (identity) and statehood (government) through ideas such as 'the national interest'. In such a view, governments preside over peoples in a complex known as the nation-state. While countries may be characterized by internal diversity, for realists they are united by common interests on the international stage, interests that are determined largely by governments. The contrary view, that Deutsch did much to develop, is that common identities are the product of intensive transactions and communications. It follows that the development of multiple interactions among different peoples may be the basis for increased mutual under-standing and, thus, of a widespread sense of security.

The contribution of Deutsch to the study of European integration is perhaps a little less clear-cut. As Peter Willets has noted, 'Deutsch asked important questions about the assimilation of different peoples into a single people and about the differentiation of one people into two or more separate peoples, through changes in communication patterns' (1994: 256). The sociological concern with security communities provided a rather distinct problematic, different from both the constitutional engineering of the federalists and the functionalists' rational pursuit of human needs. Unlike the other schools discussed in this chapter, Deutsch was much less concerned with the transcendence of the nation-state and the associated construction of international institutions. Indeed, Deutsch's work can be placed very plausibly within an approach to integration that sought to preserve nation-states as the predominant actors in international politics, but at the same time which hoped to reduce the likelihood of international conflict. The normative aspirations of such a tradition foresee, as Charles Pentland puts it, 'a felicitous combination of the values of national self-determination on the one hand, and international peace and security on the other' (Pentland, 1973: 30). Unlike his neofunctionalist contemporaries, Deutsch was not concerned with building theory out of observations of the European Communities. Post-war supranational institutional development in Europe was but one historical case among many. To some extent, transactionalism had a claim to be a better *general* theory of integration than the likes of neofunctionalism which, as will become apparent in the next chapter, quite clearly sought to theorize 'outwards' from the experience of the European Coal and Steel Community of the 1950s. Transactionalism looked at multiple historical instances of the creation of security communities to establish a set of general theoretical propositions.

In any case, Deutsch's preference was for *pluralistic* security communities of which the EC was patently not an instance. Having said that, Deutsch did develop an important argument about the evolution of *amalgamated* security communities for which the EC 'Six' offered a primary case study (Deutsch *et al.*, 1967). The development of functional linkages through informal economic and social interaction among separate

West European communities creates, in the course of time, socio-psychological tendencies and learning processes that in turn lead to assimilation and integration. In time these induce elite-led attempts to institutionalize and formalize the initial functional linkages. This formal institution-building is a means to preserve the community that intense patterns of communication has created. This argument clearly anticipated William Wallace's discussion (1990) of formal and informal integration which suggests that in certain cases region-building is accomplished in the first instance by informal economic interactions that states later consolidate and develop (see Chapters 1 and 7). Also interesting in this regard was the sharp empirical disagreement between transactionalists and neofunctionalists. The former suggested that integration – in Deutschian terms – had reached something of a high watermark by the late 1950s (Deutsch, 1966b; Inglehart, 1967) – an assertion that amounted to a vigorous refutation of neofunctionalist arguments.

Criticisms of transactionalist approaches usually begin with the observation that the processes recognized by Deutsch and his followers pose serious problems of measurement and operationalization. As Donald Puchala notes, Deutsch regarded integration and amalgamation as a 'quantitative concepts . . . to be measured with regard to degree or intensity and . . . [ranging] along continua that extend from incipience to fulfilment' (1981: 153). The main advantage of such thinking was the very large number of historical cases it generated, thereby facilitating comparative research of all kinds into attitudinal change and political identification. However, the sophisticated data needed by investigators to measure these phenomena and to test hypotheses would not be readily available. This was obviously true for attempts to undertake longitudinal/historical comparisons because mass survey data, sophisticated surveying techniques and forms of multivariate analysis were only emerging in the 1950s. In addition, while data could be obtained on various indices such as international travel and phone calls, it was not entirely clear how surveys could uncover the effects of such interaction on the identities of and mutual identifications between peoples.

A second line of criticism concerns the lack of clarity in Deutsch's work about the mechanisms through which certain key processes operated. One was the nature of the transition from 'integration' to 'amalgamation': how exactly informal interactions generate formal institution-building and how socio-psychological changes (at both elite and mass levels) feed into authoritative action. This is summed up by Donald Puchala (1981) as a failure to understand the politics of motivation in the processes described by transactionalism, which in turn becomes a problem of power. The assumption in transactionalist work was that mass sentimental change would eventually force formal policy changes on the part of governments, but it could be argued that attitudinal patterns among mass publics derive from national media in which national authorities are heavily implicated. Conventional theories of foreign policy-making clash head on with Deutschian transactionalism. Realist-inspired work emphasizes the particular character of decision-making that supposedly moves outward from governments' analyses of their strategic location in the international system of states, rather than reflecting the inner political or attitudinal dynamics of the domestic polity. While Deutsch's ontological position (i.e. his view of the basic nature of the world) was different from that of conventional realists, it would still be possible to understand foreign policy as a site of gatekeeping by state actors within a more pluralistic conception of the actor balance in international politics. In any case, if the integration process is to follow the gradual pattern of adjustment envisaged by Deutsch, then the formal construction of the pluralistic or amalgamated security communities would need to be accomplished by governments in an environment detached from sudden swings in public consciousness (Pentland, 1973: 63).

This connects to a third problem. Deutschians were attacked for the apparently complacent assumption that increased communication would *necessarily* lead to cognitive change.

The evidence of burgeoning international and intersocietal communication during the 1950s and 1960s could not be disputed. But the extent to which it was producing a deep-lying socio-psychological transformation certainly was at very best ambiguous. In some ways, this was a purely empirical problem, but one affected by the still limited capacity of social scientists to measure cognitive change and to make reasonably certain statements about the hypothesized connections between interaction, attitudes and behaviour. Insofar as measurement has been possible, the evidence seems to point to the continuing attachment of citizens to the iconography of European nation-states (Niedermeyer and Sinnott, 1995). But it was also a theoretical problem of underspecification of principal actors and decision-making dynamics that 'forces unguided inferential leaps of considerable magnitude' (Puchala, 1981: 157).

Conclusions

These early manifestations of integration theory emerged out of early attempts to produce a non-realist form of International Relations scholarship. Their guiding *problematique* (or puzzle) was the old IR question of the avoidance of war. The Europe of the inter-war and early post-war period offered an exciting empirical laboratory, even if approaches like functionalism sought to undermine the argument for the necessity for territorially defined systems of collective security. The appearance of theoretical work generated important debates within the scholarly community and subsequent work, particularly that of neofunctionalists, drew heavily on the insights and claims of functionalism and transactionalism, while at the same time thinking about the processes that might induce a federal endgame for integration (hence the occasional use of 'federal functionalism' as an alternate title for neofunctionalism). The questions raised by early integration theory were substantial and continue to be important for students of the EU and international/regional integration more generally. They are, in essence, questions about structure and agency that go well beyond the relatively narrow world of EU studies. They concern the centrality of states to processes of social change, the ability of states or other unit actors to withstand structural transformation as well as the relationship between state and non-state actors and processes of economic change.

The study of federalism, functionalism and transactionalism also begins to show how difficult it can be to draw lines in the sand between 'theory' and 'advocacy' or between 'theory' and 'practice'. This point is brought out further in the next chapter, which discusses the relationship between the strategic construction of the Communities and the theoretical project of the neofunctionalists. It is also worth noting the significance of academic styles and social scientific fashions. As the early manifestations of integration theory arose, so patterns of scholarly exegesis were clearly undergoing a significant shift associated with the 'professionalization' of the social sciences. This is important because federalist and functionalist work of the inter-war and early post-war period is often dismissed as overly normative and conceptually naïve. But the evaluation of such theoretical treatments cannot properly be accomplished without attending to important 'sociology of knowledge' questions. These are picked up in greater detail Chapter 8, but for now it is worth pointing out that the 'real' developments in the European Communities do not provide the only contextual reference points for the study of integration theory.

Neofunctionalism

For many, 'integration theory' and 'neofunctionalism' are virtual synonyms. The approach has been integral to the study of European unity in the second half of the twentieth century. The main propositions of the approach were defined, tested, reformulated and re-evaluated by some of the finest political scientists of their day. Countless doctoral researchers have used the neofunctionalist template to conduct their research on Europe and other supposed examples of regional integration and cooperation. Despite the best efforts of its finest practitioners to declare the theory 'obsolescent' (Haas, 1975a), neofunctionalism has displayed impressive qualities of obstinacy and revitalization in recent years. While there may not be many 'fundamentalist' neofunctionalists around in contemporary political science, there are certainly many who use elements of neofunctionalist logic and neofunctionalist vocabulary in their analysis (see Chapter 5 and, for example, Burley and Mattli, 1993; Cram, 1996; Marks *et al.*, 1996; Sandholtz and Stone Sweet, 1998; Sandholtz and Zysman, 1989; Tranholm-Mikkelsen, 1991).

So, like it or not, we cannot think about the analysis of European integration without confronting neofunctionalism. But there are two other important reasons why neofunctionalism is important. Firstly, a reading of neofunctionalism reveals much about theory, theory-building and the importance of particular social scientific moments for the ways in which social phenomena are studied (see also Chapter 8). If federalism and functionalism owed their impetus ultimately to the desire among groups of intellectuals to advance towards a more peaceful form of world politics, neofunctionalism – like transactionalism – was a product of new social scientific mindsets that emerged in the United States after the Second World War and grew to maturity in the late 1950s and throughout the 1960s. As this chapter indicates, much of the neofunctionalist literature carried with it the desire to explain, classify and generate hypotheses to guide further empirical inquiry. Secondly, the neofunctionalist project was evidently bound up with the strategies of the founding architects of the EC. There is an obvious resemblance between the 'Monnet method' of integration and the propositions developed by neofunctionalist writers such as Ernst Haas. Here we are confronted with the theory–practice interface that is, of course, an element of all social theory. Nonetheless, a particularly striking example is revealed in the study of neofunctionalist integration theory which might even be described as the 'authorized version' of European integration.

Neofunctionalism and the architects of European unity

As suggested above, neofunctionalism (in its early manifestations at least) might be thought of as an attempt to theorize the strategies of the founding elites of post-war European unity. Figures such as Jean Monnet and Robert Schuman were quite explicit about the path that they envisaged to an integrated Europe. Their approach represented a direct rejection of the idealism of the federalist movement. Federalists had seemingly lost the arguments about the path to post-war unity by the early 1950s. While a federal outcome might still be the ultimate goal, this would not be achieved through the pursuit of rational argument and forward-thinking constitutional design, but through incremental and strategic means. The approach has been described as technocratic and functionalist, not least by Ernst Haas, the most important neounctionalist scholar. For Haas, the Monnet method was rooted in an analysis of converging preferences and hard-nosed self-interest among policy actors in Europe. But it is also worth noting Haas's telling point about which actors matter:

> Converging economic goals embedded in the bureaucratic, pluralistic, and industrial life of modern Europe provided the crucial impetus. *The economic technician, the planner, the innovating industrialist, and trade unionist advanced the movement not the politician, the scholar, the poet, the writer.*
>
> (Haas, 1968: xix, emphasis added).

The strategy that emerged for building the European communities can be encapsulated by the following propositions:

1. Integrate modestly in areas of 'low politics' in the first instance, but ensure that these are key strategic economic sectors (coal and steel for example).
2. Create a high authority without the distracting baggage of national interests to oversee the integration process and give it the ability to act as a sponsor of further integration.
3. The integration of particular economic sectors across nations will create functional pressures for the integration of related economic sectors. This momentum is likely to continue, especially with the guiding role played by the impresario high authority. The consequence is the gradual and progressive entangling of national economies.

4. Deeper integration will not only be sponsored by the high authority. Gradually, social interests, whose loyalty hitherto has been directed to national forms of authority, will begin to perceive a shift in the location of meaningful authority. They will transfer their loyalties and redirect their activities accordingly because they seek the most effective route for the fulfilment of their material interests. These interests become vested in the European system as the new supranational European framework begins to deliver.
5. Deepening economic integration will create the need for further European institutionalization as more expansive integration will require greater regulatory complexity.
6. In other words, political integration is a more or less inevitable side-effect of economic integration.
7. It follows that this gradual economic integration accompanied by a degree of supranational institutionalization is an effective route to the creation of a long-term system of peace in Europe.

The extent to which this 'Community method' could be directly attributable to Jean Monnet's thinking is debatable, and indeed there is much discussion about whether Monnet should be thought of as a federalist, a functionalist or as a hybrid of the two (Burgess, 1989; Holland, 1996a). Monnet appears to have been most in favour of sectoral functional organizations such as the ECSC and Euratom. Consequently, the dominant role established by the EEC within the first decade of the Communities' existence would not have appealed. In spite of this, his biographer makes a strong claim to suggest that Monnet should be regarded as the 'father of the Community' (Duchêne, 1994: 392–404). His 'method was quite consciously to switch the landscape in which conflict was viewed in order to break out of a current impasse and release a new course of events' (Duchêne, 1994: 375). It also involved the instigation of dynamic processes so that the momentum of profound transformation was never lost. This logic of what Monnet called 'dynamic disequilibrium' was clearly present in the Schuman Declaration of 9 May 1950 - the foundation for the ECSC which was created by the 1951 Treaty of Paris. It is worth quoting from the Schuman Declaration at length:

> Europe will not be made all at once or according to a single plan. It will be built through concrete achievements which first create a *de facto* solidarity. The coming together of the nations of Europe requires the elimination of the age-old opposition of France and Germany. Any action which must be taken in the first place must concern these two countries. The French Government proposes that action be taken immediately on *one limited but decisive point*. It proposes that Franco–

German production of coal and steel as a whole be placed under a common High Authority, within a framework open to the participation of the other countries of Europe. *The pooling of coal and steel production should immediately provide for the setting up of common foundations for economic development as a first step in the federation of Europe* ... The setting up of this powerful productive unit, open to all countries willing to take part and bound ultimately to provide all the member countries with the basic elements of industrial production on the same terms, *will lay a true foundation for their economic unification.*
(cited in Weigall and Stirk, 1992: 58–9, emphasis added)

It was very clear that the architects of post-war integration had in mind, as their ultimate aim, some form of political unity among states on the European continent – or at the very least a settlement to provide for the integration of Western Germany into the West European mainstream and to prevent a return to Franco–German conflict (see Duchêne, 1994: Chs 6–7). This was to be achieved less by grand design and more by stealth. Political unity and, therefore, peace would be the ultimate consequence of economic enmeshment. But this would not happen without the creation of *purposeful* institutions. These should be designed with the specific intention of guiding the integration process. Supranational institutions would also develop into repositories of knowledge to ensure the continuation of integrative momentum and the durability of the integration achievement. For Monnet, institutions could embody and solidify ideas into the realm of real politics and thereby promote real and lasting change (Holland, 1996a: 98).

Nevertheless, it is rather too easy to read the events after 1951 in terms of the successful implementation of the Monnet–Schuman strategy. The six-year gap between the Treaties of Paris and Rome might be viewed as the definitive peak of the expansive logic of integration as the narrowly, based ECSC pre-empted the somewhat broader EEC. Moreover, the longer-term transition from common market to putative monetary union, with the attendant institutionalization and 'drift' of governance functions to the European level, could also be understood in these terms. Others would be quick to point out the evidence for hard-nosed intergovernmentalism in the process. For instance, Desmond Dinan has attributed the Schuman declaration to 'narrowly-defined national interest' (Dinan, 1994: 10) and the Franco–German trade-off is as easily read as a classic intergovernmental bargain in the context of emerging American dominance of the world system. From this perspective, the likes of Monnet were playing typical games of power politics, but employing the fashionable rhetoric of supranationalism and European unity. Yet an alternative reading would argue that the strategic manipulation of material and/or national interests was the only way to set about integrating the economies and polities of Western Europe. Neither of these readings appeals to idealist sentiment. Also schemes of constitutional/functional creatively could not achieve this end without latching onto and engaging with the preferences of self-interested actors.

This is an important and on-going debate and to take sides in this discussion is to adopt a particular theoretical stance as well as to favour a particular interpretation of certain historical events. However, the point to be made here concerns the undisputed existence of linkages and overlaps between (a) the political discourses and actions of the 'Europeanizing elites' of the early 1950s, (b) the processes they initiated and managed and (c) the dominant academic explanations that developed.

Neofunctionalist premises

It should already be clear that neofunctionalism arose in a set of particularly extraordinary political circumstances and it cannot really be evaluated without recognition of that fact. It is also the case that neofunctionalism was the child of a particular social scientific moment. Like Deutsch's transactionalism and Etzioni's sociological approach to unification, neofunctionalism was born amidst the behavioural revolution in (American) political science. The behavioural movement directed scholarship towards the analysis of political behaviour and, therefore, closer to the study of political processes than earlier forms of political analysis which had been heavily institutional and constitutional in their focus (Eulau, 1963; Kavanagh, 1983; Sanders, 1995). The behavioural prospectus for the analysis of these processes was associated with the growing impulse to render the study of social phenomena more 'scientific'. This meant that theories were devices for generating testable hypotheses and that theoretical evaluation would be bound up with the extent to which research driven by the theory in question produced a depiction of 'reality' that confirmed or denied the hypotheses. The development of neofunctionalist theorizing from the late 1950s through to the early 1970s needs to be understood in terms of this broad intellectual location and the self-image of the approach contributed much to its eventual rejection by some of its key practitioners.

Neofunctionalist ideas emerged most clearly in the work of Ernst Haas. His book, *The Uniting of Europe*, first published in 1958 (Haas, 1958, 1968), was a theoretically informed study of the early years of the ECSC. This was followed by Leon Lindberg's *The Political Dynamics of European Economic Integration* (Lindberg, 1963) and Haas's own *Beyond the Nation-State* (Haas, 1964), along with a series of important articles and papers throughout the 1960s that together refined and embellished the original neofunctionalist theoretical prospectus. As its name suggests, this approach to integration drew on earlier functionalism, albeit in a spirit of friendly critique and with some highly significant deviation. Perhaps the main departure from earlier functionalist approaches to international order was what neofunctionalists saw as the reinstatement of political *agency* into the integration process. The driving motivation that would lead ultimately to post-national political communities was not just the technocratic 'automaticity' suggested by Mitrany's functionalism (although this did play a role). Rather, the process would be sponsored and enacted by purposeful actors pursuing their own self-interest. Looking back on the earliest statement of his theoretical approach to integration, Haas suggested that

> [the] ECSC experience has spawned a theory of international integration by indirection, by trial and error, by miscalculation on the part of the actors desiring integration, by manipulation of elite social forces on the part of small groups of pragmatic administrators and politicians in the setting of a vague but permissive public opinion. 'Functionalism' and 'incrementalism' rather than 'federalism' and 'comprehensive planning' are key terms used in describing the theory.
>
> (Haas, 1968: xii)

The emphasis on actors and their (often haphazard) interaction was illustrative of neofunctionalists' emphasis on integration in terms of *process* rather than outcomes. The process emerged from a complex web of actors pursuing their interests within a pluralist political environment.

Thus, a second assumption was that politics is a group-based activity. Neofunctionalism's appearance coincided with the development of pluralism in political science. In many ways, neofunctionalism can be read as a pluralist theory. This is explicitly acknowledged as such by Lindberg (1963: 9). Pluralist political science explores the politics of diversity and so has tended to view society as composed of a multiplicity of interests that configure themselves into discernible groups. Politics becomes more or less the competition between different groups for input into decision-making and influence over policy outcomes (see Alford and Friedland, 1985: Chs 1–6; Dunleavy and O'Leary, 1987: Ch. 2). In the pluralist polity, the state is subject to the competing demands of these groups. For some pluralists, public policy is defined as the state's synthesis of these demands. For others, it reflects the interests of the most powerful social groups over the state. The key to pluralism, though, is its rejection of straightforward elite–mass depictions of society.

This leads to a further supposition. Early neofunctionalism imagined the transplantation of the pluralist polity from the national to the supranational level. As Heathcote (1975) points out, neofunctionalism was built around the proposition that an international society of states can acquire the procedural characteristics of a domestic political system. The interested actor and group-based politics assumptions meant that neofunctionalists held that the industrialized, pluralistic and bureaucratic nature of modern Europe ensured the inevitable presence of self-interested groups. The aggregation of the actions of these groups created patterns of behaviour that would come to constitute a system. Action by such groups would be self-regarding and goal-driven; it would not be motivated by idealistic zeal in pursuit of the common good: '[t]here is no common good other than that perceived through the interest-tinted lenses worn by the international actors' (Haas, 1964: 35). It follows that patterns of integration would become apparent in changed behaviour on the part of groups. Most obviously, integrative processes would alter the attitudes and strategies of interest groups seeking to influence policy outcomes. Perceptions by these groups of shifts in the *loci* of authority and power would be accompanied by patterns of loyalty transference where groups ceased to direct their activity towards national governments and would look to the developing supranational arena. It could also be the case that groups 'may change their political organization and tactics in order to gain access to, and to influence, such new central decision-making centers as may be developing' (Lindberg, 1963: 9). This suggests that groups might not only change their 'loyalties', but that they might also 'transnationalize' their organizational form. So the Europeanzation of the polity would also be evident in the appearance of Europe-wide interest associations.

For these changes to transpire, it was important that the institutions should be qualitatively different from those associated with a traditional intergovernmental organization. The new region-level institutions would require direct access to societal groups. There would need to be mechanisms in place to bypass the traditional gatekeeping role of national governments if the important dialogue between interests and the new institutions was to take place and thereby generate integrative processes and outcomes.

Haas's work clearly envisaged the supranational polity as a facet of modernity, as a stage beyond nationhood and, therefore, very much in tune with the trends in mid-twentieth century political life:

> The supranational scheme of government at the regional level bears a
> very striking resemblance to the prevailing nature of government at the
> level of the industrial nation in everything but constitutional
> terminology ... [It] seems to be the appropriate regional counterpart

to the national state which no longer feels capable of realizing welfare aims within its own narrow borders, which has made its peace with the fact of interdependence in an industrial and egalitarian age.

(Haas, 1964: 71)

For Haas, the supranational policy style was a genuine advance on both old modes of national governance *and* what he saw as their international corollaries: intergovernmentalism, confederation and federalism (Haas, 1964). Recent writers have tried to reclaim the idea of supranationality on behalf of largely intergovernmental patterns of behaviour (Keohane and Hoffmann, 1991), but it remains clear that Haas had something rather different in mind. His early work presented integration as bound up with types of politics that broke away from traditional patterns of international interaction.

This links to another facet of Haas's approach. In spite of its friendly critique of Mitrany's work, a further major assumption of neofunctionalism was essentially functionalist: that key issues were not those of traditional high politics, but matters of the satisfaction of welfare and material needs. This assumption was clearly present in some of Haas's work. Technocracy meant that government was increasingly becoming a set of 'managerial' tasks rather than actions driven by the grand narratives of particular ideologies:

Ideology, then, is still with us. But it manifests itself in religious, ethnic and educational policy confrontations rather than in the realm of the economy or the large issues of defense and foreign policy ... Ideology is muted to the extent that cleavages in the national populations cut across contexts rather than clustering in firm groups united on a variety of issues.

(Haas, 1963: 69)

So, in addition to the notion of the transferability of pluralist political procedures, neofunctionalists also tended to align themselves with the view that supranational decision-making would acquire the increasingly technocratic attributes of its domestic equivalent. The term 'technocracy' is traceable to the period shortly after the First World War, although the idea had its immediate ancestors in nineteenth-century utopian socialism and in early sociological analysis. Strictly speaking, technocracy is used to denote rule by those who control the means of production, or more precisely those who are endowed with the necessary expertise to understand the complex machinery of the capitalist mode of production. Technocracy is, above all, a way of theorizing government and decision-making processes in advanced industrial economies. In early integration theory, the idea that technocratic decision-making prevailed was an altogether more benign assumption. In the 1950s and early 1960s it was part and parcel of the influential 'end of ideology' thesis (Bell, 1962; Lipset, 1960). This view held that public policy-making consisted predominantly of the 'administration of things', rather than government according to ideological credo. Government was seen increasingly as a managerial process that utilized rationalistic, scientific and (perhaps above all) non-dogmatic methods.

Neofunctionalist reasoning

Building on these assumptions and confronted by the unfolding empirical evidence supplied by the ECSC after 1951 and the European Economic Community (EEC) and Euratom after 1957, neofunctionalist scholars laid down the premises of a framework for the study of regional integration. The basic argument of neofunctionalist logic went something like the following. Two or more countries agree to work for integration in a given economic sector (sector *a*). To accomplish this task more effectively, they agree to appoint a supranational bureaucracy – a 'high authority' to use the parlance of the time – to oversee operations. While the integration of sector *a* achieves some of the supposed benefits, the full advantage of integration will not be achieved unless cognate economic sectors are also drawn into the integrative web. In any case, the integration of *a* creates functional linkage pressures for related sectors *b* and *c* to become part of the game. There are two other more or less automatic processes in the neofunctionalist model. First, economic integration automatically generates an increased level of transactions between actors within the integrating region. Second, as we have seen, because of the essential group characteristic of politics, there is a tendency for new interest organizations to form at the regional level. This is particularly true of producer groups (for example, employers federations and trade unions) whose interests shift (and indeed arise) as new levels of integration are accomplished. Meanwhile, the high authority becomes a key sponsor of further integration. Thus, it develops strategies (corresponding to its own emerging interests) to accomplish the twin goals of deeper economic integration in an expanding range of economic sectors and the increased institutionalization of authority at the regional level. To some extent, the high authority achieves this by acting as a constant advocate of the advantages of integration and by pointing to the relationships that exist between sectors *a*, *b* and *c*. But, the high authority is also entrepreneurial in other ways. For example, it may sponsor the emergence of regional-level interest associations as a way of generating allegiances to itself. Thus, at the regional level, there exist both processes of functional automaticity and actions of deliberate integration-seeking agents.

Neofunctionalists also had a theory of how these processes impact upon the domestic political processes in member polities. Here the core neofunctionalist assumptions became central. The benefits of integration would become apparent to domestically located interest groups who would lobby their governments accordingly, since integration would be promising to serve their material interests. This would have an impact upon the technocratically-minded state actors, who also would tend to become aware of the mechanisms of linkage and increased transaction emerging at the regional level. The net effect would be an increase in support for integration emanating from national political systems, combined with an increased propensity on the part of state actors to negotiate integrative agreements and to cede authority where necessary to regional-level institutions.

Leon Lindberg's careful elaboration of neofunctionalist hypotheses (Lindberg, 1963: Ch. 1) began with the view that certain conditions needed to prevail before processes of political integration could occur. Firstly, central (i.e. region-level) institutions and policies would have to be present. Secondly, these institutions should be assigned the capacity to initiate social and economic processes, thereby taking their remit well beyond the normal mandate of an international organization. Thirdly, the tasks assigned to the institutions should – recalling Monnet – be 'inherently expansive'. They would not be integrative unless they generated tensions that could only be resolved by further action and they should be capable of drawing more actors into their politics. Finally, the participant states would need to perceive some congruence between their interests and the project associated with the new institutions and common policies (Lindberg, 1963: 7–8). The last requirement reinforced the extent to which neofunctionalists saw the pursuit of interests as central to the integration process and challenges the view, often expressed in recent literature, that neofunctionalists had no conception of how national governments were involved in the integration process.

Spillover

Perhaps the most important (and most discussed) concept in the neofunctionalist armoury was the idea of 'spillover' which was used to depict the mechanisms supposedly driving processes of regional integration. Two recent observers suggest that spillover 'shouldered most of the burden of explaining change' in the neofunctionalist account (Caporaso and Keeler, 1995: 83). In Haas's original formulation (Haas, 1968, particularly 283–317), spillover referred to the way in which the creation and deepening of integration in one economic sector would create pressures for further economic integration within and beyond that sector, and greater authoritative capacity at the European level. Put simply, the spillover hypothesis maintained that the integration of the coal and steel sectors of a group of industrialized West European countries would yield substantial benefits for key economic actors. But the full integration of the coal and steel sectors would not be accomplished without integration in cognate sectors of the economy. An obvious example would be transport, where at least a modicum of coordination between member-state transport policies would be needed to facilitate the movement of raw materials, products and so on. In the second book-length contribution to neofunctionalism, Lindberg defined spillover as 'a situation in which a given action, related to a specific goal, creates a situation in which the original goal can be assured only by taking further actions, which in turn create a further condition and a need for more action and so forth' (1963: 10). As David Mutimer (1989) notes, this idea of spillover presupposed that member-state economies were reasonably interdependent *prior* to the initiation of the integration programme. Not only was integration seen as a positive sum outcome for all parties, but problems in one economic sector could not be remedied without recourse to action in other sectors. So, the logic of spillover was partly about the generation of the aforementioned 'expansive logic', where a greater range of economic functions were drawn into the integrative web. But there was also a logic of 'deepening' within the idea of spillover. A customs union among a group of states (i.e. a free trade area with common tariffs levied to outsiders) could operate with greater efficiency if the participant states tried to create stable exchange rate parities. Exchange rate coordination would further imply the need for wider cooperation in monetary policy (Caporaso and Keeler, 1995: 84). In short, and on the face of it, the processes of functional spillover can be used to explain the historical transition from ECSC to Economic and Monetary Union. As Carole Webb (1983: 19) notes, the expansive functional logic laid out by Haas and Lindberg reproduced the thinking of economists writing about international economic integration at the time. This thinking held that the decision to create a free trade area would generate pressures for the establishment of respectively a customs union, a common market and monetary union. This could culminate in total economic integration among the participant economies (Balassa, 1962). Progressive economic enmeshment would have institutional consequences. Deeper economic integration would require supranational regulatory capacity; *politics would follow economics*. This staged model of economic integration came under sustained scrutiny and criticism subsequently (El-Agraa, 1997), but again it is worth noting the linkages between neofunctionalist formulations and parallel developments in social scientific thinking.

Yet, Haas – like Monnet – came to understand that the automaticity of spillover in economics required a measure of political activism. It had to be given a push in the right direction (Tranholm-Mikkelsen, 1991: 5). Thus, economics had not (entirely) vanquished politics (Haas, 1968: xix) and the processes of functional spillover required direction and coordination from a higher authority. There were clear affinities between this idea and Monnet's stated aim of modelling the ECSC's High Authority on the French *Commisariat au Plan* (which Monnet headed for a period). This 'high-powered brains trust of civil servants' (Wright, 1989: 101) was charged with soliciting and absorbing the demands of economic interests and producing medium-term economic policy agendas for France. François Duchêne's careful discussion describes Monnet's comparison here as 'unsustainably crude' (Duchêne, 1994: 398), but the observation is worth making because it demonstrates both the significance of the post-war policy-making atmosphere to the processes of institutional design in early European integration and the close parallels between the functionalist–technocratic politics of the time and the new neofunctionalist theorizing. The high authority would be the primary source of what Jeppe Tranholm-Mikkelsen (1991) has helpfully called 'cultivated spillover'. Cultivated spillover describes the high authority's actions to upgrade the common interest of the various parties engaged in the new institutional setting. This brokering would allow genuinely progressive incursions into the realm of functional spillover. Haas (1961) argued that a group of states in an international organization will, if left to their own devices, bargain down to a lowest common denominator position. (This reasoning would now be challenged by International Relations theorists with an interest in the capacity of institutional settings to provide venues for trust and the low-risk acquisition of mutual gains (for example Keohane, 1989). In the context of European integration, a number of arguments in the literature could be mobilized to challenge Haas's position. For example, scholars of the EU's intergovernmental institutions tend to suggest that the Council of Ministers is rather more than a straightforward intergovernmental bargain based upon the clash of national self-interests (see Hayes-Renshaw and Wallace, 1996). More fundamentally perhaps, Fritz Scharpf's discussion of the 'joint decision trap' (Scharpf, 1988) suggests that even in a situation where unanimous agreement is required among parties for a policy innovation, the default position will always be the status quo which itself may not reflect any of the preferences of the negotiating parties, some of whom may wish to go still further backwards.)

Consequently, the creation of a high authority with genuine powers of initiation and definite autonomy from the member-states became a vital step in explaining why some communities integrated while others did not. What mattered most for the success of an integrative enterprise, according to Haas, was that the central institutions should be able to secure enough autonomy to escape the tendencies of states to dissolve international organizations once the preferences of those states had been met and/or the policy context had changed:

> There is no dependable, cumulative process of precedent formation leading to ever more community-oriented organizational behavior, unless the task assigned to the institution is inherently expansive, thus capable of overcoming the built-in autonomy of functional contexts and of surviving changes in the policy aims of the Member States.
>
> (Haas, 1961: 376)

It was also important to understand that some sectors contained more spillover potential than others. Haas made it clear that while specific tasks had to be chosen to initiate the dynamism of integration, these tasks had to be economically significant. They had to connect to felt needs and expectations. It was on these areas of functional low politics which had a day-to-day impact upon people's lives that integrative seeds could be scattered, rather than on big issues such as culture and defence (Haas, 1961). The emphasis on functional spillover allowed neofunctionalists to account for integration through technocratic means and for large systemic consequences to flow from uncontroversial decisions in the largely technocratic realm of 'low' politics. But the transition to political consequences and the extent to which spillover was an automatic and/or unidirectional dynamic required more elaborate thinking, and neofunctionalists refined their arguments on this matter quite significantly throughout the 1960s.

The emphasis tended to move away from functional spillover towards the dynamic momentum that emerged as actors engaged with and regenerated the integration process. Whereas Haas had tended to portray elite actors as largely bound by functional imperatives, Lindberg used empirical instances to describe how actors created political pressures for deeper integration as they became involved in the process. The change of emphasis was important, but it is probably overstating it to suggest that the idea of spillover thus became 'merely an organizing concept or hypothesis about the likelihood of integration when certain specified conditions are present' (Pentland, 1973: 119). Lindberg's discussion of the acceleration of the common market timetable in the first years of the EC placed great emphasis on the pivotal role of business associations – erstwhile sceptics about rapid deepening. Once investment decisions had been made on the presumption that the common market would become a reality, so those groups became prime movers in the creation of that forthcoming reality (1963: 130–131). Similar arguments reappeared in the late 1990s as British membership of EMU was thought more likely in the context of UK businesses planning for the existence of a Euro-zone, even if governments of the time were at best ambivalent about the enterprise. With key sectors of the economy behaving in anticipation of (and presumably lobbying for) a particular economic environment, elites would be directed to add their formal stamp of approval to the deepening of economic integration. As Reginald Harrison (1974: 83) notes, Lindberg's discussion resembled the Deutschian notion of feedback, where actions emerge in response to an input of information and where information is passed through the network to take account of the new actions (and so on). It also connected the spillover idea to acts of agency and to highly complex processes of socio-psychological change. Put more crudely, it conformed to the sociological rule stating that if enough people believe something to be true then that phenomenon will become a reality.

Phillippe Schmitter worked within the emerging neofunctionalist tradition to produce a more process-oriented view that placed the emphasis firmly upon the actors involved:

> the process whereby members of an integration scheme – agreed on some collective goals for a variety of motives but unequally satisfied with their attainment of these goals – attempt to resolve their dissatisfaction either by resorting to collaboration in another related sector (expanding the *scope* of their mutual commitment) or by intensifying their commitment to the original sector (increasing the *level* of their mutual commitment) or both.
>
> (Schmitter, 1969: 162, emphasis in original)

This took the emphasis far away from automatic or inevitable processes and sought instead to show how interest-driven actors could cultivate functional linkages to satisfy their goals. The retreat from functional automaticity arose in anticipation of some fairly obvious criticisms of neofunctionalists' views of spillover dynamics. Indeed, the importance of the concept to the whole neofunctionalist project made reflection upon spillover a central preoccupation of integration theorists throughout the late 1960s and early 1970s. The spillover hypothesis seemed to suggest that integration was a linear, progressive phenomenon; that once started, dynamics would be set in place to continue the momentum. This was certainly the argumentative thrust of the first two major studies (Haas, 1968; Lindberg, 1963) and there was certainly little evidence to suggest that the EC's institutional system could suddenly collapse. Yet, their theoretical predispositions alerted neofunctionalists to the emerging tensions between the unfolding reality of the EC experience and the predictive capacity of the Haas–Lindberg model.

These issues are dealt with more squarely in the next chapter, but it is worth noting how various ingenious adaptations to the spillover hypothesis emerged. Lindberg was the first to explore the idea that progress in integration could actually *deter* further integration. Integration could be a 'source of stress among states' (Lindberg, 1966) as encroachments upon governments' competencies raised the political stakes within and between member-states. This connects to a general rethink from the late 1960s about the way in which neofunctionalists had seemingly underestimated the importance of nationalism as a prevailing sentiment in European politics (Haas, 1968: xv–xxx; Haas, 1971, and see Chapter 4 for greater detail). It led Lindberg and (particularly) Schmitter to work very hard in an attempt to rescue the idea of spillover and thus to preserve many of the central claims of neofunctionalism. The concept of 'spill-back' was a significant component of Lindberg and Stuart Scheingold's analysis in *Europe's Would-Be Polity* (Lindberg and Scheingold, 1970). It was defined as one of four possible transformative outcomes that could occur within the boundaries of treaty commitments (the others were 'forward linkage' – which replaced the idea of spillover – 'equilibrium' or the routinization of a task, and 'output failure' – situations where systems fail to process an agreement). Spill-back was defined as 'an outcome pattern which is characterized by a decrease in sectoral scope or institutional capacities or both' (Lindberg and Scheingold, 1970: 199). It loomed large in this account because it seemed to explain some of the hiccups faced by the European integration process during the 1960s. For instance, Lindberg and Scheingold explored the coal sector and concluded that after 1958, as coal production began to produce large surpluses and so infringed some of the emerging supranational rules, the ECSC appeared less relevant to the member-states' perceptions of their interests in the coal sector. Consequently, the high authority was unable to recultivate support. Thus '[s]ectoral rules were no longer regularly followed and more and more the member states sought to deal with coal problems unilaterally' (1970: 199). Schmitter went somewhat further and in a lengthy and complex paper (Schmitter, 1971) sought to reintroduce the idea of spillover as one of a number of possible 'actor integration strategies' that might emerge in the context of 'decisional cycles'. These take actors beyond normal and uncontroversial patterns of behaviour and interaction (the so-called 'zone of indifference'). For Schmitter, a dynamic theory of integration should focus upon these actor strategies and should aim to predict circumstances in which they might arise. Spillover may be the most efficient strategic route to the creation of a new political community, but actor strategies are likely to involve a mixture of 'spillover' with

Table 3.1 *Alternative actor strategies*

Strategy	Definition
Spillover	Increase both the scope and level of an actor's commitment concomitantly.
Spill-around	Increase only the scope while holding the level of authority constant or within the zone of indifference.
Buildup	Agree to increase the decisional autonomy or capacity of joint institutions, but deny them entrance into new issue areas.
Retrench	Increase the level of joint deliberation, but withdraw the institutions.
Muddle-about	Let the regional bureaucrats debate. Suggest and expostulate on a variety of issues, but decrease their actual capacity to allocate values.
Spill-back	Retreat on level and scope of authority, perhaps returning to the status quo prior to initiation of integration.
Encapsulate	Respond to crisis by marginal modifications.

Source: Schmitter 1971: 242.

alternative options. Schmitter labelled these 'spill-around', 'buildup', 'retrench', 'muddle-about', 'spill-back' and 'encapsulate' (see Table 3.1).

Schmitter also agreed with Lindberg that increased joint decision-making induces costs and that this may lead to the controversialization of that decision-making (the 'politicization hypothesis', Schmitter, 1971: 243). The shift to treating actor strategies as the central point of investigation enabled neofunctionalists to remain within the broad remit of their perspective, but allowed them to be more adaptive to changing circumstances within the EC. The social science favoured by neofunctionalists clearly held that theories stand or fall on their ability to explain empirical phenomena and the furious theoretical work of neofunctionalists from the late 1960s (of which more in Chapter 4) was testimony to the continued commitment to the achievement of a general theory of integration using the European experience as its laboratory.

Loyalties

To be accomplished, political spillover – in whatever form it took – would require a process of loyalty transference. The concept of loyalty was central to Haas's original definition of political integration (see also Chapter 1):

> Political integration is the process whereby political actors in several distinct national settings are persuaded to shift their loyalties, expectations and political activities toward a new center, whose institutions possess or demand jurisdiction over the pre-existing national states.
>
> (Haas, 1968: 16)

Haas initially defined 'loyalties' in terms of the attributes of political community, so that a population is 'loyal to a set of symbols and institutions when it habitually and predictability over long periods obeys the injunctions of their authority and turns to them for the satisfaction of important expectations' (1968: 5). Political community was defined as 'a condition in which specific groups and individuals show more loyalty to their central political institutions than to any other political authority, in a specific period of time and in a definable geographic space' (Haas, 1968: 5). Here neofunctionalist notions of process and outcome came together, with the latter defined very much in terms of a pluralist political community.

Loyalty transference was a long-standing aspect of functionalist reasoning about integration (see Chapter 2). Here the establishment of sector-specific functional organizations would lead to a movement of mass allegiances away from established modes of authority as essential human needs came to be systematically and efficiently addressed by these new entities. Neofunctionalists thought more in terms of the transfer of (significant) group and elite loyalties and less in terms of cognitive shifts among mass publics (Lodge, 1978), but it was still a vital component in the process of transition to a new form of political community. A key question for neofunctionalists was the problem of the mechanisms through which this would occur. Juliet Lodge (1978) teases out several assumptions about loyalty transference among writers in the neofunctionalist tradition. Firstly, she spots the assumption that if an organization provides for a given welfare need, then this will automatically register in the consciousness of the beneficiaries. Neofunctionalists, according to Lodge, suppose not only that the agency in question is now the agent of delivery, but that a positive sum game clearly emerges. But it is also plausible that new agencies such as the EC might remain relatively invisible to recipients of their largesse. It may be that, contrary to the reality of emergent supranational governance, actors continue to assume that their needs are *still* catered for by national agencies. If this is so, then loyalty transference will not occur in the way envisaged. Lodge's point is that neofunctionalists, especially in their early work, tended to rely heavily on highly rationalist and utilitarian notions of how agents operate. This in turn tended to more or less factor enduring political loyalties out of the analysis and to overestimate the extent to which faceless apolitical agencies could be capable of commanding loyalty. Lodge argues, using the contractarian language of liberal political theory, that these cannot be viable premises for the creation of political communities. Communities have arisen historically where loyalties are owed to an identifiable sovereign or to concrete symbols rather than to abstract ideas (Lodge, 1978: 239).

In many ways, neofunctionalism's 'loyalty problem' was an issue about politics, or more precisely about the treatment of 'politics' and political identities as residual to the integration process. The appearance of nationalism – in the form of French President Charles de Gaulle – in the EC system in the mid-1960s posed substantial problems for a theoretical framework that assumed government to be a technocratic rather than an ideological exercise and which seemed to predict the withering away of traditional allegiances to the nation-state as the logic of integration revealed itself to key societal and élite actors. The various refinements of ideas about actor strategies in an institutionalized environment were bold attempts to deal with this problem. Additionally, Haas's preface to the second edition of *The Uniting of Europe* and other pieces written in the mid to late 1960s (notably Haas, 1967) paid substantial attention to the challenges posed by the phenomenon of de Gaulle to the neofunctionalist project.

Haas argued that integration inspired by functionalist logic would be less likely to ignite the political imagination than integration led by a 'dramatic actor' articulating a unifying vision with the backing of charismatic authority. But this would also be vulnerable to reverse unless there emerged a consensus between governmental and non-governmental elites. If economic elites also sought 'dramatic political' integration outcomes then integration would occur smoothly, provided that the shared aims were supportive of community building. If the aims of political and non-governmental elites diverged, then there would be a potential for conflict or for integration to fail. In circumstances where government and non-governmental elites share incremental economic aims, integration will follow a path largely in line with the original speculations of neofunctionalists. From the vantage point of the late 1960s and in the wake of de Gaulle's disruption of the EC system, it was instances of conflict that were interesting and which required explanation. This was an important challenge because Haas reasoned that widespread consensus could not be expected to occur often, at least within pluralistic societies of the West European type. Pluralism, by definition, breeds conflict and the progress of integration would rely on the balance of goals among elites and key groups (Haas, 1968: xxv). So, greater reflection on the nature and implications of pluralism posed awkward problems for neofunctionalists. Haas also refused to abandon the view that technocratic thinking and procedures were conducive to integration, but came to recognize how this was a fragile basis for the advance of an integrative process, especially where the consummation of that process required loyalty transference:

> Pragmatic interest politics is its own worst enemy. The politician and the businessman who have abandoned an interest in high politics and devote themselves only to the maximisation of their daily welfare are compelled by virtue of that very concern to make concessions to another actor who forces him to choose so as to sacrifice welfare. Pragmatic interests, because they are pragmatic and not reinforced with deep ideological or philosophical commitment, are ephemeral. Just because they are weakly held they can be readily scrapped. And a political process that is built and projected from pragmatic interests, therefore, is bound to be a frail process susceptible to reversal. And so integration can turn into disintegration.
>
> (Haas, 1968: xxiii)

The challenges to neofunctionalism that had been exemplified by de Gaulle's attempts to alter radically the trajectory of European integration were not, in Haas's view, fatal. Rather the socio-economic and political bases of the integration project may have been flimsier than had been apparent in the late 1950s. In addition, neofunctionalists needed to deal with some of the rigidities in their approach and 'to build a theory of integration supple enough to take account of . . . disintegrative phenomena' (Haas, 1967: 316).

Beyond Europe: neofunctionalism as a general theory of regional integration

The partial re-evaluation described above sought to deal with particular questions related to the neofunctionalist idea of 'loyalty' and to the empirical experience of the EC in the 1960s. But they also emerged in the context of a broadening of the remit of neofunctionalist theories of integration to deal with analogous processes elsewhere in the world. Neofunctionalism arose as an attempt to explain the dynamic processes of integration in Europe, but Europe was seen very much as a case study of the sorts of processes that could operate in *any* regional setting. The books by Haas and Lindberg were clearly about the experiences of 'the Six' in Western Europe, and the immediate theoretical lessons to be drawn were about the trajectory of *European* integration within the context of the ECSC and the EC. Haas was perhaps rather more concerned to elaborate ideal types and general propositions than Lindberg (Lindberg, 1963: 5), but the attempt to expand the analytical reach of neofunctionalism occurred later. In some ways this was an inevitable development of the social scientific attributes of neofunctionalism which led it to generate hypotheses for wider application beyond the single European case study (Pentland, 1981: 557). The 'theory' applied to one case would become little more than a sophisticated description of that one case. Also, one of the distinguishing features of neofunctionalist analysis (as opposed to functionalism) was its claim that integration could take place within delimited territorial regions. Functionalism was primarily a theory of *post-territorial* governance, whereas neofunctionalism was an early theory of *regionalism*. Indeed, there did appear to be real signs from the early 1960s that regional integration was developing into a world-wide trend with serious proposals under way for the formation of free trade areas in the Pacific, Latin America, North America and elsewhere (Fawcett, 1995). Given neofunctionalism's apparently close fit with integrative trends in Western Europe, it was obvious that as a new International Relations literature on the new regionalizing trends emerged, it should explore the capacity of neofunctionalism to make predictions beyond its European home domain. Indeed, much of it was written by those who had cut their neofunctionalist teeth in the study of European integration (Barrera and Haas, 1968; Haas, 1961; Haas, 1967; Haas and Schmitter, 1964; Nye, 1971; Schmitter, 1969).

The question was first systematically addressed by Haas in an influential essay entitled 'International Integration: the European and the Universal Process' (Haas, 1961). Haas saw the problem in both intellectual and normative terms. The intellectual puzzle concerned the implications of the European integration process for elsewhere. Would it be imitated or would it generate transregional spillovers leading other clusters of states to embark upon projects of integration? In normative terms, Haas supposed the spread of integration schemes to be a good thing. Regional blocs had the potential to be 'islands of cooperation' that might build a bridge towards universal peace. The issue for Haas was twofold: what 'background conditions' could be said to be conducive for integration and, more specifically, what lessons could be drawn from the European experience of the ECSC and the early EEC? He identified three background conditions that made for successful integration (and which were consistent with neofunctionalist theorizing): pluralistic social structures, substantial economic and industrial development and common ideological patterns among participating units. These all existed in Western Europe and the European experience also taught that the momentum for integration could be maintained where supranational agencies were given tasks that facilitated the upgrading of common interests. Additionally, rapid integration and maximum spillover potential would occur in situations where mass interests were implicated in the specific tasks selected for the integration scheme, and particularly where those tasks dealt with the solution of imperfect compromises at the national level. Finally, the control of the integration process by rational, urban industrial elites pursuing their interests would yield most in the way of positive integrative outcomes (Haas, 1961: 377–8).

Haas concluded that integration in other regional contexts or universally through the United Nations would be seriously limited. Progress to political community would be unlikely because of the thinner spread of core preconditions. This in turn prompted a tentative generalization about integration: 'European integration will proceed at a much more rapid pace than universal integration. Further, other regions with strongly varying environmental factors are unlikely to imitate successfully the European example' (Haas, 1961: 389). Yet it was also possible that locally specific conditions (or 'functional equivalents' to the background conditions in Western Europe) might be sufficient for the generation of integrative potential in other regions. This left Haas in rather ambiguous position regarding the wider applicability of the neofunctionalist theory. It was this. If core background conditions could be identified, then it would be relatively easy to read off the integrative potential of any region. But if background conditions could be regionally specific, then attempts to generalize on a transregional basis would be relatively meaningless. It might also follow that patterns of integration would be regionally specific and the logical conclusion might be that any attempt to theorize integration as a general phenomenon might be misplaced. In essence, scholars might have been attempting to generate common theories out of radically distinct dependent variables. That is, they might actually be trying to explain different things.

The question of background conditions became a major preoccupation of neofunctionalist attempts to develop an early theoretical framework for the study of what would now be called 'comparative regionalism' (Pentland, 1973: Ch. 5). One view was to argue that integration was a more or less inevitable by-product of modernity. As societies gradually industrialized and urbanized, so trends that culminated in international political integration were set in motion. While neofunctionalists might have been sympathetic to elements of this modernity premise, their concern with political agency led them to reject the more linear or deterministic elements of such claims, even if the question of the 'automaticity' of the integration process was still important to them. The question about background conditions was formalized by Haas and Schmitter (1964) who, prompted by the emergence of proposals for a Latin American Free Trade Area (LAFTA), became interested in the background conditions necessary for the generation of spillovers from economic integration to political unity.

Table 3.2 *The Haas–Schmitter model*

Background conditions	*Conditions at the time of economic union*	*Process conditions*
• size of unit	• possible governmental purposes	• decision-making style
• rate of transactions		
		• rate of growth of transactions
• pluralism	• powers and functions of new region-level institutions	
• elite complementarity		• adaptability of governmental/ private actors

Source: Derived from Haas and Schmitter (1964).

Haas and Schmitter devised a three-stage model to allow for the investigation of conditions during the integration process. Establishing the status of the various conditions would allow for predictions to be made about the prospects for 'automatic politicization'. The model is represented in Table 3.2.

Each of these sets of conditions could be evaluated in turn and aggregate judgements could then be made for each of the categories, leading to a final judgement on the chances of 'automatic politicization' in any given regional scheme. Haas and Schmitter performed this evaluation for ten contemporary regional integration schemes and concluded that only in the EEC were the chances of 'automatic politicization' good. In Latin America during the mid 1960s, background conditions may have been partially conducive, but a mixture of ambiguous governmental purposes and weak powers for the putative regional institutions were suggestive of minimal advance beyond a simple free trade area (Haas and Schmitter, 1964: 720).

The Haas–Schmitter refinements began to develop ways in which phenomena conducive or antithetical to integration could be measured. However, they continued to assume that integration occurred in all cases through the politicization of technical–economic tasks via mechanisms of spillover. Indeed, subsequent attempts to develop criteria for the operationalization of the various 'condition variables' (Barrera and Haas, 1968; Schmitter, 1969) were explicitly geared to establishing a comparative basis for the study of political spillover dynamics. On the other hand, as Joseph Nye (1965) pointed out, spillover might not be the only integrative dynamic and so looking for conditions conducive to 'politicization' might be at best misplaced and at worst Euro-centric. Indeed, Nye argued that spillover was a limited explanatory tool, even in the West European case where it appeared to account for the formative years of the ECSC, but was less successful at explaining the politics of the EC in the mid-1960s. Integration might be 'delivered' by other means. In a series of contributions from the mid-1960s, Nye developed the idea that background conditions are indeed important, but that they must be subdivided into structural and perceptual categories (Nye, 1971a, 1971b). Structural conditions (in classic neofunctionalist mode) included the extent to which the units (states) in an integration scheme were symmetrical, the capacity of member-states to respond and adapt, levels of pluralism within member-states and the degree to which the values of economic policy elites were complementary). Nye's discussion of perceptual conditions added new layers to neofunctionalist discussions of agency by introducing the importance of subjective interpretations of objective context. The three mentioned by Nye (1971) were potentially powerful and plausible explanations of the capacity of integration schemes to proceed. The first was perceptions of the equity of the distribution of benefits deriving from integration. Widespread understandings of integration as less than positive sum would be a basis for nationalist retrenchment. Politicians like de Gaulle might dramatize inequalities and thereby retard integrative progress. Secondly, Nye argued that actors' perceptions of their external situation were important. Strategies to deal with (perceived) opportunities and threats would arise and these might be counter-integrative. Advances in integration could be explained by common perceptions of external threat combined with agreement about appropriate policy strategies. Finally, if the costs of integration were seen to be either low or exportable, then the chances of deeper integration were advanced. Nye (1965) also argued that 'accidental' historical factors needed to be taken into account. The question to be posed here was whether Western Europe was somehow special as an instance of integration.

Nye's work – while sympathetic to neofunctionalist reasoning – drew on some of the more violent critics of neofunctionalism such as Stanley Hoffmann (see Chapter 4). Moreover, his refinements in particular suggested that many of the standard tools of neofunctionalist theorizing might be of severely limited use in explaining not only changing patterns of European economic governance in the 1950s and 1960s, but also experiments in regional integration among any group of states at any time. The debate about comparative regionalism, combined with the empirical difficulties posed by the EC experience in the 1960s, highlighted some of the core dilemmas faced by neofunctionalist integration theory. As the next chapter shows, these became ever more apparent to the main 'integration theorists'.

Conclusions

Neofunctionalism was (indeed still is) important. As a theoretical prospectus, it contemplated the replacement of power politics with a new supranational style, built around a core procedural consensus which resembled that of most domestic political systems. This was a bold claim for an international theory to make and is one that struck at the heart of the realist emphasis on the perpetuity of power politics. As will become evident in subsequent chapters, these claims prompted substantial criticism that produced a strong rival intergovernmentalist alternative to neofunctionalism. Like functionalism before it, the neofunctionalist idea of the withering away of a power-based states system was open to two sorts of criticism. The first was alleged implausibility. It was argued that the empirical evidence pointed overwhelmingly to the continued relevance of states and that there was no reason to suppose that this state of affairs would change. The second emerged from a more ethical-normative set of concerns. Here the argument was that nation-states are the best vessels available to mankind for the protection of certain sorts of key values (such as justice, liberty). To dissolve the states system would be to jeopardize those freedoms. Nonetheless, neofunctionalists did have the advantage of offering a plausible account of the moves to political integration that seemed to be taking place in Western Europe. The progressive institutionalization of the EC system was difficult to account for in the terms of orthodox International Relations perspectives and, if nothing else, neofunctionalists revealed the guiding logic of some of the main protagonists in the post-war uniting of Europe.

Chapter 4

Backlash, Critique and Contemplation

It is probably true to say that the early statements of neofunctionalism came to be regarded as important largely thanks to a mixture of hindsight and the continued efforts of neofunctionalists themselves to perfect and refine their theory. Indeed, it is striking – and somewhat disarming – to examine the contemporary reception of these first contributions, not least because this shows how the evolution of an accepted narrative about the development of a theoretical discourse is often related to subsequent read-ings of its evolution. This seems particularly the case with the early theoretical contributions to EC/EU studies. To illustrate this point, reviewers of *Beyond the Nation-State* (Haas, 1964) tended to read the book as a contribution to the *empirical* study of international organizations in general and the International Labour Organization in particular. One contemporary reviewer found the book's conceptual-theoretical compo-nents to be largely unimportant, even though it was clear that Haas understood himself as importing functionalist concepts into the social scientific mainstream and exposing them to systems theory, functional sociology, pluralist political science and the like: 'he apparently enjoys the higher altitudes of theorising ... Going into orbit produces exhilaration – but also weightlessness. Haas is a weighty man when he has his feet on the ground' (Claude, 1965: 1012). Earlier, a reviewer of *The Uniting of Europe* (Haas, 1958) had described the sections of the book containing the earliest neofunctionalist theorizing as 'ponderous' (Kitzinger, 1962) and this review, like others, read the book as an *empirical* study of the ECSC rather than a major *theoretical* contribution. The leading British International Relations journal of the time was particularly acerbic about Haas's intervention: 'European unity is a subject which defies all attempts to make it interesting' (Younger, 1959: 92). Lindberg's *The Political Dynamics of European Economic Integration* (Lindberg, 1963) – now recognized as a major statement of the neofunctionalist case – was not reviewed by the *Journal of Common Market Studies*, and sat inconspicuously among a list of 'books received'.

By the early 1970s, however, neofunctionalism was widely perceived as a theoretical paradigm with its own research programme. This was partly because of the formalization of some relatively loose arguments about 'integration theory' into a cohesive set of neofunctionalist propositions, but also because of the emergence of unapologetically state-centred work on the EC which defined neofunctionalist work as its coherent 'enemy'. This chapter reviews the interaction between this intergovernmentalism and neofunctionalism, reviews the appearance of alternative approaches to European unity and examines the ways in which neofunctionalists grappled with the difficulties of their world view.

The intergovernmentalist backlash

The last chapter noted the ways in which neofunctionalists sought to deal with empirical challenges to their account of the politicization of technocratically driven, post-national enmeshment. In particular, observers of the EC from the early 1960s were able to note not only a slowdown of integrative momentum, but also the reassertion of nationalist sentiment at elite level in West European politics. The pivotal figure in the nationalist resurgence was Charles de Gaulle, the French President since the inauguration of the Fifth Republic in 1958. De Gaulle's interaction with the Communities was both acrimonious and disruptive. The French President was largely responsible for the vetoing of the British membership application in 1963 and Gaullist objections to proposals for institutional reform lay at the heart of the so-called 'empty chair crisis' when France withdrew from EC business for a portion of 1965. The 'Luxembourg Compromise' of 1966 brought the French back into the Community fold. By common consent this facilitated national vetoes in the Council of Ministers in circumstances where 'vital national interests' were deemed to be at stake. The accord is usually read as a moment when the fundamental premises of the integration experiment were renegotiated heavily in favour of the member-states and when the principle of *intergovernmentalism* trumped that of *supranationalism*. De Gaulle could not be dismissed simply as an aberrant or anachronistic throwback, or even as a representative of a purely French experiment in pompous, nationalistic politics. Even neofunctionalists were aware that the French President represented something more profound about the nature of nationalism and the enduring qualities of statehood and, therefore, were prepared to concede that this highlighted deficiencies in their original formulations (Haas, 1968: preface). This is especially important because neofunctionalists – as we have seen – placed great faith in relatively short-term empirical correspondence as the key way of verifying their predictions.

Stanley Hoffmann's work (1964, 1966) offered a systematic contextualization of these events and in so doing engaged directly with neofunctionalist arguments. Hoffmann did not seek to advance a backward looking state-centrism. He was perfectly conscious of significant social change and of real challenges to the nation-state, but he did want to provide an argument about the continued centrality of nation-states in – as well as in spite of – the post-war European experiment with integration. Hoffmann's position was consistent with the realist claim that states are the basic units in world politics (see Chapter 6). In a recent reflective essay (Hoffmann, 1995: 1–6), Hoffmann is keen to put distance between himself and the purveyors of more fundamentalist realism or neorealism. His point, he claims, was to emphasize the importance of national interests in the post-war international politics of Europe. But he also sought to advance a rather deeper notion of 'interests' than the standard realist view that treats interests as derivative of structural balance of power calculus: 'state interests . . . are constructs in which ideas and ideals, precedents and past experiences, and domestic forces and rulers all play a role' (1995: 5). His emphasis on the domestic bases of interests would place Hoffmann as an early purveyor of the 'domestic politics' approach to integration that emerged as a 'school' two decades later (Bulmer, 1983; see Chapter 6), rather than among contemporary realist scholarship. Nonetheless, Hoffmann's state-centrism was striking in the 1960s, especially given that integration theory was dominated by neofunctionalists at the time. Hoffmann's main complaint against neofunctionalists was not that they had totally misconstrued particular dynamics, but that they had failed to locate these within a proper historical picture: '[t]he emphasis on the *process* led to a certain neglect of the *context*, or at least to a view of the context that may have been too selective' (Hoffmann, 1964: 85, emphasis in original).

While Hoffmann spent much time analysing the de Gaulle phenomenon and its implications for the integration experiment, he sought to make more general points about inherent qualities of the international system in general and the logics of closer international cooperation and functional integration in particular. Any international system, argued Hoffmann, would be likely to produce diversity rather than synthesis among the units. The present system was 'profoundly conservative' of diversity (1966: 866) because it was underwritten by principles of national self-determination. But in any international system, diversity would arise out of both the natural plurality of domestic imperatives and the fact that every state's situation within the system would be unique. So, the twin pulls of the domestic and the global would tend to create centrifugal tendencies. These in turn prompted diverse rather than convergent interests among states. The tensions manifest in the West European system in the early 1960s could be explained partly by the fact that the member-states had not been able to arrive at a consensus on the appropriate location of their new supranational entity in the global order. Alternative readings of the geopolitical situation of states were reinforced by different relationships with powerful external actors such as the United States, for whom European integration was a matter of ongoing profound interest. Tension was also explained by the fact that the stakes of integration were raised by incursions of supranationality into areas of controversy. This led Hoffmann to draw on the distinction between 'high' and 'low' politics to explain why integration was possible in certain technocratic and uncontroversial areas and why it was likely to generate conflict in matters where the autonomy of governments or components of national identity were at stake. What came to be called 'negative integration' (Pinder, 1968) – the removal of barriers to the operation of markets – fitted into the low politics category because it would not threaten the position of national elites, and thus imperil particular definitions of 'vital national interests'. In areas of key importance, where national interests were deemed to be at stake, Hoffmann argued that 'nations prefer the certainty, or the self-controlled uncertainty, of national self-reliance, to the uncontrolled uncertainty of the untested blender' (1966: 882). High politics was virtually immune from the penetration of integrative impulses. Hoffmann saw this as an autonomous sphere of political activity (1966: 865). On the other hand, governments were actually prepared to cooperate in the realm of low politics because it was a way of retaining control over areas where intersocietal (as opposed to interstate) transaction was becoming the norm.

Hoffmann portrayed post-war Western Europe as grappling with the contradictory logics of integration and diversity. The former was represented by the functional approach associated with the 'Monnet method' of community building as theorized by Haasian neofunctionalism. The logic of integration implied that nationalism would wither away, not only because it was an anachronism in the post-ideological world of technocratic management, but also because supranational sentiment would begin to infect national consciousness. Hoffmann took this to be a crass underestimation of the logic of diversity (described above). He also argued that the Monnet–Haas logic would only work where integration could *guarantee* perpetual positive sum outcomes or, to use neofunctionalist terminology, where interests could be upgraded in common for perpetuity. Permanent gains over losses might work in the arena of economic integration, but Hoffmann maintained that it could never prevail for political integration. The expansion of tasks generated by functional methods brought with it uncertainty about where the whole project was going. Such uncertainty would rub up against the threshold of high politics, both internally and externally. The fact that different member-states derived their national interests from alternative bases and were located differently in the global political economy meant that the emergence of uncertainty would certainly lead to conflict between governments:

> The functional process was used in order to 'make Europe'; once Europe began being made, the process collided with the question: 'making Europe what for?'. The process is like a grinding action that can work only if someone keeps giving it something to grind. When the users start quarrelling and stop providing the machine stops.
>
> (Hoffmann, 1966: 886)

Also, the appearance of purposeful supranational institutions with their own agendas would pose clearly articulated threats to national policy actors who in turn might resist. This, in effect, was Hoffmann's explanation of the 1965 crisis. Advances in integration would also generate external uncertainties. For example, Hoffmann argued that the fears expressed in the United States of the EC becoming a rival hegemon offered a good example of this phenomenon (1964: 86–7).

Hoffmann's critique added up to an impressive interrogation of the idea of spillover and the implication of automaticity that it conveyed. His point was to suggest that functional integration followed by 'politicization' would not necessarily proceed in the prescribed manner because the centrality of state actors and the persistence of nationalist sentiments meant that important countervailing forces and logics had been sidelined in the neofunctionalist account. Additionally, spillover had teleological problems of its own:

> The whole spillover process is a fiduciary operation: 'you and I accept today a measure that gives us less than you and I have hoped for because each of us expects our concessions of today to be repaid tomorrow on another issue'. Now, a day must come when the reckoning has to be done and the credit is exhausted.
>
> (Hoffmann, 1964: 88)

Hoffmann began from very different premises to Haas, Lindberg and Schmitter. He rejected the idea that the guiding logics of West European societies had become industrialism and technocracy. His emphasis on the political (traditionally conceived) meant not just that there would be intervening variables in the spillover process, but that functional linkages were simply not as decisive as the neofunctionalists supposed. As Carole Webb (1983) has noted, Hoffmann's intervention cut at the heart of the neofunctionalist paradigm because it repudiated the idea of a continuum from economics to politics that he identified as central to the neofunctionalists' explanation. The image presented by Hoffmann was of economics and politics as relatively autonomous. Put another way, there were two distinct circuits of political economy, one characterized by 'low politics', where states were prepared to engage in integrative and cooperative activity, and one where the precepts of 'high politics' meant that states were not prepared to compromise their sovereignty.

Hoffmann's points were prescient and, as the last chapter indicated, did not go unnoticed by neofunctionalists. Yet his arguments did not pass without criticism. Most attention focused on the distinction between high and low politics. The most immediate observation here was that the autonomy of the high politics sphere was thrown into doubt by the EC experience throughout the 1970s as European Political Cooperation (EPC) developed in the foreign policy sphere (Webb, 1983). Indeed, Hoffmann's thesis might be further taken to task in light of the Treaty commitments made at Maastricht in 1991. Both the development of the Common Foreign and Security Policy (CFSP) and the commitment to enact Economic and Monetary Union (EMU) within a specified period can be seen as instances where member states *willingly* surrendered control over issues of central importance to national sovereignty. Hoffmann's critique of the automaticity of spillover process might still hold, but the EC/EU system was clearly something rather more complex than a straight intergovernmental system. As Webb notes, governments are not capable of constructing a 'consistently highly orchestrated and impenetrable national front' (1983: 23). Member-state preferences are deeply immersed in a set of domestic level bargains and trade-offs and cannot be reduced to a simple set of national interests. Such observations are now commonplace following the recent 'governance turn' in theorizing about the EU (Chapter 5), but a number of contributions from the late 1960s were beginning to make similar points about the systemic complexity of the Community (see, for example, Lindberg, 1966; Lindberg and Scheingold, 1970; Puchala, 1972; H. Wallace, 1983).

Hoffmann's arguments were used as a foundation for an important contribution to the debate about integration theory by Roger Hansen (1969). Hansen argued that neofunctionalists had made three theoretical errors which, when rectified, would yield an altogether more intergovernmental account of the integration process. The first was a collective denial of the high–low politics problem. The second was a failure to place the European integration experience into appropriate international perspective. The third was the refusal to accept that the existence of supranational institutions was not necessary to the achievement of mutual economic gains in a common market. Economic gains could just as easily arise from a system coordinated by sovereign governments.

Hansen's arguments remain interesting because, rather than asserting that neofunctionalists were 'wrong' in a crude empirical-correspondence sense, he pointed to matters of theory construction and epistemology (strategies for acquiring knowledge) to explain the alleged theoretical blind spots. This is especially true of the failure to acknowledge the importance of external factors and the global environment. These were simply not factored into the original neofunctionalists' formulation. The latter had concentrated on the dynamics within and between a group of societies. So, spillover was largely seen as a dynamic *internal* to the member-states and their societies and economies. Spillover might have had external effects, by – for example – drawing in new member-states through the export of functional imperatives and loyalty transfers, but there was no account of how the external situation of the member-states impacted upon the Community. For Hansen, there simply was not enough explanatory power in neofunctionalism to account for the events shaping the EC since the 1950s. Drawing on the work of Karl Kaiser (1967), Hansen argued that neofunctionalism could explain low politics, but it could not say anything of substance about high politics. Nor could it generate productive ideas about the interaction between high and low politics. In many ways, argued Hansen, neofunctionalists drew inappropriate conclusions from their premises. For instance, societal pluralism might actually *prevent* spillover. Spillover would occur at moments of crisis, where functional pressures reach boiling point and force further integrative steps to be taken. Pluralistic societies would be sufficiently sophisticated to temper such crisis situations. Informal economic dynamics and elaborate infrastructure would ensure peaceful adjustment rather than dramatic social and political change. It followed that *political* integration was most likely to be the consequence of deliberate political decisions and not the logical corollary of economic restructuring.

As Chapter 6 makes clear, intergovernmentalist arguments developed significantly from the early 1970s. An influential school of economic historians led by Alan Milward (1992; Milward *et al.*, 1993) combined a distaste for abstruse theorizing with detailed analysis of the formative period of post-war integration to reach heavily intergovernmental conclusions. Writers concerned to capture the particular complexities of the EC/EU system within a framework that emphasized the centrality of member-state governments developed ideas about 'confederation' (Forsyth, 1981). Others were concerned to emphasize the domestic determinants of national preference formation (Bulmer, 1983) and this later connected with ideas about 'two-level games' (Moravcsik, 1993a; Smith and Ray, 1993). Even realist scholars of International Relations continued to formulate explanations of the European experience (Grieco, 1995; Mearsheimer, 1990). The point to make at this stage is that intergovernmentalism emerged as a rival to neofunctionalism, in a broad 'paradigmatic' sense, from the mid-1960s (O'Neill, 1996). Until the mid-1960s, 'integration theory' had really been a domain for the elaboration of functionalist perspectives on international restructuring. The appearance of Hoffmann's critique signalled the opening of the field to some of the broader concerns of International Relations. Indeed, the history of integration theory since the mid-1960s is usually presented as a conversation between these two broad schools (for example George, 1996a, 1996b). So, it should be remembered that the intergovernmental 'turn' in the study of the EC was not just a matter of empirical conformity, but was also a question of disciplinary 'catch-up'. It is not stretching things too far to claim that realist (state-centric) approaches had become utterly dominant in International Relations scholarship by the mid-1960s (Brown, 1997). To a degree, journals such as *International Organization* (where many of the key refinements to neofunctionalism were published) were conspicuous havens of liberal dissent while rival approaches such as that developed by the 'English School' quarrelled with realism over method rather than the fundamental nature of the international system. Intergovernmentalists had formidable disciplinary weight behind them, and so it is not surprising that their appearance in the study of European integration created a sense of theoretical crisis.

Alternative critiques

There is no doubt that the intergovernmentalist versus (qualified) neofunctionalist argument was the most important from the mid-1960s onwards, but it is worth bearing in mind that the development of the Community attracted interest from other critically-inclined sources, notably Marxism. That said, a coherent corpus of Marxist work on the EU has never really developed and historical materialist contributions to EC/EU scholarship have been sporadic, if occasionally significant. This is partly because Marxism explores a largely different *problematique* (or guiding puzzle) from that of the International Relations debate between liberal–idealism and realism (Halliday, 1994: 50–5). Rather than investigating questions about (for instance) the avoidance of war and the possibilities for the transcendence of the state-centred international system, Marxist scholarship seeks to deal with the nature of capitalism in the context of a theory of large-scale historical change. Marxism has forced a (tenuous) role for itself within the discipline of International Relations, largely because of the need to view capitalism as operating beyond the rigid boundaries of national-territorial units. Many scholars working on the dynamics of the global political economy operate within the Marxist tradition or derivatives thereof. But 'EC/EU studies' has not been a particular venue for the elaboration of Marxist theorizing.

Marxists were certainly active in national debates about the merits of integration, but the first serious Marxist 'intellectual' contribution to the debate came from the Belgian Trotskyist Ernest Mandel (1967, 1970).

Mandel's argument sought to locate the evolution of the Community within an analysis of the dynamics of capitalism. So, rather than seeking to explain the emergence of European-level institutions, Mandel paid attention to the restructuring of firms within Europe and to issues of ownership and control. He read the EC as both the product of and the vehicle for capital concentration within Europe. Capital concentration could involve the merger of national companies, the acquisition of European firms by larger American predators or the transnational fusion of European enterprises (Mandel, 1967: 28–9). In short, there was a built-in logic of amalgamation and concentration. This should be construed as the real core matter of Western European integration. Moreover, these changes to the European economic substructure had profound consequences for the nature of state power. Armed with a fairly brutal definition of the state as the instrument of bourgeois power against the working class and the guarantor of monopoly profits, Mandel was able to suggest that the transformation of the West European bourgeoisie necessitated a reorganization of state power at the supranational level:

> The growth of capital interpenetration inside the Common Market, the appearance of large amalgamated banking and industrial units which are not mainly the property of any national capitalist class, represent the material infrastructure for the emergence of supranational state power organs in the Common Market.
>
> (Mandel, 1967: 31)

The pull of these logics was quite profound and single currencies and single taxation systems would be sure to emerge, provided that recessionary situations were not tackled with a reversion to protectionism and economic nationalism. The latter represented a counter-tendency in West European capitalism and Mandel's analysis suggested that the EC was on the cusp of either disintegration or the inauguration of a supranational capitalist state and that the real test for the EC would occur during a recessionary period. While there were powerful forces in favour of supranationalization – not least the fact that the supranational state could support the interests of dominant capital through the promotion of capital concentration – the economic nationalist scenario was also plausible:

> The other possibility is that those capitalist circles who persist in defending a national fiscal, monetary and financial policy will triumph, in which case a co-ordinated anti-recessionary policy throughout the EEC would be impossible. As a severe recession confronts each government, each in turn would put its own anti-recessionary policy into action, which would mean a massive return to protectionism ...

The entire Common Market will tear itself apart. The weakest European companies will be sacrificed to national 'egoism' and only the strongest will survive, not however as the seeds of a new economic system – but as foreign bodies within a national economic system, with a role analogous to that played today by American companies.

(Mandel, 1970: 193)

Mandel's analysis is interesting because it offered a radically different take on the relationship between the politics and economics of integration. Neofunctionalists had argued that institutionalization and political integration were more or less inevitable by-products of functional economic spillovers. The normative basis, core research questions and language were all very different, but Mandel was also arguing that shifts in the 'economic' were likely to determine the nature of changes to the 'political'.

Stuart Holland's *UnCommon Market* (Holland, 1980) represented an unusually direct interrogation of orthodox theories of economic and political integration from a Marxist standpoint. Holland was not utterly dismissive of orthodoxy and acknowledged the identification of potential dynamics of integration, but chastised both theories of economic integration and neofunctionalism for a failing to contextualize their analysis. Conventional theories of economic integration were criticized for not identifying the fundamentally capitalist nature of the process and thus for neglecting the relationship between the development of the EC and the increasingly dominant position of multinational capital in Europe (1980: Chs 3–4). Neofunctionalism was (surprisingly) commended for its understanding of dialectical mechanisms, and processes of determinism, a matter that is particularly clear for Holland in his discussion of spillover: 'Lindberg defines spillover in a way which Engels himself could have approved' (1980: 92). Holland was attracted by the economism of neofunctionalism: its emphasis on explanations of political change rooted in changing economic circumstances and behaviour. This was not a unique observation. Writing a few years earlier, Reginald Harrison had argued that '[n]eofunctionalism might, in the last analysis, be summed up as neo-Marxian in the very loose sense that it assumes that economic imperatives will impose themselves on the political arrangements of society' (Harrison, 1974: 185). However, the crucial distinction, as Holland pointed out, was the basic disagreement about the fundamentals of societal composition. Marxists continued to emphasize the centrality to capitalism of a dichotomous logic of class polarization, whereas neofunctionalists drew on the pluralist position of societal diversity. Moreover, the adoption of pluralism as a premise had been done without serious thought being given to the assumptions thereby imported from liberal economic orthodoxy. Holland maintained that this uncritical and perhaps unwitting acceptance of this premise had led neofunctionalists into unrealistic depictions of economic growth as 'linear, smooth and homogeneous, rather than staggered, uneven, highly diverse and differentiated between firms and industries, regions and countries, and social groups and classes' (1980: 93). The other problem was the emphasis placed by neofunctionalists on the role played by elites in the integration process. This led to a 'failure to relate the role of élites to a given class structure, and to follow through or parallel the link in Marxist analysis between political superstructure and economic base' (1980: 90). Armed with class analysis, Holland felt equipped to reread neofunctionalist interpretations of some of the key moments in the Community's history. So, where Lindberg saw 'business interests' being proactive in the integration cause, Holland saw cohesive and dominant sections of capital. Where Haas observed coincidences between the preferences of public and private elites, Holland depicted alliances between sections of the state and key sections of capital driven by common ideological purposes.

Probably the most serious attempt to develop a genuinely Marxist theoretical standpoint on integration came from Peter Cocks (1980). Cocks was concerned to place the developments in post-war Western Europe within a Marxist concern for long-term historical development and maintained that 'the EC is systematically connected to earlier cases of integration in Europe' (1980: 1). The problem with 'integration theory' was that it had an unhealthy obsession with the specificities of the EC experiment in the post-war period. Where some work, such as that of Deutsch, was concerned to develop a theory based upon the treatment of the EC as an example of integration, there was a failure to establish the connections between past and present instances of the phenomenon: 'they avoid the question of whether integration is qualitatively different in different socio-economic formations, why it emerges at some historical periods and not at others, and what the connection is between different levels of integration in distinct social systems' (Cocks, 1980: 2). Cocks instead argued that European integration needed to be located as a phenomenon associated with interdependence, but where interdependence was understood as a capitalist phenomenon. The core guiding question was to be historical: why do particular patterns of interdependence arise in particular periods? For Cocks, integration should be understood as an attempt to deal with dilemmas arising in the course of capitalist development. To that end, integration facilitated the growth of the productive forces (which capitalism as a dynamic system needed) and also helped to legitimize the exploitative social relationships at the core of capitalist societies. Thus, integration – whether national or international – could be seen as an exercise in state-building where the growth of political institutions represented an attempt to impose capitalist state functions in ways commensurate with the development of capitalist relations of production.

This long-run view allowed the direct comparison of trends towards regional economic and political integration in the late twentieth century with the (uneven) evolution of national markets (defined as territorially-bound free trade and common currency areas with unified communications) and national-territorial states from the sixteenth century onwards. The development of national markets coexisted initially with a variety of state forms, some of which were more permissive of capitalism than others, but gradually national political unification came to be the natural accompaniment of national markets. Twentieth-century regional integration was based upon the need to ensure continued capital accumulation leading to the interpenetration of and growing interdependencies between national markets. Supranationalism became a powerful economic and political ideology as well as an institutional configuration designed to meet the needs of late capitalism. The consolidation of nation-states in the earlier period was often a reaction to the dominant competitive position of hegemonic states and a similar process was observed in terms of the EC's relationship to the competitive advantages of the United States in the post-war period.

The criticisms that might be levelled against these contributions are of the sort normally associated with critiques of Marxism. For instance, there is a heavy dependence on economic determinism to explain the changes to political configurations, thereby placing analytical restrictions on the significance of political autonomy. So, for example, the capacity of the state (in either national or supranational form) to detach itself from economic imperatives is rather downplayed and the role of ideas as shapers of both economic and political processes might be marginalized. In some ways it has been unfortunate that integration scholars have not taken up the gauntlets periodically tossed in their direction by historical materialists because these issues have never really been debated extensively in EU studies circles.

Neofunctionalist contemplation and the end of integration theory?

The previous chapter gave some sense of how, throughout the 1960s, neofunctionalists thought seriously about how to take account of nationalism, how to incorporate the troublesome obstinacy of governmental actors in the face of functional pressures and how precisely low-level economic integration could become politicized. Some of this rethinking took into account the intergovernmentalist points being raised by writers like Hoffmann and some of it was a reflex to developments within the evolving EC system. Yet Haas, Schmitter, Lindberg and others certainly saw the refinement of concepts, the quest to clarify and operationalize key variables and the development of comparative frameworks for the study of regional integration as part and parcel of their theory-building project. There was certainly no sense that 'integration theory' was in dramatic crisis when its leading lights met at Madison, Wisconsin in 1969 for a colloquium on regional integration. The conference generated perhaps the most important collection of theoretical papers on integration, published first as a special issue of *International Organization* and then as a book (Lindberg and Scheingold, 1971). To quote from the preface of the resulting collection:

> Our research frontier was defined with various goals in mind: the development of more sophisticated theory and methodology, the acceleration of comparative regional integration analysis, and the exploration of inchoate links to the problems of nation building and political change ... In a sense we see this volume as ringing down the curtain on the first act of integration studies. Our hope is that these essays answer some questions about where we have been and what we have accomplished ... But we are really more interested in raising questions than in answering them. We look back only in order to look ahead, to prepare for the second act.
>
> (Lindberg and Scheingold, 1971: ix–x)

The contributions to the volume were shot through with a preoccupation to make integration theory more rigorous and to conform to the canons of 'good' social science. The studies also connected to modish concerns with, for example, multivariate analysis (Lindberg) and transaction flow analysis (Puchala). The authors sought to make connections with important prevailing questions in the social sciences such as the attempt by Hayward Alker to use nation-building as an analogue for regional integration. There was also the hope that theoretical frameworks could be refined so as to generate research on new questions such as the nature of the link between mass attitudes and the direction of elite decisions about integration (Inglehart) and the impact (as opposed to the causes) of integration (Scheingold). There was also the alluring promise that Alker, Haas, Nye, Schmitter and Lindberg were working on computer simulations of the integration process. In short, it was clear that the aim was to build a more robust integration theory within the context of cognate questions of importance in political science and International Relations.

Haas's keynote contribution to the volume (Haas, 1971) offered an elegant statement of the state of the art in integration studies at the turn of the 1970s. It included a thorough account of the empirical generalizations advanced by then in comparative studies of regional integration. But the real heart of the paper consisted of its reflections on the state integration theory in general and neofunctionalism in particular. The latter was relegated to the status of a 'pretheory', along with federalism and the communications approach (Haas's term for transactionalism). They were pretheories because they 'do not now provide an explanation of a recurring series of events made up of dimensions of activity causally linked to one another' (1971: 19). Each pretheory was founded on a set of basic axioms about the nature of social processes. Federalists assumed that institutional formats could be transferred from the national to the regional level and that this could be accomplished in situations where actors developed common purposes and needs. Deutschians believed that social processes mimicked cybernetic laws and neofunctionalism was built around the resemblance of actor behaviour in national pluralistic polities and in instances of region-building (1971: 18–20).

Haas noted several limitations of neofunctionalism. Two stood out. First, the transferability of the theory to non-European cases of integration was in doubt because of neofunctionalism's deep roots in the analysis of processes of social change and decision-making in pluralistic industrialized societies. Second, neofunctionalism suffered seriously from the 'dependent variable problem' (see Chapter 1). It was simply impossible to establish accurately what a successful prediction might be, given that the theory had a highly ambiguous notion of the terminal condition of integration (1971: 24). The dependent variable problem was central to the limitations of integration theory. Neofunctionalism was constructed as a theory of large-scale economic and political transformation that aspired to reveal the dynamics associated with the politicization of functional economic integration. But it was also a theory about incrementalism and pluralism, about the triumph of short-term interest fulfilment over the politics of grand design. In effect, it was caught between a rock and a hard place. This was an inherent contradiction and as the 1970s progressed, neofunctionalists clearly moved decisively towards the second aspect of the theory at the expense of the first.

The dependent variable problem was deeply complex and Haas went some way to thinking it through. If it could be agreed that the end-state of integration was a supranational community, then it might be possible to achieve such an outcome without the means described by neofunctionalism, in which case the latter would be falsified. Also, the problem for integration theorists was that while terminal conditions had been advanced, they could at best be speculative ideal types. In other words, integration theory was trying to explain something that did not yet exist and whose existence could only be postulated. 'At best,' wrote Haas, 'we have a putative dependent variable' (1971: 27). Indeed, the capacity to imagine possible outcomes was inevitably conditioned by historical experiences so that the conceptualization of terminal conditions might be restricted to analogues of previous instances of community building. This might be wholly inappropriate for the novel transformations gripping the European political economy in the post-war period. Finally, the many instances of 'actually existing' regional integration in Western Europe, East Africa, Central America and so on indicated that a multiplicity of outcomes was possible and thus, that the attempt to theorize on behalf of a particular, common terminal condition might be seriously mistaken.

The logic of this position would suggest that the guiding puzzle of integration theory was misconceived, a conclusion to which Haas was later drawn (see below), but for the time being he was committed to rescuing integration theory as a discrete pursuit. His proposed solution was the identification of multiple dependent variables, the definition of which would be bound up with alternative dispersals of legitimate authority. This in turn would allow for rather more fluid theorizing about European integration.

By the mid-1970s Haas had declared integration theory 'obsolescent' (Haas 1975a, 1976). This is sometimes misread as Haas effectively falling on his neofunctionalist sword. Haas's intention was rather more subtle and the choice of the adjective 'obsolescent' rather than 'obsolete' was significant. Some of 'integration theory's' core concepts did appear to possess considerable explanatory power, but it was no longer appropriate given the conspiracy of 'real world' events and developments in the social sciences to conduct integration theory as a self-contained intellectual pursuit (1975a: 2–6). Haas was categorically *not* saying that the study of integration had ceased to be relevant. Rather, he was signalling a turning-point in the way in which phenomena such as the EC should be conceptualized. The built-in assumption of neofunctionalism and the other pretheories was that European integration was an instance of a deliberate attempt to bring about regional economic (and thus political) enmeshment among a group of West European countries. Moreover, integration theory had built on that premise to look for the mechanisms through which this enmeshment occurred. It also sought orderly processes to explain how regional integration occurred in practice in Western Europe and elsewhere. But the Community could also be read in other crucial ways, and by the mid-1970s two important qualifications had shifted the core questions away from the ground occupied by full-blown neofunctionalism. The first was the conceptualization of the EC as a complex political system in possession of guiding logics other than those associated with 'integration'. The second was the location of the EC within the changing global order.

The EC as a system and 'turbulence'

The issues raised by the first point were dealt with in a much-cited paper by Donald Puchala (1972). Puchala's objection to the approaches to integration of the early 1970s is that they each characterized the Communities in particular terms and generated narrow research agendas with limited capacities to explain:

> Our conventional frameworks have clouded more than they have illuminated our understanding of international integration. No model describes the integration phenomenon with complete accuracy because all the models present images of what integration could be or should be rather than here and now.
>
> (Puchala, 1972: 276)

Of course, this observation relied heavily on the empiricist idea that the full objective reality of integration would be discernible to an observer equipped with the right conceptual telescope. Alternatively, Puchala could be read as an advocate of rewriting our narratives of the processes and institutions of European integration with a view to opening up new analytical avenues. His alternative reading portrayed the EC as a 'concordance system', a term preferable in his view to any of the available alternatives (federalism, regional level nationalism, a functional international organization à la Mitrany and a zone of power politics). A concordance system was a complex entity where nation-states remained important and were still probably the primary actors, but where arenas of political action operated at several levels (subnational, national, transnational and supranational) and where levels of influence varied from issue area to issue area. A concordance system was also a forum for positive sum interaction and for the development of mutual understandings. Where there was conflict, it would not derive from cleavages based on antithetical interests, but from disagreements about modes of cooperation. Bargaining was not zero-sum in character, but about the construction of convergent goals. This in turn follows from what Puchala described as the 'distinctive attitudinal environment' of the concordance system (1972: 276–83). This amounted to an atmosphere of prevailing pragmatism, where actors were attentive to the requisites set by international interdependence and where they operated with a high level of mutual sensitivity and responsiveness. This was a groundbreaking article that prefigured some of the themes of multi-level governance and new institutionalist approaches by the best part of two decades (see Chapter 5).

Moves towards thinking about the Community as a political system had been apparent for some time in the work of Lindberg. With Stuart

Scheingold, he went on to produce a book-length treatment of the EC in these terms (Lindberg and Scheingold, 1970). *Europe's Would-Be Polity* offered a detailed mapping of the functional scope and institutional capacity of the EC, along with an analysis of its standard operating procedures (or norms). In empirical terms, Lindberg and Scheingold's key message also anticipated the themes of the later multi-level governance literature (Chapter 5). They noted unevenness in the Community, both in terms of integrative peaks and troughs and of asymmetries in European-level governance capacity across policy sectors. The core research problem was how to explain change within the EC system. To do this, Lindberg and Scheingold drew upon the (then fashionable) systems theory of David Easton (1965). They made it abundantly clear that their purpose was not to develop a theory of regional integration. That could only be done by comparing the EC with other cases, a task attempted already by Haas and Schmitter (Haas, 1967: Haas and Schmitter, 1964) (see Chapter 3). This was not to dismiss the value of this sort of integration theory:

> [Haas and Schmitter's] analysis provides insights into why the European Community *took off* as a venture in political integration, why it was more successful than the other efforts, but it says little about what accounts for variations in success after take off.
>
> (Lindberg and Scheingold, 1970: 107, emphasis in original)

What was clear was the perception that 'integration theory' was not capable of dealing with important matters of system change as well as rival theoretical apparatuses. Lindberg and Scheingold's preference was to deploy the heuristic simplicity of Eastonian systems theory to the EC. Their diagrammatic depiction of their model is reproduced here as Figure 4.1

The point of such analysis is not to explain why a system arises, but how it transforms itself, or indeed maintains a stable equilibrium, over time. This can be explained by variables external to the system (demands, supports, leadership), but also by features of the system itself:

> The kinds of decision outcome that result, and we have classified these for our purposes in terms of their contribution to increasing (or decreasing) the functional scope and institutional capacities of the Community system, will be a function of five clusters of variables: demands; the existing functional scope; institutional capacities, and level of systemic support; and finally leadership. By thus relating outcomes to the scope of the political system and to its institutional capacity via feedback, we can transform a static system model into a model of *system change*.
>
> (Lindberg and Scheingold, 1970: 114, emphasis in original)

Figure 4.1 *Lindberg and Scheingold's model of the EC political system*

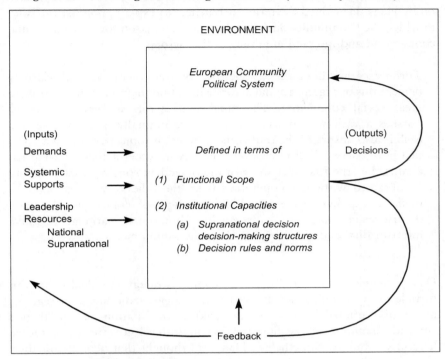

Source: Lindberg and Scheingold, 1970: 113.

The implication is that scholars of the EC need to turn their attention to understanding the nuances and implications of evolving patterns of collective decision-making (see also Lindberg, 1967). The consequent research programme might be construed as a decisive move away from the disciplinary homeland of International Relations. Having said that, there were still strong neofunctionalist tendencies in Lindberg and Scheingold's prospectus. For instance, they were still interested in how decision-making processes could be stimulated to involve wider circuits of actors and to embrace new policy sectors (1970: 117). But their argument was that the study of spillover could be given greater nuance by recognizing the uneven patterns of practice within the EC and the particularities of policy-making in different sectors. The use of this model allowed for the clear differentiation between the Community political system and its 'environment'. The environment was treated by Lindberg and Scheingold as the context provided by the member-states with all other external factors deemed to be channelled through the political systems of the Six.

The issue of complexity in the EC policy process was eventually taken up by Haas. He coined the term 'turbulence' to explain, not just the ways in which the Community operated, but also the reason for creating greater cooperation and interaction among policy actors:

> Turbulence is the term we bestow on the confused and clashing perceptions of organizational actors which find themselves in a setting of great social complexity. The number of actors is very large. Each pursues a variety of objectives which are mutually incompatible; but each is also unsure of the trade offs between the objectives. Each actor is tied into a network of interdependencies with other actors which are as confused as the first. Yet some of the objectives sought by each cannot be obtained without co-operation from the others. A turbulent field, then, is a policy space in which this type of confusion dominates discussion and negotiation. It can be sub-national, national, regional, inter-regional and global – and all at the same time.
>
> (Haas, 1976: 179)

Haas's depiction of the EC as a 'coping strategy' to deal with this turbulence, rather than an avowed and strategic experiment in regional integration offered another quite striking anticipation of the themes currently explored in the literature on multi-level governance, explored here in Chapter 5. Nonetheless, Haas still thought that neofunctionalism had something to say about the internal dynamics of the EC system. Indeed, its emphasis on incrementalism, now rechristened as 'disjointed incrementalism', was able to capture the subtleties of the system and to make predictions until about 1968. Disjointed incrementalism was about the flexible use of means to attain a goal that remained more or less constant. Thus Haas defined integration in Deutschian terms, as the achievement of a pluralistic security community. What then kicked in – and here is where neofunctionalism's problems in explaining the internal tensions in the EC began – was 'fragmented issue linkage'. The fragmentation occurred because actors (unlike neofunctionalist scholars!) did not see problems as part of an overall process. Issue linkage happened 'when older objectives are questioned, when new objectives clamour for satisfaction, and when the rationality accepted as adequate in the past ceases to be a legitimate guide for future action' (1976: 184). The question of how turbulent fields link to regional integration led Haas to pose questions that were central themes in much of his subsequent work (notably Haas, 1990). The questions now crucial for students of integration, he argued, concerned a series of relationships between objectives, knowledge, learning, strategies, bargaining styles and institutions. The emphasis was still largely on matters of agency and there was no great concession to state-centric forms of analysis. Haas was trying to understand how and why actors interact in new institutional settings in the face of radical uncertainty.

Externalization

The failure of neofunctionalists to deal with the exogenous context of regional integration had been integral to Hoffmann's critique (Hoffmann, 1966). This was the second area in which the guiding questions shifted during the early to mid 1970s. As we saw in Chapter 3, Schmitter (1971) attempted to redefine the dependent variable of integration studies as 'the range of alternative actor strategies' and this came to be related to the scope of integration in the context of 'crisis-induced decision cycles'. This drew attention to the importance of external context, and more concretely to the geo-economic and geo-political shocks that might prompt actors into creating (and for that matter refining) regional economic and political institutions. While there was a tendency in Schmitter's revised theory to treat these external happenings as 'givens' or background variables, he did develop an 'externalization hypothesis', which

> predicts that external conditions will become less exogenously determined if integration rather than disintegration strategies are commonly adopted. The 'independent' role of these conditions should decline as integration proceeds until joint negotiation vis-à-vis outsiders has become such an integral part of the decisional process that the international system accords the new unit full participant status.
>
> (Schmitter, 1971: 244)

Schmitter's formulation was not really about the impact of structural changes in the international economic and political systems. It was more concerned with processes of socialization in the international system and the mechanisms through which (a) the integrated entity could be accorded actor status in the international system and (b) how the interaction of regional units with the international system can be a stimulus for the closer integration of those units.

The permeation of the inside and the outside was taken up, inevitably, by Haas (1975a; 1976) who suggested that attention needed to be drawn to external contexts because they might help to explain why other regional integration schemes took different evolutionary paths from the European model. In the European context, it was also (empirically) apparent that the difficulties faced by the EC were related to factors that originated beyond the collective jurisdiction of the member-states. In theoretical terms, it was necessary to work through the implications of member-state transactions with outside parties to understand the consequences in terms of incentives for collective action among members of regional units. At one level, the need to develop a common negotiating posture *vis-à-vis* outsiders in the context of a customs union would provide strong incentives for collective action (and thus deeper integration). But, on the other hand, exchanges between individual member-states and non-members might only be beneficial to the particular member-state(s) concerned. It would follow that they would have little incentive to engage in any collective action that might jeopardize those bilateral ties (Haas, 1975a).

Summing the debate up, Haas (1976) identified two uses of the term 'externalization'. The first treated externalization as the perception and fear of powerful non-regional actors that induced regional actors to engage in closer policy coordination. The second – Haas's preferred sense – was externalization as a situation where 'regional policy-making is more and more constrained by the extra and inter-regional economic calculations of the actors' (1976: 176). Here harmonization, institutionalization and politicization may all be slowed down by the perception of individual member-states of interdependencies beyond the region.

Interdependence

Bringing together these strands, Haas argued that the study of integration should cease to be a subject in its own right, and should become an aspect of the study of interdependence. To think about European integration in these terms would help to explain why the EC had come to be beset by such problems in the 1970s: 'In the learning mode of fragmented issue linkage, then, the treatment of the externalization issue is inimical to continued regional integration' (1976: 199). Interdependence quickly became a core concept in International Relations during the 1970s. The key works on interdependence, such as those of Keohane and Nye (1971, 1975, 1977) sought to challenge the dominant state-centric image of realism by presenting a picture of a diffuse global order characterized by multiple actors among whom states were important, but not alone. Supranational entities, along with multinational corporations, transnational interest organizations and subnational entities were all key shapers of the world order, and their operation contributed to the blurring of traditional distinctions between the 'domestic' and the 'international' and between national politics and foreign policy-making. Relations were *transnational* as well as *international*. The depiction of interconnected world order was suggestive of change and adaptation from previous patterns of international relations and that 'regional integration' might be thought of as one way in which actors sought to reconstitute elements of the international system. Indeed, interdependence theory tried to show how realism's emphasis on power, force and the primacy of military security should be challenged. Keohane and Nye (1977) argued that the growth of interdependence would force states to reconsider the meaning of the 'national interest' to the point where this might become convergent with the idea of building common positions with other states. This would be aided in part by the growth of international institutions that offered incentives for close ties between states and which themselves were created because the processes of interdependence motivated states to solve common problems. There was also more than an echo of the old commercial liberal argument that increased commerce between states lessens the rationale of territorial conflict.

Thinking about the EC through the lens of interdependence analysis enabled students of the EU to capture the multi-actor complexity of the system, thereby avoiding the pitfalls of both crude intergovernmentalism and the unidirectionality of neofunctionalism. There was no pre-assumed endpoint for the integration process. Moreover, the possibilities for comparative work would survive strongly, given that it would not be necessary to compare the EC with other instances of regional integration, but with any relatively ordered set of responses to 'turbulent fields'. However, as Carole Webb (1983), pointed out, there was also a danger of missing the peculiar nature of the EC polity which had rather more order about it than the somewhat chaotic image of international life thrown up by some interdependence and transnational relations literature.

Writing in 1983, Webb argued that the study of integration had come to be dominated by two camps: intergovernmentalism and theories of interdependence, both of which ascribed more weight to the forces of governmental actors than neofunctionalism. Interdependence thinking appealed in two specific ways. Firstly, 'interdependence' was a condition in the global political economy that might, but would not necessarily, produce a regional integrative response. So the growth of international or transnational interdependence would not necessarily lead to 'deeper' integration. Secondly, there was no normative linkage between interdependence theory and any form of international institution. This was a problem with neofunctionalism which had been too tightly associated with the Community model and method. Focusing on formal institutions such as the EC potentially distorts the picture of intergovernmental exchange (Webb, 1983: 32–33). In short

> the concept of interdependence has been used to explain the conditions under which governments and other economic actors have to contemplate some form of collaboration; but, unlike the approach of integration theory, it does not necessarily help to define the outcome

very precisely. Interdependence seems to be the answer for scholars and politicians who wish, for different reasons, to keep their options open on the evolution of the EC.

(Webb, 1983: 33)

In her review, Webb goes on to suggest that framing intellectual discussion of the Community in terms of interdependence raises questions about policy dilemmas that face all governments, not just those in Western Europe. Furthermore, it discourages parochial discussion of the minutiae of EC institutional issues. In other words, the deployment of the vocabulary of interdependence is a potential route out of the $n = 1$ dilemma. Rather than being a *sui generis* phenomenon, the Community could be viewed as an attempt to grapple with some of the trends affecting all modern interdependent capitalist economies.

While the concept of interdependence is nowadays less central to the discourse of International Relations, the application of the concept to the EU in the 1970s and 1980s foreshadowed some interesting developments that are explored here in subsequent chapters. Firstly, the firm location of this approach to the EC in International Relations implied that all was not lost for that discipline as a feeder for EC/EU studies (Chapter 7). Secondly, addressing the EU in terms of broader policy questions rather than the specificities generated by the Community's unique institutional structure anticipated one of the key themes of the 'governance turn' discussed in Chapter 5.

Conclusions

The debates of the late 1960s and early 1970s suggested two conclusions about the analysis of the EC, the net effect of which was to cast serious doubt on the helpfulness of the term 'European integration'. The first was that the EC was usefully thought of as a political system in the making. The second was that 'integration theory' could not really be sustained as a separate branch of International Relations. Many saw the emerging literature on international interdependence to be a better location to theorize about interstate cooperation and the emergence of alternative modes of governance in world politics. What is interesting is the extent to which these conclusions emerged from the deliberations of the integration theorists themselves. That is not to say that external critique was of no importance, but even Hoffmann's fulsome rebuttal of neofunctionalism (if read carefully) was clearly not the work of an atavistic realist. The cautionary tale to emerge from this chapter is that it pays to read this literature carefully – for two reasons. Firstly, the decline of neofunctionalism is rather too often understood as a theory collapsing under the weight of 'real world' events or suffering from a kind of intellectual market failure. The evidence presented here at least points to the substantial theoretical refinements undertaken by the neofunctionalists. The crisis was as much epistemological as ontological and the explanation for integration theory's obsolescence could reside as easily in the 'sociology of knowledge' as it might in the deviation of prediction from 'truth'. The second reason is that many of the themes of later literatures – notably the new institutionalism and multi-level governance (Chapter 5) – were clearly anticipated in these debates. The work of Haas, in particular, stands out in this regard.

It is especially interesting to chart where the core neofunctionalist scholars went intellectually after integration theory's 'denouement' in the mid-1970s. Haas continued to contribute to International Relations debates about international organizations and was an early contributor to the literatures on interdependence (Haas, 1970), regime theory (Haas, 1975b, 1975c, 1980) and the role of knowledge in world politics (Haas, 1990). Thus, Haas continued to work with and help to define the trajectory of liberal International Relations throughout the 1970s and 1980s. Lindberg took the route from neofunctionalism to the study of EC policy-making and offered some of the earliest attempts to conceptualize the EC in political systemic terms (Lindberg, 1965, 1966, 1967). This was consistent with the thrust of his later work on economic governance (Campbell, Hollingsworth and Lindberg, 1991; Lindberg, 1975). Schmitter's interest in Latin American integration fed into a long-standing concern with democratization (O'Donnell *et al.*, 1980) and his neofunctionalist roots were evident in his pioneering work on interest intermediation and neo-corporatism (Lehmbruch and Schmitter, 1982; Schmitter and Lehmbruch, 1979). In recent years, he has re-emerged as a powerful discussant on the conceptualization of European integration and governance (Schmitter, 1996a, 1996b). The point to make is that even if it is accepted that neofunctionalism failed or was discredited, it is clear that the study of European integration had generated significant spillovers into the development of mid-range theories in both International Relations and political science. The emphasis on non-state actors fed into the study of governance as pluralist political science developed layers of sophistication, and the interest in the politicization of economic interaction sat at the core of much work in the realm of non-realist International Political Economy (IPE) as it developed throughout the 1970s and 1980s.

Theorizing the 'New Europe'

The changing context of European integration

The 1990s witnessed a substantial revival in academic interest in European integration. While it would be entirely unfair to characterize the field of EC studies in the 1970s and 1980s as sterile, it is probably true to say that political scientists and scholars of International Relations were unlikely to be drawn to the Communities as anything other than a *sui generis* phenomenon. The Communities may have been intrinsically interesting, but it was difficult to mount a case that profound social processes were unfolding within the framework of, or because of, the EC. Not only had 'integration theory' apparently failed (Haas, 1975a, 1976), but also the widespread perception took root that little of substance was occurring within the Communities themselves. Economic crises following the oil shock of 1973 had been met by recourse to nationally oriented policy programmes and not by EC-sponsored projects for economic recovery. Following British accession to the EC in 1973, the Communities seemed to be bogged down by cyclical wrangles over apparent iniquities in the distribution of budgetary responsibilities, a matter itself related to the huge portions of the Community budget consumed by the deeply controversial Common Agricultural Policy (CAP). This stasis and lack of progress in institution-building at the European level – a perception, incidentally, that is now often disputed – did not lend itself to high theorizing. This was certainly not a fertile time for supranational institutionalists or for those seeking to theorize the conditions for the transformation away from national forms of governance.

Theoretical renewal coincided with the apparent revival in European integration beginning in the mid to late 1980s. The most obvious manifestation was the Single European Act (SEA) of 1987 that provided the first set of major amendments to the founding Rome Treaties. This followed the resolution in 1984 of the long-standing dispute about the UK's contribution to the EC budget, the coming to office of a new, purposeful Commission under Jacques Delors (Ross, 1995), a renewed sense of institutional activism within the European Parliament (Lodge, 1984) and significant interaction between institutions, such as that between the Commission's policy entrepreneurship and the Court's jurisprudence in the wake of the latter's famous *Cassis de Dijon* decision (1979)(Alter and Meunier-Aitsahalia, 1994; Armstrong, 1995; Dehousse, 1999; Wincott,

1996). The SEA, aside from facilitating institutional reform and the expansion of the EC's policy competence, was most notable for the way in which it laid down a timetable for the completion of the Community's internal market. It also resuscitated Europe-wide debates about the nature and scope of future integration. The SEA sought to create, in the words of Article 13, 'an area without internal frontiers in which the free movement of goods, persons, services and capital is ensured'. The single market programme carried with it significant spillover expectations. The attachment of a so-called 'social dimension' to the internal market programme was seen by some as essential to ameliorate the worst effects of the substantial market restructuring which would occur. Moreover, the liberal logic of seeking to complete the internal market could be followed to the point where the member-states could, to all intents and purposes, share a single economic space with a single currency and a centralized monetary authority. The unravelling of such logic provided an obvious rationale for the decisions regarding Economic and Monetary Union (EMU) taken at the Maastricht European Council in December 1991, which in turn produced the Treaty on European Union (1992). Finally, the legislative agenda of the SEA was suggestive of the need to reform the decision-making processes of the EC in such a way as to minimize intergovernmental gridlock and maximize the scope for swift and efficient decision-making. So, in neofunctionalist terminology, there was great spillover potential in the social, economic and political domains.

This chapter examines the theoretical response to these developments, beginning – as the last paragraph suggests – with a discussion of the attempt to revive neofunctionalist explanations of the trajectory of European integration. This is followed with a discussion of the emergence of a new set of perspectives derived largely from the literatures on public policy analysis and comparative political science that began to question the traditional International Relations problematic around which theoretical debate on integration had hitherto revolved. The development of inter-governmentalist responses is held over until the next chapter.

The revival of old paradigms: towards theoretical synthesis?

One of the most evident consequences of the appearance of the empirical 'new Europe' was the revival of the long-standing theoretical conversation between neofunctionalism and intergovernmentalism (George, 1996a, 1996b). The impetus for the resuscitation of neofunctionalist thinking was obvious. As suggested above, the renewed dynamism of the EC from the mid-1980s had coincided with significant activism by supranational institutions. Moreover, the single market initiative and its accompanying logic smacked of functional spillover (see Chapter 3). It was also possible to apply a quasi-neofunctionalist reading to the newly Europeanized activities of some traditionally nationally-bound interest associations. For analysts of intergovernmental persuasions, on the other hand, renewed integration could and should be read as a state-led process. Some of the most significant accounts of this sort deliberately juxtaposed intergovernmental readings of integration in the 1980s with the alleged errors of neofunctionalism, or supranational institutionalism as it was sometimes called (Keohane and Hoffmann, 1991; Moravcsik, 1991, 1993).

The variants of contemporary intergovernmentalism are discussed in the next chapter. The reappearance of neofunctionalism as a way of thinking about integration received some sympathetic, if rather qualified hearings. What was clear, though, was that the idea of neofunctionalism as obsolescent (Haas, 1975a) was something of an exaggeration. A number of texts on European integration published in the 1970s and 1980s recognized the contribution that the school had made and the concept of spillover in particular was clearly thought to retain significant explanatory power, albeit as part of a wider-ranging and rather more eclectic approach to the subject (George, 1996a). Having said that, the idea that a full-scale revival of unadulterated neofunctionalism was imminent was a non-starter. For one thing, neofunctionalists such as Haas, Lindberg and Schmitter had clearly recognized the ontological and epistemological limits of the approach in their own self-critiques. If neofunctionalism were to make a comeback, it would represent a significant modification of the premises laid down by its founding fathers (see Chapter 3). The real question in the empirical context of the mid–late 1980s was whether neofunctionalist reasoning could say something significant about the trajectory of integration and not whether it could assume the status of grand theory once again.

Jeppe Tranholm-Mikkelsen's careful analysis of neofunctionalism's past and its possible applicability to the contemporary situation makes this very point (Tranholm-Mikkelsen, 1991). There is first and foremost compelling empirical evidence to suggest, at the very least, an amount of neofunctionalist logic at work. Tranholm-Mikkelsen argues that there is evidence of three forms of spillover in European integration since the mid-1980s. Functional spillover is apparent in several spheres. Even the 'negative integration' proposed by the 1992 project (i.e. the removal of barriers and regulatory controls as opposed to the positive construction of an integrated market space) requires legal harmonization as well as enhanced cooperation among states in areas such as policing. For the single market's potential to be realized, pure economic logic would contend that EMU is a necessity to maximize economic efficiency. Additionally, economic restructuring will have uneven consequences, thereby creating strong pressures for European-level activity to ameliorate its worst effects (1991: 12–13). In short, '[t]hese functional links between negative and positive integration are creating exactly the sort of pressures identified by Lindberg. The only difference is that the more radical conception of the common market inherent in the 1992 project provides even stronger functional links now than in the early 1960s' (1991: 13).

Evidence of political spillover is more circumstantial, but Tranholm-Mikkelsen points to the positive orientations to the 1992 programme held by interest groups as diverse as the European Round Table of Industrialists and the British Trades Union Congress (for greater detail see respectively Cowles, 1995; Rosamond, 1993, 1998) and to the conversion of erstwhile opponents of the EC such as the British Labour Party. Cultivated spillover – the deliberate sponsorship of integrative initiatives by supranational actors – is displayed by the entrepreneurial actions of the Delors Commission (Tranholm-Mikkelsen, 1991: 13–16).

Therefore, concludes Tranholm-Mikkelsen, '[t]he obstinacy of the logic of spill-over implies that neofunctionalism is by no means obsolete' (1991: 19). But neofunctionalism cannot explain everything: '[t]he integration process encompasses factors which can be more adequately handled with the tools of intergovernmentalism and interdependence theory' (1991: 19). These factors are identified as diversity among the member-states and the presence of 'dramatic actors' (i.e. key shapers of change) on the one hand and the need to attend to the imperatives for integration set by the context of the external security environment on the other.

The implication of this sort of reasoning is that scholars of integration should strive to achieve a theoretical synthesis in which certain components of neofunctionalism have a place. Michael O'Neill delves a little deeper by arguing that the process of integration is 'endemically syncretic' (O'Neill, 1996: 144). It is driven, he argues, by coexistent yet contradictory logics such as economic globalization on the one hand and the urge to retain the primacy of national governance on the other. The actors involved in the process operate with different sets of expectations and interests. This means that the theorization of integration requires a corresponding degree of eclecticism (see also Webb, 1983). The implications of this point are taken up in greater detail in Chapter 8, but for now it is clear that quite a lot of work in contemporary EU studies operates in a climate of relative theoretical eclecticism. To take one particularly notable example, the work of Wayne Sandholtz and John Zysman (1989) on the single market initiative contains obvious neofunctionalist overtones. For instance, they argue for the importance of ascribing significance to the enterprise of supranational institutions: '[t]he renewed drive for market unification can be explained only if theory takes into account the policy leadership of the Commission' (Sandholtz and Zysman, 1989: 96). Moreover, the interaction between the Commission and groups with an interest in the creation of conditions of market harmonization played a vital role in the mobilization of national governmental elites on behalf of the cause of the single market. But such neofunctionalist reasoning cannot, they argue, carry the full weight of explanation. In an echo of neorealist thinking (see Chapter 6), they maintain that structural changes in the international economy provided an essential trigger for both supranational activism and for activity in a further crucial arena: the domestic politics of the member-states. In particular, states became persuaded of the feasibility and value of Europeanization strategies in the context of the manifest failure of *national* economic strategies, the decline of the political left and the strategies of Keynesian welfare statism with which it was associated, along with the rise of neoliberal political economy as a framework of ideas shaping policy choices. Supranational entrepreneurship and coalition-building were important, and perhaps merit theoretical primacy, but Sandholtz and Zysman's point is that the integrative steps taken in the mid 1980s cannot be completely understood without adding theories of the structural change in the international political economy and of domestic politics.

The alternative to syncretism is to use theoretical frameworks such as neofunctionalism in a rather more circumscribed manner. Perhaps the most innovative attempt to reactivate neofunctionalism can be found in Anne-Marie Burley and Walter Mattli's discussion of the legal dimensions of European integration (Burley and Mattli, 1993). Burley and Mattli argue that neofunctionalism provides an economical framework for the generation of real insights about the nature and dynamics of legal integration in the Communities. Burley and Mattli do not rely exclusively on neofunctionalism, arguing for the development of a complementary sophisticated legalism, but they do use its core concepts. In particular, they claim that 'the core insight of neofunctionalism – that integration is most likely to occur within a domain shielded from the interplay of direct political interests – leads to the paradox that actors are best able to circumvent and overcome political obstacles by acting as nonpolitically as possible' (Burley and Mattli, 1993: 57). But non-political action does not exclude supranational entrepreneurship and Burley and Mattli present plenty of evidence to show how the European Court of Justice has been an activist on behalf of the development of an effective, legitimate and quasi-constitutional EC-level system of law. Moreover, processes of spillover aid the construction of an EC legal system. Functional spillover can be used to describe the ways in which the relatively modest provisions of the Treaty of Rome have received expansive judicial interpretation, notably via the doctrines of direct effect and supremacy (Dehousse, 1999: Ch. 2). The corollary is the gradual encroachment of EC law beyond the narrow economic domain.

There is also substantial evidence of shifting expectations (i.e. political spillover) as various actors learn to operate within the rule-bound environment set by the ECJ.

The single market programme also prompted a partial resuscitation of federalist theory and of normative arguments about the desirability of a constitutional settlement to accompany the deepening of the integration process. John Pinder's work offers a particularly good example of this normative-analytic crossover. His position is that federalists continue to be well-equipped to understand the dilemmas facing nation-states and the institutional configurations that might help to confront them:

> The common problems are in the fields of trade, money, security, and now, evidently, the environment; the institutions are those of constitutional government to deal with the common affairs, leaving the member states to manage their own affairs with their own institutions. The problems have been identified through observation and analysis of the capacity of states to deal with them; and it has been assumed that democracies would not wish to entrust important functions of government to institutions other than those of representative government, in a framework of the rule of law.
>
> (Pinder, 1991: 213–14)

Such sentiments latched onto the renewed political activism of European federalists such as Altiero Spinelli, a veteran member of the European Parliament and prime mover behind the Parliament's bold Draft Treaty on European Union of 1984 (Lodge, 1984). Pinder advocates what he calls 'neo-federalism' as a way of combining theoretical reflection upon and policy advice about the trajectory of the Communities (Pinder, 1986; 1991: 216–218). Neofederalism is built around the idea that a federal settlement continues to be a *rational* solution in light of both the problems faced by European states and the quasi-federal solutions already in existence. Contrary to 'classical' federalism, which placed too great an emphasis on the convening of a powerful European representative assembly with the power to design a constitution for the United States of Europe, Pinder is more attentive to the power of countervailing forces and, thus, more aware of the need to follow incrementalist strategies to spur on unifying forces and to lend legitimacy to protofederalist institutions. What emerges, according to Pinder, is an alliance between neofunctionalism's emphasis on economic and political linkages and federalism's concern with constitutional principles and problems.

The renewed interest in 'federalism' also began to draw political philosophers into the debate about the 'new Europe' and 'Europe future'. This development stemmed partly from an engagement with the ethical dimensions of political restructuring following the end of the Cold War

(Brown, 1994) and partly from an emerging strain of democratic theory dealing with the issue of whether the nation-state continues to be the most appropriate capsule for democratic governance (Archibugi and Held, 1995). On occasions, this debate taps directly into the analysis of federalism (Forsyth, 1994), but usually develops into a philosophical conversation between 'communitarians' and 'cosmopolitans' (Brown, 1994). The debate is too nuanced and multifaceted to be done justice here, but the implicit message of such exchanges is that federalist thinking has much to offer in the analysis of European change. Cosmopolitans tend to argue for universal human values against which the institution of the nation-state is often seen as an unhelpful barrier. For federalists, the issue here is whether universalism can in some way be delimited into projects of regional political integration. Communitarians include defenders of the nation-state (Miller, 1994), but the real message is the value of human communities which find institutional expression in statehood. States do not necessarily require nations, but this does mean that intellectual energies need to be directed towards constitutional creativity in the light of the sorts of economic and political pressures that threaten the integrity of the nation-state.

The value of federalist theory to the study of the EU is given a different but no less important spin by Alberta Sbragia (1992). Sbragia is not at all concerned with advancing arguments about the virtues of a federal solution. Her point is that federalist theory offers important analytical tools without the normative baggage. The debate about whether the EU is on course to a federal destination is largely irrelevant from this point of view. It is also misplaced to think of the Communities and their evolution as analogous to the development of existing federal systems such as the United States. Rather, Sbragia describes federalism as 'an exercise in institutional creativity ... not necessarily a replication of existing institutional designs' (1992: 261). The political science literature on comparative federalism can offer insights into the dilemmas that an organization such as the EU is likely to face in the context of this climate of ongoing creativity. As a process of institution-building in this sense, European integration is quite anachronistic. Most contemporary instances of federalization appear to represent the disintegration of existing entities, rather than the integration of a new body.

With these considerations in mind, Sbragia uses federalist theory to shed new light on the politics of territoriality in the context of political integration at the European level. Her core concern is to dissolve the opposition between federalism and intergovernmentalism: 'In their wish to see a "United States of Europe", European federalists railed against a confederation of sovereign states to such an extent that they tended to conceptualize a federal Europe without the institutionalization of territorial politics' (Sbragia, 1992: 279). To juxtapose intergovernmentalism and federalism – particularly as integration *outcomes* – is, therefore, fundamentally misconceived. Federal systems are all about the institutionalization of territorial cleavages – in this case international cleavages – and not their eradication or transcendence.

Another important conclusion to be taken from Sbragia's work is that comparative political science has a central role to play in the analysis of integration. In this case 'the study of the Community could both be incorporated into and contribute to the study of comparative politics rather than be isolated from the general conceptual and theoretical concerns of political scientists interested in comparing political systems' (1992: 267–8). This addresses directly the matter of whether the 'old' paradigms can be usefully revamped to deal with the analysis of the contemporary EU.

The limits of the old debate

One consequence of revisiting the old debate may be viewed as both a strength and a weakness. Although contemporary writers are nervous about falling into a teleological trap, the neofunctionalist–intergovernmentalist dispute tends to pose two diametrically opposed scenarios for the European future: the EU as an intergovernmental organization *versus* the EU as a putative supranational state. Additionally, as Schmitter (1996a) notes, a variety of intermediate outcomes are possible between these two poles. So, this directs attention to the big picture about the nature of the EU and the trajectory of European integration. If handled sensitively and rigorously, this might provide a useful framework for the ordering of data and for prediction. The polarization continues to explore the fundamental question of the role of the nation-state and national governments, both as agents of integration and as plausible ways of organizing and ordering social and political life. Now this debate is clearly of major importance, yet there are two objections to the continuation of discussion on these established terms. The first objection, explored in the remainder of this chapter, is that the continuing theoretical joust between neofunctionalists and intergovernmentalists fails to pose all of the possible questions about contemporary European integration because it problematizes the EU and integration in the preferred disciplinary terms of International Relations. While the two paradigms have much to say about process, they are unable to capture the sheer complexity and dynamism of the emerging Europolity. The second, addressed in Chapter 7, is that this debate marginalizes significant and important strands of international theory. Here the argument is that 'International Relations' approaches are far from irrelevant and that a wider IR canvas is capable of posing interesting and important questions about integration. Here we explore the first of these objections in greater detail as a prelude to examining some of the theoretical perspectives that have migrated into EU studies in recent years.

A substantial literature has emerged to reflect upon the 'comparativist' or governance turn in EU studies (for example Hix, 1994, 1998; Marks, Hooghe and Blank, 1996; Marks *et al.*, 1996; Richardson, 1996a, 1996b; Risse-Kappen, 1996). The basic thrust in this writing is that the discussion between comparative policy analysis and EU studies is likely to generate a mutually beneficial intellectual conversation. From the viewpoint of scholars of the EU, drawing from the insights of public policy literatures will avoid two fundamental caricatures of the EU: the focus on singular moments of change or crisis and the tendency to portray the dynamics of integration as centering on an opposition between the poles of nation-state and 'superstate'. Established approaches, it is argued, focus our attention upon so-called history-making moments such as treaty revisions or major crises and thereby neglect the day-to-day patterns of politics within the EU system. The consequence is that responsibility for integration outcomes is ascribed to either national governments or purposive supranational institutions, rather than to the gradual accretion of competence that is associated with the regulatory thicket of European policy-making and in evolving processes of institutional interaction (Wincott, 1995b). Also, the sheer complexity of the Euro-polity militates against the treatment of European integration as revolving around the matter of nation-state versus superstate. The pro-comparativist argument asserts quite vigorously that this is not all that European integration is about (see, for example, Richardson, 1996b). The vocabulary of the old debate can capture neither the dynamics of the process, nor indeed the range of possible 'Euro-futures' that may lie between '*Europe des Patries*' and '*United States of Europe*'.

The argument is partly that the EU makes authoritative decisions and that this 'centralization of governance functions' is continuing apace (Dunleavy, 1996; Pollack, 1994). The consequence is a policy-making process characterized by – amongst other things – conflicts of a distributional nature, resource dependencies and various 'nested games'. Such conflicts embrace a variety of interested actors – not just states. In any case, the European institutional environment in which states are compelled to participate renders old-fashioned notions of national interest difficult to sustain. Institutions may constrain or indeed mould the preferences of state actors (Caporaso and Keeler, 1995). There is no single central question at the core of this complex political process. The politics of European integration are not just about whether there should be more or less *integration*. There are multiple issues embedded in the policy process. Indeed, the EU political game is not simply about matters of high politics such as the pooling or retention of national currencies or the development of a common European foreign policy and defence identity. Much (perhaps most) of what goes on in the EU game is about day-to-day technical, regulatory policy-making. As Richardson puts it

> Low politics this may be ... but it is probably the nine-tenths of the EU 'policy iceberg' that is below the water line. There is an increasing amount of political activity at this level within the EU and some means has to be found of analysing and conceptualising it.
>
> (Richardson, 1996b: 5)

The idea that the study of European integration should not be confined purely to established integration theory is actually not an entirely novel insight. As suggested in the previous chapter, the idea formed the centrepiece of a notable and still-cited paper by Donald Puchala (1972) and the treatment of the Community as a system had been a fairly recurrent and ever more important theme in the literature since the mid-1960s. These contributions, while lacking the vocabulary of modern institutionalism and concepts such as 'multi-level governance' and policy communities, pre-empted many of the themes discussed below in this chapter. Interventions such as Puchala's cut to the heart of the long-standing issue of what 'EU studies' and European integration are all about. The debate is certainly accentuated by the *sui generis* character of the EU. The theory-building possibilities of adapting traditional approaches are severely limited by the so-called '$n = 1$ problem', because there is no other apparently comparable instance of international integration in the global political economy (though see Chapter 7). This is a particular problem for neofunctionalism that evolved in the empirical context of the EU, but which aspired to develop a generally applicable theory of regional integration (Risse-Kappen, 1996: 56).

The case for comparative politics approaches is also bolstered by the claim that the EU harbours many political games that resemble politics within national polities. Simon Hix (1994, 1999) takes this point further than most by showing how different research problems in comparative political science can be transplanted into the EU context. These may include questions about the authoritative allocation and distribution of resources – the classic 'who gets what, when, how' issue raised by Harold Lasswell (1950) – and questions about the representation and intermediation of interests in a political system. They may also include the matter of the formation of political cleavages within the Euro-polity. Hix's argument boils down to the observation that because there is a politics other than the politics of 'integration', the student of the EU has a duty to pursue these alternative lines of inquiry using the appropriate conceptual tools. The bolder claim, explored in Chapter 7, is that a substantial shift of focus is required away from International Relations to comparative political science as the 'parent discipline' of EU studies. The theoretical implications of Hix's intervention are twofold. Firstly, the reconceptualization of the EU as a political system deals with the '$n = 1$ problem' by allowing comparison with other instances of processes such as redistribution or cleavage formation. This reinforces – and perhaps widens – the arguments of Sbragia (1992) outlined above. Secondly, in addition to thinking about the problem in terms of 'IR versus CP', Hix also directs attention to the distinction between 'grand theory' and middle-range theory. He points to the absurdity of looking for a general theory of the EU (the alleged sin of neofunctionalism) and how this would be analogous to a quest for a general theory of, say, German politics. The alternative is to use the EU as a productive venue for testing theories of politics and policy-making, which themselves may be sub-theories of broader paradigms such as pluralism. So, just as the theory-driven study of the United States has taught political scientists much about the intersection between organized interests and the machinery of government, the study of the EU may help to perfect the likes of policy network and institutionalist analysis (Richardson, 1996b).

One particularly notable contribution is found in the work of Giandomenico Majone (1991, 1993, 1994, 1996) who treats the EU as an instance of a 'regulatory state' or at least as if it is on the pathway to becoming such an entity. A regulatory state 'may be less of a state in the traditional sense than a web of networks of national and supranational regulatory institutions held together by shared values and objectives, and by a common style of policy-making' (Majone, 1996: 276). Majone's aim is to understand the EU in terms of the policy-making functions of states. Regulation is one of three functions normally undertaken by states. The others are redistribution (resource transfers, welfare provision) and stabilization (the use of fiscal and monetary instruments to ensure economic growth, price stability and satisfactory employment levels). Regulation is defined as measures to address problems of market imperfection or failure and it is here that the EU – with its emphasis on the regulatory harmonization needed to ensure the efficient operation of the single market – is most active. Indeed, it is much less developed in terms of the other two functions, a fact that distinguishes the EU from the normal model of European statehood. A potentially valid comparison is with the United States (Majone, 1991). In part, the regulatory emphasis can be explained by the fact that it is a low cost method of policy-making, an important consideration in the resource-constrained EU context. This means that there are significant incentives for the Commission in seeking to 'supply' regulation. On the demand side, various state and non-state actors are said to acquire interests in the development of European regulatory capacity and action. But the rationale for supranational regulation also arises because of the fragility of international regulation – bilateral and multilateral agreements struck by governments. The Commission has powers of scrutiny over the implementation of regulatory legislation and therefore provides a better 'bet' for the successful execution of regulatory policy-making (Majone, 1996).

Majone's important contribution is easily linked to some of the perspectives discussed later in this chapter, notably institutionalism. But his work also focuses attention on the fact that the study of the EU has, to a large extent, shifted from the study of *integration* to the study of *governance*. Governance is usually defined as being about the exercise of authority with or without the formal institutions of government. In recent years, however, the term has come to be used to note the drift of authority away from government, hence the term 'governance without government' (Rosenau and Czempiel, 1992). The idea has significant purchase in International Relations, but it also has been a huge theme in recent policy analytical literature. As the editor of one significant collection notes:

> Governance can be seen as the pattern or structure that emerges in socio-political systems as 'common' result or outcome of the interacting intervention efforts of all involved actors. This pattern cannot be reduced to one actor or group of actors in particular ... No single actor has all knowledge and information required to solve complex, dynamic and diversified problems, no actor has sufficient overview to make the application of needed instruments effective, no single actor has sufficient action potential to dominate unilaterally in a particular governing model.
>
> (Kooiman, 1993: 4)

This is portrayed as a pervasive feature of all advanced states, but it is an image which has become increasingly acceptable in EU studies circles (see Hix, 1998; Jachtenfuchs, 1995, 1997; Marks, Scharpf *et al.*, 1996). The governance 'turn' in EU studies is certainly about deploying policy analytical tools to the EU, but it also encourages serious thinking about our use of the conventional categories of politics (Schmitter, 1996b). So, while the theoretical literature on governance treats the EU as a polity, it also uses the EU as a laboratory for the exploration of possible transformations in policy-making on a much wider scale.

Theorizing complex policy-making and multi-level governance

The foregoing hints that the EU is best treated as an empirical venue for the pursuit of the ongoing preoccupations of political science. Put another way, the purpose of EU studies should be to say something about politics more generally, rather than developing a series of specific claims about the EU. There are echoes here of the migration of Haas and others away from the neofunctionalist analysis of European integration towards the study of interdependence in the 1970s (see Chapter 4). Thus, what might be called the 'governance turn' in EU studies may reflect an alternative answer to the perennial question: 'Of what is the EU an instance?' (see Chapter 1). Yet, in spite of the efforts to use the EU to answer broader questions about politics, it remains stubbornly distinctive. Any full-scale attempt to plunge the study of the EU into the waters of comparative politics and policy analysis leaves itself open to the observation that the EU is not necessarily a precise analogue for the processes of politics *within* nation-states. Indeed, the EU may be read as a hybrid form: neither political system nor international organization, but something in-between.

Attempts to combine a reading of the EU in policy process terms with an acknowledgement of its peculiarities are captured by the compelling metaphor of 'multi-level governance'. The multi-level governance literature seeks to avoid two traps: state-centrism and the treatment of the EU as only operating at the European level in the institutional arena of Brussels and Strasbourg:

> The point of departure for this multi-level governance (MLG) approach is the existence of overlapping competencies among multiple levels of governments and the interaction of political actors across those levels. Member state executives, while powerful, are only one set among a variety of actors in the European polity. States are not an exclusive link between domestic politics and intergovernmental bargaining in the EU. Instead of the two level game assumptions adopted by state-centrists [see Chapter 6], MLG theorists posit a set of overarching, multi-level policy networks. The structure of political control is variable, not constant, across policy areas.
>
> (Marks, Nielsen *et al.*, 1996: 41)

MLG analysis amounts to the claim that the EU has become a polity where authority is dispersed between levels of governance and amongst actors, and where there are significant sectoral variations in governance patterns. It is suggestive of a process that is 'a horizontally as well as vertically asymmetrical negotiating system' (Christiansen, 1997b: 65). Wolfgang Wessels describes the EU as 'a system of complex, multitiered, geographically overlapping structures of governmental and non-governmental élites' (1997: 291). The emphasis on governance takes the debate about authority away from the zero-sum notions associated with discourses of sovereignty. The normal politics of sovereignty is, therefore, a politics of absolutes. Theoretical treatments that engage with this notion fall into the trap of imagining either the withering away of the state or its stubborn resilience. Analysts associated with MLG do not maintain that states are unimportant. Indeed, MLG is consistent with a rather more pluralistic view of the state as an arena in which different agendas, ideas and interests are contested. Autonomy and control may be at stake (Kassim and Menon, 1996), but states remain crucially important, but they 'are melded into the multi-level polity by their leaders and the actions of numerous subnational and supranational actors' (Marks, Hooghe and Blank, 1996: 371; see also Chapter 8). Moreover, MLG is understood as a pattern of politics that has arisen in *recent* years (Marks, Hooghe and Blank, 1996: 373), meaning that other dominant patterns may emerge in time, just as the supranational–intergovernmental partnership model that dominated in the formative years of the Communities was displaced by Gaullist modes of decision-making in the 1960s (Wallace, 1996b).

Of course, all of this makes 'grand theorizing' difficult. Researchers working under the auspices of MLG admit that they do not have particular expectations of the dynamics of the Euro-polity beyond a sense that the boundaries between various levels of governance (European, national, local, etc) will become less clear-cut. If anything, MLG is an attempt to depict *complexity* as the principal feature of the EU's policy system and its emphasis on variability, unpredictability and multi-actorness tends to set adherents of this approach in opposition to the contemporary intergovernmentalists discussed in the next chapter (Marks, Hooghe and Blank, 1996). Expressed in more radical language, MLG may give substance to John Ruggie's claim that 'the EU may constitute nothing less than the emergence of the first truly postmodern international political form' (Ruggie, 1998: 173). While there may appear to be echoes of federalist thinking in MLG language about tiers of authority, MLG does not seek to depict a polity governed by constitutional rules about the location(s) of power (Warleigh, 1998: 11). Pushing Ruggie's observation a little further, federalism (as a normative project as well as a form of political settlement) may be viewed as a *modernist*, given its preference for rule-bound closures and a tight definition of authority. MLG is about fluidity, the permanence of uncertainty and multiple modalities of authority – suggesting an association with postmodernity.

If anything, MLG offers a (dis)ordering framework for the use of policy network analysis (see below), but the recognition of 'multi-levelness' has produced one or two attempts to impose theoretical order on the complex Euro-polity. For example, John Peterson (1995a) explores the possibility of separating the study of European integration into different levels of analysis. At each level, different sorts of theoretical approach are appropriate (see Table 5.1).

Table 5.1   *Peterson's approach*

Level	Decisive variable	Best model
Super-systemic	Change in the wider political/economic environment	'Macro theories' (intergovernmentalism, neofunctionalism)
Systemic	Institutional change	New institutionalism
Meso level	Resource dependencies	Policy network analysis

Source: Peterson, 1995 (adapted).

Peterson argues that each level is characterized by different decision types, and that different sorts of rationality operate in each. The super-systemic level is the domain of 'history-making' decisions that modify the way that the EU works as a system of governance (Peterson and Bomberg, 1999). Significantly, this level is the arena of European *integration*, whereas the other levels are arenas of European *policy-making* or, more specifically, policy-setting (the systemic level) and policy-shaping (the meso level). This is not just a neat semantic exercise, but has real implications for the potential scope of particular theories. The likes of liberal intergovernmentalism (Chapter 6) and neofunctionalism (Chapters 3 and 4) become quite tightly circumscribed.

An alternative is offered by Jeremy Richardson (1996b) who – in line with orthodox policy analysis – separates the policy process into distinct stages. Again, particular theoretical tools are suitable at different points in the policy process (see Table 5.2).

Both interventions assume that alternative theories can coexist in the study of the European Union. The difference resides in the ways in which

Table 5.2   *Richardson's approach*

Stage of the policy process	Theoretical tools
Agenda setting	epistemic communities
Policy formulation	policy communities/networks
Policy decision	institutional analysis
Policy implementation	interorganizational/behavioural analysis

Source: Derived from Richardson (1996b: 5).

each slices the EU studies 'cake'. Peterson divides the sub-discipline into different analytical levels (on levels of analysis, see Buzan, 1995), allowing for the discussion of the broad trajectory of the EU plus the dynamics of institutional change and detailed analysis of identifiable policy sectors. Richardson offers a recipe for the mapping of a particular policy area (or indeed a single piece of legislation) over time. Both also attempt to circumscribe the boundaries of usefulness for any given theoretical approach. Peterson's argument limits neofunctionalism to the 'supersystemic' level of analysis, so that supranational activism and functional spillovers are best at explaining change in the context of decisive changes in the global environment. This raises questions about the usefulness and the propriety of deriving explanations from different theoretical starting points. This is a problem for any exercise in theoretical synthesis and relates to whether the perspectives to be merged are respectively ontologically and epistemologically compatible (i.e. do they have divergent views about the nature of social reality and processes of knowledge gathering?). Of the two models, this is a bigger challenge for Richardson. Peterson's proposals could be read as an attempt to partition EU studies off into a further series of sub-disciplines, each with its prevailing 'normal science', whereas Richardson's argument looks to a varied theoretical toolkit to map the development of a piece of legislation or the emergence of European-level policy competence in a given area. For the most part, Richardson's proposals are for the deployment of what he calls actor-based models (1996a and 1996b) in a context of thinking beyond politics as a purely interest-driven process. The emphasis on ideas and knowledge, which he recommends, is potentially central to all of the approaches he identifies. But this in itself can push up against some fairly formidable ontological and epistemological thresholds associated particularly with constructivist notions of social reality (Jørgensen, 1997b; Risse-Kappen, 1996 and Chapter 7 below). With these cautionary sentiments in place it is necessary to proceed to the two most important theoretical strands to emerge from the 'governance turn' in EU studies: institutionalism and policy network analysis, both of which lay claim to giving a firmer conceptual underpinning to the multi-level governance metaphor (Armstrong and Bulmer, 1998: 316; Richardson, 1996a, 1996b).

New institutionalism

Institutionalist approaches are built around (but expand upon) the apparently banal claim that 'institutions matter'. They matter particularly because of the ways in which institutional configurations have an impact upon political outcomes. The revival of institutionalism in political science represents an attempt to counter both the behaviouralist emphasis upon political outcomes as the product of aggregated societal behaviour and a crude emphasis on political outputs as derivatives of the straightforward interplay of actors' interests. Much of the impetus for the arrival of the so-called 'new institutionalist' political science of the 1980s and 1990s came from a concern that the discipline had for too long neglected the importance of the state as a shaper of outcomes (Evans *et al.*, 1985). Orthodox political science was taken to task for failing to attend to the importance of the organization of political life generally and to the relatively autonomous quality of political institutions in particular (March and Olsen, 1984; Thelen and Steinmo, 1992). Rather than being simple and passive vessels within which politics occurs, institutions provide contexts where actors can conduct a relatively higher proportion of positive sum bargains. Institutions offer 'information-rich' venues where transparency prevails and where trust is high. They act as intervening variables between actor preferences and policy outputs.

The institutionalist literature is diverse and certainly does not constitute a single research programme. It is usual to subdivide institutionalist analysis into *historical* and *rational choice* variants (Armstrong and Bulmer, 1998; Bulmer, 1994). While this certainly captures two very different ways of dealing with institutions, other reviewers prefer to make a further distinction between historical and *sociological* institutionalism (most notably, Hall and Taylor, 1996). Indeed Hall and Taylor see the three institutionalisms as largely autonomous developments linked to-gether by a renewal of interest in institutions in several areas of the social sciences. Historical institutionalism grew out of critiques of conventional group theories of politics, while rational choice institutionalism reflects the successful import of the axioms of microeconomics into political science. At the same time, sociologists became interested in the capacity of cultural and organizational practices (institutions) to mould the preferences, interests and identities of actors in the social world (hence 'sociological institutionalism'). Therefore, given such diverse disciplinary starting points, it is perhaps disingenuous to talk about new institutionalism as a movement. Indeed, as suggested below, different institutionalisms operate with quite different views about the nature of reality and the relationship between structure and agency. Yet, there is clearly some significance to be gleaned from the facts that such sustained critical attention is devoted to *the* new institutionalist political science and that several EU studies contributions reflect on the place of institutionalism(s) in the study of integration and EU governance (Aspinwall and Schneider, 1998; Peterson, 1995a; Pierson, 1996; Pollack, 1996, 1997a). The EU, with its rich mixture of formal and informal institutions is often seen as an ideal testing ground for the various forms of institutional analysis.

This leads to the obvious (but crucial) question of what is meant by 'institutions'? Rational choice institutionalism tends to define institutions as formal legalistic entities and sets of decision rules that impose obligations upon self-interested political actors. An example in the EU would be the voting rules in the Council of Ministers where the nuances of qualified majority voting (QMV) force governments into strategic coalition games in pursuit of their interests. The existence of rule-bound interaction also creates incentives for actors to shape the formal rules under which they operate. As two recent commentators put it, '[a]ctors bump into institutions, go "ouch", and then recalculate behavior and strategies' (Aspinwall and Schneider, 1998: 5). Historical institutionalists tend to operate with wider definitions. Peter Hall's much cited work on Britain and France (1986: 19) defines institutions as 'formal rules, compliance procedures and standard operating practices that structure relationships between individual units of the polity and the economy'. This means that institutions comprise not just formal constitutional entities, but also instances of established informal interaction and aspects of what Ikenberry calls 'normative social order' (Ikenberry, 1988: 226) such as conventions, codes of behaviour and standard constraints upon behaviour (see also North, 1990). The fact that institutions may be defined as systems of norms gives the institutionalist a fairly wide remit. For example, Kenneth Armstrong and Simon Bulmer's study of the single market defines institutions 'as meaning formal institutions; informal institutions and conventions; the norms and symbols embedded in them; and policy instruments and procedures' (Armstrong and Bulmer, 1998: 52).

It follows that institutionalists may focus on a huge variety of attributes of the EU and the integration process. These include – amongst others – the formalities of the legislative process as laid down in the treaties; the long-term consequences of historic acts of institutional architecture; the styles of intergovernmental bargaining that prevail within the different Councils of Ministers; the institutional cultures of the Directorates General of the Commission and the institutional activism of the European Court of Justice. To take one example, Thomas Christiansen (1997a) offers what he calls a 'neo-institutionalist' analysis of the European Commission. His aim is to move beyond the formalistic analysis of the Commission in terms of its role or its functions by exploring the interaction of multiple organizational logics within the institution. So, there are internal tensions between the logics of politicization and bureaucratization on the one hand, and between diplomacy and democracy on the other. This serves as an example of how institutionalism, in all of its guises, poses new research questions for students of integration and European governance. It is not just that institutionalism is thought to be *better* at understanding the EU. Rather the choice of an institutionalist perspective tends to redefine what the EU 'is an instance of' and, therefore, the sorts of question that we should be asking about it.

Nonetheless, perhaps the majority (but by no means all) of the institutionalists working on the EU would side with Mark Pollack (1996, 1997) who claims that the new institutionalism has the virtue of beginning with the intergovernmentalist claim about member-state primacy, but then taking account of the way in which institutions structure individual and collective policy choices. EU outcomes cannot be read off from an analysis of preferences and relative state power alone.

Not surprisingly, the different institutionalisms have alternative accounts of how institutions actually matter. One way into this issue is to think about the views taken by each variant of actor preferences and in particular of the way in which preferences are formed. Rational choice institutionalists regard preference formation as exogenous to the institutional venue. It is assumed that actors will undertake the rational pursuit of self-interest. Institutions in this context are a decisive constraint upon self-interested action: 'political and economic institutions are important for rational choice scholars interested in real-world politics because the institutions define (or at least constrain) the strategies that political actors adopt in pursuit of their interests' (Thelen and Steinmo, 1992: 7). The rationalist position on institutions holds that institutions are created by states because states see benefits accruing to themselves from the functions performed by those institutions (Keohane, 1984; see also Chapter 6). A particularly important function is the reduction of 'transaction costs' – those risks and penalties that arise when actors engage in negotiation with one another. As Wayne Sandholtz notes, this runs the risk of treating institutions as empty vessels lacking any autonomy from the states that create them. But at the same time this rationalist (sometimes confusingly 'functionalist') view of institutions offers an account of why states actually create them in the first place. They 'allow ... governments to become intimately acquainted with the goals, aversions, tastes and domestic constraints of each other' (Sandholtz, 1996: 406).

Historical institutionalists are normally associated with a more generous interpretation of the influence of institutions. Institutions certainly constitute 'intervening variables', but they also govern the wider context within which political action occurs. Actors are less likely to pursue rational instincts than socially defined rules. As a consequence, institutions also have the capacity to shape the goals and the preferences of actors and in so doing 'structure political situations and leave their own imprint on political outcomes' (Thelen and Steinmo, 1992: 9). In historical institutionalist terms, actors are not perfectly knowledgeable about institutional consequences. That is to say, actors may not be aware of the full implications of participating in institutional venues. Indeed, actors engaging in acts of institutional creativity at moment '*t*' are not likely to understand the long-term implications of that act, but the preferences of actors at '*t* + *n*' will have to operate in a context defined by those institutions. Institutions tend to lock into place and create 'path dependencies'. In the context of European integration, historical institutionalists tend to argue that the construction of supranational institutions was rooted in a very particular historical context (post-war reconstruction and looming bipolarity in the case of the ECSC). So, the institutional architects of the Community made their decisions to formalize integration on the basis of particular motivations and preferences. But, the very act of creating particular sorts of institutions, with identifiable competencies and powers, unleashed logics that could not necessarily be predicted at the time. The path of subsequent European integration is determined, therefore, by these context-bound decisions. The 'lock-in' of formal institutions meant that bodies such as the Commission acquired distinctive and ongoing agendas. The European Court of Justice became a forceful and effective advocate of the quasi-constitutionalization of the treaties, the general expansion of European-level policy competence and the supremacy of Community law over that of the member-states (Alter, 1996: Wincott, 1996). Meanwhile, less formal patterns of interaction developed and evolved norms of behaviour that tended to persist beyond the short-term occupancy of institutions by particular actors. In short, subsequent actors have to operate within these self-reproducing institutional scripts. So, the single market programme that emerged in the EC in the mid-1980s cannot simply be put down to a neoliberal turn in economic thinking across Western Europe. This may well be a powerful explanation, but its precise manifestation can only be understood within the already existing EC institutional context. Such thinking opens up comparative possibilities because it isolates institutions as independent variables that help to explain the specificities of the European response to the global situation of the 1980s. This period is often read as one where regionalizing tendencies came to the fore within the world economy (see also Chapter 7). It is not just that the extensive and heavily supranational EC version of market-led regional integration can be explained with reference to the imperatives set by and the bargains made within institutions. Institutions were also arguably a constraint on what was politically possible in terms of (West) European regionalization from the late 1980s. From the outside at least, it might have seemed more rational to pursue a rather looser form of regional integration, with the emphasis on interstate agreements to remove the impediments to factor movements and an open stance *vis-à-vis* the outside. But this form of action was never open to EC. As Charlie Dannreuther puts it: '[i]nstitutions tend to perpetuate certain forms of decision making activity that are not derived from political debate, consultation exercises or interest group activity' (Dannreuther, 1997: 4). This sort of reasoning offers a very powerful explanation for why governance functions have drifted out of national control in the evolving EU system. After all, it would seem irrational for a state to cede aspects of its autonomy or its ability to control dimensions of its domestic polity and/or the external environment. Yet they do. Paul Pierson's account emphasizes the historical logic of unintended consequences: 'the short-term preoccupations of institutional designers have led them to make decisions that undermined long-term member-state control' (Pierson, 1996: 156).

There is no necessary incompatibility between the rational choice and historical variants. It is perfectly possible to be a rational choice historical institutionalist. This is true, for example, of Pierson (1996) who works clearly within a framework that understands the preferences of actors and the reasons behind their institutional choices as exogenous to the processes of integration (Aspinwall and Schneider, 1998: 21). Other historical institutionalists offer a less rationalist starting point. Armstrong and Bulmer's major case study of the single market is a case in point (Armstrong and Bulmer, 1998). They draw on the pioneering work of March and Olsen (1984) which sought to distance itself from a universe of rational utility maximizers and began to explore the potential for institutions to be thought of as 'normative vessels'. That is to say, institutions were to be seen as carriers of beliefs, knowledge, understandings, values and established ways of doing things. From this standpoint, prevailing ideas and institutional cultures are seen as very important shapers of the behaviour of actors. Moreover, these cultural attributes tend to stabilize over time, thereby inducing the reproduction of behavioural patterns. This offers a potentially powerful account of how institutions tend to replicate patterns of policy over time and how different institutional cultures emerge and coexist within the same policy-making system. Armstrong and Bulmer insist that this form of institutional analysis is especially well suited to the discussion of the EU's regime of economic governance. It is able to identify systemic norms and the differentiation of norms within particular segments of the policy system (such as Directorates General of the Commission). It also helps to bring law back into the study of European integration (see also Armstrong, 1995: Wincott, 1995a):

> Thus, just as we can consider the issue of the autonomy of the EU's political institutions, so we can examine the way in which the institutionalisation of legal norms has created some autonomy for the EC legal system. The interaction of the legal and political systems is facilitated in a way that is not possible with the predominant approaches [neofunctionalism and intergovernmentalism].
>
> (Armstrong and Bulmer, 1998: 62)

The empirical applications of this approach are legion, as Armstrong and Bulmer show, and the claim to foster the interdisciplinary study of EU governance promises real added value.

There are also clear hints of sociological institutionalist themes in the form of historical institutionalism favoured by Armstrong and Bulmer. The role of institutional norms and conventions is certainly a big theme for many contemporary sociologists and indeed many of the shaping capacities of institutions described by other institutionalists could be rewritten in the rubric of socialization. However, as Hall and Taylor note, sociological institutionalism places yet greater emphasis on the cognitive dimensions of institutions: 'they emphasize the way in which institutions influence behaviour by providing the cognitive scripts, categories and models that are indispensable for action, not least because without them the world and the behaviour of others cannot be interpreted' (Hall and Taylor, 1996: 948). In addition, sociological institutionalists often place emphasis on the 'mutual constitution' of institutions and the actors that populate them. Institutions (which are very broadly defined) become the mechanisms through which the world is rendered meaningful to social actors. This is a vast step beyond the rational choice view of institutions as formal sets of rules that mediate the interaction of exogenously derived interests. For sociological institutionalists, interests and identities are *endogenous* to (emanate from within) the processes of interaction that institutions represent. Interests as well as the contexts of action are socially con-structed – given meaning to actors – by institutional 'scripts':

> When faced with a situation, the individual must find a new way of recognizing it as well as responding to it, and the scripts or templates implicit in the institutional world provide the means for accomplishing both of these tasks, often more or less simultaneously.
>
> (Hall and Taylor, 1996: 948–9)

There are clear affinities here with social constructivism, a movement that emerged most fully in sociological circles in the mid-1960s (Berger and Luckmann, 1967) and which has recently been influential within International Relations (see Chapter 7). The idea that reality is socially constructed rather than objectively given directs the researcher towards the subjective aspects of social life: how actors construe the world in which they operate and what the implications of those construals might be in terms of choices and constraints on action. The institutionalist take on these arguments is that institutions perform a 'symbolic guidance function' (Jachtenfuchs, 1997: 46). They supply actors with their bearings in a turbulent world, and thereby contribute to actors' senses of who they are and what their interests must be.

In terms of EU studies, sociological institutionalist approaches are evident in various constructivist contributions (Checkel, 1998; Dannreuther, 1997; Rosamond, 1999) and in the somewhat wider notion of 'reflective' approaches to European governance (Jørgensen, 1997). Perhaps the most distinctive 'sociological' contribution (as distinct from historical institutionalism broadly defined) emanates from the interest displayed by some writers in frameworks of ideas or discourses. These are treated as cognitive institutions that shape the 'boundaries of the possible' for actors in the European context. As Markus Jachtenfuchs notes, 'institutions create theories about themselves which have, in turn, consequences for the interaction of actors' (Jachtenfuchs, 1997: 47). It may also be that these 'theories' extend to the world outside; to the environment in which action takes place. Moreover, for some, discourses should be seen as institutions in their own right insofar as they can guide political action by denoting appropriate or plausible behaviour in light of an agreed environment. Such ideas can be applied to the prevailing narratives within institutions such as the European Commission where a prevailing neoliberal ethos is discernible in some of the main 'economic' Directorates General such as DGs I, II and III, whereas DG XI has been characterized as being infused with preferences for 'ecological modernization' (Weale and Williams, 1992). The thesis here is not only that the discourses are shapers of policy initiative (e.g. neoliberal policy frames exclude the sponsorship of Keynesian-style reflation packages), but that the capacity to shape and deploy these ideas is a powerful strategic tool. For example, the Commission has shown a tendency in recent years to define the external environment as 'globalized' and, therefore, threatening to the competitiveness of the European economy. This not only coincides with and supports preferences for market liberalization, but also helps to legitimize European-level action (as opposed to a reversion to national solutions) (Rosamond, 1999 and, to some extent Cameron, 1995). Others have moved down the multi-level polity to explore the significance of different national discourses of European integration for alternative patterns of domestic-EU linkage (for example, Holm, 1997; Larsen, 1997).

The ideational dimension of sociological institutionalism is linked to a more general move away from rational choice theories of action (Wind, 1997). This produces several routes into the study of ideas, beliefs, knowledge and discourses and their application to EU policy-making (Jachtenfuchs, 1997; Richardson, 1996a; Risse-Kappen, 1996). The central question here is how ideas and discourses become embedded. Thomas Risse draws attention to the role of communicative action: 'the processes by which norms are internalized and ideas become consensual ... communicative processes are a necessary condition for ideas to become consensual (or fall by the wayside for that matter)' (Risse-Kappen,

1996: 69). Theories of communicative action – which draw especially on the work of Jürgen Habermas – focus on processes of deliberation and argumentation, which in turn are seen as manufacturing the basic epistemic 'glue' that binds actors together. Looking for argumentative manoeuvres based purely on the 'rational' pursuit of material interests threatens to misdirect the study of EU institutions into the analysis of formal bargaining procedures. Also, it is hard to see why institutions perpetuate themselves if actor interaction is *only* based upon instrumental rationality. Once preferences diverge, then there would be no *rational* reason for the continued existence of the institution. For Risse, the EU is better understood as an evolving polity, held together by the binding power of normative consensus. Research inspired by theories of communicative action should focus upon non-hierarchical processes of informal transnational exchange. This is not to say that instrumental calculus does not exist within the EU polity, but that a fuller picture will be gained through investigating patterns of communicative behaviour. The EU is a potentially fruitful setting for this kind of work because it has an unusual level of institutionalization for an international organization. Risse hypothesises that 'deliberative processes are more likely to occur in highly institutionalized settings providing norms, rules and procedures that establish some degree of trust among the actors, as well as the possibility of informal contacts' (Risse-Kappen, 1996: 71). It follows that policy progress is more likely to occur in situations where this holds and is less likely when it does not. Thus, the difficulty of moving towards the Common Foreign and Security Policy (CFSP) envisaged in the Treaty on European Union would, from a instrumental rationalist viewpoint, be seen as resulting from divergent policy goals among the member-state governments plus the high premium normally placed upon foreign policy autonomy. A non-rationalist, communicative action approach would identify the 'lack of opportunities for discursive policy deliberation' (Risse-Kappen, 1996: 71).

The search by communicative action theorists for conditions where ideas and discourses stabilize creates an affinity with the policy network literature discussed below. However, it is worth pausing to consider one broader theoretical issue that is raised by the appearance of institutionalist approaches into the political science of European integration: the relationship between structure and agency. The agent–structure problem is an old chestnut of social science (Hay, 1995: Wendt, 1987). It revolves around the extent to which actors (or agents or subjects) have the space to be creative, and the extent to which the formal and informal properties of structure impose constraints and define the boundaries of possible behaviour. The debate is deeply philosophical and inevitably raises some fundamental questions about the nature of social reality. The issue is important because it also raises questions about the mechanisms of and possibilities for social change. To use institutionalist terminology is to suggest that institutions are shapers of behaviour and perhaps cognition, thereby exhibiting a 'structuralist bias' (Hay and Wincott, 1998). But it is important to recognize that while this may hold across the institutionalist spectrum, there are some subtle variations. Sociological institutionalism is usually thought of as privileging structure over agency, although some of its strands do give space to actors to be innovative and thus potentially subversive of prevailing institutional norms. This is particularly true of constructivism which tends to begin from a depiction of social reality where agency and structure are 'mutually constitutive'. Neither is 'ontologically primitive' (Checkel, 1998: 326). This position is largely consistent with the structurationist position of Anthony Giddens (1984). This builds on the premise that agents may make structures, but are also subject to the behavioural modifications that are imposed by those structures (see also Bhaskar, 1979 and Cerny, 1990; Archer, 1988 offers a more structuralist variant). This is important because of the implications that it has for interests. Interests and identities do not exist exogenously to a context of interaction between structures and agents. This contrasts markedly with rational choice perspectives, as we have seen. The emphasis on rational utility maximizing agents does not seem to make rational choice institutionalism obviously structuralist. However, it is an approach that explores rational strategic action within particular contexts. Thus, as Tsebelis points out 'the prevailing institutions (rules of the game) *determine* the behaviour of the actors, which in turn produces political or social outcomes' (cited in Hay and Wincott, 1998: 952, emphasis in original).

The structure–agency debate is especially pertinent for historical institutionalism which, as suggested above, seeks to account for the effects of decisions to create institutions that were made in previous historical contexts. So, as Colin Hay and Daniel Wincott note, this perspective is purporting to explore the relationships between 'institutional architects, institutional subjects and institutional environments' (1998: 957). This is a particularly important and challenging project from the point of view of EU studies since it can incorporate an explanation of the origins of the institutions as well as accounting for ongoing institutional logics and changes in the EU system. It is also true, as Laura Cram (1997) points out, that institutions can be construed as purposive agents. In the EU there is plenty of evidence of Commission entrepreneurship, activism on the part of the European Parliament and expansive jurisprudence on the part of the European Court of Justice. All of this indicates that institutions (as actors) can create institutions (as structures).

Policy networks and actor-based models

As we have seen above, policy network analysis is recommended by Peterson (1995a) for the study of the meso or sectoral level of analysis and by Richardson (1996b) for the analysis of various 'moments' in the EU's decision-making process. Perhaps here more than anywhere we see the significance of the input of policy-analytical approaches into the study of the EU and also concepts and frameworks that have very little to do with *integration*. The image of networks is an attempt to depict the highly segmented nature of EU policy-making in which advice, consultation, expertise and technocratic rationality are the means used to cope with the regulatory thicket of day-to-day decision-making. It also aims to make sense of the multi-actor way in which sectoral policy-making operates and how these multiple 'stakeholders' in the policy process play their 'nested games' (Tsebelis, 1990). Policy network analysis is also consistent with the MLG view that power has become dispersed within the EU polity.

The origins of the approach are firmly rooted in the political science of British government from the late 1970s. The pressing problem here was how to explain continuity in policy-making. Jeremy Richardson and Grant Jordan's studies revealed that stability was enhanced by the existence of closed and stable communities of actors organized into interlocking and overlapping networks (Richardson and Jordan, 1979). The aim of this literature was to place emphasis on the decisive impact of *informalities* in the policy process and, therefore, to direct empirical research attention away from formal, parliamentary institutions of government. 'Policy community' became the conventional label for these particular kinds of network based upon commonly held assumptions about interests and methods of operation. It has also become conventional to speak of policy communities as specific instances of the wider phenomenon of policy networks.

Policy networks are defined in many ways and there is substantial debate in policy studies literature about what they are (Richardson, 1996a and b). John Peterson describes a policy network as 'an arena for the mediation of the interests of government and interest groups' (1995b: 391; see also 1995a: 76). He goes on:

> The term 'network' implies that clusters of actors representing multiple organisations interact with one another and share information and resources. 'Mediation' implies that the networks usually are settings for the playing of positive sum games: they facilitate reconciliation, settlement or compromise between different interests which have a stake in outcomes in a particular policy sector.
>
> (Peterson, 1995b: 391)

So, policy networks are usually understood as venues for the pooling and/ or exchange of information and resources. They are useful because they give actors access to information and resources that they could not otherwise obtain and they facilitate policy-making by reinforcing norms. The most stable form of policy network is said to be the policy community. Here actors are bound together in a series of relations of dependency (i.e. actor *a* needs *x* from actor *b* and actor *b* needs *y* from actor *a*) and networks remain largely impenetrable to outside actors. Membership is ongoing. In these situations policy outcomes reflect the stability of the community. On the other hand, in some sectors policy outcomes are often less predictable. Here policy network analysis hypothesizes that open 'issue networks' are the norm rather than closed policy communities. These are characterized by a fluidity of members and permeable boundaries.

Applied to the EU, it is argued that this form of analysis focuses attention on the actors involved in the policy process, along with their motivations and their interests. As Richardson notes: 'If EU politics is about who gets what, how and when ... then identifying the range of actors involved and trying to see if they can realistically be described as networks is at least a starting point for understanding how the system of making EU policy works' (1996a: 10). On the face of it, policy network analysis has the apparent advantage of generating a framework that is testable through detailed empirical investigation. However, a cautionary note is sounded by Hussein Kassim (1994) who expresses serious reservations about the usefulness of policy network analysis in the EU context. Kassim suggests that the 'elusive fluidity' of the EU policy process means that there is little continuity and much fragmentation. However, policy network analysis requires situations of ongoing policy reproduction to work properly. Moreover, Kassim argues that the policy network approach loses sight of the potentially important relationships between the Community institutions. Policy network analysis only works when the institutional dimensions of policy-making are quite weak. Finally, there is the problem of actually identifying discrete networks empirically. The last is a serious issue for any theory that seeks empirical verification. Does the heuristic device (in this case 'policy network') lend itself to observation and measurement? In response, Peterson (1995b) asserts that the 'elusive fluidity' problem is precisely the sort of thing that policy network analysis would want to identify in the EU. Stability is not assumed as a condition, but as a variable and policy networks are just as likely to be absent as they are to be identifiable. Whether policy communities arise is dependent on the existence of resource dependencies among actors and their ability to perform some sort of closure on access to the network. In response to the question of the significance of institutions, Peterson reiterates his discussion of the levels of analysis question, which places policy network analysis firmly into the meso (or sectoral) level of analysis. Policy network analysis claims to capture the dynamics of regulatory decision-making on a sector by sector basis and thus purports to offer a theory of the everyday politics of the EU.

That said, network-type models are not always confined to sectoral analysis. The literatures on epistemic communities and advocacy coalitions bring actor-based analysis into the issue of agenda setting. The literature on epistemic communities arose largely in International Relations circles. Peter Haas (1992) describes increasingly numerous networks of experts who supply knowledge to authoritative policy actors. This knowledge not only helps to legitimize the decisions made by actors (by giving them an external source of 'scientific' authority), but it also helps to influence the interests of actors and to frame coherent positions for bargaining. Even if the crucial decisions are made through negotiations between national executives, Haas's arguments suggest that there exist influential forms of non-state authority that acquire power through access to and expression of knowledge. Epistemic communities are bound together by shared beliefs, shared understandings of cause and effect within their particular domain of knowledge and shared notions of what actually constitutes valid knowledge. States require the input of epistemic communities, explains Haas, because

> In international policy coordination, the forms of uncertainty that tend to stimulate demands for information are those which arise from the strong dependence of states on each other's policy choices for success in obtaining goals and those which involve multiple and only partly estimable consequences of action.
>
> (Haas, 1992: 4)

Such an approach to EU policy-formulation challenges the intergovernmentalist emphasis on the primacy of governmental preferences (see Chapter 6). The choice made by member-states to pursue Economic and Monetary Union (EMU) could be treated as a puzzle to be solved through a forensic analysis of preferences, bargains and trade-offs among states. The epistemic community approach asks the prior question about the forms of knowledge upon which governmental preferences for EMU were based (Verdun, 1999).

The knowledge–interests relationship also lies at the heart of the advocacy coalition framework developed for policy analysis by Paul Sabatier (1988). This approach looks at how aggregations of individuals with shared belief systems (a mixture of knowledge, perceptions and core values) operate within policy-making. Unlike the largely technocratic character of epistemic communities, advocacy coalitions purposefully seek policy goals. Sabatier's approach is not only distinctive because it identifies a new form of influential non-state actor, but also because it rejects the idea that the influence of groups will be determined by their relative endowments of power. Rather, what Sabatier calls 'policy oriented learning' within and across coalitions is important (see Radaelli, 1999). Moreover, these learning processes are likely to occur in environments where the prestige of expertise is acknowledged. The receptiveness of the Commission to external input may provide one such venue (Richardson, 1996b: 18). Moreover, the tendency of the EU system to periodically dredge itself up by creating new decision rules and expanding the range of policy competence could be construed as an ideal venue for the strategic intervention of advocacy coalitions (Peterson and Bomberg, 1999: 24).

These actor-based approaches have the effect of emphasizing the role of agency within the EU system, often (deliberately) at the expense of structural explanations of polity development and change (Peterson and Bomberg, 1999). This sets up an interesting (though far from perfect) contrast between institutionalist and actor-based approaches in the con-temporary literature. But the approaches are united in other ways. Most obviously, they tend to question intergovernmentalist narratives about the EU. In addition, both institutionalist and actor-based approaches insist that 'politics' matters and that crude economistic readings of development and change do not assist a full understanding of EU governance.

Bringing it all together? Theorising supranational governance

One clear outcome of the governance turn in EU studies has been the widespread disposal of 'grand theory' and the migration of theoretical work to the 'middle range'. As Peterson (1995a) notes, neither institutionalism nor policy network analysis aspires to explain everything. Rather, they are theories which purport to explain elements or particular slices of the EU polity. Yet the renewed emphasis on governance (rather than integration) and the recognition of segmentation and diversity across the policy spectrum has not deterred some writers from thinking in grander terms. A case in point is Alec Stone Sweet and Wayne Sandholtz's theory of supranational governance (Stone Sweet and Sandholtz, 1997; Sandholtz and Stone Sweet, 1998). They pitch their framework as a less state-centric and more supranational alternative to the influential work on liberal intergovernmentalism developed by Andrew Moravcsik (1993) (see Chapter 6 below). To do this, Stone Sweet and Sandholtz deploy the image of demand and supply sides to integration. The role of transnational exchange is central to generating demands for regulation and governance capacity at the European level. Supranational institutions work to supply these things. The emphasis on transnational exchange and the development of social interaction between actors across borders recalls Karl Deutsch's thinking about the sociology of community building in the international system (see Chapter 2). Stone Sweet and Sandholtz are less interested in the extent to which these transactions create identities or have major cognitive impacts. Rather, they are concerned with how these transactions become institutionalized and, thus, how they create effective channels for demands to be generated. This is the key variable in their analysis. Variability in levels of transborder transaction and intra-EU exchange may help to explain why some policy areas are more supranationalized than others. But differing levels of transnational interaction do not explain patterns of supranationalism in their own right. Demands generated in the transnational domain stimulate a response from the decision-making institutions. Here Stone Sweet and Sandholtz borrow from the institutionalist vocabulary to consider how institutions can reproduce tendencies to expand governance and rule-making:

> We view intergovernmental bargaining and decision-making as embedded in processes that are provoked and sustained by the expansion of transnational society, the pro-integrative activities of supranational organizations, and the growing density of supranational rules. And ... these processes gradually, but inevitably, reduce the capacity of the member states to control outcomes.
>
> (Stone Sweet and Sandholtz, 1997: 299–300)

Haasian neofunctionalism is reread here as a form of institutionalist analysis. Institutions acquire legitimacy through both their own efforts to promote supranational norms and the lobbying activities of interests that seek access to public officials in pursuit of their goals.

This leads Stone Sweet and Sandholtz to the depiction of a continuum from intergovernmental politics through to supranational politics. Intergovernmental politics represents the ideal type of international bargaining among states where the EU operates as an international regime in the strictest sense of the term (see Chapter 7). The supranational end of the continuum represents centralized control of governance capacity over policy areas across the constituent member-states. Different policy domains can then be placed at relevant points along the continuum in relation to three variables: the intensity of formal and informal EU-level rules, the EU-level governance structures and the level of development of transnational society. Moreover, '[g]rowth in one element of the supranational trio ... creates conditions that favor the growth of the other two' (Stone Sweet and Sandholtz, 1997: 305). There are heavy echoes of institutionalist thinking here, but there remains the question of how these mechanisms click into place. Here Stone Sweet and Sandholtz place great emphasis on the role of non-state actors operating in transnational space. A mixture of cross-border interactions and organized interest group activity is seen as an important stimulus for change largely because actors in rational pursuit of their interests begin to engage in various forms of transnational activity. So, firms engaging in significant amounts of cross-border activity have an interest in the regionalization of various relevant aspects of economic governance. Similarly, transnational activity is the generator of spillovers because the growth of supranational rules and the increased responsiveness of central institutions of governance reduces the costs of transactions. Moreover, the existence of particular patterns of rules and rule-making creates a strong institutional logic for persistence of those patterns. There is also an emphasis on external economic stimuli, most notably in the form of changes to the global economic environment that are captured by the idea of 'globalization'. Transnational actors are seen as the agents who bring the agendas set by globalization into the EC system. Again, firms facing competitive threats on world markets may lobby for the further liberalization of the European market space. The emphasis on transnationalism also poses a direct challenge to intergovernmentalist accounts (Chapters 4 and 6). At the heart of Stone Sweet and Sandholtz's argument is the claim that 'rather than being the generator of integration, intergovernmental bargaining is more often its product' (1997: 307).

This is a challenging proposal for a research programme to test the extent to which non-state actor transactions drive the growth of European-level governance. What is interesting about it from the point of view of this chapter is the way in which Stone Sweet and Sandholtz incorporate elements of earlier integration theory, emphasize governance rather than integration as their dependent variable and attempt to generate something akin to a grand theory.

Conclusions

The reinvigoration of EU studies has coincided with the deepening of integration that began in the mid-1980s with the single market programme. There have been serious attempts to think again about classical models of integration. Neofunctionalist reasoning seemed to have found a degree of new legitimacy as the logics of the single market project became apparent. Renewed thinking about federalism has been widespread and Deutschian notions of transactionalism have also found a place as some analysts seek to make linkages between the emergence of informal transnationalism and the formal drift of governance functions to the European level. However, any notion that integration theory in unexpurgated form has been revived needs to be tempered for two reasons associated with the evident 'governance turn' in EU studies. Firstly, there has been much contemplation of the extent to which theories such as neofunctionalism can be used to explain the whole of the EU system, with some arguments going as far as to confine such grand theorizing to the super systemic level. This leads to the second qualification. The governance turn has consisted of significant inward migration of policy analytic and comparative political science perspectives into EU studies. This has led to a serious interrogation of the utility of perspectives supposedly derived from International Relations and the growth of research inspired by a collection of mid-range theories, including the various institutionalisms and actor-based approaches such as policy network analysis. This has meant a gradual transformation of the techniques through which knowledge about the EU is acquired and the lenses through which it is studied. It is probably fair to say that outright neofunctionalism is no longer a norm amongst scholars of European integration. But there is still some resilience of intergovernmentalist accounts and these are explored in greater detail in the next chapter.

Perhaps the most provocative claim to emerge from some discussions of the 'governance turn' is the alleged obsolescence of International Relations as a disciplinary base for EU studies. This argument is taken up again in Chapter 7, but in anticipation it might be noted that institutionalism in its various guises has become a substantial part of the international studies intellectual repertoire. The emphasis on ideas and norms, found in both institutionalism and actor-based approaches, is similarly prevalent. So, in some ways, the intellectual trajectories of political science and International Relations have followed similar pathways. This then raises the question about whether there is still utility in plundering the resources of contemporary international theory to shed light upon the EU.

One of the implications of rejecting International Relations is that the EU defies categorization and comparison in international terms. It is argued that there can be no general theory of international integration or at least that the EU experience cannot be used for that purpose. One of the features of the development of multi-level governance models is that they focus specifically on the *sui generis* aspects of the EU. But the models which have been deployed, from Majone's thoughts about the regulatory state, through the various institutionalist contributions to the detailed meso-level studies inspired by policy network theory, all make clear that the EU can be treated as an instance of a polity or a policy system or a regime of governance. The question for International Relations is whether this image of the EU is the only one available or whether we need to think in more detail about the super-systemic level of analysis and the place of European integration therein.

Chapter 6

Intergovernmental Europe?

As Stanley Hoffmann (1966) suggested, the European nation-state has been rather more obstinate in the face of the processes of European integration than the early neofunctionalists might have expected. The formal institutions and policy-making processes of the EU might represent the emergence of a new and complex polity, but most analysts – including those discussed in the previous chapter – find it difficult to factor the state out of their frameworks completely. Indeed, a large proportion still regards the state as *the* primary actor in the development of European integration. William Wallace (1990), for example, sets up a useful distinction between so-called 'formal' and 'informal' integration. The latter denotes the sorts of economic and social interdependencies and interpenetrations that develop without the sanction of deliberate political decision. Formal integration consists of those acts of institution-building which emerge from the cooperative deliberations of national elites. It is possible to argue that formal integration is a reaction to informal integration – perhaps to promote, capture or constrain it. There are two routes to arguing for state primacy here. The first is to say that formal integration matters more than informal integration, because it is these decisions which determine the nature and scope of European-level governance and, thus, hold the most crucial implications for the survival of the nation-state and national governments as authoritative entities. The second is to argue that formal integration is the process through which informal integration is promoted. From this point of view, the latter is not possible without the former. Networked market interactions across borders are not possible without political decisions such as those embodied in the Single European Act. To understand the transformations of the contemporary European economy, runs this argument, it is necessary to understand the complex national-interest driven negotiations that produced the SEA.

This chapter has two purposes: firstly to re-emphasize the idea that there is rather more to the present theoretical debate than the extension of the long-standing conversation between intergovernmentalists and modified neofunctionalists and secondly to note, nonetheless, the continuing significance of state-centric formulations. These take many forms and embellish in crucial ways the 'classical' version of intergovernmentalism that flows from realist International Relations. It also lays some of the groundwork for the following chapter which argues for the usefulness of a

130

return to 'international theory' for fruitful theoretical developments in the analysis of European integration and EU governance. It is common to argue that contemporary EU studies divides into two broad theoretical camps: multi-level governance and state-centrism (Marks, Hooghe and Blank, 1996; Pollack, 1996: 430). The multi-level governance school is really the province of the type of work discussed in the previous chapter. The state-centric view generates a series of propositions about the centrality of nation-states – or more precisely, national governments – to the development of the EU.

The assertion that states should be regarded as the primary actors in the integration process is a commonplace well beyond the specialist realm of EU academic studies. The language of international exchange is the staple of most (if not all) media coverage of the European Union. Treaty revisions are presented as moments when the course of the integration process is debated, decided, altered and/or consolidated. The negotiations leading to these crucial junctures are shown as *inter*governmental; any politics here is *inter*national. The literature on 'multi-level governance' has begun to offer an empirical challenge to this position, but this is rather more than a matter of what 'really' happens in the 'real world' of European integration. There are also crucial theoretical issues at stake here. Therefore, it is important to get to grips with the sorts of assumptions that reside at the core of state-centred accounts of integration and to begin to dwell on how and why it is that states are thought to occupy a primary position in the explanation.

Realism and neorealism

The dominant strand of theoretical work in the last 50 years or so of International Relations scholarship has been realism. Realist theory developed as a systematic account of international politics through the work of writers such as Hans Morgenthau (1985) in the period after the Second World War. Realism grew out of a critical engagement with the inter-war idealist emphasis on the perfectibility of humanity and the virtues of collective security, post-national systems for peace and the advocacy of international organizations. At the core of the realist prospectus is the idea that international politics is about the interaction of self-interested actors (states) in an essentially anarchic environment – a situation where there is no overarching authority to provide order on a global scale. States are seen as rational, unitary actors that derive their interests from an evaluation of their position in the system of states. In classical realism, these interests are defined in terms of survival which in turn generates an interstate politics built around questions of security and military capabilities. In the context of anarchy, rational state policy-making involves minimizing risk and maximizing benefits. But the quest for security by any state by necessity leaves all other states less secure. Forms of international cooperation can be seen as attempts to deal with this core security dilemma, but any attempt to bring about the dissolution of the states system through institutions of post-national governance is misguided. The self-help system is a natural, often self-regulating and even, perhaps, a highly ethical way of conducting international affairs (Murray, 1997).

The realist approach has undergone something of a revival in the past twenty years with the onset of neorealist work. Neorealist International Relations is usually associated with Kenneth Waltz's *Theory of International Politics* (Waltz, 1979). The book is a bold attempt to give realist thinking rigour and a parsimonious edge over rival perspectives. More specifically, Waltz updates realist analysis by paying attention to the *systemic* level of analysis. The conduct of international relations cannot simply be explained with reference to human nature or the inherent properties of states. It must also take structure into account. Neorealism is thus a theory of how the structural properties of anarchy provide particular sets of limitations upon possibilities for action in international politics.

For Waltz the international system is characterized by anarchy rather than hierarchy. It is composed of units that are formally and functionally equal (states) and the key variable is 'the distribution of capabilities across units' (a system level attribute). This refers to how much power state a possesses *in relation to* states b, c and so on. State behaviour will vary with this distribution of capabilities so that structural change will alter patterns of conflict and cooperation. Anarchy *can* produce order, but it inhibits effective and long-standing cooperation amongst states because of the essentially competitive and rational nature of the interstate game. In other words unit (state) survival is always in question. Rational states realize this, and so seek to maximize the possibilities for their survival. This is not to say that cooperation never occurs. The emergence of alliances and forms of cooperation is a well-established rational means to the end of survival and the nature of this balancing behaviour is bound up with the issue of relative capabilities. The interests and actions of the most powerful states constitute the nature of the system and any alteration in this distribution of capabilities is likely to induce alterations in unit behaviour (for critical discussions see Keohane, 1986; Buzan, Jones and Little, 1993).

It is far from straightforward to construct a neorealist theory of European integration (but see Grieco, 1995, 1996). As one commentator puts it, 'neorealists like Waltz have not been much interested in European integration processes' (Stone, 1994: 457). Put another way, which allows us to impute the sort of arguments which neorealists might make, 'neorealism is a theory of why, in "international political" society, the establishment of stable norms is either unlikely or impossible, why formal institutions do not develop meaningful autonomy, and therefore why a constitutional international regime is unimaginable' (Stone, 1994: 449). Because of the emphasis upon the systemic level, the impulse of neorealism is to place the formation of bodies like the EU into the wider structural context. Post-war European integration is seen very much as a creature of the move to a bipolar system, responding to the dynamics of superpower rivalry (Waltz, 1979: 71; Stone, 1994: 458). In historical terms then, contemporary European integration represents an intensification of interstate cooperation within the overall context of the Cold War. The pursuit of this logic has led some contemporary realists to speculate about the consequences of the end of superpower bipolarity. For instance, the notably apocalyptic scenario offered by John Mearsheimer (1990) contends that cooperation amongst European states will become less easy in the absence of both a tangible threat from the communist bloc and the protective wing of the United States. International suspicion will emerge as a consequence of both lost autonomy and imbalances in gains from cooperation (Mearsheimer, 1990: 47). Europe in the context of multipolarity is more likely to be a venue for conflict rather than cooperation.

The neorealist emphasis on system should not distract us from its biases in terms of agency. The stories it tells are about states playing fairly traditional interstate games. The EU is viewed as a mechanism for interstate cooperation that fulfilled the survival imperatives of a group of West European states in the context of an emerging bipolar order, and perhaps was driven by the preferences of the most powerful states in that game. It would be slightly unfair to accuse neorealists of failing to explain the complexities of EU governance. This does not really form part of the research agenda of neorealism and it might be argued that this approach can be confined to providing a possible system-level explanation which neither seeks nor needs to explain other levels of the integration process or EU governance functions (Peterson, 1995a).

The neorealist Joseph Grieco (1995) tackles head-on the apparent abdication of neorealism from EU studies. Taking the successful negotiation of the Treaty on European Union (TEU) (1992) and the prospect of Economic and Monetary Union as his point of departure, Grieco acknowledges that neorealist theory faces serious challenges if it is to continue to offer an explanation of the trajectory of international politics in Europe. This would be the case even if the processes envisaged at Maastricht were to collapse. Neorealists still had to explain why such a bold and risk-laden exercise in innovation was even envisaged. The TEU project seems to counteract neorealist assumptions about the low esteem in which states are likely to hold international institutions. Fears about 'cheating, dependency and relative gains' are not likely to be quelled by the mere existence of an international institution (Grieco, 1995: 27). Moreover, as we have seen, neorealists can explain the anomalous longevity of the EU in terms of post-Second World War balances of power politics.

Grieco identifies four problems for neorealists. The first concerns the core neorealist assumption of instrumental rationality among states. One way would be to regard the Maastricht negotiations as 'irrational', but then it would be necessary to develop an argument about why such an abandonment of state rationality occurred. Alternatively, neorealists could assume that instrumental rationality did operate in this case, but this would leave them having 'to acknowledge that rational states may sometimes assign importance to international institutions' (Grieco, 1995: 28). Secondly, the progressive assignment of powers to Community institutions suggests that anarchy is not the main structural feature of international politics in this region. Thirdly, the increasing significance of Germany in the Community throughout the 1980s creates expectations, from a neorealist perspective, that the other member-states would seek to rectify these growing asymmetries. Yet, if anything, the Maastricht process consolidated the hegemonic status of Germany within the EU. Finally, the relative position of neorealism as a serious research programme is put into jeopardy as functionalism, institutionalism and other theoretical starting points are able to generate more empirically plausible propositions.

Grieco's response to this crisis is to develop an alternative hypothesis derived from core neorealist assumptions that not only offers a potential explanation for the intensification of European integration in the 1980s and 1990s, but also – in his view – has greater merit than rival accounts. He reads the EMU negotiations as an interstate bargain without initial supranational sponsorship. This creates the puzzle of how and why states came to choose the mode of EMU developed in the TEU. He offers a 'voice opportunities hypothesis' which states that

> if states share a common interest and undertake negotiations on rules constituting a collaborative arrangement, then the weaker but still influential partners will seek to ensure that the rules so constructed will provide sufficient opportunities for them to voice their concerns and interests and thereby prevent or at least ameliorate their domination by stronger parties.
>
> (Grieco, 1995: 35)

This is an ingenious attempt to use neorealist premises to explain institutionalization, but it does rest on deeply contentious assumptions, notably that states are the primary actors and that they are best conceived of as unitary entities deploying instrumental rationality. The validity of these assumptions is not just challenged by non-state-centrists. Other largely state-centric accounts of integration begin from alternative starting points, notably those that emphasize the significance of domestic politics.

Domestic politics and two-level games

A rather more pungent criticism would address neorealism's version of the origin of state interests and preferences. This is one of the main thrusts of the recent debate in International Relations between neorealism and neoliberalism (Baldwin, 1993; Kegley, 1995). Neoliberals tend to be more interested in the *interaction* of state preferences rather than in the distribution of capabilities among states (Stone, 1994: 460). As a consequence, neoliberals are as interested in the formation of state preferences as they are in the bargaining processes that take place between states. Such theories of preference formation almost inevitably begin to factor in processes of domestic politics.

Realists have tended to downplay the significance of politics *within* nations for the operation of politics *among* nations. As suggested above, for realists foreign policy is not the product of political pressures and negotiations at the domestic level, but rather interests are derived from foreign policy executives' perceptions of external context. One of the central features of contemporary state-centred scholarship has been the way in which the neoliberal concern with domestic factors has been brought into the analysis. Simon Bulmer's attempt to construct a domestic politics approach to EC policy-making was an early attempt to do just this (Bulmer, 1983). Bulmer maintained that national governments were clearly the key actors in the Community system and that the interaction of national governmental preferences was the most effective way of under-standing the dynamics of integration. However, Bulmer also pointed to the fact that governments acted as gatekeepers at the cusp of the EC and national political systems. This is the key to Bulmer's intervention which also offers a theory of the formation of national preferences or, to put it another way, a government's 'European policy'. Bulmer's reasoning is bottom up. That is to say that he begins with the view that the basic unit of the EC system is the national *polity* – not member-state executives. The national polity is the source of legitimacy for state actors. It follows that in order to understand the bargaining that occurs between governments at the European level, we need to attend to the domestic roots of the state preferences which are negotiated in those bargains. Andrew Moravcsik's (1991) analysis of the origins of the Single European Act (SEA) offers a case study that is consistent with some of the ideas developed by Bulmer. Moravcsik's basic point is that the SEA arose because of the converging preferences of the three most important member-states of the EC (France, Britain and the Federal Republic of Germany) around versions of neoliberal political economy. In each case, the preference for a more liberal and Europeanized market space was rooted in very specific sets of domestic circumstances. There is a continued quasi-realist emphasis on the centrality of states and relative power in bargaining dynamics (Cornett and Caporaso, 1992). Note one of Moravcsik's most forthright conclusions: 'the primary source of integration lies in the interests of the states themselves and the relative power each brings to Brussels' (1991: 75). Yet there is also a liberal–pluralist emphasis which allows intergovernmental analysis to acquire one of the key advantages of neofunctionalist integration theory and theories of International Political Economy more generally: the exploration of the interface between the domestic and the international (Underhill, 1994).

More recent work has drawn on Robert Putnam's influential idea of two-level games (Putnam, 1988). The idea of two-level games is an attempt to offer a metaphor for the linkages between domestic (national level) politics and international relations. Putnam's core point is that national executives play games in two arenas more or less simultaneously. At the domestic level, power-seeking/enhancing office holders aim to build coalitions of support among domestic groups. At the international level, the same actors seek to bargain in ways that enhance their position domestically by meeting the demands of key domestic constituents. In many ways this simply formalizes Bulmer's point about the domestic sources of legitimacy. In terms of the debate discussed in the next chapter, the two-level games analogy could be used to show the importance of interdisciplinarity between International Relations and Comparative Politics. Nonetheless, it continues to assert the primacy of national governmental actors in creating integration outcomes and uses Comparative Politics to ascertain the origins of those state preferences.

Liberal intergovernmentalism, the rescue of the nation-state and the logic of intergovernmentalism

Perhaps the ultimate example of an attempt to theorize European integration as a two-level game is provided by Andrew Moravcsik's liberal intergovernmentalist analysis (Moravcsik, 1993, 1998). Moravcsik offers a model of a two-level game to explain European integration consisting of a liberal theory of national preference formation and an intergovernmentalist account of strategic bargaining between states. The former, which theorizes the demand side (that is the demand for integration outcomes), sees national preferences arising in the contexts provided by the domestic politics of the member-states. This again represents a departure from classic intergovernmentalism which sees national interests arising in the context of the sovereign state's perception of its relative position in the states system. For Moravcsik, national interests are best viewed as consequences of a state–society interaction:

> National interests ... emerge through domestic political conflict as societal groups compete for political influence, national and transnational coalitions form and new policy alternatives are recognized by governments. An understanding of domestic politics is a precondition for, not a supplement to, the analysis of strategic interaction among states.
>
> (Moravcsik, 1993: 481)

So, once formulated, interests are then bargained in an intergovernmental fashion (the supply side). While the demand side of the process highlights the advantages of cooperative activity and the coordination of policy, the supply side demonstrates the restricted range of possible integration outcomes. At the heart of Moravcsik's framework is – again – an assumption of state rationality. This is an assumption shared with realist International Relations, but Moravcsik develops the idea that rational state behaviour does not emerge from fixed preferences, but rather from dynamic political processes in the domestic polity. According to Moravcsik, his approach avoids the twin perils of 'demand side reductionism' and 'supply side reductionism', in which analysts unnecessarily privilege one or other of the two arenas in their explanation. The demand side is characterized as highly complex processes of national preference formation and the nature of these games will most likely vary on a case by case basis. Nonetheless, certain sorts of dynamic are common across states:

> The primary interest of governments is to maintain themselves in office ... this requires the support of a coalition of domestic voters, parties, interest groups and bureaucracies, whose views are transmitted, directly or indirectly, through domestic institutions and practices of political representation. Through this process emerges the set of national interests or goals that states bring to international negotiations.
>
> (Moravcsik, 1993a: 483)

The supply side – the domain of interstate bargaining – is equally complicated and again Moravcsik recommends the application of detailed empirical analysis. Nonetheless, he makes three assumptions about the particular bargaining environment of the EU. Firstly, it is a situation that states enter into voluntarily and which is non-coercive, particularly since the major 'history-making' decisions are made by unanimity rather than by majority voting. Secondly, echoing institutionalism (see Chapter 5), interstate bargaining in the EU takes place in an 'information-rich' setting. The environment is information-rich in two ways: there is widespread knowledge about the technicalities of EU policy-making and states have a clear idea of the preferences of and constraints upon other states. Thirdly, the transaction costs of EU bargaining are low because of the long time-frame of negotiations and the innumerable possibilities for issue linkages, trade-offs and sub-bargains (Moravcsik, 1993a: 498).

The processes of intergovernmental bargaining at the European level also strengthens states *vis-à-vis* their home polities:

> National governments are able to take initiatives and reach bargains in Council negotiations with relatively little constraint. The EC provides information to governments that is not generally available ... National leaders undermine potential opposition by reaching bargains in Brussels first and presenting domestic groups with an 'up or down' choice ... Greater domestic agenda-setting power in the hands of national political leaders increases the ability of governments to reach agreements by strengthening the ability of governments to gain domestic ratification for compromises or tactical issue linkages.
>
> (Moravcsik, 1993a: 515)

This apparently paradoxical claim that international integration actually *strengthens* the state has been developed considerably in recent literature. Elsewhere Moravcsik himself has argued at length about the ways in which membership of organizations such as the EU enhances the domestic autonomy of governments (Moravcsik, 1994; see also Taylor, 1991). This provides one possible answer to the ongoing puzzle of why states should agree to processes that would ultimately make them less autonomous.

These ideas echo the alternative brand of state-centred analysis found in the work of the economic historian Alan Milward. Milward, along with a group of like-minded colleagues, has undertaken detailed empirical analysis of the origins of contemporary European integration in the 1940s and the 1950s which develops the thesis of integration as the *rescue* of the European nation-state (Milward, 1984, 1992; Milward et al., 1993). Milward's empiricism is self-consciously and quite explicitly sceptical about the claims of 'theory' and draws sustenance from a vituperative critique of neofunctionalism (Milward, 1992: 1–20; Milward and Sørensen, 1993; see also Chapter 8). Nonetheless, his analysis carries with it quite important theoretical implications, not least the resemblance to the more formally theoretical work of liberal intergovernmentalists.

The Milward hypothesis is built around the perception that post-war West European governments were faced with the twin dilemmas of growing interdependence and increased societal demands and disaffection (the latter in the context of economic hardship in the 1930s and wartime austerity in the 1940s). In particular, governments were faced with the question of how to deliver national policy programmes to important domestic constituencies. These policy programmes were not simply packages of measures designed to construct coalitions supportive of a particular set of governing elites. Rather their successful implementation was essential for the long-run survival of the nation-state as the primary agent of governance. Out of necessity, some policy areas were best managed through international bargains, but traditional forms of inter-state cooperation had an air of obsolescence in the post-war environment. Integration, therefore, became one means through which certain sorts of policy programme could be delivered. The idea of integration as a progressive transfer of power away from the state managed by emerging supranational elites is given little credence by this hypothesis. The key actors remain governmental elites and the motivation for integration is the preservation of executive capacity at the national level, not its erosion. However, read in a particular way, Milward's work can be seen as challenging the standard polarization of intergovernmentalism and supra-nationalism. Integration does not necessarily entail the drift towards supranational statehood and states can be seen as controlling agents with an interest in the promotion of degrees of integration.

The whole matter of the relationship between states, state autonomy, domestic politics, interdependence and international cooperation has been a major theme in comparative and international political economy for some time (see, for example, Gourevitch, 1978; Katzenstein, 1985). The emergence of liberal intergovernmentalism can partly be understood as the feeding in of these debates into the discourse of EU studies. Nonetheless, it is possible to develop alternative accounts about state autonomy within the same broad framework. For example, against what he calls 'the newest intergovernmentalism' of Moravcsik and others, Karl-Orfeo Fioretos (1997), maintains that surges in integration such as the EC's *relance* of the late 1980s occur because states are forced to accommodate to the demands of key domestic constituencies. These are powerful domestic coalitions of actors that have been liberated by the intensification of international economic interdependence and whose preferences coincide with the widespread liberalization of the European economic space. This is an important challenge to Moravcsik's demand side image and is one that bears some resemblance to Stone Sweet and Sandholtz's (1997) notion of transnational society as the main stimulus for integrative activity (see Chapter 5). At stake here is the appropriate account of domestic politics. For Moravcsik, this seems to be a relatively insulated domain, whereas others see the boundary between the domestic and the external as increasingly perforated. National governments are less able to be the exclusive mediators between domestic groups and the global environment.

An interesting perspective on these issues is developed by Wolfgang Wessels. His 'fusion hypothesis' (Wessels, 1997) grows out of a concern to search for dynamic mid-range theory in the context of the EU. The guiding puzzle for Wessels is how integrative momentum accrues over time. He rejects on the one hand the idea – associated most obviously with neofunctionalism – that integration is a matter of linear progress to a pre-ordained endpoint. At the same time, neither the realist prediction that integration is destined to collapse nor the 'governance view' of the EU polity as an unstable equilibrium really capture the very real drift of governance capacity to the European level. Wessels depicts integrative momentum accumulating over time. But it occurs in fits and starts and cannot be associated with any particular end state. His explanation is both rationalist and statist in that integration can be explained by the self-regarding actions of nation-state actors. Governments seek integration as a way of solving problems that they have in common. These problems emanate from both citizen demands in domestic politics and the imperatives set by global economic interdependence (see also Wallace, 1996a). Interestingly, Wessels also locates his analysis in the context of the widespread evolution of the welfare or service-state. This has directed government in the direction of servicing human needs and seems to factor in the old functionalist arguments about the key tasks of government (see Chapter 2). As Wessels notes, this takes things well beyond Milward's explanation of integration as the 'rescue' of the nation-state. Rather 'it is a crucial factor and dynamic engine in the fundamental changes in the statehood of Western Europe' (Wessels, 1997: 274). Whereas Milward sees integration as a way of ensuring the survival of the established order, Wessels links the growth of the EU to fundamental alterations in the style and emphasis of governance that are occurring *within* the member-states.

Wessels reads integration as the gradual pooling of sovereignties across sectors with a view to joint problem solving. This leads to 'an ever closer fusion', defined as 'a merger of public resources at several "state" levels for which the "outside world", i.e. the average European citizen, but also many experts, cannot trace the accountability, as responsibilities for specific policies are diffused' (Wessels, 1997: 274). This has two important implications. Firstly, as with some analysts of consociation (see below), the fusion hypothesis offers an explanation of the EU's democratic short-falls in terms of the actions of national elites. Secondly, Wessels is keen to show how integration 'locks in'. While he is adamant that states sit at the centre of the process, his analysis treats this interstate interaction as considerably more than an instance of diplomatic exchange. If this were so, intergovernmental bargains would be fragile and would dissolve –

in line with realist predictions – when the balance of interests among states changed.

Wessels draws comparisons between the EU system and the interlocking qualities displayed by German federalism. In a similar vein, Fritz Scharpf's discussion of the 'joint decision trap' draws analogies between Germany and the Communities to explain the largely irreversible nature of integration and its associated institutionalization in state-centred terms (Scharpf, 1988). Scharpf offers a rather pessimistic view of this process. The decision-making arrangements of the Community system give states the opportunity to devise ways of solving joint problems. Yet the outcomes of these deliberations are likely to be 'sub-optimal' and will not emerge from a rational appraisal of the best available solutions. This is because the institutional structure of the EU system has installed a distinctive 'decision logic'. Rational governmental actors are responsible for the crucial shaping decisions in the EU system. The deepening of integration and the growth of European-level policy competence is propelled by the attractiveness of seeking joint solutions to common problems. That said, even the most zealous advocates of an expansionary Europeanization are likely to be reluctant to surrender their powers of veto. At the same time, states with less pro-integration preferences will be prepared to make compromises sufficient to ensure that they have input into future shaping decisions. Decisions that emerge are unlikely to satisfy any particular state preference. Nor will they amount to a rational optimum of the various preferences that the governments offer. This does not make for great acceleration in the drift of governance capacity to the EU level, but at the same time it also ensures that retreat or reverse is impossible. Scharpf describes this joint decision trap as

> an institutional arrangement whose policy outcomes have an inherent (non-accidental) tendency to be sub-optimal – certainly when compared to the policy potential of unitary governments of similar size and resources. Nevertheless the arrangement represents a 'local optimum' in the cost-benefit calculations of all participants that might have the power to change it. If that is so, there is no 'gradualist' way in which joint-decision systems might transform themselves into an institutional arrangement of greater policy potential.
>
> (Scharpf, 1988: 271)

Intergovernmentalism and institutions

Intergovernmentalists of various persuasions are distinguished from realists because they are attentive to the fact that the (international) politics of European integration takes place within a very specific institutional environment. As an entry point into thinking about how intergovernmentalists deal with the institutional 'thickness' of the EU, it is instructive to use the work of Andrew Moravcsik as a starting point. It is fairly clear throughout his detailed analysis and in other work (Moravcsik, 1993b), that Moravcsik sees himself working in the *liberal* tradition. For Moravcsik, such work has three core assumptions:

1. the basic actors in politics are rational, autonomous individuals and groups which interact on the basis of self-interest and risk-aversion;
2. governments represent a subset of domestic society whose interests constrain the interests and identities of states internationally;
3. state behaviour and patterns of conflict and co-operation reflect the nature and configuration of state interests.

(Moravcsik, 1993b: 7, 11, 13)

It is manifestly unfair to categorize Moravcsik's work as realist or neorealist, but it is decidedly intergovernmentalist – and quite aggressively so. Moravcsik's work on European integration draws on a sustained critique of neofunctionalism (or supranational institutionalism as he calls it) and is obviously influenced by the developing body of neoliberal institutionalist work associated in particular with Robert Keohane (1989). Keohane's work tries to cope with the obvious acceleration of institutionalization in world politics. The stuff of contemporary international relations is evidently rather more than sovereign self-interested states clashing in line with the billiard ball analogy of classical realism. Institutions can take several forms. They may be purposive quasi-constitutional orders such as the EU, they may be issue-specific regimes or they may be simply established norms for interstate interaction. What is clear for Keohane is that levels of institutionalization affect state behaviour. He maintains that prevailing institutional arrangements can affect state actions by influencing

the flow of information and opportunities to negotiate; the ability of governments to monitor others' compliance and to implement their own commitments – hence their ability to make credible commitments in the first place; and prevailing expectations about the solidity of international agreements.

(Keohane, 1989: 2)

Put another way, 'Neoliberal institutionalism seeks to add (or more precisely integrate) institutions into this explanatory equation. By this account, states pursue their interests within an anarchic environment, but one notably modified by the presence of institutions' (Cornett and Caporaso, 1992: 233). Moravcsik's liberal intergovernmentalism goes beyond his earlier work (Moravcsik, 1991) by assigning an important role to institutions as facilitators of positive sum bargaining. States benefit from and use the institutional environment of the EU for purposes of domestic legitimation and the pursuit of preferences. This seemingly applies to supranational institutions such as the Commission, the European Parliament and the Court of Justice as well as intergovernmental fora such as the Council of Ministers. Indeed, 'only where the actions of supranational leaders *systematically* bias outcomes away from the long-term self-interest of member-states can we speak of a serious challenge to an intergovernmental view' (Moravcsik, 1993a: 514).

These arguments are taken a little further by scholars working within the framework of the 'new institutionalism'. This body of work has already been discussed at length in Chapter 5, but here it is worth pointing out again that many institutionalist analysts take the primacy of state preferences as given. For example, working within a rational choice institutionalist perspective, Mark Pollack maintains that institutionalism 'accepts the fundamental intergovernmentalist insight about the initial primacy and continuing centrality of member governments in the creation and amendment of EC institutions' (Pollack, 1996: 430). The step beyond intergovernmentalism is the potential role assigned to these institutions in structuring the choices of member-states thereafter. Supranational institutions tend to operate within the boundaries set by member-state preferences, although the exploitation of differences between member-states provides a definite opportunity for entrepreneurial supranational activity (see also Pollack, 1997a).

A good deal of institutionalist analysis explores the relationship between states and European-level institutions. In particular, scholars have focused on the question of institutional choice – roughly why states have opted to create the particular mixture of institutions that now characterize the EU. Like many others, Geoffrey Garrett (1992) is puzzled by the apparently sub-optimal way in which member-states have constrained their autonomy. For Garrett, the Single European Act – a change to the Treaties and, therefore, wholly within the remit of national governments – presented an institutional logic meaning that the power of national executives would be severely circumscribed. The most obvious example of this was the increased use of qualified majority voting (QMV) sanctioned by the Treaty. This, he insists, cannot be modelled using traditional state-centred approaches to cooperation. These would expect efficient outcomes based upon the exercise of rational policy calculus. The point, emphasizes Garrett, is not just to explain outcomes, but to look at the reasons why particular outcomes (or sets of rules), that may appear to be irrational are selected over others. Additionally, traditional theories of bargaining hold that states will do nothing to disrupt either the fabric of the state-centred international order or the core principles which underwrite that order (e.g. sovereignty). Garrett argues that the environment provided by intergovernmental institutions enables certain states, or coalitions of states, to bring particular preferences to the fore. In the case of QMV in the SEA, both France and Germany expected considerable economic gains from the completion of the internal market in the light of a series of external incentives. The two governments used the mechanisms of intergovernmental bargaining to manoeuvre themselves into a position where their common preferences came to the fore.

Such ideas about institutions are often described as 'functional' (although not in the sense understood by Mitrany or Haas) because they think about how institutions are used by states (i.e. what functions they perform). One important function is the role they play in the dynamics of intergovernmental bargaining where governments are seeking to establish advantageous positions, secure their preferences and ensure compliance from other governments. As Moravcsik explains '[g]overnments transfer sovereignty to international institutions where potential joint gains are large, but efforts to secure compliance by foreign governments through decentralized or domestic means are likely to be ineffective' (Moravcsik, 1998: 9). Even in Moracvsik's most recent theoretical statement (Moravcsik, 1998), there is still a tendency to marginalize the significance of supranational institutions (for critiques see below). In an argument that continues to focus on states, but which manages to take account of the institutional complexity and multiple decision rules of the EU, Geoffrey Garrett and George Tsebelis (1996) chastise liberal intergovernmentalism for its emphasis of strategic rationality among states. The institutional complexity of the EU is a factor and should not be 'bracketed'. To be sure, the way in which states arrange themselves into coalescent groups has something to do with the convergence or divergence of their preferences. But the actual decision rules that apply for particular decisions also need to be taken into account. The variable involvement of the European Parliament and the Commission across policy areas and between different pillars of the EU means that it is not just the distance of preferences of states in relation to each other that has to be factored in. The preferences of institutions also figures as an important variable influencing the style and substance of intergovernmental bargaining.

Wayne Sandholtz (1996) goes further still by arguing that the functional approach retains the intergovernmentalist neglect of significant action amongst non-state actors. There is a danger of treating supranational institutions in particular as mere expressions of state preferences. Moreover, the links that supranational institutions develop with societal interests have the effect of inserting extra non-state preferences into the EU's decision-making system. Also, these connections open a route for the

EU to embed itself in the domestic politics of the member-states via a route that bypasses the gatekeeping of national governments. This leads to a situation that '[brings] about changes in domestic policies and institutions. The states themselves are changed as a result of their participation in European integration' (Sandholtz, 1996: 426).

Critiques of liberal intergovernmentalism

Moravcsik's liberal intergovernmentalism has been a major influence upon contemporary work in EU studies. Most, if not all, conceptually-informed work on the EU engages with his work (see, for example, Stone Sweet and Sandholtz, 1997). Students conducting empirical analyses of aspects of European integration have found liberal intergovernmentalism to be a useful heuristic device to assist in the ordering of data and the testing of hypotheses. Moreover, the formality with which the tenets of liberal intergovernmentalism are laid out offers an explicit challenge for sympathetic as well as rival frameworks to do the same (Lindberg, 1994: 81). Needless to say, the stimulation provided by the articulation of the liberal intergovernmentalist approach has also encouraged significant critical reflection, both upon Moravcsik's work and upon the broader theoretical perspectives that lie beneath it.

The erstwhile neofunctionalist Leon Lindberg suggests that portions of Moravcsik's reasoning can actually be used to bolster certain neofunction-alist claims. In particular, he draws attention to Moravcsik's discussion of the ways in which participation at the European level allows states to manoeuvre themselves into positions of relative autonomy in relation to their domestic constituencies: 'exactly the same analysis can be applied to an understanding of the Commission in this process of national interest formation! This is ... what neofunctionalists were trying to do or what I think I was certainly trying to do' (Lindberg, 1994: 83). In pursuit of this point, Lindberg draws on contemporary institutionalist literatures to reinstate the importance of supranational bodies. While Moravcsik's analysis gives space to the socializing qualities of intergovernmental institutions, Lindberg is seeking to draw an analogy between the Commission's ability to gain entrepreneurial advantage from the diversity of preferences among member-states on the one hand, and member-state governments' abilities to play off divided domestic interests on the other.

A similarly-inclined but rather more trenchant critique is developed by Daniel Wincott (1995b). Wincott is also concerned by Moravcsik's emphasis upon the primacy of intergovernmentalism on the 'supply side' and discusses the specific empirical anomaly of the role of the European Court of Justice (ECJ) in the integration process. In part, this represents a corrective to the tendency, apparent in Moravcsik's work, to treat the supply side almost exclusively in terms of nodal 'history-making moments' such as treaty revisions (Wincott, 1995b: 602–3). Indeed, liberal inter-governmentalism could be viewed as out of touch with the movement in the direction of the sorts of theoretical analysis described in the previous chapter. Perhaps this is because it seeks to offer a theory of *integration* rather than an analysis of EU *governance*.

Wincott's boldest claim – and the one most contested by Moravcsik in his reply (Moravcsik, 1995) – is that liberal intergovernmentalism should be thought of as an 'approach' rather than a 'theory'. This is because liberal intergovernmentalism as laid down by Moravcsik does not lay out the circumstances in which it could be empirically refuted. Because of this, it is impossible to treat the clear intergovernmental biases of liberal inter-governmentalism as working assumptions. Moravcsik is not attempting to make deductions on the basis of a few carefully selected assumptions. Rather, he is performing an act of closure upon certain potential sources of explanation. This contention allows Wincott, grounding himself in policy analysis, to develop an alternative account of the recent history of European integration, emphasizing the everyday practices of the EC/EU as important to its unravelling trajectory (i.e. 'integration'). This reinstates the signifi-cance of supranational institutions in general and the ECJ in particular (1995b: 603–6). The point here is not to assert the importance of stand-alone entrepreneurial institutions, but to emphasize the significance of the interaction *between* institutions. Moreover, Wincott points to liberal intergovernmentalism's failure to theorize the significance of policy feed-backs into the EU system that are the consequence of previous decisions.

Wincott also addresses the rationality assumption at the heart of LI:

> Rather than assuming that the players in the EC game can review the alternatives before them synoptically and choose between them rationally, the approach presented here is based on the radical imperfection of knowledge. In such a world the position of an institution at the centre of a network of knowledge (in this case the Commission) gives the individuals working in it an advantage to be weighed against the advantages of other players (for example the member-states).
>
> (Wincott, 1995b: 607)

The point of the sort of critique developed by Wincott is not simply to raise matters of empirical dispute, but rather to contemplate matters of epistemology that hold highly significant implications for empirical enquiry. Indeed, Moravcsik's rebuttal of Wincott's criticisms contains the claim that liberal intergovernmentalism does not stand or fall upon whether it fulfils the standard criteria for characterization as a deductive theory. Its application to grand bargains is described by Moravcsik as 'a theoretically justified first step', but there is nothing to rule out the use of liberal intergovernmentalism for the analysis of everyday decisions (Moravcsik, 1995: 613).

In addition, the two-level game approach adopted by the likes of Moravcsik has attracted substantial scrutiny, often from reasonably sympathetic quarters. Putnam's original formulation, it has been argued, constitutes little more than a metaphor. Therefore, the approach is lacking in explanatory power and has no core propositions from which hypotheses might be generated. Its greatest usefulness is in the description of the outcomes of international exchange. It might be that the application of game theory might rectify the situation by injecting formal theoretical components into the basic metaphor. However, as two recent writers point out, 'the application of formal game theory to international relations requires a variety of information, which has to be gained *ex ante*, otherwise the hypotheses cannot be tested' (Wolf and Zangl, 1996: 356). The point here is that circular reasoning will quickly ensue as the results of the interactions need to be known before they can be predicted.

Others argue that the two-level game analogy is too simplistic. Smith and Ray (1993) begin to chip away at the association between two-level games and intergovernmentalism by expanding upon the number of levels at which significant games are played. Their notion of multi-level games clearly links with the literature on multi-level governance discussed in the previous chapter by (a) recognizing the distinctive bargaining environment offered by European institutions and (b) opening the possibility for exchange between non-state actors as a potentially decisive shaper of integration outcomes. Putnam's original formulation suggested the significance of the following levels:

Level 1: international exchange (government–government)
Level 2: domestic politics (government–national polity).

Smith and Ray's schema inserts three extra levels:

Level 3: institutionalized intergovernmental exchange (EC member-state–EC member-state)
Level 4: EC–non-member government exchange
Level 5: subnational exchange (national polity–national polity)
(adapted from Smith and Ray, 1993: 8–9)

The recognition that states play games at many levels simultaneously, along with the observation that various non-state actors are also players, brings the study of multi level games close to the multi-level governance position described in the previous chapter. What is clear is that even intergovernmentalists have to grapple with their well-established concepts in order to capture the distinctiveness of the EU system.

Confederalism and consociationalism

Moravcsik's adaptation of the two-level game idea is so significant in part because it makes connections with work in the mainstream of international political economy. But liberal intergovernmentalism is by no means the only way in which state-centric accounts about integration have been developed. Confederal theory and the depiction of the EU as a consociation have both been long-standing themes in the literature, even if they have been unjustly confined to the margins of theoretical debate (Warleigh, 1998). Both positions make claims about what the EU represents ('of what it is an instance') and both do so with a state-centric vocabulary.

The most complete rendition of the view of the EU as a confederation is found in Murray Forsyth's *Unions of States* (Forsyth, 1981). His basic claim was that the Community was best seen as the latest instance of a common theme in European history: the voluntary association of states with a common interest in building larger markets. It is one option in a repertoire of three strategies used by states in pursuit of their economic interests. The others, the exercise of hegemony and the manipulation of the balance of power, were not readily available to any of the EU member-states. Therefore, what others call European integration arose because of the common interests of a small group of states to secure their interests in the international system. Institutionalization is necessary to supply stability and longevity to the system. Alex Warleigh (1998) teases out some of the implications of Forsyth's argument. The first, and most significant, is that if we think of the EU as an instance of unification, then there is no longer a need for a separate theory of integration. Second, the dominance of the intergovernmental institutions (notably the European Council) can then be reinterpreted as fitting the imperatives of a confederal international arrangement. Yet, it has to be said that just because the EU cannot be thought of as a federation or as an intergovernmental regime (see Chapter 7), it does not follow that it is, therefore, a confederation. It is certainly the case that the intergovernmentalist analysis of integration can make some interesting inroads into thinking about the dynamics of the EU's intergovernmental institutions. Jacob Øhrgaard (1997) uses the case study of foreign policy coordination that was formalized in the processes of European Political Cooperation (EPC). This was a sphere in which supranational institutions had little or no role to play. As a consequence, developments had to be attributed to intergovernmental dynamics. Given, therefore, that neofunctionalism could not explain the development of EPC (which arose originally as an extra-Treaty mechanism), Øhrgaard looks to construct a conceptualization of intergovernmental integration based around three processes: socialization, cooperation and formalization:

Integration through socialisation becomes a precondition for the establishment of a sufficient level of trust. The level of trust allows for co-operation on the basis of upgrading common interests, which might eventually create a platform from which further formalisation – in scope or level – might be undertaken.

(Øhrgaard, 1997: 18)

Again we see the powerful ideas associated with institutionalist political science, although Øhrgaard's explanation places quite a lot of emphasis on the agency of states in setting these processes in motion.

The view of the EU as a consociation is most associated with the work of Paul Taylor (1993, 1994b). The idea of consociation grew out of political scientists' concerns with how deeply divided societies could achieve governing stability. The work of Arend Lijphart (1977, 1991) was instrumental in showing how judicious institution-building and the development of a consensual political culture among elites could be a sufficient condition for the successful governance of societies with deep sub-cultural divisions. Lijphart's model of consociational decision-making anticipates government by 'grand coalition' (rather than by majority) and the existence of veto powers for each of the constituent elites. Power should be distributed amongst the governing elites in proportion to the size of the population they represent. Moreover, to work, society has to be divided, with minimal communication between the separate segments. This means that the predominant lines of communication are between societies and elites on the one hand and between respective elites on the other.

The applications to an international body like the EU are fairly self-evident. The Council of Ministers utilizes the principle of proportionality with qualified majority voting and the veto principle is given some purchase by the operation of the Luxembourg Compromise (see Chapter 4). If domestic politics or two-level game images of the 'demand side' of integration prevail, then the constituent societies can be seen in the segmented manner of consociational theory. Taylor uses consociational vocabulary because in his view, 'integration in the sense of the strengthening of the regional functional systems may help to sharpen rather than soften the cleavages in the existing society of nations' (Taylor, 1994b: 176). His logic is interesting, partly because it posits the development of elite-led resistance to the development of sub-state, cross-border transnational exchange. Using rationalist argumentation, Taylor hypothesises that elites are pulled by two sets of countervailing incentives. The first set consists of incentives to expand the resource capacities of the supranational level in the hope of securing gains for their own segment. The second set of incentives derives from the need to protect the integrity and autonomy of their segment. This arises because the growth of supranational functional capacity is likely to promote intersocietal activity as a side effect. The growth of such exchange would weaken the elites' constituencies. This is problematic for the elites because '[t]he status and authority of the members of the cartel are dependent upon their capacity to identify segmental interests and to present themselves as leaders and agents of a distinct and clearly defined community' (Taylor, 1994b: 176). What this gives the student of integration is an explanation of how the in-built incentives for states to engage in self-preservation and how the ring fencing of their own power bases can be reconciled with integration. Again, we have another possible answer to why states might seek an apparently irrational or sub-optimal outcome. But we also have an account of how states might react against the integrative momentum for which they may have been responsible in the past.

Confederational and consociational approaches also direct attention to what James Caporaso (1996) calls the 'ontological phase' of EU studies: the troublesome question of 'what sort of entity is the EU?'. The two depictions of the EU are fused together by Dimitris Chryssochoou (1994; Chryssochoou *et al.*, 1999) who develops the notion of 'Confederal Consociation' as a way of steering between the alternate poles of intergovernmental and federal understandings of the EU polity in the post-Maastricht period. This is defined as

> a compound polity whose distinct culturally defined and politically organised units are bound together in a consensually pre-arranged form of 'Union' for specific purposes, without losing their national identity or resigning their individual sovereignty to a higher central authority.
>
> (Chryssochoou *et al.*, 1999: 49)

The strength of this thesis is that it is readily connected to the empirical reality of contemporary European integration. The commitments made at Maastricht that led to the Treaty on European Union (1992), if read through the confederal–consociational thesis, make sense because the growth of EU-level policy competence can be reconciled with the securing of significant degrees of autonomy *by the member-states themselves*. They are driven to collective decisions as a result of common pressures, but the chosen models of integration and institution-building seem to allow a maximum degree of autonomy for national governments. Thus, the confederal emphasis on voluntary association is married to the consociational concern with 'segmental autonomy' (Chryssochoou *et al.*, 1999: 49–50). Additionally, the model claims to offer a linkage between the elite-led nature of European integration and the EU's manifest lack of democratic character. The institutional and decision-making architecture of the EU has manipulated the integration process so that states continue to manage the processes of community building. Thus, the pro-activity of elites seriously inhibits the capacities of integration from below that could help to create a European *demos*. This could be taken as a negative attribute of the EU and as a way of developing a critique of the so-called 'democratic deficit' (Lord, 1998). But the confederal–consociational character of the EU might also be taken in a positive sense as the way in which national democratic institutions are actually preserved in the context of deepening European integration.

Dilemmas of state-centrism

State-centrism is clearly still big business in EU studies. Varieties of intergovernmental analysis remain popular in spite of the growth of a literature on governance that poses serious challenges to the view that states are the controlling agents of integration. Put another way, intergovernmentalism has to find an answer to the question of why it is that states should invest in an enterprise that results in a *de facto* clipping of their policy autonomy. In this regard, intergovernmentalists have been highly creative in developing rationalizations for such apparently 'irrational action'. As we have seen, these usually involve some sort of trade-off between state and society. Indeed, the view that the agency of the nation-state is central to the making of Europe yields a variety of discrete research programmes which say much about the interstate bargains and the political game which takes place within the EU. To study the interaction of national governments within the institutions of the EU makes considerable sense. The EU game – a mixture of grand summitry and furious behind-the-scenes bargaining – reveals itself as one which is played by intergovernmental rules and whose key institution (the Council of Ministers) is a forum for the interchange of and compromise between *national* interests. Not surprisingly, state-centric authors see integration outcomes (that which 'makes' the EU) as the consequence of the interplay of interests, perhaps mediated by institutions of the EU.

We have also seen that there are penetrating challenges to intergovernmentalism that draw on actor-based policy-analytic models and new institutionalist reasoning to question the basic image of the EU offered by intergovernmentalists. There is also the question of how well state-centrism can explain the EU at the super-systemic level of analysis, and this question is held over until the next chapter, where the discussion moves to the relationship between current developments in international theory and the EU.

For now, we explore how the critique of intergovernmentalist state-centrism can cut deeper. The remainder of this chapter raises three interrelated dilemmas of state-centric accounts of European integration. These raise issues related to the social science of intergovernmentalism. They are, respectively, the problem of 'sovereignty discourse', argumentative circularity, and problematic conceptions of the state (see also Rosamond, 1995, 1996).

Intergovernmentalists have intuition on their side. Intergovernmentalism sounds empirically valid because it accords with a widely held and often reproduced image of what the world is like. We might even say that state-centrism provides a kind of 'authorized version' of European integration in that it reflects the understanding of the process *held by political actors themselves*. It might even be argued that state-centric versions of events have displaced neofunctionalist depictions as the officially sanctioned view of integration (see the arguments in Chapter 3). Justin Rosenberg makes the point well in his discussion of realist international relations:

> Realism *sounds plausible* because it articulates commonly held, common sense assumptions about world politics. This is not surprising since it mimics the vocabulary of the state's rationalization of its own behaviour, and forms in that sense a ruling ideology *par excellence*.
> (Rosenberg, 1990: 297, emphasis in original)

The notion that the world operates via the interaction of sovereign nation-states is, as Camilleri and Falk note, invested with almost commonsensical properties. As they put it, this is the way in which the European mind deals with its experience of space and time (Camilleri and Falk, 1992: 11). Therefore, we need to be conscious that discussions about European integration seem to take place within a pervasive 'sovereignty discourse'. This is a discourse infecting not only academic analyses of integration, but also the self-image of governmental actors who operate within the European institutions.

This is not to say that state-centric imagery is necessarily 'wrong', but the observation opens up the discussion, pursued more fully in Chapter 8, of the relationships between prevailing theories, their ontologies and the self-image of actors engaged in the integration process. Rather, this is a route into a more radical critique of two aspects of integration theory: widespread positivism (essentially: 'reality' is what we observe empirically) and its attendant rationalism. These theoretical starting points mean that theory is presented as an attempt to secure an 'objective capture' of the world, by outlining a set of propositions that can be tested empirically.

But this intersects with the second 'deep' issue: theoretical circularity. This relates to the way in which some state-centric approaches carry assumptions that tend to pre-empt their conclusions. For liberal inter-governmentalists, the chosen level of analysis is national governments and the key research questions concern the ways in which these emissaries of national interests interact when placed in the institutional confines of the EU. What is studied as integration outcomes is the product of these games. This may be a route to theoretical parsimony, but it also threatens a circular form of argument that excludes alternative explanations which might emphasize the importance of non-state variables (Christiansen and Jørgensen, 1999; Rosamond, 1996; Wincott, 1995b). Nation-states are deemed to be the primary agents of any transformation in international politics. Therefore research, especially on multi-state entities such as the EU, is directed to the roots, articulation, representation and interaction of national interests. The outcomes of these interactions are noted and explanations are offered in state-centric terms. Confronted with alternative explanations of the origins of recent integration in Europe, nation-state-centrists claim that states are the primary agents of transformation. This is accomplished by defining integration as the consequence of intergovernmental bargains.

Thus, one issue here is the capacity of intergovernmentalism to explain anything but intergovernmental bargains, which themselves can easily be construed as non-decisive or at least responsive to the 'real' motors of integration (perhaps supranational institutional activism or the accumulation of everyday regulatory incrementalism or the emergence of transnational society). But a deeper issue concerns the normative status of intergovernmentalism or state-centric forms of analysis. Theories can be construed as rather more than heuristic constructions through which academics order the world. They can also be seen as forces in the world that they describe (Gill and Law, 1988; Neufeld, 1995). So, to put it crudely, intergovernmentalism is a *political preference* held by a range of actors within the EU. But it also consists of a set of propositions that help to provide rationalizations for what particular actors do. So, a more 'subjectivist' position of the sort associated with some forms of sociological institutionalism (see Chapter 5) would seek to criticize the 'objectivist' assumptions that approaches like liberal intergovernmentalism carry. This does not mean that intergovernmentalism *per se* has to be abandoned. Indeed, as the instructive example of constructivism in International Relations shows, it is possible to encounter subjectivism and emerge with a critically attuned state-centrism (see Chapter 7, plus Wendt, 1992, 1994).

The third dilemma is about the state and what is meant by that term. It is frequently pointed out that the EU is not a state. This can only be a valid statement if we know what we mean by a state, and what is usually intended here is that the EU does not reproduce the national institutional form of the state at the supranational level. This is a point made with some force by John Ruggie, who argues that nation-state-centric approaches to world politics appear to understand challenges to the authority of the state and the interstate system 'only in terms of entities which are institutionally substitutable for the state' (Ruggie, 1993: 143). The danger for intergovernmentalists is to conclude that because the organs of supranational governance have not developed into nation-state-like repositories of power and authority, it follows that there has been no meaningful displacement in the authority of the member-states. The development of significant transnational networks of non-state actors may not appear to be significant because it fails to fit a particular conception of significant authority. There are several routes to dismantling this claim. One would be to develop Majone's (1996) discussion of the emergence of the regulatory state to show that 'state' capacity at the EU level is overdeveloped in the area of regulation and underdeveloped in terms of redistribution and stabilization functions. This could be added to a general discussion of the trajectory of the state under globalization, which for some authors has left the state with residual functions, particularly those geared to ensuring competitiveness (Cerny, 1996). So it might be that the most crucial functions of the state in the contemporary period have been 'Europeanized'. The whole literature on governance and particularly that on multi-level governance presents a challenging picture of the dispersal of authority. Again, governments obviously continue to engage in bargaining in intergovernmental institutions, but this does not necessarily mean that the outputs of those deliberations are as significant or as primary as might be supposed. Neither does it mean that particular national executives in particular bargaining forums necessarily represent 'the state' or, for that matter, an agreed national interest. Institutionalists would hypothesize that individual Councils of Ministers, far from being crude arenas for instrumental interstate bargaining, would tend to produce particular collective norms, a conclusion that seems to have some basis in empirical research (Edwards, 1996; Hayes-Renshaw and Wallace, 1996).

Some order is given to these issues in James Caporaso's (1996) discussion of the EU and forms of state. His starting point is that the state is often reified and even seasoned analysts mistake a very partial understanding of the recent histories of a handful of West European states for transnational and trans-historical truths about the state. It is better, argues Caporaso, to think in terms of state forms, which he defines as 'emanations of social formations that rest on specific clusters of social interests' (1996: 33). With that in mind, he considers the application of three ideal type forms of state to the EU experience and concludes that the Westphalian, regulatory and postmodern variants each shed light on distinctive qualities of the EU system. More interestingly perhaps, viewing the EU through the lenses of the respective ideal types leads to quite different sorts of research question. The Westphalian state form is the conventional image of the national territorial state, secure in its monopoly over the means of violence. Deployment of the Westphalian model is consistent with comparative research on the differences between established national forms of governance and the regime of the EU. It also prompts us to consider European integration as an instance of state-building analogous to process undertaken within national territories over the past three to four centuries. Yet, a critical engagement with the powerful Westphalian creed is likely to conclude that 'we should not expect the EU to look like a traditional nation-state at all, nor its future development to follow the beaten path from intergovernmental relations to confederation and federation' (Caporaso, 1996: 41). The regulatory state model raises the possibility of more variegated patterns of political authority with – at best – a tenuous relationship to conventional understandings of democracy, while the postmodern model captures the weakness of the EU's core institutions and the considerable decentralization of authority. Caporaso's discussion shows how a critical reading of a concept – in this case 'the state' – can open all sorts of conceptual possibilities. But it also opens up alternative meanings of state-centrism. The particular value of his contribution is the way in which it reveals the close relationship between a lot of intergovernmental analysis and the Westphalian model of statehood.

This discussion of statehood brings us back to the matter of 'sovereignty discourse'. Much of the public debate about the EU in the member-states is framed in terms of sovereignty. Witness, for instance, the vocabulary of British Euroscepticism since the late 1980s and the foundations of the British left's erstwhile hostility to the Community from the late 1950s. Sovereignty is about absolutes: states either have it or they do not. Moreover, the present international system is founded on the principle of sovereign statehood. States are self-determining, legally equal entities. In *de jure* terms they are sovereign (i.e. free from external restraint). Yet, in *de facto* terms, there appear to be multiple challenges to states' authority – of which the EU is but one instance. The discrepancy between *de jure* sovereignty and *de facto* authority has led some students of the EU to deploy the concept of autonomy rather than sovereignty. As Kassim and Menon put it: '[a]utonomy ... is a ... flexible conception, able to capture the freedom of the state in relation to, for example, domestic social forces, developments in the economy and international pressures' (Kassim and Menon, 1996: 3). Using the concept of autonomy directs research into thinking about how the powers of states have been circumscribed even if no formal transfer of sovereign authority has been granted. This allows for a more nuanced, sectoral analysis to take place. It also takes the pressure away from thinking about 'sovereignty versus integration' as a zero-sum game (Hoffmann, 1993) and provides a serious and on-going research programme for those with a preference for ascribing analytical primacy to the state.

Conclusions

To be fair, these deep dilemmas apply to any attempt to theorize European integration. However, they matter particularly to intergovernmental accounts because these perspectives tend to reassert the importance of the 'national' versus the 'supranational'. Notwithstanding the densely fascinating plethora of issues raised by the governance literature, the survival of the nation-state as the primary authoritative unit in European politics remains the most compelling question. One common observation is that European integration or the growth of European-level governance capacity has arisen because states have come under pressure from both above and below (Wallace, 1996a). From above there are external pressures, nowadays described by the idea of 'globalization', that constrain the state's autonomy and limit its capacity to act (Armingeon, 1997; Kurzer, 1997 and Chapter 7 below). Theories that retain the idea of states (or governments or national executives) as the primary actors in the EU system need to grapple with this problem. If the state is guided by external forces, then how constrained is its agency? If domestic imperatives force the state into pro-integrative bargains, how effective is the state as a gatekeeper between the domestic policy and the world 'outside'? Or, intriguingly, does the state's pursuit of autonomy from troublesome domestic forces lead it into the arena of integration? If this is so, are states conscious of the trade-offs that they make at these points? Do they perceive themselves recapturing sovereignty, albeit collectively? Or is this the starting point for the historical institutionalist discussion of path dependencies and unintended consequences? The fact that these questions are all raised by state-centric and intergovernmental analyses of the EU renders these approaches valuable in their own right. Engagement with these issues will make intergovernmentalists more reflexive and self-aware. Whether they can remain intergovernmentalists depends upon their ability to keep supplying answers to the regular anomalies thrown up by the EU.

Europe and the World: Contemporary International Theory and European Integration

The previous chapters have indicated that there is considerable richness in contemporary theoretical analyses of European integration. An implication, often amplified by students of policy analysis, is that the EU is no longer a subject simply for students of 'International Relations'. The argument here is quite compelling. After all, the focus of 'International Relations', by definition, concerns interactions among states or at least between members of national executives. In terms of integration, the only questions it is capable of asking are those about whether there should be more or less of it, or those about the interaction of national interests in an intergovernmental arena. International Relations is an academic discourse dealing with the polarities of nation-states or superstates and envisages the state of 'integration' as lying somewhere along a continuum between those two poles (Caporaso and Keeler, 1995). IR, runs the argument, is particularly ill equipped to deal with the complexity of the contemporary EU game. It lacks the tools to deal with the coexistence of multiple actors playing nested games and whose interests are not simply bound up with the final destination of the integration project. The EU is rather more than an international organization; it has a mature internal politics or 'normal politics' to borrow Caporaso and Keeler's phrase (Caporaso and Keeler, 1995: 56). The EU is not provisional; it is well established and heavily institutionalized. It follows that many political practices are embedded in its everyday games. Such things, it is argued, cannot be captured by IR paradigms.

This chapter begins with a more detailed scrutiny of this type of argument, thinks about the ways in which it has been countered and questions whether an 'International Relations' versus 'comparative politics' dichotomy is a helpful way of thinking about the analysis of integration and the EU more generally. It suggests that this is a largely false and highly constraining way of contemplating the disciplinary possibilities for studying the EU and integration processes. Moreover, it is argued that the 'IR–CP debate' rests on a narrow and largely anachronistic view of 'International Relations' in general and international theory in particular.

The critique of International Relations as a 'home discipline' for EU studies

What is the problem with International Relations as a vehicle for the study of the European Union? The most usual argument is that IR is at best partial and at worst downright misleading in its depiction of the processes which sustain and develop the European Union. The usual view of how IR develops its picture of the EU is put with some clarity by Paul Pierson:

> Despite significant internal disputes, the dominant paradigm in IR scholarship regards European integration as the practice of ordinary diplomacy under conditions creating unusual opportunities for providing collective goods through highly institutionalized exchange. From this 'intergovernmentalist' perspective, the EC is essentially a forum for interstate bargaining. Member-states remain the only important actors at the European level. Societal actors exert influence only through the domestic political structures of member-states. Policy making is made through negotiation among member-states or through carefully circumscribed delegations of authority. Whether relying on negotiation or delegation ... Chiefs of Government are at the heart of the EC, and each member-state seeks to maximise its own advantage.
>
> (Pierson, 1996: 124)

The point here is that IR is a discipline capable only of contemplating the interactions between states – and in the ways associated with 'conventional' forms of diplomacy at that. This means that even some of the 'intergovernmentalist' positions discussed here in Chapter 6 would not be appropriate for the formal IR canon. This leads some writers to play their trump card and to declare IR as largely irrelevant to EU studies. One variant of this 'International Relations is moribund' argument has been put most forcefully by Simon Hix (1994). Hix argues that the tendency in the academic community has been to study the Communities as instances of either interstate cooperation or emergent supranationalism. Such approaches, he argue, share the presumption that there is one significant line of political cleavage operating in the EU: advocacy of or hostility to further supranational integration. However, at the same time, the EU has gradually acquired many of the qualities normally associated with national political systems. In other words, alternative lines of political conflict concerned with (in particular) distributional questions ('who gets what, when, how' to recall some classic political science vocabulary) have become important. Like all political systems, the EU generates questions of interest articulation, representation and intermediation. Hix's point is that political science has an established set of tools for unravelling these issues and that these can be systematically imported and adapted for the study of the EU. This is not just a matter of disciplinary preference; the EU has become a genuine polity. IR may still work in areas where sovereign statehood is retained in the EU system. But 'where decisions are taken which involve cross-cutting party-political and national interests, decision and coalition theories from comparative politics are likely to have higher explanatory value ... this will probably be true for most areas of EC politics' (Hix, 1994: 23; see also Richardson, 1996b). It is this politics *within* the EC system (as opposed to politics *among* the member-states) that Hix identifies as important. The repertoire of 'comparative politics' approaches offers key insights into many aspects of the EU system such as the operation of interests, the relative influence of different actors and the importance of formal and informal institutions (see also Hix, 1999).

There are several presumptions here, but two stand out. Firstly, it is argued that the Euro-polity questions have supplanted the 'integration issue' as the most important for investigation in EU studies. Secondly, International Relations as a disciplinary starting point is incapable of asking the sorts of question necessary to unravel the complexity of EU politics because it is a disciplinary discourse of interstate interaction and little else. This chapter focuses on these claims. The first is, to some extent, a matter of argument and relies on the view that the EU has become rather more than an interstate forum. Even if one accepts the multi-actor complexity of the EU, it is still possible to assert the dominance of the member-state governments and the primacy of intergovernmental decisions. Whether this involves an adherence to 'International Relations' as a disciplinary home domain is quite another matter. As Chapter 6 tried to indicate, there are several intergovernmental approaches and many of these set their sights on the sorts of political games described by Hix as important. What is at stake for Hix is an issue of explanation – essentially 'CP' explains the EU better than 'IR'. Yet this claim also depends largely on the sorts of question that are regarded as important and this, in turn, is a derivative of particular disciplinary or theoretical starting points. So, to be pedantic, it could be argued that Hix's objection to IR (as he sees it) could be reduced to his own preference for the theoretical models of comparative political science and the questions thereby generated. Of course, there is a little more to the objection than this. In particular, the Hix position also threatens to expel IR-inspired integration theory from the EU studies repertoire because the latter allegedly seeks to develop a general theory of regional integration from very particular European experiences.

In response, Andrew Hurrell and Anand Menon (1996) have argued that Hix underestimates the importance of international theory. They accuse him of making an untenable separation between the processes of 'integration' (where IR has some utility) and EU politics (the important domain where the tools of comparative analysis should hold sway). Moreover, they assert the continuing centrality of member-states to EU politics and, by extension, see a continuing role for theories which deal with the mechanics of interstate exchange. Finally, Hurrell and Menon argue that there are compelling reasons to use IR theories because of the necessity of locating the EU and its internal politics within the international system. The EU is not hermetically sealed from the international system and it is, therefore, proper to consider the impact of the international system by leaving space in EU studies for theoretical perspectives that account for its nature.

This response carries with it all kinds of assumptions of its own. One is that interstate exchange is largely the same as intergovernmental bargaining. Yet the assumption of much realist-inspired International Relations is that states are unitary actors, whereas much intergovernmentalist analysis presents a much less homogeneous image of the state. Liberal intergovernmentalists place emphasis upon the permeability of the state from below as domestic groups shape the bargaining preferences of national governments (Moravcsik, 1993, 1998), while scholars of the intergovernmental institutions – by implication – develop a much more pluralistic account of the state with their depiction of segmentation in Council cultures and severe coordination problems for different branches of national governments (Edwards, 1996; Wright, 1996). The second brand of scholarship does not deny that state actors are important, but throws open the question of how we are to best construe 'state actors'. A second assumption resident in the Hurrell–Menon critique is that the international environment is exogenous to the EU game. This may well be a route to parsimonious theorizing, but to make the assertion that EU actors are stimulated by external imperatives or pressures opens up its own particular can of worms. The immediate question is how external threat perceptions are realized and, to all intents and purposes, this is a theoretical question that raises substantial questions of the relationship between 'inside' and 'outside' which are far from unproblematic.

Hix's response (Hix, 1996) is accommodating to the extent that it acknowledges the usefulness of keeping the IR channels open for the analysis of the external determinants of actions within the Euro-polity. He also recognizes the difficulties of drawing boundaries between International Relations and Comparative Politics as disciplines. Yet, he adds a provocative rider to suggest that comparative political science may be better at answering some of the important and on-going normative questions in EU studies. When it comes to thinking about how we increase the welfare of the citizens of the EU, Hix suggests:

> We may learn more from the ideas of Madison, Dahl, Easton, Rokkan, Olson, Lijphart, Schmitter, Rose and Majone than either from the likes of Morgenthau, Haas, Hoffman [sic], Waltz, Keohane and Moravcsik, or from the likes of Lodge, Wallace, Wessels and Nugent.
>
> (Hix, 1996: 804)

There may be some objections to assigning particular authors to specific categories, but Hix is trying to take the argument further, by differentiating his notion of comparative politics from the general school of EU studies. His point is not elaborated, but it seems to mean that EU studies should not just be accumulating a cache of information about the EU. Rather, it should receive a further conceptual injection from conventional political science, the message being that the EU raises issues of concern to pluralists, systems theorists, students of public policy-making, analysts of party systems, and scholars of political cleavage formation.

Another slant on the question is offered by Bernhard Ebbinghaus (1998) who points out that the IR and CP approaches differ because of their tendency to generate different kinds of research question. However, it is also the case that, in their conventional guises at least, they share the imagery of the nation-state. In conventional (realist) IR, the world is composed of self-regarding unitary states, whereas comparative political science has tended to engage in the comparison of states and their political systems as discrete entities. Ebbinghaus is concerned that neither convention is able to capture the dynamics of a changing world with increasing transnational interpenetration of polities and societies. His recommendation is the mobilization of the multi-level governance metaphor (see Chapter 5) which has the virtue of recognizing both the multi-actor complexity of contemporary politics and the fact that political action occurs at and between several tiers of action. His argument echoes that of James Caporaso (1996; see Chapter 6) who intimates that much EU scholarship is hooked up with traditional Westphalian conceptions of the state.

The 'IR versus CP' question to some extent revolves around the issue of what is the important stuff of EU studies. It is a matter of what scholars of the EU *should* be studying and how these phenomena are theorized. If the student of integration follows a writer like Majone and opts to treat the EU as an instance of a regulatory regime that can be compared fruitfully with other regulatory regimes (see Chapter 5), then it is unlikely that orthodox

IR-derived theory will be of primary use. The student is much more likely to find theories of regulation the most useful route to explanation. However, the IR–CP question is rather more than a matter of choice. Most would argue that International Relations does not have the equipment to respond to the most compelling questions about the formal and semi-formal institutions of the EU and crucially cannot explain the emergence of policy outcomes, particularly of the day-to-day regulatory variety. Another point to bolster the CP case might be that the EU is unique, so in effect is nothing other than an instance of itself (and thereby incomparable with any other phenomenon in the contemporary international system). The only theoretically valid route from here would be to engage in longitudinal comparisons of different phases in the EU's history or perhaps to develop counterfactual methods (Anderson, 1995). Such thoughts open up the question of the time-frame of European integration. The overwhelming tendency has been to date the origins of the present EU to the period following the Second World War. However, others have traced European integration to processes of social and political mobilization dating back to the mid-nineteenth century (Klausen and Tilly, 1997). As with all comparative work, the longitudinal option must face the question: what to compare?

As we have also seen in Chapter 5 and with Hurrell and Menon's argument above, some analysts are prepared to give IR a role, albeit limited, in the generation of explanations about integration and EU/EC governance. For some, IR's role should be confined to the analysis of the systemic level – essentially the analysis of the external structural environment within which entities such as the EU evolve and operate (Peterson, 1995). Others see utility in thinking about integration as an *inter*national issue for particular stages in the EU policy process, notably those where interstate bargaining takes hold (say Treaty revisions). It is also evident that even in cases where intergovernmental bargaining is being analysed, there has been a serious attempt to wrestle analytical primacy away from traditional IR. This has been a particular project of institutionalists (Bulmer, 1994; Pierson, 1996; Pollack, 1996, 1997a).

Theorists, according to Rosenau and Durfee (1995) should be engaged in journeys up and down what they call the 'ladder of abstraction'. The question that should define all social enquiry and which must stand at the start of all theoretical work is: 'Of what is this an instance?' The fact that we are able to identify a particular set of events as, say, a military coup or as a revolution allows us to compare our set of events with other instances of *coups d'etat* or revolutions. This is also a crucial stage in theory building. In the case of revolutions, for example, writers such as Theda Skocpol (1979) have developed persuasive theories of revolution through exercises in comparative historical analysis. 'Of what is the EU an instance' is an interesting question with no shortage of potential answers. As suggested in the introduction to this book, the answer offered is likely to be crucial to the sort of theoretical analysis that emerges. Concept formation stands prior to investigation and further theory-building (Sartori, 1970). Advocates of the CP approach to the EU are offering the foundational proposition that the EU is an instance of a political system analogous to modern national polities (or at least that elements of the EU polity resemble significantly elements of the subject matter of 'conventional' political science). But that is not the only conceivable answer to this question. Indeed it is quite a stark assertion, given the tendency of some to treat the EU as something rather more complicated, provisional and atypical. For example, William Wallace and others have thought carefully about the extent to which the EU might be thought of as either a confederation or a regime (Wallace, 1983) and the erstwhile neofunctionalist Philippe Schmitter (1996b) has offered a considerable range of present and possible future characterizations of the EU. European integration first attracted the attention of scholars of International Relations because it appeared to be an early instance of post-national institution-building, or at least of quite intensive interstate cooperative activity. The fact that the European nation-state has not withered away in the way predicted by some functionalists and the fact that the EU is rather more complicated than a grand interstate bargain, does not in itself render the CP school's answer to the question triumphant. IR is quite capable of generating interesting research questions from newer bodies of theoretical work. It is possible then that there may be a multiplicity of answers to the question, 'Of what is the EU an instance?'

So what use is IR? It seems that to prove its utility international theory needs to be able to demonstrate its worth to EU studies in four ways:

1. 'IR' must transcend the 'would be polity'-nation-state continuum – or at least it must offer evidence that this polarity can be given new intellectual energy and can continue to pose meaningful questions about the EU
2. 'IR' must be able to pose interesting questions about the ways in which actors in institutionalized environments such as the EU derive their interests and thereby generate policy outcomes.
3. 'IR' must be able to pose alternative questions of the 'Of what is this an instance?' variety. The EU may be an instance of a polity and it may be an instance of interstate cooperation/bargaining/conflict, but these may not be the only alternatives.
4. 'IR' must show that it has the best tools to locate the EU within the dynamics of global change. This is an undeniable weakness of CP theories as they tend to treat exogenous input as largely given.

International Relations: not just about states?

The remainder of this chapter offers an assessment of the extent to which IR theories might be able to do these things. Having said that, and as an important precursor to this discussion, it is also necessary contemplate the meaning of 'international theory'. After all, one accusation that might be levelled at advocates of the CP school is that they misunderstand the scope of International Relations as a discipline by caricaturing it as exclusively concerned with the interaction of states and/or governmental elites.

This is certainly one view of the substance of IR. However, as one recent introductory text notes, there are other views such as the idea that International Relations is about cross-border transactions or about the development of forms of world society – reflecting the fact that there is no real world essence that is 'international relations' (Brown, 1997). Any definition of what IR is 'the study of' is likely to be partisan and exclusionary. It is true, as Brown notes, that many scholars within the discipline think of themselves as students of the interaction of states through diplomacy or violence within an overall context of structural anarchy (i.e. a situation without overarching authority on a world scale). Indeed, this is the starting point for much work, even that which self-consciously seeks to reconstruct and reform the discipline. Martin Griffiths (1992) begins his recent re-elaboration of realist IR with the claim that the discipline conventionally revolves around two assumptions: that there is a fundamental distinction between domestic and international forms of governance and that explanations of the long-term patterns of state behaviour follow from this preliminary distinction. The claim here is that politics *among* states is quite different to politics *within* states. So, while writers in the idealist traditions of IR may be prepared to countenance the possibilities for collective security through interstate cooperation rather more than their realist counterparts, an IR purist would still argue that the domain of international politics cannot be viewed through the devices used by the political science of domestic polities.

But it is equally true that many others would dispute this basic image of IR, portraying themselves perhaps as observers of the sorts of global actors and post-national institutions that explicitly rival or threaten both the states system and the anarchic structural environment. Others prefer to think about the development of transnational social forces. Indeed, some scholars refuse to use the term 'international relations' on the grounds that the phrase presupposes an overly state-centric ontology (Rosenau, 1989; 1990). To use the term 'international relations' automatically privileges particular categories of actor in the mêlée of political activity above the nation-state. So, to some extent, an ever-present question in IR is the issue of the basic units that constitute the international or global system and how these units relate to one another (Hoffmann, 1961). Such issues were at the core of the discipline's first great debate in the inter-war period where idealist conceptions of global society locked horns with an emergent hard-nosed proto-realism (Long and Wilson, 1995). What seems to be occurring in recent IR thinking is a re-opening of this particular 'Pandora's box' with the additional input of more critical theoretical sentiments (Cox and Sjolander, 1994; Smith, Booth and Zalewski, 1996). At the same time, the discipline of IR is being connected to some of the wider currents in social theory (Booth and Smith, 1995). Another way of posing the same issue is through so-called 'post-positivist' IR's depiction of the conventional terms of IR discourse as loaded in favour of Euro-centric or Westphalian assumptions about how the world operates. The paradox, of course, is that arguably the most telling challenges to these conventions is unravelling in the heartland of Westphalian Euro-centrism. All of this opens possibilities for the incorporation of non-state actors and non-state forms of authority into the IR analytical canon and at first sight the EU polity is swarming with such things.

It is certainly something of a straw man exercise to castigate IR and the theoretical work it generates as inappropriate tools for the analysis of European integration simply because the discipline is essentially *about* states and that the processes and practices of European integration and EU governance amount to rather more than interstate exchange. The primacy of particular actors is a matter for intellectual argument. Whether a focus on actors, their interests and preferences and their relations with other actors is enough is another matter entirely. Here the tendency to connect IR with broader currents in social theory has some importance. This is particularly true of those international theorists who have explored the agent–structure problem. This has been a central feature of constructivist International Relations and has direct applicability to the study of the EU and the questions that we ask about European integration (discussed later in this chapter).

It is also important to recognize that theoretical movements generated within the discipline of International Relations can have considerably wider applications. IR and its intellectual discourses are not separable from what goes on elsewhere in the social sciences. For instance, the resuscitation and re-invention of institutionalist work in political science, which (as Chapter 5 indicated) has been so influential in recent scholarship on the EU, was partially accomplished within the domain of comparative public policy. Yet it also owed something to developments in neoliberal institutionalist international relations, the growth of regime theory and the so-called neorealist/neoliberal synthesis (particularly Keohane, 1989; and see Chapter 6). Now, while much of the emphasis of institutionalist International Relations has been placed on the impact of institutions, norms and regimes upon state behaviour, the fact that particular actors tend to be given primacy does not obliterate the entire theoretical discourse. Similarly, constructivist IR has been especially concerned with rethinking state-centrism (see Wendt, 1992; 1994; 1995), but constructivist insights have also been applied to the rather more fluid and multi-actor Euro-polity (Jørgensen, 1997a, 1997b, 1997c; Rosamond, 1999).

The argument so far, therefore, is that International Relations deserves more than summary dismissal. The rest of the chapter explores more fully what IR might be able to do for EU studies in terms of supplying useful theoretical concepts. The growth of regime theory and other thinking about cooperation in International Relations is the first port of call and this is followed by a discussion of the utility of constructivism as a theoretical perspective. This is followed by an exploration of how the EU's role in the global political economy can be given greater theoretical purchase and how the study of integration might usefully be attached to the current concerns with globalization and regionalization in world politics.

International cooperation, regimes, security communities and the EU

An on-going issue for scholars of international politics has been the question of why states cooperate and with what consequences? The problem for much IR has been to understand the rationale for cooperation. The neorealist answer is to suggest that the construction of international institutions may serve the mutual interests of the parties involved, or it might indicate the power of a hegemon to exercise its preferences. Either way, institutions in international politics tend to be regarded as both secondary to the real issues of power and inherently unstable. Institutions, like alliances, may dissolve once the interests of the involved parties or power balances alter. Liberals have traditionally seen the emergence of institutions, organizations and forms of cooperation as signals of a transformation from a state-bound world order towards a more peaceful settlement. More recently, and less idealistically perhaps, neoliberal institutionalists have tried to think about how to explain the undoubted existence of institutionalization of international politics in spite of (a) the persistence of a largely state-centred system (Keohane, 1989) or (b) the alleged decline of American hegemony in recent years (Keohane, 1984).

Regime theory

In this intellectual context, the development of regime theory has been one of the major currents in International Relations scholarship since the early

1980s. The idea began to have some purchase in the 1970s, notably in the context of John Ruggie's attempt to develop ideas about the importance of cognitive factors in international politics. These included symbols and referents shared by actors, particularly where exogenous shocks challenged the utility of particular relationships (see Ruggie, 1975). Later regimes came to be less thought of as exclusively 'ideational' phenomena and much more as mechanisms for delivering the effective governance of international or transnational relations. This came to be a theme in the literature on interdependence (Keohane and Nye, 1977; see also Chapter 4) and scholars such as Keohane developed the idea as they laid the groundwork for contemporary liberal institutionalism (Keohane, 1989; Suhr, 1997). Regime theory draws on several strands of scholarship, from IR and elsewhere (Zacher, 1991). Neorealist ideas about rational action can be used to show that states pursuing security can be persuaded to construct regimes to safeguard their interests. These have combined with imported ideas from microeconomics that aim to explain how frameworks of regulation can induce shifts in the behaviour of actors. The English school of IR, associated with writers such as Hedley Bull (1977), can be mobilized to explore the emergence of norm-governed behaviour. Even functionalism's emphasis on sector-specific organizations is an intellectual ancestor.

Regimes are usually thought of as established and acknowledged practices, as ongoing patterns of behaviour. The definition most often cited is that of Stephen Krasner:

> Regimes can be defined as sets of implicit or explicit principles, norms, rules and decision-making procedures around which actors' expectations converge in a given area of international relations. Principles are beliefs of fact, causation and rectitude. Norms are standards of behaviour defined in terms of rights and obligations. Rules are specific prescriptions or proscriptions for action. Decision-making procedures are prevailing practices for making and implementing collective choice.
>
> (Krasner, 1983: 2)

This has almost become a consensus definition (though see Milner, 1993). The concept is usually applied to systems of rules that oversee more specific agreements (Keohane, 1993), where rules are defined very broadly. The issue at stake in the regime literature is how regimes make a difference (Levy *et al.*, 1995). Where the involved actors are treated as utility-maximizers, regime theory tends to argue that the creation of a regime will alter the cost-benefit calculus of action. Put another way, regimes are an intervening variable between the structure of the international system and the behaviour of actors (Krasner, 1983). Others might go further and argue that the output of regimes is to reconfigure the international system. They may reinforce the power of a hegemon or they may emasculate its capacity to exercise authority. Indeed, for some, regimes are the basis for the modification of the anarchic international system. Under anarchy, states make short-term calculations based upon self-interest. In a system infested with regimes the calculus becomes longer-term and actors begin to expect reciprocity from others (Levy *et al.*, 1995: 287–90).

Can the EU be studied as an instance of a regime? This has been the subject of some discussion. For the most part, analysts have expressed scepticism about the fit between the EU and the definition offered by regime theorists. Most argue that the EU occupies a plateau well above that of an international regime. William Wallace (1993) notes that the peculiar legal personality of the Community, with its capacity to override national law, is an important difference, while Keohane and Hoffmann (1991) point out that the level of institutionalization, the spread of policy competence and the centralization of authority are all denials of the efficacy of regime analysis. An alternative interpretation has been offered more recently by Robert Breckinridge (1997). His argument is that comparing the EU with regimes is a false comparison because, according to the regime literature, international organizations are embedded *within* regimes. The function of international organizations, he argues, is to monitor, manage and modify regimes. So:

> The regime aspects of the EU have not ceased to exist, replaced by the confederation, as Wallace would argue. On the contrary, the economic confederation is embedded in the regime as the international organisation was and as any future federation or unitary state will be.
> (Breckinridge, 1997: 180)

Therefore, Breckinridge's argument is that the EU is embedded within a regime and that regime theory can help to unravel the nature of the rules and patterned behaviour that constitute the regime. With that in mind, he draws attention to the practices and norms of the 'Community method' as exemplified by the long-term reproduction of bargaining methodologies and forms of package dealing within the Community institutions, along with the persistence of basic unwritten rules of membership. This, he argues, allows scholars to engage in direct comparisons involving the EU and other instances of regional blocs in the global political economy. The EU may be functionally and organizationally different from NAFTA, Mercusor and the like, but all of these formations have an associated regime underwriting their activities and development.

The objections to this line of thinking might include the claim that perspectives such as constructivism (see below) are better able to capture the normative basis of the EU, because, unlike regime analysis, they are not wedded to rationalistic accounts of utility-maximizing actors. They might also latch onto one of the classic critiques of regime theory which argues that the study of regimes is a distraction from the more important analysis of the forms of power that lie in the background (Strange, 1983). It is certainly possible to discern changes in what might be called the EU's governing regime as alternative modes of decision-making rise and fall (Wallace, 1996b), but it might be just as (if not more) plausible to examine these shifts in terms of alterations to the balance of forces within the EC system and in the global environment.

Security communities revisited

The study of norms and rules in International Relations has also re-ignited interest in the Deutschian idea of security communities (see Chapter 2). This has been attributed to the shifting agenda of International Relations following the end of the Cold War. According to one account, IR has produced a number of distinct perspectives that seek to account for the absence of war (perhaps, in so doing, turning the traditional *problematique* of IR on its head) (Adler and Barnett, 1998a). This accounts for the growth of perspectives such as regime theory and liberal institutionalism. Deutsch had defined security communities as groupings of states where war was no longer a tenable means of dispute settlement. As a result, the concept might appear to have obvious purchase in the contemporary world. It might have added spice for students of the EU because the investigations of Deutsch and his colleagues had spawned a distinctive theory of integration in transactionalism. Might there be some utility in taking a second look? The answer from Adler and Barnett (1998a) is a decisive yes, but they qualify their argument by pointing to certain deficiencies in Deutsch's original formulation. They note that the transactionalist account was heavily reliant on behavioural reasoning (see Chapter 3). As a consequence, Deutsch became preoccupied with the achievement of security communities through intersocietal transactions. Furthermore, he was convinced that these transactions could be measured and quantified. So, his attention was focused on measurable indices of communication such as international phone calls and the cross-border traffic of tourists. The renewal of interest in security communities should, they contend, be attentive to the sociological origins of transactions and to the processes of social learning and communicative action that produce mutual identification among actors. This emphasis puts Adler and Barnett's deliberations firmly within the constructivist camp (see below). They develop a three-tier model of the development of security communities (Adler and Barnett, 1998b: 38). The first tier concerns the identification of conditions that precipitate the emergence of security communities. These include broad environmental factors such as demographic or technological change, shifts in the global economy or alterations in the pattern of external threats. But precipitating conditions also include broad epistemic shifts, what Adler and Barnett call 'developments of new interpretations of social reality'. Thus, ideational change as well as material change is considered an important factor. A similar story holds at tier two: the emergence of factors conducive to the development of mutual trust and collective identity. Here, there are structural and process variables including power (structure) and transactions and organizations (process). But Adler and Barnett also include knowledge as a component of the structure and social learning as one of the key processes. By knowledge, they are referring to 'cognitive structures ... [or] shared meanings and understandings ... part of what constitutes and constrains state action is the knowledge that represents categories of practical action and legitimate activity' (Adler and Barnett, 1998b: 40). It is these things that are transmitted via processes of social learning and socialization. The third tier, necessary conditions of dependable expectations of peaceful change, consists of mutual trust and collective identity among involved actors.

The transactionalist account originally developed between the 1950s and mid-1960s was distinctive because its notion of 'integration' was rather different from that of rival theories such as neofunctionalism. This also meant that its notion of European integration was less associated with the European Communities than other perspectives, in part because the accomplishment of a security community among a group of states was not dependent upon supranational institutional expression. Deutsch's theories directed researchers into quite particular empirical directions. Adler and Barnett's approach requires the development of indicators to measure communication and collective identification, and it also opens another route to comparative possibilities. The question remains though: what contribution does the study of the EU offer the literature on security communities? One answer would be to say that the use of the security community concept opens up renewed possibilities for thinking otherwise about 'European integration', so that the study of integration need not be coincident with the analysis of the EU.

To some extent, this is inescapable. Any reasonable definition of the geography of European security communities (or the European security community) would have to include non-EU members. But it would be difficult to factor the EU out of the equation. However, what emerges is the use of the EU as an *independent variable* used to explain the absence of war (or the persistence of a European security community), rather than the conventional theoretical twist of EU studies which is, to all intents and purposes, to explain the EU. The post-war European instance of a security community is examined by Ole Wæver (1998) who argues that the achievement of a security community was accomplished through a process of 'desecuritization'. This consists of the emergence of other issues of mutual concern to European states taking precedence and guiding their interactions. Needless to say, this development owed much to the emergence and growth of the European Communities. Paradoxically, however, the deepening of formal European integration has brought 'security' back onto the agenda, most obviously with the formalization of foreign policy cooperation and the aspiration to create a Common Foreign and Security Policy (CFSP). This could become a threat to the stability of the security community because it 're-securitizes' the agenda, which, in turn, may be the source of insecurity. Wæver's analysis relies on the idea of security as rooted in discursive action. The connection of an issue to security concerns brings with it meanings and expectations:

> Security discourse is characterized by dramatizing an issue as having absolute priority. Something is presented as an existential threat: if we do not tackle his, everything else will be irrelevant ... By labeling this a security issue, the actor has claimed a right to handle it with extraordinary means, to break the normal rules of the political game.
>
> (Wæver, 1998: 80)

It follows that the framing of an issue in non-security terms allows the continued pursuit of 'normal' procedures. Not only will actors have alternative notions of what 'security' is, they may also have absorbed different ideas about the 'Europe' that is now threatened. Wæver's use of the security community literature suggests that the EU can be used to explain both the rise and possible decline of security communities and also adds interesting new dimensions to the study of integration. Many of these are bound up with the constructivist turn in International Relations.

Constructivism and European integration

Constructivism has become difficult to ignore in contemporary International Relations scholarship, certainly since the early 1990s, although a number of writers have been exploring constructivist themes, without using the heading, for many years (see, for example, Ruggie, 1998). It is bound up with the move towards greater meta-theoretical reflection upon international politics and the desire to interrogate established categories and concepts. It represents the connection of international theory with long-standing sociological concerns with the social construction of reality (Berger and Luckmann, 1967). Moreover, constructivism connects IR to some important strands in social theorizing. With so much to draw on, it is hardly surprising that rather than there being a single constructivist approach, there are many constructivisms. The disputes are quite profound and tend to revolve around the epistemological implications of ontological starting points – in effect, can we use conventional rationalistic research procedures to investigate a world that we regard as socially-constructed? (Matláry, 1997). That said, most constructivists working within contemporary International Relations agree that the structures of world politics are *social* rather than *material* (Checkel, 1998). This means that structural properties such as anarchy are not fixed and external to the interaction of states. Rather, anarchy is a social construct (Wendt, 1992), something that is inter-subjectively understood by states and which is reproduced through their interaction. So, state behaviour does not just derive from the anarchic international environment; it also helps to make it. So constructivists

> all agree that the structures of international politics are outcomes of social interactions, that states are not static subjects, but dynamic agents, that state identities are not given, but (re)constituted through complex, historical overlapping (often contradictory) practices – and therefore variable, unstable, constantly changing; that the distinction between domestic politics and international relations are tenuous.
>
> (Knutsen, 1997: 281–2)

This places constructivism in a particular position in the debates about agency and structure, normally labelled structurationist (Duvall, Wendt and Muppidi, 1996; Hay, 1995; Wendt, 1987). Structurationists write about the complex relationships between structures and agents, so that neither structural determinism nor intentionalism are viable theoretical starting points. Agents are bound by structures, but they are also capable through action of altering the structural environment in which they operate, albeit in ways that may be structurally contained. This duality of structure and agency, first explored by Giddens (1984), has been summed up as follows:

> The structurationist points of departure are the rules, norms and patterns of behaviour that govern social interaction. These are structures, which are on the one hand, subject to change if and when the practice of actors changes, but on the other hand structure political life as actors re-produce them in their every day actions.
>
> (Christiansen and Jørgensen, 1999: 5)

Social interaction is the mechanism for the reproduction of structures. This means that constructivists object to the rationalism that characterizes the mainstream perspectives in international relations. This is because constructivists treat the interests and identities of actors as *endogenous* to interaction. Rationalists, including neorealists and liberal institutionalists derive their accounts of actors' interests from an analysis of their material position. Institutions, such as those formal and informal environments provided by the EU, are arenas (often created by states) in which those interests are bargained. For institutionalists, this usually means that institutions facilitate the procedures of bargaining by providing atmospheres of transparency and trust. Constructivists, on the other hand, treat interests as socially constructed – as derivatives of processes of social interaction. They also maintain that identities are socially constructed, that actors' accounts of self and other and of their operational context are also the products of interaction (Checkel, 1998; Wendt, 1992, 1994; Wind, 1997).

This begins to show how constructivist approaches might make a difference in the study of European (Union) governance. As Janne Haaland Matláry points out with some vigour, such a research programme poses some fairly fundamental challenges to mainstream contemporary theories of integration such as intergovernmentalism:

> It is state-centred and hence privileges the state conceptually and even reifies it; it is centred on instrumental interests that are *a priori* assumed to be the most important ones; and it exogenises interest formation. By privileging one type of actor – the state – and one type of interest – that of money and/or power, it imposes categories on the empirical material that select and limit what can be found.
>
> (Matláry, 1997: 206)

Having said that, Matláry argues that there are some issue areas (she mentions fishing quota disputes between the EU and Norway) that do not require constructivist methods to produce an explanation. In some cases, it might be possible to generate plausible and verifiable accounts of events using rationalistic methods. The key, she implies, is to practise theoretical reflexivity. That is to say that investigators should always be theoretically aware and conscious of the assumptions that underlie their arguments. Of course, it is also true that rationalism and constructivism are ontologically opposed. Constructivists would shift the research agenda of EU studies into the analysis of the role of ideas, the impact of shared beliefs, the effects of dominant discourses and the processes of communicative action (Risse-Kappen, 1996). In conventional rationalistic accounts, such factors are treated as epiphenomena – matter explained by other, more crucial factors.

The linkages between constructivist investigation and the fluid image of multi-level governance offers an obvious way in which the insights of a branch of International Relations can connect with policy work that deals with symbols, norms, understandings and belief systems (Christiansen, 1997b; Radaelli, 1999; Richardson, 1996b: Risse-Kappen, 1996). Thomas Christiansen argues that the emerging reality of post-territorial, multi-level governance in Europe cannot be captured by conventional concepts. It is important, he argues, to depict the fluidity of the system that is structured through institutions, the economy and identity: and whose agents operate at and between several levels of action. Yet it is also imperative to understand how 'Europe' comes to be understood as a legitimate space for political action:

> A constructivist epistemology ... must conceive of territorial units on all levels as social constructs ... view the political significance of [these] in the processes for which they provide containers, and such research must address the agency/structure problem, meaning that no level in the studied process must, ex ante, be assumed to be primary.
>
> (Christiansen, 1997b: 54)

Another potential way of using constructivist work is through the development of more critically attuned notions of intergovernmentalism. In many ways, the central achievement of constructivist International Relations has been the substantial re-evaluation of state-centred concepts (Wendt, 1992, 1994). In the EU context, writers have begun to argue that processes of intergovernmental bargaining can be better captured through a non-rationalistic frame. Knud-Erik Jørgensen (1997c) has argued the depiction of the EU's Common Foreign and Security Policy (CFSP) as 'intergovernmental' may relate the formal institutional reality, but it cannot capture the emerging norms and rules of the game, in short the governance regime of CFSP. Christiansen and Jørgensen (1999) look at one of the principal focal points of liberal intergovernmentalists: the processes of Treaty reform. They argue that conventional models are inherently actor-centred in that they read treaty reforms as the product of bargains based upon the negotiations of actor's (exogenously derived) interests. This has the twin failing of losing sight of the structural environment in which the bargains take place and aggregating and unifying actors into implausible collectivities such as 'the state'. The actors in the process of treaty negotiations and the preceding Intergovernmental Conferences (IGCs) are diverse 'civil servants, Commission officials, MEPs, national ministers and Prime Ministers, rather than personified states' (1999: 3). The structure includes the established formalities and routine practices of IGCs and the mosaic of path-dependent institutionalization, which defines and contains the preferential possibilities of the involved actors. They also introduce the structural component of IGC discourses, a set of signifying themes within which the whole process occurs. Such approaches allow for the understanding of integration as an international process, but within a framework that is able to capture the institutional complexity and maturity of the EU.

The EU and international 'actorness'

'International Relations' is often assigned importance because of a need to understand the environment within which the restructuring of European governance is taking place. But it also has to be remembered that the EU has a presence on the global stage and that it can be construed as an actor in the global system in its own right. This 'external' presence is manifested in four broad ways: trade policy, development cooperation, foreign policy and interregional dialogue. Foreign policy has a treaty basis (the Common Foreign and Security Policy occupies title V of the Treaty on European Union), but is conducted through heavily intergovernmental decision rules that are quite distinct from the possibilities for multiple actor interaction found within 'pillar one' of the treaty (European Community). On occasions this yields joint positions among the member-states, but it remains difficult to make the case for construing the EU as a unitary foreign policy actor. Probably the most important manifestation of the EU's external presence is its role in trade issues. Because the EU is a customs union with a common commercial policy and a common external tariff, it has long been clear that the Commission should conduct trade relations with outside parties through agreements conducted under the rubric of the General Agreement on Tariffs and Trade (GATT) and, more recently, the World Trade Organization (WTO). The Commission also negotiates economic cooperation agreements that establish privileged relations with third countries and association agreements creating particular sets of reciprocal rights and obligations. In all of these circumstances the EU acts as a bloc and negotiates with single states, with blocs of states and within international agreements such as GATT. Relations with other regional groupings remain embryonic, but processes such as the biennial Asia–Europe Meetings (ASEM) certainly operate with the presumption that 'Europe' has some kind of distinctive presence (Camroux and Lechervy, 1996).

Viewing these elements of EU activity suggests that the governance turn and its associated public policy perspectives do not have the tools to achieve explanation or understanding in this domain. The most obvious issue is that the appearance of actor-like entities such as the EU challenges traditional state-centred images of the 'international system'. However, the literature on EU external relations has been conspicuously cautious about possible transformations of the international system. Instead, attention is focused upon the EU's *capabilities* as an international actor and, by extension, to the capacity of the EU to mimic the features of a nation-state within the international system (Allen and Smith, 1990; Hill, 1994; Sjostedt, 1977; Smith, 1996; Whitman, 1997). The usual conclusion of such deliberations is to recognize that the EU is not a state, or at least that its

external attributes do not resemble those of a state as normally understood. As Martin Holland remarks,

> the notion of an international actor is wedded, at least historically, to
> the concept of the nation, sovereignty and the broad tenets of *realpolitik*
> ... the mismatch between the language of international affairs and the
> institutional and procedural realities of the EC has created an oasis for
> theoretical dispute and occasional obfuscation.
>
> (Holland, 1996b)

As Taylor (1982) notes, even while there are discernible external 'products'
of the EU, they do not arise from a unified policy-making process (that
which would be expected from a state), but via a form of loose
intergovernmentalism.

Here, of course, there is synergy with much of the new governance
literature's claim that the EU cannot be placed on a continuum running
from loose intergovernmentalism to 'superstate'. The multi-level governance metaphor is an emphatic attempt to break with the rigid imagery
associated with such a continuum (Marks, Scharpf *et al.*, 1996; Marks,
Hooghe and Blank, 1996; Richardson, 1996a). Indeed, the external
relations issues are not really amenable to exploration through what is
usually thought to be the traditional IR *problematique* on the EU (more or
less integration?/nation-state or superstate?). But the question remains: if it
is not a state, what is the EU in the global system? This is, of course, a
fundamentally theoretical question.

Christopher Hill's discussion of foreign policy cooperation in the EU
(Hill, 1994) attempts to conceptualize the EU's world role through a
discussion of 'actorness' and 'presence'. 'Actorness' is about (a) the
delimitation of one unit from others, (b) the autonomy of a unit to make
its own laws and (c) the possession of various structural prerequisites for
action at the international level (including a legal personality, a set of
diplomatic agents and the capability to conduct negotiations with third
parties). Presence is about 'the reality of a cohesive European impact upon
international relations despite the messy way in which it is produced' (Hill,
1994: 107). Hill chooses to represent the Community as a subsystem of the
international system that generates international relations 'collectively,
individually, economically and politically'. This is rather distinct from an
entity – like a normal state – that produces a foreign policy. Richard
Whitman (1997) seeks to take the debate further by actually mapping the
capabilities of the EU in a variety of manifestations that reveal the
structural facts of the EU's actorness and presence. For Whitman, these
various exhibits (which include the formation of rationales for external
action, the existence of established procedures for developing relations
with the outside world, the issuing of communiqués of external relevance,

the provision of forms of assistance to the outside world and the placement of EU representatives in other parts of the world) represent steps towards the fulfilment of an international identity for the EU. This theme is taken up by Dave Allen and Mike Smith's discussion of the EU's 'structured presence' in the international arena (Allen and Smith, 1990; Smith, 1996). They make the point that this presence has two elements. The first is that the EU exhibits distinctive forms of external behaviour. The second is that the EU is perceived to be important by other actors within the global system. So, actorness is not only about the objective existence of dimensions of external presence, but also about the subjective aspects embodied in the validation of a collective self by significant others.

These considerations all have important theoretical implications and, while serious theoretical analysis is still very much in its infancy, Knud-Erik Jørgensen (1992) has gone some way to laying out clearly the theoretical possibilities. At one level, of course, these external dimensions of European integration defy conventional classification. In its global activities the EU would seem to be in the $n = 1$ category. Jørgensen's solution is to pay attention to the deeper questions of epistemology and ontology. He presents a typology of potential theoretical treatments of the external dimensions of the EU, which is illustrated in Table 7.1.

Alternative ontological positions are represented by the choice of agency versus structure, whereas the broad epistemological alternatives are presented by the interpretative–objectivist distinction. Different categories of theory can be located in each box. So, agency–objectivistic theories ask about the motivations of actors and, by posing such questions, tend to seek rationalizations of actor behaviour. This in turn feeds into a preoccupation with understanding the linkages between interests and action, where behaviour is understood in terms of exogenously defined interests. As a starting point, this runs into some difficulty because the identification of these interests presupposes – to a degree at least – unitary actors. It might be possible to assert that the EU is a customs union and therefore, that it possesses definite and definable interests in external trade matters. But the obvious empirical objection is that the positions held by the EU in

Table 7.1 *Possible ontological and epistemological positions on the EU's external role*

	Interpretative	Objectivistic
Agency		
Structure		

Source: Jørgensen, 1996: 6.

international trade matters are always the consequence of delicate negotiations and that different member-states can have radically different positions on matters associated with trade. For example, certain member-states might be happy to open their markets to the import of cheap Japanese automobiles; whereas others with threatened indigenous car manufacturers may be more inclined to support measures to constrain such incoming trade. The argument boils down to a level of analysis issue. It is indeed possible to read the EU as an agent with articulated preferences, but the basis of those preferences may best be understood as the product of the interaction of interests *below* EU level and not in terms of the generation of specific 'EU interests'.

Structural objectivism operates at the systemic level of analysis (rather than focusing on the interests and behaviour of identifiable agents). The point here is to treat the international system as a 'deep structure' within which activity occurs and by which it is contextualized. So, the EU acts externally because of imperatives set by, amongst other things, global markets and shifts in the global security structure. Such a 'structure-primitive' account still requires the identification of the EU as an agent. But because agents are seen as being constituted by structural imperatives, this may have greater theoretical purchase. After all, the galvanization of market integration in Europe from the mid-1980s is often seen as the consequence of changes in the logic of global markets (Sandholtz and Zysman, 1989) and, by extension, the motivation for the development of external activities such as ASEM could also be read in these terms. (Specifically, ASEM might be seen as a way of responding to (a) the competitive challenges posed by East Asian economies and (b) a response to the development of various forms of Asia–Pacific regionalism). The other advantage of the structuralist position is that it does not necessarily require the privileging of particular actors. Structural imperatives can be seen as impacting upon the interests of states, firms and supranational bureaucracies. The key is how these imperatives interact with the interests of these actors and how actors work in concert or in opposition to one another thereafter.

One major objection to structural objectivism, however, is the criticism supplied by constructivists about the treatment of interests as exogenous givens rather than endogenous to the processes of interaction. The key research question in terms of the EU is how is its 'actorness' constituted? The problem with rigidly structuralist accounts is that they presuppose the existence of the actor. Interpretative approaches may be better at identifying how agents or structures come to be constituted. Yet, as Jørgensen argues, this is best accomplished through the development of a structurationist dissolution of the structure–agency dichotomy. Investigation from this premise would think about how the global structural environment contributes to the collectivization of an EU identity, but also about how actors within the EU define the global structural environment so as to create the rationale for a cohesive EU identity (Rosamond, 1999). It would also investigate the extent to which the development of EU cohesion in external affairs related to the perceptions of other (external) actors about the EU's actorness.

One of the central problems with thinking about the EU as an international actor is that the whole idea of actorness in the global political economy has been thrown into confusion in recent years by the extensive debates about globalization. It is to these that we now turn.

Globalization, regionalization and European integration

The phenomena of globalization and regionalization have attracted huge attention in recent years in the literatures of International Relations and International Political Economy (IPE). Both are posed as challenges to the traditionally state-centric Westphalian order. Globalization is said to reduce the capacity of the state to govern effectively in key policy areas, while the appearance of regional orders might suggest that new sites of authority are emerging. Neither term begs easy definition. Regionalism, or the processes of regionalization, has been used since the late 1980s to refer to the appearance and consolidation of various economic arrangements among groups of geographically proximate countries. These include the North American Free Trade Agreement (NAFTA), Mecusor in South America, Asia–Pacific Economic Cooperation (APEC), Southern African Development Cooperation (SADC), along with the relatively venerable Association of South East Asian Nations (ASEAN). The revitalization of the EC/EU following the single market initiative of the late 1980s usually brings European experiences into wider discussions of regionalism (Coleman and Underhill, 1998; Fawcett and Hurrell, 1997; Mansfield and Milner, 1997; Mattli, 1999). The appearance of regional blocs or trading areas is a phenomenon that demands the attention of international theorists (Hurrell, 1995).

The same is true of globalization, a yet more slippery and elusive concept. Globalization is usually used to describe the breakdown of discrete economic spaces (economies). Moreover, it is often said to herald the consequent loss of executive capacity by territorially bound national governments, or at least radical residualization of the state in economic governance (Cerny, 1995, 1996; Strange, 1996). Globalization, in this sense, is bound up with the liberalization of global finance and the rapid rise of instant transborder dealings in financial commodities. It is associated with the multi- and transnationalization of production activities and the growth of global trade. Globalization theorists portray a world where the conventions of territorial space have been rendered meaningless by the proliferation of transborder economic activity (Scholte, 1996). For some, globalization is a recent phenomenon occasioned by a mixture of techno-logical innovation and progressive market liberalization, particularly since the early 1970s. For others, it is a rather longer-run phenomenon, bound up with earlier technological innovations and/or the unfolding logic of capitalism as a world economic system.

Needless to say, the debates about these phenomena – particularly globalization – are incredibly wide-ranging. Considerable doubt has been cast on whether the image of globalization is a valid depiction of the changing economic order. For some talk of globalization is wild hyperbole. The consequence is that political agency, and that of the state in particular, is rather less constrained than might be supposed (for a flavour of the debate see *inter alia* Boyer and Drache, 1996; Held *et al.*, 1999; Hirst and Thompson, 1996; Kofman and Youngs, 1996; Strange, 1996). But this also raises questions of the relationship between agency and the processes of globalization. Is globalization sponsored by particular actors? Or is it best conceived as an external process that impacts upon actors' interests and thereby affects their preferences and the possibilities they enjoy for strategically motivated behaviour? If globalization is conceived as the world-wide spread of neoliberal ideas and economic practices, then the authorship of globalization might be associated with the possession of power. Once again, issues both of structure and agency and of the relationship between economics and politics are predominant.

It is impossible to do justice to the full range of debate here. The questions most pertinent for the purposes of this chapter seem to be the following:

1. What is the relationship between globalization and regionalization?
2. How does the EU relate to both of these phenomena?

The first question tends to beg the second. It is often supposed that the wave of regionalizing activity that began in the mid-1980s was occasioned by the challenge of globalization. So, to include recent European integration in the equation presupposes that the activities of the EU can be treated as an instance of regionalization. If regionalization is defined as the consolidation and formalization of economic integration among a group of geographically proximate economies, then the EU fits the pattern, although the stage of economic integration reached could be said to be more advanced than other counterparts. By the end of the 1990s, the EU was well on the road to the achievement of a common market and was embarking on the first stages of monetary integration, while the likes of

NAFTA and APEC were still only aspirant free trade areas (Dent, 1997). Also, the EU exhibited altogether more institutionalization and patterns of supranational governance than other regionalisms. These may be significant divergences, but it is still possible to argue that globalization has been a significant stimulus to both integrative activity and the widespread questioning of established patterns of governance.

In international economics and much IPE, the norm is to think about regionalism in terms of its effects on trade. Regions are seen either as inward-looking fortresses that impede the progress to a global free-trading order or as accelerators of free trade. On the latter option, by promoting intra-regional liberalization, regional orders can be seen as stepping-stones to the globalization of the precepts of liberal trade. The key is whether regions remain open or closed to the outside and whether they can be shown to create new trade rather than simply diverting international transactions (Anderson and Blackhurst, 1993; Cable and Henderson, 1994). This raises the broader question of whether regionalization is merely a territorially-bound form of globalization – that, to all intents and purposes, regionalization and globalization are manifestations of the same process of economic integration and heightened interdependence. In this way regions might be read as globalizing entities. On the other hand, regions could be construed as *loci* of resistance to globalization, as protective blocs erected by economic actors confronted with the 'chill winds' of globalizing imperatives. Here, the very existence of regions, as well as the tendency in some instances to pool elements of authority, could be seen as the attempt of actors (most obviously states) to recapture executive capacity that has been lost domestically. This feeds into a further set of issues concerned with the origins of regionalizing tendencies. Are regions deliberate and controlled acts of institutional design by policy actors or do the political decisions that institutionalize regionalism represent a kind of catch-up by policy-makers? This debate taps into the distinction made by William Wallace (1990) between formal and informal integration and by others between *de facto* and *de jure* regionalization (Bressand and Nicolaides, 1990; Higgott, 1997) (see also Chapter 1). Placing emphasis upon formal integration (cooperative agreements, treaties, acts of collective legislation) suggests that regionalization is guided by the deliberate agency of identifiable actors (usually states). This then creates the space for non-state, private economic actors to engage in regionalizing activity. For example, the creation of the Organization for European Economic Co-operation (OEEC) and the European Payments Union (EPU) in the late 1940s are usually seen as the stimulus for a substantial growth in intra-European trade (Tsoukalis, 1997: 9–10). On the other hand, the growth of cross-border economic activity in terms of production, investment and trade could be taken as the stimulus for political decisions to institutionalize or gain control over the regionalizing process. Approaches to this problem come in different theoretical guises, but essentially the issue boils down to which actors analysts choose to nominate and the capacities they are willing to ascribe to political agency. One argument often used is that globalization engenders outward policy orientations for states and that this often manifests itself through the emergence of regional accords. The impact of globalization may also manifest itself via the 'internationalization' of the state as particular ministries become closely connected to or find themselves at the behest of the forces of global finance. Such arguments found in the IPE literature often portray states as involved in *three*-level games (domestic politics, regional cooperation and global engagement) and generate research questions about the capacities for state autonomy in this context (Coleman and Underhill, 1998). These sometimes generate the counter-intuitive proposition that globalization actually strengthens the autonomy of the state, by reorienting its imperative activity away from traditionally troublesome domestic constituencies (which in turn become marginalized). One way in which states pursue this autonomy is via the institutionalization of cooperative activity and the cooperative sponsorship of formal economic integration. The point here is that an IPE frame of reference offers a coherent set of research questions, which link the internal dynamics of the EU, the domestic politics of member-states and the processes of global change. An exercise of this sort is carried out by Helen Milner (1998) who draws on rational choice and two-level game assumptions to compare the processes behind the Treaty on European Union and the North American Free Trade Agreement (NAFTA). She argues that national leaders are likely to seek international agreements in circumstances where their economies are interdependent and where domestic conditions allow. Thus, the processes of financial liberalization in key EC member-states created imperatives for the governments to seek international cooperation. Financial liberalization was the product of particular domestic imperatives, but its execution meant that governments lost effective control over key areas of economic governance. But the successful accomplishment of the international negotiations could only be achieved if national leaders had the support of key domestic constituencies – hence the multiple protocols and opt-out clauses in the TEU.

Many studies cite the importance of global economic change as a crucial determinant of the advances in formal economic integration. What might be called 'globalization', competitive threat', 'informal integration' or 'global economic change' often appears in the literature as a form of external 'regulatory shock' that forces a policy response from within the EU. These changes 'outside' impact upon the interests of key policy actors and are said to have accelerated the momentum towards the liberalization of the European economy and galvanized the deeper institutionalization of governance functions at the European level. This breaks down into a number of more specific accounts. One is that global economic change – especially technological changes – affected the preferences of key sections of European business and opened a strategic opportunity for the development of alliances with the Commission, which in turn generated the momentum for the single market programme in the mid to late-1980s. This combined the de-fragmentation and liberalization of the European economy with the enhancement of supranational regulatory capacity (Sandholtz and Zysman, 1989). More state-centred accounts observe the impact of global shifts upon either the executive capacities of (member-state) national governments (Armingeon, 1997) or the interests of domestic constituencies that are central to the formulation of governmental preferences (Moravcsik, 1993a). Another common line of argument is that the Europeanization of economic governance arose as national models of economic policy-making manifestly failed to cope with the pressures of globalization, a perception aided and abetted by the growth of informal transnational networks within high technology sectors (Bressand, 1990). A way of combining some of these insights is to see European integration, and especially that since the mid-1980s, in terms of the dilemmas of nation-states emasculated on the one hand by the forces of globalization and overloaded by demands from the domestic arena on the other:

> European integration can be seen as a distinct west European effort to contain the consequences of globalisation. Rather than be forced to choose between the national polity for developing policies and the relative anarchy of the globe, west Europeans invented a form of regional governance with polity-like features to extend the state and to broaden the boundary between themselves and the rest of the world.
>
> (Wallace, 1996a: 16)

This proposition is attentive to the specificities of the European experience, but also recognizes the advantage of treating the EU as an instance of region-building in the context of globalization.

These studies tend to make a sharp separation between the EU and the outside. Globalization, therefore, becomes a set of dynamics generated outside the EU that *impact* upon the *inside*. This sharp analytical separation works best if integration is viewed as a response or a form of resistance to globalization. It works less well if European integration is treated as a facilitator of globalization. If the EU is a globalizing project, then analysts clearly need to think about how the linkage between the European and the global is accomplished (Rosamond, 1995). Work here remains in its infancy, but a number of possibilities are being canvassed. One method is to reject the image of the EU as a unitary entity and note how different components of the EU polity and different actors within the EU polity have distinct relationships with globalization. This would amount to looking for ways to combine the insights of the branches of globalization theory emphasizing diversification rather than homogenization, with the powerful metaphor of multi-level governance (Ebbinghaus, 1998: Rosamond, 1999). Constructivist insights might also be used to think about how knowledge about globalization is socially constructed within the EU polity and how this in turn might promote particular policy possibilities while downgrading others. This could then be attached to a wider set of theoretical propositions about how intersubjective understandings of external context influence policy choice (Rosamond, 1999).

One significant recent attempt to give European regionalism a comparative and historical gloss is provided, from a rather different vantage point, by Walter Mattli (1999). Defining integration as 'the process of internalising externalities that cross borders within a group of countries' (1999: 199), Mattli argues that the demand for regional rules arises amidst a variety of circumstances. These include the potential for gains arising out of increased cross-border transaction which in turn grows as technology improves. That said, greater cross-border economic activity heightens uncertainty for market actors and imposes – in the parlance of economics – 'externalities' upon them. Therefore, like Stone Sweet and Sandholtz (1997), Mattli's argument is that the impetus for integration is rooted amongst market actors. Where these demands for integration are lacking, then regional integration schemes are unlikely to prosper. Mattli's argument also insists that authoritative actors need to have some rationale for integration to proceed. Additionally, the presence of a regional hegemon to lead, coordinate and broker the activity of other states is important (Mattli, 1999: 50–7). Mattli's contribution brings together several strands of literature in political economy, though the real added value of his contribution lies in his thoughts about the external effects of regional integration (Mattli, 1999: 59–64). Actors excluded from the initial delineation of the region are likely to lose market access and, therefore, to undertake compensatory action. This has two historical variants. The first is to seek to join the integration scheme, an option. The second is to set up a rival regional organization (which itself must satisfy the demand and supply conditions).

Mattli's discussion shows how far rationalistic perspectives can take us in the search for a general theory of regionalism, but it inevitably runs into the sort of objections raised by critics of rationalism such as constructivists (see above). That said, he does indicate the interesting questions that can be followed using a 'political economy' frame of reference. Whereas the governance literature is largely preoccupied with the political activities of multiple actors pursuing their interests in the context of the institutionalized environment of the EU, the political economy literature begins with a focus on private market behaviour and draws conclusions about political outcomes. The governance literature seems to be good at providing a kind of 'steady state' theory of European governance. Political economists cannot provide the equivalent of a 'big bang' theory to act as a rival, but there is a sense that they can do a better job at explaining the initiation, collapse and expansion of regional integration schemes.

Conclusions

International theory is not easily dismissed. This is not because traditional IR *problematiques* continue to be relevant to the study of European integration. Rather, recent reflections in the International Relations literature have thrown up new ways of thinking about old concepts and have provided substantial challenges to images of the world built around images of the Westphalian nation-state. This has not just been a matter of exploring new ontologies of world politics, but it has also included the critical examination of established concepts. With the study of European integration in mind, these developments have several implications. Firstly, the imagery of dispersed authority and multi-actor complexity present in much IR seems to connect well with some of the developing themes in EU studies. Secondly, the growth of critical investigations of established concepts has meant that even relatively staid depictions of the EU such as intergovernmentalism can be given new life. Thirdly, and probably most importantly, there are clear possibilities for making productive theoretical connections between elements of the 'governance turn' outlined in Chapter 5 and some of the main themes in contemporary international theory. It follows that the use of 'International Relations' need not necessarily imply rigid *a priori* depictions of what the world is like which correspond poorly to the complexity of EU governance. Rather, receptiveness to IR suggests receptiveness to themes and methods that open exciting possibilities for the study of the EU.

Chapter 8

Integration Theory and Social Science

Integration theory is an elusive concept. What to include under this heading is a matter for some debate and is likely to revolve around how we define 'integration'. This book has sought to show that integration theory has been tightly bound up both with the evolution of what is now called the European Union and with the efforts of successive generations of scholars to grapple with this entity. It also shows that a narrow focus on 'EU studies' and the conceptual work thereby generated is not enough and that the theorization of European integration is only fully understood with reference to wider currents in the social sciences. The theoretical analysis of European integration and shifting patterns of European governance has happened amidst several mood-swings in the academy. The earliest work discussed in this book (Chapter 2) arose in two contextual environments. On the one hand, the inter-war period saw only marginal disciplinary formalization in the political sciences. The 'theories' of writers such as Coudenhove-Kalergi (1926) were not theories in the contemporary understanding of that term, but normative visions which contained several propositions about the dynamics of the (European) international system. They are not 'functionally-equivalent' to latter day theories. On the other hand, early functionalism found expression in the early stirrings of formal International Relations and its first great debate about the essence of the international system (Long and Wilson, 1995).

The 'classic' integration theorists, Deutsch and Haas most notably (Chapters 2 and 3), developed their work in the context of key movements in the American social scientific *zeitgeist*. Deutschian transactionalism is an expression of the behavioural movement that came to be dominant from the 1950s (Eulau, 1963). In a fascinating autobiographical account, Deutsch (1989) explains the various intellectual intersections that led him to think as he did about international integration. His formative encounters with behaviouralism occurred as a series of behaviouralist scholars arrived at MIT in the early 1950s, and his interest in the use of large-scale computer modelling was ignited by a year's study leave at the Center for Advanced Study in the Behavioral Sciences at Palo Alto. He also recalls the happy occurrence of Talcott Parsons walking into his office at Palo Alto:

[Parsons] began to explain to me his view of the basic functions of every social system – pattern maintenance, adaptation, goal attainment, and integration. I found this idea fascinating. Soon the small blackboard in my office was covered with their graphic representations, and we kept discussing them for several days.

(Deutsch, 1989: 19)

These reflections raise a number of issues about the significance of individuals to theoretical development and the reliability of autobiographical reconstructions of personal intellectual journeys. Yet, this example shows clearly how a theorist of integration developed ideas within broader academic movements. The input of Parsonian ideas gave direction to the processes Deutsch and his colleagues wrote about and the emphasis on the quantitative study of behaviour supplied means to conceptualize and measure transactions. More broadly still, these influences also imported a particular brand of positivism that suggested possibilities for mapping the social world according to the criteria of natural science (Hollis and Smith, 1991: 28–29; Adler and Barnett, 1998a). Indeed, International Relations' second great debate was that between realists and behaviouralists. This sometimes ferocious encounter saw behaviouralists attacking realists for importing *a priori* assumptions into their analysis rather than relying upon that which was observable. The fact that both schools saw themselves as occupying radically distinct intellectual terrain should be a lesson to those who might seek to package together IR as a discipline united by particular guiding themes.

Similarly, the neofunctionalism of Haas and others drew heavily of the imagery and logic of pluralist political science (Harrison, 1974: 237). As the school developed, so theoretical structures were formalized and re-interrogated (see especially Lindberg and Scheingold, 1971). This found expression in the increasing resort to quantification and the use of mathematical notation, all trends in political science in general and US political science in particular. The point to make here is that the neofunctionalists were not simply trying to do a better job at explaining regional integration. They were also following rules and norms about how theoretical enquiry should be conducted; rules that were standard working practices well beyond the small community of neofunctionalists. 'Routine models of conduct' (Christiansen and Jørgensen, 1999: 6) are not just subjects to be studied. They are also part and parcel of the process of studying.

The rise of intergovernmental critiques from the mid-1960s (Chapter 4) was certainly – though perhaps not exclusively – connected to the dominant position established by realism within International Relations. In fact, both the early intergovernmentalism of Hoffmann (1966) and the later liberal intergovernmentalism of Moravcsik (1991; 1993a; 1998) are quite distinct from traditional state-centred accounts of international politics, not least because of their emphasis upon the domestic roots of national preferences and the operation of two-level games. The fact that intergovernmental theories of integration do not equate to realism/neorealism is given substance by the existence of a separate small body of distinctively neorealist scholarship on the EU (see Chapter 6). Hoffmann, often thought of in EU studies circles as the apologist for realism *par excellence*, is perhaps better categorized as a dissident realist, an impression confirmed by reading some of his autobiographical reflections (Hoffmann, 1989: 1993). Moravcsik sees himself working squarely within the liberal tradition (1993b) and more specifically within the neoliberal institutionalism most associated with Robert Keohane (1989). It is also worth noting that intergovernmentalist contributions to the debates about European integration have tended to appear following neofunctionalist or supranational institutionalist flourishes. It may be an obvious point, but theoretical accounts do not develop in isolation as hermetically sealed bodies of knowledge. Each theoretical 'self' has its theoretical 'other(s)' and for intergovernmentalist work on European integration, the other has most definitely been neofunctionalism. The initial reception of neofunctionalist work (see Chapter 4) suggested that its *theoretical* significance was not immediately apparent. Neofunctionalism was given substance as *the* primary theoretical account of integration by the efforts of neofunctionalist scholars, but its *visibility* and salience as 'integration theory' has had much to do with its intergovernmental critics. A recent scholar of the history of International Relations (Schmidt, 1998) makes a similar point in a broader context. The history of IR, it is argued, is reconstructed periodically to legitimize particular positions in contemporary debates. This means that central concepts and ideas, such as 'anarchy', need to be understood less as facts out there in the real world and more as the product of intradisciplinary conversations. This does not mean that intergovernmentalists and neofunctionalists have been engaging in inward-looking conceptual jousts without concern for the unfolding developments of the European Communities. What it does suggest, is that we need to be conscious about the way in which theoretical trajectories are influenced by the interaction between alternative perspectives.

Intergovernmentalist work on the EC/EU has also been sustained by developments beyond the study of integration. Some of the rationalistic state-centred work on the interplay between domestic politics and international bargains (for example, Milner, 1997, 1998) owes much to the development of International Political Economy, where scholars have tended to question the firmness of the boundary between the 'domestic' and the 'international' (Underhill, 1994). The emergence of IPE-style approaches to integration has clearly opened up the possibilities for comparative discussion and, in many ways, challenges the old realist–liberal dichotomy in international studies (Mattli, 1999). Yet, at the same time, it leaves open the 'rationalist–reflectivist' divide that has become such an issue (Keohane, 1988; Jørgensen, 1997a). Indeed, as Chapter 7 showed, the substantial turbulence in international theory in recent years has opened new avenues of thinking and forced significant re-evaluation of old cherished concepts.

The 'governance turn' in EU studies discussed in Chapter 5 draws on a wide array of theoretical developments in public policy analysis and comparative political science. In part, this has consisted of an insistence that traditional questions of politics can be applied to the EU *because* the EU is a polity (Hix, 1994). But it also reflects innovation and development in the policy sciences where there is renewed interest in the impact of institutions, the role of ideas and the place of symbols, norms and rules in political life (Richardson, 1996a). These approaches, which question exclusively interest-driven accounts of politics and policy change, connect well with movements in IR such as constructivism and open possibilities – as yet not fully explored – for the transcendence of the disciplinary divide between International Relations and Comparative Politics (Ebbinghaus, 1998; Jørgensen, 1997a; Risse-Kappen, 1996; Rosamond, 1999).

All of this suggests – obviously perhaps – that theories of integration need to be contextualized and that 'contextualization' means rather more than the idea that theories should be understood in relation to developments in the 'real world' of integration. They are only properly understood if we comprehend the broader social scientific concerns that gave rise to them and the social scientific environments in which they operate(d). In short, there are important 'sociology of knowledge' questions to consider when writing an intellectual history. It is not just the success of a theoretical enterprise in relation to the object of its studies that matters, but the ability of that enterprise to play the requisite academic 'games' successfully.

Evaluating integration theory

The few paragraphs above have suggested that there are complex issues involved in the evaluation of theories and that a proper appreciation of the significance and success of a theory needs to pay attention to the intellectual context in which it arises and operates. Theories can be evaluated in a number of ways. Pentland (1973: 19–20) argues that there are three sites of evaluation for any theory or, put another way, three avenues down which any theory may travel. One is the internal logic of theories. This relates to how well they develop their concepts, how rigorous they are in their quest to explain and how well they follow good practice in theory building. As we have seen in Chapters 3 and 4, neofunctionalists put a lot of effort into specifying and refining the concept of spillover in an effort to give scholars the capacity to measure that phenomenon and thereby activate the supposed explanatory power of their theory. The development of Andrew Moravcsik's work is also instructive in this regard. He has long maintained the primacy of intergovernmental bargains in European integration and the importance of domestic politics in the member states (Moravcsik, 1991), but his work has matured and become nuanced over time by thinking about the mechanics of national preference formation (Moravcsik, 1993a) and institutional choice (Moravcsik, 1998). It reflects a self-conscious attempt to follow a model of theoretical good practice. Too much work on integration, he argues, is *un*-theoretical and, therefore, flawed. It selects evidence to fit a pre-ordained conclusion, accepts at face value the *ex post* justifications of politicians and other involved actors and uses secondary sources that have drawn on similarly dubious methods to reach their conclusions:

> One can find abundant support for any plausible conjecture about the causes of European integration. Only by deriving competing hypotheses from general theories, multiplying observations, and paying attention to the quality of primary sources can we transcend such indeterminacy and bias.
>
> (Moravcsik, 1998: 11)

Moravcsik goes on to think about the limitations of neofunctionalism. He mentions its empirical deficiencies (see also below), but notes how the tortuous, yet necessary, re-evaluations of the late 1960s and 1970s stripped away so much of the theory's original power, that it ended up lacking the coherence to make predictions that could be tested. Neofunctionalists themselves acknowledged this (Haas, 1975a; 1976). But their 'failure' was not an isolated instance. Moravcsik suggests that the 'obsolescence' of neofunctionalism was symptomatic of a wider malaise afflicting most attempts to capture politics in terms of an overarching theory.

Such lessons are the staple of graduate classes in political science methods (King, Keohane and Verba, 1994) and they draw on Karl Popper's ideas about good theoretical practice (Popper, 1969; see also Hollis and Smith, 1991: 52–7). Popper's most famous argument is that theories should be constructed so as to render them capable of falsification. Empirical confirmation of a theory is not enough in itself – a point illustrated by the arguments made by Moravcsik about much EU studies work. One conclusion might be to suggest that what really matters is not how well the theory fits the reality (see also below), but the extent to which the scholarship is reflective about its own assumptions and how rigorously the process of theorizing is conducted.

The second point of evaluation is the theory's intellectual context. This enables the evaluator to explore the family history of the theory and to check its resemblance and its debts to its living relatives. In some cases, the observer of theories will be able to identify theoretical cousins with whom productive contact might be made. This sort of contextualization – the kind of exercise carried out briefly above – has various uses. Historians of political thought often follow the dictums of Quentin Skinner (1978) who is most associated with the position that ideas and concepts are inseparable from their historical and intellectual contexts. Theories, ideas and concepts do not necessarily have timeless, trans-historical qualities. Their authors were burdened with preoccupations of the time and made their arguments by deploying particular forms of intellectual rhetoric in the context of the historically rooted intellectual games in which they were engaged. So, to read Hobbes as a defender of arbitrary dictatorship or Machiavelli as an apologist for amoral *realpolitik* might make the mistake of importing our contemporary concerns into the analysis without appreciating the contexts in which Hobbes and Machiavelli operated (Cox, 1981). In a rather different vein, writers influenced by Michel Foucault have argued that we need to be more attentive to the relationship between knowledge and power and how, in particular, dominant intellectual discourses are related to prevailing structures of power (see Devetak, 1996). In terms of integration theory, the general lesson would be well learned.

The fact that, for the most part, the theories under discussion have all arisen in the second half of the twentieth century removes the need for painstaking historical reconstruction. But any attempt to evaluate a theory has to be attentive to the social scientific and intellectual concerns of the time as well as to the prevailing political discourses of the period. So, from the comfort of a millennial armchair, armed with the sophisticated theoretical technology of the new governance literature, it is not enough to say that functionalists, neofunctionalists or transactionalists were *wrong* or *naïve*. For example, we have to recognize that David Mitrany (Chapter 2) wrote in a particular way for an audience that was not as formally 'academic' (at least when he wrote *A Working Peace System*). True, his work was located within a broad intradisciplinary discussion, but he also wrote to intervene in practical policy debates at a time when thinking otherwise about structures of governance was widely practised. Andrew Moravcsik can be read as a careful adherent of widely accepted (if not always widely practised) theoretical norms. His is not a theoretical exercise in trying to change the world. His point is, as it were, to explain it. To say this is not to make a pejorative judgement, but to recognize that intellectual interventions are rule-bound and that intellectual work is a social exercise, influenced by dominant patterns of discourse and accepted modes of academic behaviour. At the same time, his state-centrism has the ring of familiarity about it. Politicians, especially members of national executives, view the integration process as an exercise in bargaining and diplomacy and these perceptions are reinforced through media coverage which is not inclined to explore the 'everyday' political economy of the EU (Richardson, 1996b; Wincott, 1995b). State-centric explanations have a 'common sense' feel to them, but that should not substitute for theoretical or empirical verification.

In other words, the search for knowledge, indeed the establishment of what counts as valid knowledge, is socially located and socially constructed. Interestingly, Haas has reflected on these questions with characteristic insight:

> Progress has occurred in international politics, but I also want to argue that progress has occurred *because* our conceptions of what constitute political problems, and of solutions to these problems have been increasingly informed by the form of reasoning we label 'scientific'.
>
> (Haas, 1991: 189)

This view recognizes the ultimate contingency and social-rootedness of human knowledge. But it does not take this observation to a relativistic conclusion (where judgements about anything become impossible). Rather, for Haas, the social construction of knowledge becomes the means through which progress is achieved. Not all would agree with the explicit celebration of 'science', the logic of which might be to exclude heterodox or critical thinking, but Haas's position connects with a view of knowledgeable progress associated with Thomas Kuhn (1970). Kuhn's argument was that science can be periodized into phases where particular paradigms dominate research. Paradigms define the guiding assumptions of research, what counts as valid knowledge and how work should proceed. Work at the margins or beyond these working assumptions is not regarded as scientific or (therefore) valid. Work progresses on the basis of these assumptions until the results produced challenge the paradigm to the point of unsustainability. There then follows a period of scientific revolution as a new paradigm displaces the old. There have been periodic attempts to apply the idea of paradigms to social science and even to integration theory. Michael O'Neill (1996) writes about the shifts from a supranational to an intergovernmental paradigm with a further shift towards a 'syncretic' paradigm as the insights of multiple perspectives become synthesized. But the real strength of Kuhn's account lies in his depiction of the way in which intellectual activity becomes institutionalized into sets of acceptable practices. In any case, neither 'integration theory' nor 'EU studies' are disciplines in the sense of physics or, for that matter, political science and International Relations. It should be patently clear by now that all theoretical work on integration or EU governance draws on external referents. If we are looking for paradigms, then they are likely to be embedded in those broader disciplinary environments (Hollis and Smith, 1991).

The third and final point of evaluation concerns the ability of a theory to connect to reality. At first sight this seems to be the most straightforward criterion for judging the merits of respective theoretical accounts. It is true that theories develop and sometimes collapse in accordance with how well their propositions match what goes on in 'the real world'. Neofunctionalism provides a very obvious example from the work discussed in these pages. By the late 1960s, neofunctionalists ran into a series of empirical difficulties. The first was the residual obstinacy of the nation-state, manifested most starkly by the increasing impression made upon EC affairs by President de Gaulle. At the same time, the logic of functional spillover and the teleological account of the development of integration were also much less discernible. Ultimately, neofunctionalists were presented with the more plausible alternatives: (a) that national and nationalistic forces matter, (b) that the pattern of activity exhibited within the Communities might owe more to traditional international relations than they had first allowed and (c) that the Community displayed a politics that organized itself around multiple *loci* and not just questions of 'integration'. The upshot was that state-centred International Relations, theories of international interdependence and perspectives derived from policy analysis all seemed to be better candidates to offer explanatory power. It is very important to recognize that this was a game that neofunctionalists were prepared to play (Haas, 1975; 1976) because the evaluative standards they set for themselves were largely ones of empirical correspondence. The partial revival of neofunctionalism in the context of the Single European Act and the acceleration in formal integration in the 1980s showed the process in reverse. As the empirical winter thawed, so neofunctionalism re-emerged (Mutimer, 1989; Tranholm-Mikkelsen, 1991).

But the 'truth as correspondence' issue is not as simple as it might seem. In *Modern Political Analysis* Robert Dahl remarks that '[w]hether [an empirical] proposition is true or false depends on the degree to which the proposition and the real world correspond' (cited in Neufeld, 1995: 34). This relies on the positivist supposition that the 'object' (the real world) can be separated from the 'subject' (the investigator). If accepted, this means that objective knowledge about the world is possible. This is not an issue to which those inclined towards positivistic and rationalistic investigation are indifferent. The comments of Moravcsik (cited above) indicate that there are ways through the minefield and that objectivism is possible provided that investigators follow certain rules. However, Mark Neufeld's study of International Relations takes the issue rather deeper into the realms of discourse analysis, hermeneutics and the philosophy of science:

> If the paradigm (language game/tradition/discourse) tells us not only how to interpret evidence, but also determines what will count as valid evidence in the first place, the tenet of 'truth as correspondence' to the facts can no longer be sustained.
>
> (Neufeld, 1995: 42)

The uncomfortable conclusion is that 'objective' facts are difficult to know because theories help to define the world that they describe. They have different answers to the question, 'Of what is this an instance?' and different criteria for selecting independent variables. Neufeld (1995) recommends theoretical reflexivity as the most useful way to encounter this problem. This involves being conscious about the status of our concepts and the rootedness of our theories. But it also requires reflection about our strategies and the politico-normative context of what scholarship entails. Social sciences and theories have different value bases. Robert Cox's famous dictum merits another citation:

> Theory is always for someone and for some purpose. All theories have a perspective. Perspectives derive from a position in time and space, specifically social and political time and space. The world is seen from a standpoint definable in terms of nation or social class, of dominance or subordination, of rising or declining power, or a sense of immobility or of present crisis, of past experience, and of hopes and expectations for the future. Of course sophisticated theory is never just the expression of a perspective. The more sophisticated a theory is, the more it reflects upon and transcends its own perspective; but the initial perspective is always contained within a theory and is relevant to its explication. There is, accordingly, no such thing as theory in itself, divorced from a standpoint in time and space. When any theory so represents itself, it is the more important to examine it as ideology, and to lay bare its concealed perspective.
>
> (Cox, 1981: 128)

Going back to integration theory, there is always the danger that theoretical work and the derivative empirical investigation follows the logic of particular values that are rooted in the object of enquiry. So intergovernmentalism might at times become the 'authorized version' of what national executive actors say and think that they are doing

(Chapter 6, also Rosamond, 1996). What's more, it can be an exercise in circular reasoning. As Christiansen and Jørgensen note: ' "Proving" that member states are in control of "intergovernmental bargaining" by starting with the input from member states is a tautology which ultimately obscures much of what is analytically relevant' (1999: 5).

Of course, we have also seen the close links between neofunctionalist theory and the strategies embedded in the Schuman Plan, the ECSC and the whole community method (Chapter 3). So, neofunctionalism could also be called an authorized version. Indeed, this accusation has been levelled by Milward and Sørensen (1993) who add spice to their quite venomous critique by making linkages between the largely American thrust of early integration theory and US foreign policy priorities of the time. For them, Haas and the other neofunctionalists were too eager to assemble grand theory at the expense of detailed attention to the historical record. Attentiveness to the minutiae of post-war reconstruction and the origins of the European Communities has been a long-standing preoccupation of Milward (see also Milward, 1984, 1992). Perhaps his major work on the period contains the most telling indictment of 'integration theorists' from this perspective. For Milward, the likes of Deutsch, Haas and Lindberg

> simplified history unacceptably ... they all did so in the same way, by greatly exaggerating the incapacity of the state. From the beginnings *of detailed historical research* into the origins of the European Community, it became clear that nation-states had played the dominant role in its formation and retained firm control of their new creation
>
> (Milward, 1992: 12)

A similar way of thinking informs another recent contributor to the archive-based history of European integration. Keith Middlemas (1995) is similarly dismissive of the partiality of theories of integration: 'I have tried not to confine myself to any one interpretation, whether federal, functional or intergovernmental, and to proceed empirically, *taking account of all the significant players*' (Middlemas, 1995: xiv, emphasis added). To argue from this position requires the establishment of an opposition between 'history' and 'theory', where the former is objective, empirical and inclusive and the latter is value-laden, conceptual and partial. Now both Milward and Middlemas are careful historians and are attentive to the quality of their sources and the contexts in which utterances are made. But, they rely heavily on the premise of 'truth as correspondence' to separate the subject and object. What count as valid facts? Who are 'all of the significance players'? To attend to these questions requires some kind of *a priori* judgement. Even historians are theoreticians – whether they know it or not.

Concluding comments

The general arguments of this book have been stated often enough, but a final rehearsal might be worthwhile. Firstly, the study of European integration, the transformation of European governance and the politics of the EU polity has been a very fertile site for theoretical development. This is partly because European integration is an intrinsically interesting process and partly because creative scholars have flocked to study it. Secondly, in many ways, the identification of sub-fields called 'integration theory' or 'EU studies' is less than helpful. Obviously scholars specialize, but to map disciplines too much in this way artificially cordons them off from the wider social scientific contexts within which they arise and develop. A full appreciation of theories of European integration, therefore, has to be attentive to 'sociology of knowledge' issues. This will deepen understanding of the contexts of integration theory and help us to understand debates between different schools in their own terms. It will also help to give us a sense of theoretical family trees. It is tempting to portray integration theory's main cleavage as a long-standing confrontation between intergovernmentalism and neofunctionalism. This has obvious merits, but could lead to an overly static picture both of the positions themselves and the nature of the debate between them. Understanding these positions as they evolve in a broader social scientific context helps us to avoid basic simplifications such as the equation of intergovernmentalism with (neo)realism and helps us to trace theoretical lineages (for example, the relationship between neofunctionalism and regime theory, or domestic politics approaches and neoliberal institutionalism). Thirdly, attention to these sociology of knowledge issues connects to deeper reflection on the processes of theorizing. The observation that theory is inescapable is not meant to drive all students of the EU into metatheoretical frenzy. Rather, solid empirical work should be rooted in an understanding of the investigator's assumptions and the theoretical suppositions upon which they draw. We can choose how far to take this requirement. It might be a matter of careful theory building to ensure that hypotheses are properly generated and that conclusions are not drawn from inherently biased reasoning. Alternatively, it might lead to a break with rationalistic assumptions, not only about ontology (the nature of the world that we are investigating), but also about epistemology (the process through which we acquire knowledge about that world). Fourthly, the question of whether EU studies is an 'International Relations' or a 'Comparative Politics' question is a non-problem, relying on a false dichotomy between these two disciplinary domains. Of course, scholars from different vantage points in the disciplinary universe will see the EU differently and conceptualize it in different ways. But they may also use similar methods to shed light on different things. For example, there is nothing to prevent constructivist analyses of the internal sociology of the European Commission, the processes of intergovernmental bargaining and the construction of the EU's identity as an international actor.

There is no doubt that 'integration theory' (if it can be called that any more) is in a good state of health. It was not always so, and the recent phase of theoretical reflexivity and innovation owes much to the spillover into EU studies of creative thinking across the political sciences. Grand theories of European integration have certainly had their day. In one sense they were never meant to exist! The neofunctionalists *always* intended to generate general theories of regional integration from the European case study and virtually all other 'theories' discussed here have slotted their analyses of the EU into broader theoretical contexts. Even the multi-level governance literature which, at face value, looks to be an attempt to depict a *sui generis* phenomenon does not fall into this trap. This is partly because MLG is more metaphor than theory, which allows alternative theoretical accounts to colonize it. Also, MLG analysis fits well with the increasing number of scholars depicting governance as fluid and authority as dispersed, in terms of both domestic politics and transnational relations. Therefore, theoretical endeavours on European integration are likely to develop most fully as sub-sets of other concerns. These include theories of regulation, epistemic communities, institutional choice, policy networks, path dependency, the role of ideas in policy-making, regionalism and regionalization, two-level games, transnational relations and constructivism – to name but a few. European integration may well be a totally unique enterprise without either historical precedent or contemporary parallel, but it is a ready source for comparative study in some of the most energizing and lively social science currently going on.

Theories of integration are also important because they grapple with one of the most remarkable experiments of the twentieth century. To contemplate the sources of apparently radical dislocations in patterns of governance in Europe and to seek to shed light upon the processes of institutional creativity and economic enmeshment that have been occurring is a vitally important enterprise – not just an academic game. Long may it continue. And long may it be theoretically astute.

Glossary of Theoretical Terms

Advocacy coalition framework

An approach from policy analysis that identifies (a) the significance of knowledge in the policy process and (b) the role of groups of like-minded activists united by common belief systems who seek to influence policy agendas.

Behaviouralism

A movement of great significance in post-war political science that sought to produce law-like generalizations about political life based upon sophisticated, often quantitative, research into individual and collective political behaviour. A major influence on both *neofunctionalism* and *transactionalism*.

Constructivism

Increasingly influential theoretical approach in contemporary International Relations. It begins from the premise that the world is social rather than material. Actors' interests and identities are not 'given'. Rather, they arise in situations of interaction and are thereby socially constructed. This means that stable patterns in international politics are the consequence of shared understandings among actors about their environment, their respective roles and so on.

Dependent variable

The phenomenon analysts are trying to explain. An issue of some confusion in EC/EU studies.

Domestic politics approach

A framework that retains the idea of states as central players in the integration process, but which – unlike *realist* International Relations – sees governmental preferences arising within processes of domestic politics. Governments remain the 'gatekeepers' between national politics and the EU system.

Epistemic communities

An approach to agenda setting, particularly in global politics, that places a premium on the role of expertise and knowledge more generally. Epistemic communities are transnational groups united by their shared beliefs and conceptions of scientific validity. They supply knowledge, usually about technical policy matters, and thereby help to frame the interests and preferences of policy actors (notably states).

Epistemology

The strategies through which a particular theory gathers knowledge and ensures that its reading of phenomena is superior to rival theories.

Federal functionalism

Another term for *neofunctionalism*.

Federalism

A theoretical project closely linked to the movement to create a 'United States of Europe'. Traditionally, federalists have been interested in the creation of constitutional settlements that define the relationships between several layers of authority (European, national and local). Some federalists took the view that this was a rational way to order human affairs (a) because different tasks could be accomplished best at different levels and (b) because a federal settlement would eradicate the rationale for war in Europe. More recently, federalist theory has become interested in (a) the processes through which federalist polities arise and (b) the extent to which the EU can be compared usefully to existing forms of federalism.

Functionalism

A theory proposing the radical transformation of international politics associated most notably with David Mitrany. Functionalists argue that the primary motivation of government should be the fulfilment of human needs. Unfortunately, the territorial nation-state is an irrational mechanism for this purpose, based as it is on the perpetuation of particular dogmas. The effective management of human need requires agencies geared specifically to individual tasks. The form that these agencies take will be dependent upon the function that they are required to perform. This means that functionalists espouse flexibility and are particularly reluctant to support large-scale schemes of regional integration.

Functional approach to institutions

A recent approach from International Relations that explores the reasons why states opt to create international institutions. It assumes that institutions arise because they fulfil certain collective interests among states such as the need to reduce transaction costs in international bargains.

Globalization

A term with many complex implications usually used to describe widespread and far-reaching social, economic and political change in the contemporary world. In particular, globalization describes the radical interpenetration of economies to the extent that states are no longer able to exercise meaningful authority over their territories.

Historical institutionalism

An approach that investigates the long-term implications of institutional choices made at a particular time. It assumes that actors are not perfectly knowledgeable about the consequences of their choices and suggests, therefore, that present behaviour is constrained by the locking into place of past choices.

Independent variables

Those factors that may provide explanations for phenomena under investigation.

Interdependence

A term used to describe the increasing array of interconnections in the international system, particularly between economies and societies. In International Relations, the idea has been used as the foundation for explaining the appearance of international institutions and regimes. These are often explained as the product of attempts by states to 'manage' interdependence.

Intergovernmentalism

An approach to integration that treats states, and national governments in particular, as the primary actors in the integration process. Various intergovernmentalist approaches have been developed in the literature and these claim to be able to explain both periods of radical change in the EU (because of converging governmental preferences) and periods of inertia (due to diverging national interests). Intergovernmentalism is distinguishable from *realism* and *neorealism* because of its recognition of both the significance of institutionalization in international politics and the impact of processes of domestic politics upon governmental preferences.

Liberal–idealist International Relations

A view of international relations that is firmly optimistic about the prospects for human progress and the end of war. Liberals are keen to emphasize that the states system so beloved of *realism* is neither inevitable nor desirable. The construction of international institutions and the spread of commerce and human interaction across borders form the basis for the transcendence of the *Westphalian* order.

Liberal intergovernmentalism

A variant of intergovernmentalism developed in the work of Andrew Moravcsik. Demands for integration arise within processes of domestic politics whereas integration outcomes are supplied as consequence of intergovernmental negotiations. Supranational institutions are of limited importance to processes of integration.

Marxism

Large-scale theory of political economy and social change that tends to focus on changing patterns of production and economic relations more generally as the basis for explaining political forms. However, Marxism is not susceptible to easy definition and in many accounts the state and ideas are granted more autonomy. Nonetheless, most Marxist work is rooted in a critique of the inequities of capitalism and seeks to reveal the prospects for significant ruptures with the existing order of things.

Multi-level governance

A metaphor used to depict the mature stage of the EU polity. Authority is dispersed rather than concentrated and political action occurs at and between various levels of governance. The idea also implies that the number of significant actors within the EU polity has multiplied and, therefore, that state-centric conceptions of integration carry only limited explanatory power.

Neofunctionalism

Important and influential theory of regional integration first formulated in the light of the early experiences of the European Communities. Neofunctionalists maintain that political integration and the growth of authority at the supranational level occur as a long-term consequence of modest economic integration. Integration in one sector creates pressures for integration in related sectors, and so on. This process is called functional spillover. The success of integration initiatives draws self-interested groups of actors into the game (political spillover) and both forms of spillover are promoted by purposeful supranational institutions. The theory suffered significant criticism throughout the 1960s but has proved to be resilient and influential.

Neoliberal institutionalism

A school in International Relations that seeks to account for the growth of institutionalization in world politics without losing sight of the centrality of states and the operation of rational self-seeking action.

Neorealism

Sophisticated restatement of *realism* that explains the perpetuation of the states system with reference to the structural properties of 'anarchy' rather than the inherent characteristics of states.

New institutionalism

A broad movement in contemporary political science that seeks to reinstate and refine the study of institutions as important variables in political life.

Normative

An approach to theory that seeks to validate certain claims and to use reasoning to support them.

Ontology

The view held by a theory about the nature of the world.

Pluralism

An approach to political science that emphasizes groups as the core matter of politics. Pluralists depict society as composed of various interests that coalesce into groups to pursue political goals. Policy outcomes reflect the state's processing of group demands. A major influence upon *neofunctionalism*.

Policy-network analysis

An approach to policy-making that looks for the existence of relatively stable and closed communities of actors that effectively control policy-making in particular sectors. This shifts emphasis away from the study of formal decision-making procedures.

Rational choice institutionalism

An approach to institutions concerned with how actors use such venues to pursue their interests. Institutions may constrain actors' abilities to realize these interests, but they also reduce the risks of interaction by lowering transaction costs.

Realism

Hugely important theory of international politics that emphasizes the centrality of states and the prevailing condition of anarchy. States are self-interested to the extent that they value survival above all else, thereby ensuring the primacy of security as the main issue in international politics. Realists are (a) pessimistic about the capacity of international institutions to change these basic premises and (b) adamant that international and domestic politics are very different types of political arena.

Regime theory

A close relation of *neoliberal institutionalism* that explores the growth of issue-specific rules, norms and procedures that seem to influence the expectations of actors in international politics They are normally seen as providing guiding frameworks for joint problem-solving in international politics.

Regionalism

The tendency of geographically-proximate territories or states to engage in economic integration and to form free trade areas and (possibly) common markets.

Security community

A group of states amongst whom the prospect of war is eradicated. A situation achieved via processes described by *transactionalism*.

Sociological institutionalism

An approach to institutions emphasizing their capacity to socialize actors and thereby influence interests and identities.

Sociology of knowledge

A phrase suggesting that intellectual activity is a social process like any other, characterized by norms and rules that are likely to be specific to particular periods, environments and places. A sociology of knowledge approach requires that the broader intellectual and academic contexts of theories are identified.

Structure–agency debate

A key theoretical debate in the social sciences, raising important questions about the nature of social change and the capacities for human action. It explores the issue of how agents (individual and collective human actors) and structures (the various facets of the human environment) are related. Agent-centred theories give scope to the capacity of action to transform structures, whereas structuralists see agents largely bound by the imperatives of their environment. Others, notably structurationists, have argued that while structures constrain agents, they are nevertheless the product of human creativity. This means that structures and agents simultaneously enable and constrain each other. The latter position is a major premise of *constructivism*.

Supranationalism

The development of authoritative institutions of governance and networks of policy-making activity above the nation-state.

Technocracy

Government by expertise rather than by ideological precept. The view that the tasks of government had become largely managerial and technical was a significant influence on both *functionalism* and early *neofunctionalism*.

Transactionalism

A theory of change in international politics associated largely with Karl Deutsch. Sometimes called 'pluralism' or the 'communications' approach, transactionalism explores the development of multiple linkages between societies as the basis for integration. Integration is defined as a condition where war as a means of dispute settlement between states becomes obsolete. See also *security communities*.

Two-level games

A popular approach suggesting (a) that governments are faced with strategic dilemmas in both domestic politics and international negotiations and (b) that government actions at one level feed into the other level. Governmental preferences in international negotiations are determined by processes of domestic political bargaining. At the same time, the policy outputs of international negotiations feed back into domestic politics. An influence on *liberal intergovernmentalism*.

Westphalian

The Treaty of Westphalia (1648) which ended the 'Thirty Years War' in Europe established the territorial nation-state as the dominant and preferred mode of political authority. In particular, the Treaty ensured that national monarchies were sovereign over their national territories and thus that the power of external bodies (notably the Church) over the internal affairs of kingdoms was seriously truncated. Therefore, a Westphalian view of the state describes a government with internal sovereignty over its own territory and an international system made up of these authoritative units and lacking serious authority above the nation-state.

References

Adler, E. (1997) 'Seizing the Middle Ground: Constructivism in World Politics', *European Journal of International Relations* 3 (3).

Adler, E. and Barnett, M. (1998a) 'Security Communities in Theoretical Perspective', in E. Adler and M. Barnett (eds), *Security Communities* (Cambridge: Cambridge University Press).

Adler, E. and Barnett, M. (1998b) 'A Framework for the Study of Security Communities', in E. Adler and M. Barnett (eds), *Security Communities* (Cambridge: Cambridge University Press).

Agnelli, G (1989) 'The Europe of 1992', *Foreign Affairs* 68.

Alford, R. A and Friedland, R (1985) *Powers of Theory: Capitalism, the State, and Democracy* (Cambridge: Cambridge University Press).

Allen, D and Smith, M. (1990) 'Western Europe's Presence in the Contemporary International Arena', *Review of International Studies* 16 (1).

Alter, K. A. (1996) 'The European Court's Political Power', *West European Politics* 19 (3).

Alter, K. A. and Meunier-Aitsahalia, S. (1994) 'Judicial Politics in the European Community: European Integration and the Path Breaking *Cassis de Dijon* Decision', *Comparative Political Studies* 24 (4).

Anderson, B. (1991) *Imagined Communities: Reflections on the Origins and Spread of Nationalism*, 2nd edn (London: Verso).

Anderson, J. J. (1995) 'The State of the (European) Union: From the Single Market to Maastricht, from Singular Events to General Theories', *World Politics* 47 (3).

Anderson, K. and Blackhurst, R. (eds) (1993) *Regional Integration and the Global Trading System* (New York, Harvester Wheatsheaf).

Angell, N. (1938) *The Great Illusion – Now* (Middlesex: Penguin Books).

Archer, M. (1988) *Culture and Agency: the Place of Culture in Social Theory* (Cambridge: Cambridge University Press).

Archibugi, D. and Held, D. (eds) (1995) *Cosmopolitan Democracy: An Agenda for a New World Order* (Cambridge: Polity Press).

Armingeon, K. (1997) 'The Capacity to Act: European National Governments and the European Commission', in A. Landau and R. Whitman (eds), *Rethinking the European Union: Institutions, Interests and Identities* (Basingstoke: Macmillan).

Armstrong, K. (1995) 'Regulating the Free Movement of Goods: Institutions and Institutional Change', in J. Shaw and G. More (eds), *New Legal Dynamics of European Union* (Oxford: Oxford University Press).

Armstrong, K. and Bulmer, S. (1998) *The Governance of the Single European Market* (Manchester: Manchester University Press).

Aspinwall, M. D and Schneider, G. (1998) 'Same Menu, Separate Tables: The Institutionalist Turn in Political Science and the Study of European Integration', paper to Joint Sessions of the European Consortium for Political Research, University of Warwick, March.

Axford, B. (1995) *The Global System: Economics, Politics and Culture* (Cambridge: Polity Press).

Axford, B., Browning, G., Huggins, R., Rosamond, B. and Turner, J. (1997) *Politics: An Introduction* (London: Routledge).

Balassa, B. (1962) *The Theory of Economic Integration* (London: Allen and Unwin).

Baldwin, D. A. (ed.) (1993) *Neorealism and Neoliberalism: The Contemporary Debate* (New York: Columbia University Press).

Banks, M. (1985) 'The Inter-Paradigm Debate', in M. Light and A. J. R. Groom (eds), *International Relations: A Handbook of Current Theory* (London: Pinter).

Barrera, M. and Haas, E. B. (1968) 'The Operationalization of Some Variables Related to Regional Integration: A Research Note', *International Organization* 23.

Bell, D. (1962) *The End of Ideology: On the Exhaustion of Political Ideas in the Fifties* (New York: Free Press).

Berger, P. and Luckmann, T. (1967) *The Social Construction of Reality* (Harmondsworth: Penguin).

Beveridge, W. (1942) *Social Insurance and Allied Services* (London: HMSO) Cmd 6404.

Bhaskar, R. (1979) *The Possibility of Naturalism* (Brighton: Harvester Wheatsheaf).

Booth, K. and Smith, S. (1995) *International Relations Theory Today* (Cambridge: Polity).

Bosco, A. (ed.) (1991) *The Federal Idea. The History of Federalism from Enlightenment to 1945. Vol I* (London: Lothian Foundation Press).

Boyer, R. and Drache, D. (eds) (1996) *States Against Markets* (London: Routledge).

Breckinridge, R. E. (1997) 'Reassessing Regimes: the International Regime Aspects of the European Union', *Journal of Common Market Studies* 35 (2).

Bressand, A. (1990) 'Beyond Interdependence: 1992 as a Global Challenge', *International Affairs* 66 (1).

Bressand, A. and Nicolaidis, K. (1990) 'Regional Integration in a Networked World Economy', in W. Wallace (ed.), *The Dynamics of European Integration* (London: Pinter/RIIA).

Brown, C (ed.) (1994) *Political Restructuring in Europe: Ethical Perspectives* (London: Routledge).

Brown, C. (1997) *Understanding International Relations* (Basingstoke: Macmillan).

Brugmans, H. (1948) *Fundamentals of European Federalism* (London: British Section of the European Union of Federalists).

Brugmans, H. (1969) *La Pensée Politique du Fédéralisme* (Sijthott-Leyde).

Bull, H. (1977) *The Anarchical Society: A Study of Order in World Politics* (New York: Columbia University Press).

Bulmer, S. J. (1983) 'Domestic Politics and European Community Policy-Making', *Journal of Common Market Studies* 21 (4).

Bulmer, S. J. (1994) 'The Governance of the European Union: A New Institutionalist Approach', *Journal of Public Policy* 13 (4).

Bulpitt, J. (1996) 'Federalism', in I. McLean (ed.), *The Oxford Concise Dictionary of Politics* (Oxford: Oxford University Press).

Burchill, S. (1996) 'Introduction' in S. Burchill and A. Linklater with R. Devetak, M. Paterson and J. True, *Theories of International Relations* (Basingstoke: Macmillan).

Burgess, M. (1986) 'Federalism and Federation in Western Europe', in M. Burgess (ed.), *Federalism and Federation in Western Europe* (London: Croom Helm).

Burgess, M. (1989) *Federalism and European Union: Political Ideas, Influences and Strategies in the European Community, 1972–1987* (London: Routledge).

Burgess, M. (1993) 'Federalism and Federation: A Reappraisal', in M. Burgess and A. G. Gagnon (eds), *Comparative Federalism and Federation* (Hemel Hempstead: Harvester Wheatsheaf).

Burley, A.-M. and Mattli, W. (1993) 'Europe Before the Court: A Political Theory of Legal Integration', *International Organization* 47 (1).

Buzan, B. (1995) 'The Level of Analysis Problem in International Relations Reconsidered.' in K. Booth and S. Smith (eds), *International Relations Theory Today* (Cambridge: Polity Press).

Buzan, B., Jones, C. and Little, R. (1993) *The Logic of Anarchy: Neorealism to Structural Realism* (New York: Columbia University Press).

Cable, V. and Henderson, D. (eds) *Trade Blocs? The Future of Regional Integration* (London: Royal Institute of International Affairs).

Cameron, D. (1992) 'The 1992 Initiative: Causes and Consequences', in A. Sbragia (ed.), *Euro-Politics* (Washington, DC: Brookings Institution).

Cameron, D. (1995) 'Transnational Relations and the European Economic and Monetary Union', in T. Risse-Kappen (ed.), *Bringing Transnational Relations Back In: Non-State Actors, Domestic Structures and International Institutions* (Cambridge: Cambridge University Press).

Camilleri, J. A. and Falk, J. (1992) *The End of Sovereignty: the Politics of a Shrinking and Fragmenting World* (Aldershot: Edward Elgar).

Campbell, J. L., Hollingsworth, J. R. and Lindberg, L. N. (eds) (1991) *Governance of the American Economy* (Cambridge: Cambridge University Press).

Camroux, D. and Lechervy, C. (1996) 'Encounter of a "Third Kind"? The Inaugural Asia–Europe Meeting of March 1996', *The Pacific Review* 9 (3).

Caporaso, J. A. (1996) 'The European Union and Forms of State: Westphalian, Regulatory or Post-Modern?', *Journal of Common Market Studies* 34 (1).

Caporaso, J. A. (1997) 'Does the European Union Represent an *n* of 1?', *ECSA Review* 10 (3).

Caporaso, J. A. (1998) 'Regional Integration Theory: Understanding Our Past and Anticipating Our Future', in W. Sandholtz and A. Stone Sweet (eds), *European Integration and Supranational Governance* (Oxford: Oxford University Press).

Caporaso, J. A. and Keeler, J. (1995) 'The European Union and Regional Integration Theory', in S. Mazey and C. Rhodes (eds), *The State of the European Union Volume 3: Building a European Polity?* (Boulder, CO: Lynne Rienner).

Cerny, P. G. (1990) *The Changing Architecture of Politics: Structure, Agency and the Future of the State* (London: Sage).

Cerny, P. G. (1995) 'Globalization and Changing Logic of Collective Action', *International Organization* 49 (4).

Cerny, P. G. (1996) 'International Finance and the Erosion of State Policy Capacity', in P. Gummett (ed.), *Globalization and Public Policy* (Cheltenham: Edward Elgar).

Checkel, J. T (1998) 'The Constructivist Turn in International Relations Theory', *World Politics* 50.

Christiansen, T. (1997a) 'Tensions of European Governance: Politicized Bureaucracy and Multiple Accountability in the European Union', *Journal of European Public Policy* 4 (1).

Christiansen, T. (1997b) 'Reconstructing European Space: From Territorial Politics to Multilevel Governance', in K.-E. Jørgensen (ed.), *Reflective Approaches to European Governance* (Basingstoke: Macmillan).

Christiansen, T. and Jørgensen, K.-E. (1999) 'The Amsterdam Process: A Structurationist Perspective on EU Treaty Reform', *European Integration On-Line Papers* 3 (1), http://eiop.or.at/eiop/texts/1999-001a.htm.

Chryssochoou, D. N. (1994) 'Democracy and Symbiosis in the European Union: Towards a Confederal Consociation', *West European Politics* 17 (4).

Chryssochoou, D. N., Tsinisizelis, M. J., Stavridis, S. and Ifantis, K. (1999) *Theory and Reform in the European Union* (Manchester: Manchester University Press).

Church, C. and Phinnemore, D. (1994) *European Union and European Community: A Handbook and Commentary on the Post-Maastricht Treaties* (New York: Harvester Wheatsheaf).

Claude, I. (1965) 'Review of E. B. Haas: *Beyond the Nation State*', *American Political Science Review* 59 (4).

Cocks, P. (1980) 'Towards a Marxist Theory of European Integration', *International Organization* 34 (1).

Coleman, W. D. and Underhill, G. R. D. (1998) 'Introduction: Domestic Politics, Regional Economic Co-operation, and Global Economic Integration', in W. D. Coleman and G. R. D. Underhill (eds), *Regionalism and Global Economic Integration: Europe, Asia and the Americas* (London: Routledge).

Cornett, L. and Caporaso, J. A. (1992) ' "And Still it Moves"! State Interests and Social Forces in the European Community', in J. N. Rosenau and E.-O. Czempiel (eds), *Governance without Government: Order and Change in World Politics* (Cambridge: Cambridge University Press).

Coudenhove-Kalergi, R. N. (1926) *Pan-Europe* (New York: Knopf).

Cowles, M. G (1995) 'Seizing the Agenda for the New Europe: the ERT and EC 1992', *Journal of Common Market Studies* 33 (4).

Council of the European Communities/Commission of the European Communities (1992) *Treaty on European Union* (Luxembourg: Office for Official Publications of the European Communities).

Cox, R. W. (1981) 'Social Forces, States and World Orders: Beyond International Relations Theory', *Millennium: Journal of International Studies* 10 (2).

Cox, W. S. and Sjolander, C. T. (1994) 'Critical Reflections on International Relations', in W. S. Cox and C. T. Sjolander (eds), *Beyond Positivism: Critical Reflections on International Relations* (Boulder, CO: Lynne Rienner).

Cram, L. (1996) 'Integration Theory and the Study of the European Policy Process', in J. Richardson (ed.), *European Union: Power and Policy-Making* (London: Routledge).

Cram, L. (1997) 'The European Commission and the "European Interest": Institutions, Interaction and Preference Formation in the EU Context', mimeo, University of Strathclyde.

Dannreuther, C. (1997) 'Explaining Small Business Policymaking – an Evolutionary Perspective for Political Science', Evolutionary Political Economy Association, Athens.

Dehousse, R. (1999) *The European Court of Justice* (Basingstoke: Macmillan).

Dent, C. (1997) *The European Economy: the Global Context* (London: Routledge).

Deutsch, K. W. (1963) *The Nerves of Government: Models of Political Communication and Control* (New York: Free Press of Glencoe).

Deutsch, K. W. (1964) 'Communication Theory and Political Integration', in P. E. Jacob and J. V. Toscano (eds), *The Integration of Political Communities* (Philadelphia: J. P. Lippencott and Co.).

Deutsch, K. W. (1966a) *Nationalism and Social Communication* 2nd edn (Cambridge, MA: MIT Press).

Deutsch, K. W. (1966b) 'Integration and Arms Control in the European Environment: A Summary Report', *American Political Science Review* 60 (2).

Deutsch, K. W (1968) *The Analysis of International Relations* (Englewood Cliffs, NJ: Prentice Hall).

Deutsch, K. W. (1989) 'A Path among the Social Sciences', in J. Kruzel and J. N. Rosenau (eds), *Journeys through World Politics: Autobiographical Reflections of Thirty-four Academic Travelers* (Lexington, MA: Lexington Books).

Deutsch, K. W., Burrell, S. A., Kann, R. A., Lee, M., Lichterman, M., Lindgren, R. E., Loewenheim F. L., and Van Wangeren, R. W. (1957) *Political Community and the North Atlantic Area: International Organization in the Light of Historical Experience* (Princeton, NJ: Princeton University Press).

Deutsch, K.W., Edinger, L. J., Macridis, R.C. and Merritt, R. L. (1967) *France, Germany, and the Western Alliance: A Study of Elite Attitudes on European Integration and World Politics* (New York: Charles Scribner's Sons).

Devetak, R. (1996) 'Critical Theory', in S. Burchill and A. Linklater with R. Devetak, M. Paterson and J. True, *Theories of International Relations* (Basingstoke: Macmillan).

Dinan, D. (1994) *Ever Closer Union? An Introduction to the European Community* (Basingstoke: Macmillan).

Duchêne, F. (1994) *Jean Monnet: The First Statesman of Interdependence* (New York: Norton).

Dunleavy, P. (1996) 'The Allocation of Governance Functions in the European Union: Explaining the "Drift to Brussels"', mimeo, London School of Economics and Political Science.

Dunleavy, P. and O'Leary, B. (1987) *Theories of the State: The Politics of Liberal Democracy* (Basingstoke: Macmillan).

Duvall, R., Wendt, A. and Muppidi, H. (1996) 'Institutions and Collective Representations in International Theory: the Global Capital Regime and the Constitution of Capitalist State Identities', Minnesota–Stanford–Wisconsin Consortium Workshop on Globalization and Global Governance, March.

Easton, D. (1965) *A Systems Analysis of Political Life* (New York: John Wiley and Sons).

Ebbinghaus, B. (1998) 'Europe Through the Looking Glass: Comparative and Multi-Level Perspectives', *Acta Sociologica* 41 (4).

Edwards, G. (1996) 'National Sovereignty vs Integration? The Council of Ministers', in J. Richardson (ed.), *The European Union: Power and Policy-Making* (London: Routledge).

El-Agraa, A. M. (1997) 'The Theory of Economic Integration' in A. M El-Agraa (ed.), *Economic Integration Worldwide* (New York: St Martin's Press).

El-Agraa, A. M. and Jones, A. J. (1981) *Theory of Customs Unions* (Oxford: Philip Allan).

Etzioni, A. (1965) *Political Unification: a Comparative Study of Leaders and Forces* (New York: Holt, Rinehart and Winston).

Eulau, H. (1963) *The Behavioral Persuasion in Politics* (New York: Random House).

Evans, P. R., Ruesschmeyer, D. and Skocpol, T. (eds) (1985) *Bringing the State Back In* (Cambridge: Cambridge University Press).

Fawcett, L. (1995) 'Regionalism in Historical Perspective', in L. Fawcett and A. Hurrrell (eds), *Regionalism and World Politics* (Oxford: Oxford University Press).

Fawcett, L. and Hurrell, A. (eds) (1995) *Regionalism and World Politics* (Oxford: Oxford University Press).

Fioretos, K.-O. (1997) 'The Anatomy of Autonomy: Interdependence, Domestic Balances of Power and European Integration', *Review of International Studies* 23 (3).

Forsyth, M. (1981) *Unions of States: The Theory and Practice of Confederation* (Leicester: Leicester University Press).

Forsyth, M. (1994) 'Federalism and Confederalism', in C. Brown (ed.), *Political Restructuring in Europe: Ethical Perspectives* (London: Routledge).

Forsyth, M. (1996) 'The Political Theory of Federalism: the Relevance of Classical Approaches', in J. J. Hesse and V. Wright (eds), *Federalizing Europe? The Costs, Benefits, and Preconditions of Federal Political Systems* (Oxford: Oxford University Press).

Friedrich, C. J. (1968) *Trends in Federalism in Theory and Practice* (New York: Praeger).

Friedrich, C. J. and Bowie, R. (eds) (1954) *Studies in Federalism* (Boston: Little, Brown and Co.).

Gallie, W. B. (1956) 'Essentially Contested Concepts', *Proceedings of the Aristotelian Society* 56.

Gamble, A. and Payne, A. (eds) (1996) *Regionalism and World Order* (Basingstoke: Macmillan).

Garrett, G. (1992) 'International Cooperation and Institutional Choice: the European Communities Internal Market', *International Organization* 46 (2).

Garrett, G. and Tsebelis, G. (1996) 'An Institutionalist Critique of Intergovernmentalism', *International Organization* 50 (2).

George, S. (1996a) *Politics and Policy in the European Union*, 3rd edn (Oxford: Oxford University Press).

George, S. (1996b) 'The European Union: Approaches from International Relations', in H. Kassim and A. Menon (eds), *The European Union and National Industrial Policy* (London: Routledge).

Giddens, A. (1984) *The Constitution of Society* (Cambridge: Polity Press).

Gill, S. and Law, D. (1988) *The Global Political Economy: Perspectives, Problems and Policies* (New York: Harvester Wheatsheaf).

Gourevitch, P. (1978) 'The Second Image Reversed: the International Sources of Domestic Politics', *International Organization* 32 (4).

Grant, W. (1997) *The Common Agricultural Policy* (Basingstoke: Macmillan).

Green, A. (1969) 'Mitrany Re-read with the Help of Haas and Sewell', *Journal of Common Market Studies* 9.

Grieco, J. M. (1995) 'The Maastricht Treaty, Economic and Monetary Union and the Neo-Realist Research Programme', *Review of International Studies* 21 (1).

Grieco, J. M. (1996) 'State Interests and International Rule Trajectories: A Neorealist Interpretation of the Maastricht Treaty and European Economic and Monetary Union', *Security Studies* 5 (2) .

Griffiths, M. (1992) *Realism, Idealism and International Politics – a Reinterpretation* (London: Routledge).

Groom, A. J. R. and Taylor, P. (eds) (1975) *Functionalism: Theory and Practice in International Relations* (London: University of London Press).

Groom, A. J. R. and Taylor, P. (eds) (1994) *Frameworks for International Cooperation* (London: Pinter).

Haas, E. B. (1958) *The Uniting of Europe. Political, Social and Economic Forces, 1950–1957* (Stanford: Stanford University Press).

Haas, E. B. (1961) 'International Integration: The European and the Universal Process', *International Organization* 15.

Haas, E. B. (1964) *Beyond the Nation State: Functionalism and International Organization* (Stanford: Stanford University Press).

Haas, E. B. (1967) 'The "Uniting of Europe" and the "uniting of Latin America"', *Journal of Common Market Studies* 5.

Haas, E. B. (1968) *The Uniting of Europe: Political, Social and Economic Forces 1950–1957* 2nd edn., containing author preface (Stanford CA: Stanford University Press).

Haas, E. B. (1970) *The Web of Interdependence: the United States and International Organizations* (Englewood Cliffs, NJ: Prentice Hall).

Haas, E. B. (1971) 'The Study of Regional Integration: Reflections on the Joy and Anguish of Pretheorizing', in L. N. Lindberg and S. A. Scheingold (eds), *European Integration: Theory and Research* (Cambridge, MA: Harvard University Press).

Haas, E. B. (1975a) *The Obsolescence of. Regional Integration Theory* (Berkeley: Institute of International Studies working paper)

Haas, E. B. (1975b) 'On Systems and International Regimes', *World Politics* 27 (2).

Haas, E. B (1975c) 'Is there a Hole in the Whole? Knowledge, Technology, Interdependence and the Construction of International Regimes', *International Organization* 29 (3).

Haas, E. B (1976) 'Turbulent Fields and the Study of Regional Integration', *International Organization* 30 (2).

Haas, E. B. (1980) 'Why Collaborate? Issue Linkage and International Regimes', *World Politics* 32 (3).

Haas, E. B. (1990) *When Knowledge is Power: Three Models of Change in International Organizations* (Berkeley, CA: University of California Press).

Haas, E. B. (1991) 'Reason and Change in International Life: Justifying a Hypothesis', in R. L. Rothstein (ed.), *The Evolution of Theory in International Relations* (Columbia, SC: University of South Carolina Press).

Haas, E. B. and Schmitter, P. C. (1964) 'Economics and Differential Patterns of Political Integration: Projections About Unity in Latin America', *International Organization* 18 (4).

Haas, P. M. (1992) 'Introduction: Epistemic Communities and International Policy Co-ordination', *International Organization* 46 (1).

Hall, P. (1986) *Governing the Economy: The Politics of State Intervention in Britain and France* (Cambridge: Polity Press).

Hall, P. and Taylor, R. C. R. (1996) 'Political Science and the Three New Institutionalisms', *Political Studies* 44 (5).

Halliday, F. (1994) *Rethinking International Relations* (Basingstoke: Macmillan).

Hansen, R. D. (1969) 'European Integration: Reflections on a Decade of Theoretical Efforts', *World Politics* 21 (2).

Harrison, R. J. (1974) *Europe in Question. Theories of Regional International Integration* (London: George Allen and Unwin).

Harrison, R. J. (1975) 'Testing Functionalism', in A. J. R. Groom and P. Taylor (eds), *Functionalism: Theory and Practice in International Relations* (London: University of London Press).

Harrison, R. J. (1994) 'Neo-functionalism' in A. J. R. Groom and P. Taylor (eds), *Frameworks for International Co-Operation* (London: Pinter).

Hay, C. (1995) 'Structure and Agency', in D. Marsh and G. Stoker (eds), *Theory and Methods in Political Science* (Basingstoke: Macmillan) .

Hay, C. and Wincott, D. (1998) 'Structure, Agency and Historical Institutionalism', *Political Studies* 46 (5).

Hayes-Renshaw, F. and Wallace, H. (1996) *The Council of Ministers* (Basingstoke: Macmillan).

Heater, D. (1992) *The Idea of European Unity* (Leicester: Leicester University Press).

Heathcote, N. (1975) 'Neofunctional Theories of Regional Integration', in A. J. R. Groom and P. Taylor (eds), *Functionalism: Theory and Practice in International Relations* (London: University of London Press).

Held, D., McGrew, A., Goldblatt, D. and Perraton, J. (1999) *Global Transformations: Politics, Economics and Culture* (Cambridge: Polity Press).

Héraud, G. (1968) *Les Principes du Fédéralisme et la Fédération Européene* (Paris: Presses d'Europe).

Higgott, R. (1997) '*De Facto* and *De Jure* Regionalism: The Double Discourse of Regionalism in the Asia Pacific', *Global Society* 11 (2).

Hill, C. (1994) 'The capability–expectations gap, or conceptualizing Europe's international role', in S. Bulmer and A. Scott (eds), *Economic and Political Integration in Europe: Internal Dynamics and Global Context* (Oxford: Blackwell).

Hirst, P. and Thompson, G. (1996) *Globalization in Question* (Cambridge: Polity Press).

Hix, S. (1994) 'The Study of the European Community: The Challenge to Comparative Politics', *West European Politics* 17 (1).

Hix, S. (1996) 'CP, IR and the EU! A Rejoinder to Hurrell and Menon', *West European Politics* 19 (4).

Hix, S. (1988) 'The Study of the European Union II: the "New Governance" Agenda and its Rival', *Journal of European Public Policy* 5 (1).

Hix, S. (1999) *The Political System of the European Union* (Basingstoke: Macmillan).

Hodges, M. (1972) 'Introduction' in M. Hodges (ed.), *European Integration* (Harmondsworth: Penguin).

Hoffmann, S. (1961) 'International Systems and International Law', in K. Knorr and S. Verba (eds), *The International System* (Princeton, NJ: Princeton University Press).

Hoffmann, S. (1964) 'The European Process at Atlantic Crosspurposes', *Journal of Common Market Studies* 3.

Hoffmann, S. (1966) 'Obstinate or Obsolete? The Fate of the Nation State and the Case of Western Europe' *Daedalus* 95.

Hoffmann, S. (1989) 'A Retrospective', in J. Kruzel and J. N. Rosenau (eds), *Journeys through World Politics: Autobiographical Reflections of Thirty-four Academic Travelers* (Lexington, MA: Lexington Books).

Hoffmann, S. (1995) *The European Sisyphus: Essays on Europe, 1964–1994* (Boulder, CO: Westview).

Holland, M. (1996a) 'Jean Monnet and the Federal Functionalist Approach to European Union', in P. Murray and P. Rich (eds), *Visions of European Unity* (Boulder, CO: Westview).

Holland, M. (1996b) 'European Foreign Policy Transition in Theory and Practice', *International Relations* 13 (3).

Holland, S. (1980) *UnCommon Market: Capital, Class and Power in the European Community* (London: Macmillan).

Hollis, M. and Smith, S. (1991) *Explaining and Understanding International Relations* (Oxford: Clarendon Press).

Holm, U. (1997) 'The French Garden is No Longer What It Used to Be', in K.-E. Jørgensen (ed.), *Reflective Approaches to European Governance* (Basingstoke: Macmillan).

Howe, G. (1990) 'Sovereignty and Interdependence: Britain's Place in the World', *International Affairs* 66 (4).

Hurrell, A. (1995) 'Explaining the Resurgence of Regionalism in World Politics', *Review of International Studies* 21 (4).

Hurrell, A. and Menon, A. (1996) 'Politics Like Any Other? Comparative Politics, International Relations and the Study of the EU', *West European Politics* 19 (2).

Ikenberry, G. J. (1988) 'Conclusion: An Institutional Approach to American Foreign Economic Policy', in G. J. Ikenberry, D. A. Lake and M. Mastanduno (eds), *The State and American Foreign Economic Policy* (Ithaca, NY: Cornell University Press).

Imber, M. (1984) 'Rereading Mitrany: a Pragmatic Assessment of Sovereignty', *Review of International Studies* 10 (2).

Inglehart, R. (1967) 'An End to European Integration?', *American Political Science Review* 61 (1).

Jachtenfuchs, M. (1995) 'Theoretical Approaches to European Governance', *European Law Journal* 1 (2).

Jachtenfuchs, M. (1997) 'Conceptualizing European Governance', in K.-E. Jørgensen (ed.), *Reflective Approaches to European Governance* (Basingstoke: Macmillan).

Jørgensen, K.-E. (1992) 'EC External Relations as a Theoretical Challenge: Theories, Concepts and Trends', Pan-European Conference in International Relations, Heidelberg, 16–20 September.

Jørgensen, K.-E. (ed.) (1997a) *Reflective Approaches to European Governance* (Basingstoke: Macmillan).

Jørgensen, K.-E. (1997b) 'Introduction: Approaching European Governance', in K.-E. Jørgensen (ed.), *Reflective Approaches to European Governance* (Basingstoke: Macmillan).

Jørgensen, K.-E. (1997c) 'PoCo: The Diplomatic Republic of Europe', in K.-E. Jørgensen (ed.), *Reflective Approaches to European Governance* (Basingstoke: Macmillan).

Kaiser, K. (1967) 'The US and the EEC in the Atlantic System: the Problem of Theory', *Journal of Common Market Studies 5*.

Kassim, H. (1994) 'Policy Networks and European Union Policy-Making: A Sceptical View', *West European Politics* 17 (4).

Kassim, H. and Menon, A. (1996) 'The European Union and State Autonomy', in H. Kassim and A. Menon (eds), *The European Union and National Industrial Policy* (London: Routledge).

Katzenstein, P. J. (1985) *Small States in World Markets: Industrial Policy in Europe* (Ithaca, NY: Cornell University Press).

Kavanagh, D. (1983) *Political Science and Political Behaviour* (London: George Allen and Unwin).

Kegley, C. W. (1995) *Controversies in International Relations Theory: Realism and the Neoliberal Challenge* (New York: St Martin's Press).

Keohane, R. O (1984) *After Hegemony: Cooperation and Discord in the World Political Economy* (Princeton, NJ: Princeton University Press).

Keohane, R. O. (ed.) (1986) *Neorealism and its Critics* (New York: Columbia University Press).

Keohane, R. O. (1988) 'International Institutions: Two Approaches', *International Studies Quarterly* 32 (4).

Keohane, R. O. (1989) 'Neoliberal Institutionalism: A Perspective on World Politics', in R. O. Keohane, *International Institutions and State Power: Essays in International Relations Theory* (Boulder, CO: Westview).

Keohane, R. O. (1993) 'The Analysis of International Regimes: Towards a European–American Research Program', in V. Rittberger (ed.), *Regime Theory and International Relations* (Oxford: Clarendon Press).

Keohane, R. O. and Hoffmann, S. (1991) 'Institutional Change in Europe in the 1980s', in R. O. Keohane and S. Hoffmann (eds), *The New European Community: Decisionmaking and Institutional Change* (Boulder, CO: Westview).

Keohane, R. O. and Nye, J. S. (eds) (1971) 'Transnational Relations and World Politics', *International Organization* 25 (3) (special issue).

Keohane, R. O. and Nye, J. S. (1975) 'International Interdependence and Integration', in F. Greenstein and N. Polsby (eds), *Handbook of Political Science, Volume 8* (Reading, MA: Addison-Wesley).

Keohane, R. O. and Nye, J. S. (1977) *Power and Interdependence: World Politics in Transition* (Boston, MA: Little, Brown and Co.).

Keynes, J. M. (1936) *The General Theory of Employment, Interest and Money* (London: Macmillan).

King, G., Keohane, R. O and Verba, S. (1994) *Designing Social Enquiry: Scientific Inference in Qualitative Research* (Princeton, NJ: Princeton University Press).

King, P. (1982) *Federalism and Federation* (London: Croom Helm).

Kitzinger, U. W. (1962) 'The State of the Literature in 1960', *Journal of Common Market Studies* 1.

Klausen, J. and Tilly, L. A. (1997) 'European Integration in Social and Historical Perspective', in J. Klausen and L. A. Tilly (eds), *European Integration in Social and Historical Perspective: 1850 to the Present* (Lanham, ML: Rowman and Littlefield).

Knutsen, T. L. (1997) *A History of International Relations Theory*, 2nd edn (Manchester: Manchester University Press).

Kofman, E. and Youngs, G. (eds) (1996) *Globalization: Theory and Practice* (London: Pinter).

Kohler, M. (1995) *Regional Frontiers and Transnational Economic Relations* (Washington, DC: Council on Foreign Relations).

Kooiman, J. (ed.) (1993) *Modern Governance: New Government–Society Interactions* (London: Sage).

Krasner, S. D. (1983) 'Structural Causes and Regime Consequences: Regimes as Intervening Variables', in S. D. Krasner (ed.), *International Regimes* (Ithaca, NY: Cornell University Press).

Kratochwil, F. (ed.) (1995) *International Organization: A Reader* (Boulder, CO: Westview).

Kuhn, T. (1970) *The Structure of Scientific Revolutions* 2nd edn. (Chicago: University of Chicago Press).

Kurzer, P. (1997) 'Decline or Preservation of Executive Capacity? Political and Economic Integration Revisited', *Journal of Common Market Studies* 35 (1).

Larsen, H. (1997) 'British Discourses on Europe: Sovereignty of Parliament, Instrumentality and the Non-Mythical Europe', in K.-E. Jørgensen (ed.), *Reflective Approaches to European Governance* (Basingstoke: Macmillan).

Lasswell, H. D. (1950) *Politics: Who Gets What, When, How* (New York: Peter Smith).

Lehmbruch, G. and Schmitter, P. C. (eds) (1982) *Patterns of Corporatist Policy-Making* (London: Sage).

Levy, M. A., Young, I. R., and Zürn, M. (1995) 'The Study of International Regimes', *European Journal of International Relations* 1 (3).

Lijphart, A. (1977) *Democracy in Plural Societies: A Comparative Exploration* (New Haven, CT: Yale University Press).

Lijphart, A. (1981) 'Karl W. Deutsch and the New Paradigm in International Relations', in R. W. Merritt and B. M. Russett (eds), *From National Development to Global Community: Essays in Honour of Karl Deutsch* (London: George Allen and Unwin).

Lijphart, A. (1991) 'Consociational Democracy', in V. Bogdanor (ed.), *The Blackwell Encyclopedia of Political Science* (Oxford: Blackwell).

Lindberg, L. N. (1963) *The Political Dynamics of European Economic Integration* (Stanford: Stanford University Press).

Lindberg, L. N. (1965) 'Decision Making and Integration in the European Community', *International Organization* 19 (1).

Lindberg, L. N. (1966) 'Integration as a Source of Stress on the European Community System', *International Organization* 20 (2).

Lindberg, L. N. (1967) 'The European Community as a Political System: Notes toward the Construction of a Model', *Journal of Common Market Studies* 5 (4).

Lindberg, L. N. (ed.) (1975) *Stress and Contradiction in Modern Capitalism: Public Policy and the Theory of the State* (Lexington, MA: D.C. Heath).

Lindberg, L. N. (1994) 'Comment on Moravcsik', in S. Bulmer and A. Scott (eds), *Economic and Political Integration in Europe: Internal Dynamics and Global Context* (Oxford: Blackwell).

Lindberg, L. N. and Scheingold S. A. (1970) *Europe's Would-Be Polity: Patterns of Change in the European Community* (Englewood Cliffs, NJ: Prentice Hall).

Lindberg, L. N. and Scheingold, S. A.(eds), (1971) *Regional Integration; Theory and Research* (Cambridge, MA: Harvard University Press).

Lipset, S. M. (1960) *Political Man* (New York: Doubleday).

Lodge, J. (1978) 'Loyalty and the EEC: the Limits of the Functionalist Approach', *Political Studies* 26.

Lodge, J. (1984) 'European Union and the First Elected European Parliament: the "Spinelli Initiative"', *Journal of Common Market Studies* 22 (4).

Long, D. and Wilson, P. (eds) (1995) *Thinkers of the Twenty Years' Crisis: Inter-War Idealism Reassessed* (Oxford: Clarendon Press).

Lord, C. (1998) *Democracy in the European Union* (Sheffield: Sheffield Academic Press)

Luard, E. (ed.) (1992) *Basic Texts in International Relations* (Basingstoke: Macmillan).

MacKay, R. W. G. (1940) *Federal Europe: Being the Case for European Federation Together With a Draft Constitution of the United States of Europe* (London: Michael Joseph).

Majone, G. (1991) 'Cross-National Sources of Regulatory Policy-Making in Europe and the United States', *Journal of Public Policy* 11 (1).

Majone, G. (1993) 'The European Community between Social Policy and Social Regulation', *Journal of Common Market Studies* 31 (2).

Majone, G. (1994) 'The Rise of the Regulatory State in Europe', *West European Politics* 17 (3).

Majone, G. (1996) 'A European Regulatory State?', in J. Richardson (ed.), *European Union: Power and Policy-Making* (London: Routledge).

Mandel, E. (1967) 'International Capitalism and "Supra-Nationality"', in R. Miliband and J. Saville (eds), *The Socialist Register 1967* (London: Merlin).

Mandel, E. (1970) *Europe versus America? Contradictions of Imperialism* (London: New Left Books).

Mansfield, E. D. and Milner, H. V. (eds) (1997) *The Political Economy of Regionalism* (New York: Columbia University Press).

March, J. G. and Olsen, J. P. (1984) 'The New Institutionalism: Organizational Factors in Political Life', *American Political Science Review* 78.

Marks, G. (1997) 'Does the European Union Represent an *n* of 1?', *ECSA Review* 10 (3).

Marks, G., Hooghe, L. and Blank, K. (1996) 'European Integration from the 1980s: State-Centric v. Multi-Level Governance', *Journal of Common Market Studies* 34/3.

Marks, G., Nielsen, F., Ray, L. and Salk, J. (1996) 'Competencies, Cracks and Conflicts: Regional Mobilization in the European Union', in G. Marks *et al. Governance in the European Union* (London: Sage).

Marks, G., Scharpf, F., Schmitter, P. C. and Streeck, W. (1996) *Governance in the European Union* (London: Sage).

Matláry, J. H. (1997) 'Epilogue: New Bottles for Old Wine?', in K.- E. Jørgensen (ed.), *Reflective Approaches to European Governance* (Basingstoke: Macmillan).

Mattli, W. (1999) *The Logic of Regional Integration: Europe and Beyond* (Cambridge: Cambridge University Press).

Mearsheimer, J. J. (1990) 'Back to the Future: Instability in Europe after the Cold War', *International Security* 15 (1).

Merritt, R. L. and Russett, B. M. (1981), 'Karl W. Deutsch and the Scientific Analysis of World Politics', in R. W. Merritt and B. M. Russett (eds), *From National Development to Global Community: Essays in Honour of Karl Deutsch* (London: George Allen and Unwin).

Middlemas, K. (1995) *Orchestrating Europe: the Informal Politics of the European Union, 1973–1995* (London: Fontana Press).

Miller, D. (1994) 'The Nation-State: a Modest Defence', in C. Brown (ed.), *Political Restructuring in Europe: Ethical Perspectives* (London: Routledge).

Milner, H. V. (1993) 'International Regimes and World Politics: Comments on the Articles by Smouts, de Senarchens and Jönsson', *International Social Science Journal* 45 (4).

Milner, H. V. (1997) *Interests, Institutions and Information: Domestic Politics and International Relations* (Princeton, NJ: Princeton University Press).

Milner, H. V. (1998) 'Regional Economic Co-operation, Global Markets and Domestic Politics. A comparison of NAFTA and the Maastricht Treaty', in W. D. Coleman and G. R. D. Underhill (eds), *Regionalism and Global Economic Integration: Europe, Asia and the Americas* (London: Routledge).

Milward, A. S. (1984) *The Reconstruction of Western Europe, 1945–51* (London: Methuen).

Milward, A. S. (1992) *The European Rescue of the Nation State* (London: Routledge).

Milward, A. S. and Sørenson, V. (1993) 'Integration or Interdependence: A National Choice', in A. Milward *et al. The Frontiers of National Sovereignty: History and Theory* (London: Routledge).

Milward, A. S., Lynch, F. M. B., Romero, F., Ranieri, R. and Sørensen, V. (1993) *The Frontiers of National Sovereignty. History and Theory 1945–1992* (London: Routledge).

Mitrany, D. (1933) *The Progress of International Government* (London: George Allen and Unwin).

Mitrany, D. (1948) 'The Functional Approach to World Organisation', *International Affairs* 24 (3).

Mitrany, D. (1965) 'The Prospect of Integration: Federal or Functional?', *Journal of Common Market Studies* 4.

Mitrany, D. (1966) *A Working Peace System* (Chicago: Quadrangle Books) (first published 1943).

Mitrany, D. (1971) 'The Functional Approach in Historical Perspective', *International Affairs* 47 (3).

Mitrany, D. (1975a) *The Functional Theory of Politics* (Introduction by Paul Taylor) (London: Martin Robertson).

Mitrany, D. (1975b) 'The Making of the Functional Theory: A Memoir', in D. Mitrany, *The Functional Theory of Politics* (Introduction by Paul Taylor) (London: Martin Robertson).

Mitrany, D. (1975c) 'The Prospect of Integration: Federal or Functional', in A. J. R. Groom and P. Taylor (eds), *Functionalism: Theory and Practice in International Relations* (London: University of London Press).

Moravcsik, A. (1991) 'Negotiating the Single European Act', in R. O. Keohane and S. Hoffmann (eds), *The New European Community: Decisionmaking and Institutional Change* (Boulder, CO: Westview Press).

Moravcsik, A. (1993a) 'Preferences and Power in the European Community: A Liberal Intergovernmentalist Approach', *Journal of Common Market Studies* 31 (4).

Moravcsik, A. (1993b) 'Liberalism and International Relations Theory', Harvard University Center for International Affairs (Paper No. 92–6).

Moravcsik, A. (1994) 'Why the European Community Strengthens the State: Domestic Politics and International Cooperation', Harvard University Center for European Studies (Paper No. 52).

Moravcsik, A. (1995) 'Liberal Intergovernmentalism and Integration: A Rejoinder' *Journal of Common Market Studies* 33 (4).

Moravcsik, A. (1998*) The Choice for Europe: Social Purpose and State Power from Messina to Maastricht* (London: UCL Press).

Morgenthau, H. J. (1985) *Politics Among Nations: The Struggle for Power and Peace* 6th edn. (New York: Knopf).

Murray, A. (1997) *Reconstructing Realism: Between Power Politics and Cosmopolitan Ethics* (Edinburgh: Edinburgh University Press).

Mutimer, D. (1989) '1992 and the Political Integration of Europe: Neofunctionalism Reconsidered ' *Journal of European Integration* 13 (4).

Navari, C. (1995) 'David Mitrany and International Functionalism', in D. Long and P. Wilson (eds), *Thinkers of the Twenty Years' Crisis: Inter-War Idealism Reassessed* (Oxford: Clarendon Press).

Neufeld, M. (1995) *The Restructuring of International Relations Theory* (Cambridge: Cambridge University Press).

Niedermeyer, O. and Sinnott, R. (eds) (1995) *Public Opinion and Internationalized Governance* (Oxford: Oxford University Press).

North, D. (1990) *Institutions, Institutional Change and Economic Performance* (Cambridge: Cambridge University Press).

Nye, J. S. (1965) 'Patterns and Catalysts in Regional Integration', *International Organization* 19 (4).

Nye, J. S. (1968) 'Comparative Regional Integration: Concept and Measurement', *International Organization* 22 (4).

Nye, J. S. (1971a) *Peace in Parts: Integration and Conflict in International Organization* (Boston, MA: Little, Brown and Co.)

Nye, J. S. (1971b) 'Comparing Common Markets: A revised Neo-Functionalist Model', in L. N. Lindberg and S. A. Scheingold (eds), *Regional Integration: Theory and Research* (Cambridge, MA: Harvard University Press).

O'Donnell, G., Schmitter, P. C. and Whitehead, L. (eds) (1980) *Transitions from Authoritarian Rule: Comparative Perspectives* (Baltimore, ML: Johns Hopkins University Press) .

Øhrgaard, J. C. (1997) 'Less than Supranational, More than Intergovernmental': European Political Cooperation and the Dynamics of Intergovernmental Integration', *Millennium: Journal of International Studies* 26 (1).

O'Neill, M. (1996) *The Politics of European Integration: A Reader* (London: Routledge).

Pentland, C. (1973) *International Theory and European Integration* (London: Faber and Faber).

Pentland, C. (1975) 'Functionalism and Theories of International Political Integration', in Groom, A. J. R. and Taylor, P. (eds), *Functionalism: Theory and Practice in International Relations* (London: University of London Press).

Pentland, C. (1981) 'Political Theories of European Integration: Between Science and Ideology', in D. Lasok and P. Soldatos (eds), *The European Communities in Action* (Brussels: Bruylant).

Peterson, J. (1995a) 'Decision-Making in the European Union: Towards a Framework for Analysis', *Journal of European Public Policy* 2 (1).

Peterson, J. (1995b) 'Policy Networks and European Union Policy Making: A Reply to Kassim', *West European Politics* 18 (2).

Peterson, J. and Bomberg, E. (1999) *Decision-Making in the European Union* (Basingstoke: Macmillan).

Pierson, P. (1996) 'The Path to European Integration: A Historical Institutionalist Analysis', *Comparative Political Studies* 29 (2).

Pinder, J. (1968) 'Positive Integration and Negative Integration: Some Problems of Economic Union in the EEC', *The World Today* 24 (3).

Pinder, J. (1986) 'European Community and the Nation-State: A Case for Neo-Federalism?', *International Affairs* 62 (1).

Pinder, J. (1991) *European Community: The Building of a Union* (Oxford: Oxford University Press).

Pollack, M. A. (1994) 'Creeping Competence: the Expanding Agenda of the European Community', *Journal of Public Policy* 14 (2).

Pollack, M. A. (1996) 'The New Institutionalism and EC Governance: the Promise and Limits of Institutional Analysis', *Governance* 9 (4).

Pollack, M. A. (1997a) 'Delegation, Agency, and Agenda Setting in the European Community', *International Organization* 51 (1).

Pollack, M. A. (1997b) 'Does the European Union Represent an *n* of 1?', *ECSA Review* 10 (3).

Popper, K. (1969) *Conjectures and Refutations: The Growth of Scientific Knowledge*, 3rd edn (London: Routledge and Kegan Paul).

Puchala, D. J. (1972) 'Of Blind Men, Elephants and International Integration', *Journal of Common Market Studies* 10.

Puchala, D. J. (1981) 'Integration Theory and the Study of International Relations', in R. W. Merritt and B. M. Russett (eds), *From National Development to Global Community: Essays in Honour of Karl Deutsch* (London: George Allen and Unwin).

Putnam, R. D. (1988) 'Diplomacy and Domestic Politics', *International Organization* 42.

Radaelli, C. (1999) *Technocracy in the European Union* (London: Longman).

Richardson, J. (1996a) 'Actor-based Models of National and EU Policy Making', in H. Kassim and A. Menon (eds), *The European Union and National Industrial Policy* (London: Routledge).

Richardson, J. (1996b) 'Policy-making in the EU: Interests, Ideas and Garbage Cans of Primeval Soup', in J. Richardson (ed.), *European Union: Power and Policy-Making* (London: Routledge).

Richardson, J. and Jordan, G. (1979) *Governing Under Pressure: the Policy Process in a Post-Parliamentary Democracy* (Oxford: Martin Robertson).

Riker, W. (1964) *Federalism* (Boston, MA: Little, Brown and Co.).

Riker, W. H. (1996) 'European Federalism: the Lessons of Past Experience', in J. J. Hesse and V. Wright (eds), *Federalizing Europe? The Costs, Benefits, and Preconditions of Federal Political Systems* (Oxford: Oxford University Press).

Risse-Kappen, T. (1996) 'Explaining the Nature of the Beast: International Relations and Comparative Policy Analysis Meet the EU', *Journal of Common Market Studies* 34 (1).

Robson, P. (1998) *The Economics of International Integration* (London: Routledge).

Rosamond, B. (1993) 'National Labour Organizations and European Integration: British Trade Unions and "1992"', *Political Studies* 41 (3).

Rosamond, B. (1995) 'Mapping the European Condition: the Theory of Integration and the Integration of Theory', *European Journal of International Relations* 1 (3).

Rosamond, B. (1996) 'Understanding European Unity: the Limits of Nation-State-Centric Integration Theory', *European Legacy: Towards New Paradigms* 1 (1).

Rosamond, B. (1998), 'The Integration of Labour? British Trade Union Attitudes to European Integration', in D. Baker and D. Seawright (eds), *Britain For and Against Europe* (Oxford: Clarendon Press).

Rosamond, B. (1999) 'Globalization and the Social Construction of European Identities', *Journal of European Public Policy* 6 (4).

Rosenau, J. N. (1989) 'Toward a Postinternational Politics for the 1990s', in E.- O. Czempiel and J. N. Rosenau (eds), *Global Changes and Theoretical Challenges: Approaches to World Politics in the 1990s* (Massachusetts: Lexington Books).

Rosenau, J. N. (1990) *Turbulence in World Politics: A Theory of Change and Continuity* (Princeton, NJ: Princeton University Press).

Rosenau, J. N. and Czempiel, E.-O. (eds) (1992) *Governance without Government: Order and Change in World Politics* (Cambridge: Cambridge University Press).

Rosenau, J. N. and Durfee, M. (1995) *Thinking Theory Thoroughly: Coherent Approaches in an Incoherent World* (Boulder, CO: Westview).

Rosenberg, J. (1990) 'What's the Matter with Realism?', *Review of International Studies* 16 (4).

Ross, G. (1995) *Jacques Delors and European Integration* (Cambridge: Polity Press).

Ruggie, J. G. (1975) 'International Responses to Technology: Concepts and Trends, *International Organization* 29.

Ruggie, J. G. (1993) 'Territoriality and Beyond: Problematizing Modernity in International Relations', *International Organization* 47 (1).

Ruggie, J. G. (1998) *Constructing the World Polity: Essays on International Institutionalization* (London: Routledge).

Sabatier, P. (1988) 'An Advocacy Coalition Model of Policy-Making and Change and the Role of Policy-Oriented Learning Therein', *Policy Sciences* 1.

Sanders, D. (1995) 'Behavioural Analysis', in D. Marsh and G. Stoker (eds), *Theory and Methods in Political Science* (Basingstoke: Macmillan).

Sandholtz, W. (1996) 'Membership Matters: Limits of the Functional Approach to European Institutions', *Journal of Common Market Studies* 34 (3).

Sandholtz, W. and Stone Sweet, A. (1998) *European Integration and Supranational Governance* (Oxford: Oxford University Press).

Sandholtz, W. and Zysman, J. (1989) '1992: Recasting the European Bargain', *World Politics* 27 (4).

Sartori, G. (1970) 'Concept Misinformation in Comparative Politics', *American Political Science Review* 64 (4).

Sayer, A. (1992) *Method in Social Science: A Realist Approach*, 2nd edn (London: Routledge).

Sbragia, A. (1992) 'Thinking about the European Future: the Uses of Comparison', in A. Sbragia (ed.), *Euro-Politics* (Washington DC: Brookings Institution).

Scharpf, F. (1988) 'The Joint Decision Trap: Lessons from German Federalism and European Integration', *Public Administration* 66.

Schmidt, B. C. (1998) *The Political Discourse of Anarchy: a Disciplinary History of International Relations* (Albany, NY: SUNY Press).

Schmitter, P. C. (1969a) 'Three Neo-Functional Hypotheses about European Integration', *International Organization* 23 (1).

Schmitter, P. C. (1969b) 'Further Notes on Operationalizing Some Variables Related to Regional Integration', *International Organization* 23 (2).

Schmitter, P. C. (1971) 'A Revised Theory of European Integration', in L. N. Lindberg and S. A. Scheingold (eds), *Regional Integration: Theory and Research* (Cambridge, MA: Harvard University Press).

Schmitter, P. C. (1996a) 'Examining the Present Euro-Polity with the Help of Past Theories', in G. Marks, F. W. Scharpf, P. C. Schmitter and W. Streek, *Governance in the European Union* (London: Sage).

Schmitter, P. C. (1996b) 'Imagining the Future of the Euro-Polity with the Help of New Concepts', in G. Marks, F. W. Scharpf, P. C. Schmitter and W. Streek, *Governance in the European Union* (London: Sage).

Schmitter, P. C. and Lehmbruch, G. (eds) (1979) *Trends Toward Corporatist Intermediation* (London: Sage).

Scholte, J.-A. (1996) 'Globalisation and Social Change', in B. Axford and G. K. Browning (eds) *Modernity–Postmodernity: From the Personal to the Global* (Oxford: Thamesman).

Scruton, R. (1983) *A Dictionary of Political Thought* (London: Pan).

Sewell, J. P. (1966) *Functionalism and World Politics* (London: Oxford University Press).

Sjostedt, G. (1977) *The External Role of the European Community* (Farnborough: Saxon House).

Skinner, Q. (1978) *The Foundations of Modern Political Thought* (Cambridge: Cambridge University Press).

Skocpol, T. (1979) *States and Social Revolutions* (Cambridge: Cambridge University Press).

Smith, D. L. and Ray, J. L. (1993) 'The 1992 Project', in D. L. Smith and J. L. Ray (eds), *The 1992 Project and the Future of Integration in Europe* (New York M. E. Sharpe).

Smith, M. (1996) 'The European Union as an International Actor' in J. Richardson (ed.), *European Union: Power and Policy-Making* (London: Routledge).

Smith, S., Booth, K. and Zalewski, M. (eds) (1996) *International Theory: Positivism and Beyond* (Cambridge: Cambridge University Press).

Spinelli, A. (1972) 'The Growth of the European Movement since the Second World War', in M. Hodges (ed.), *European Integration* (Harmondsworth: Penguin).

Steinmo, S., Thelen, K. and Longstreth, F. (eds) (1992) *Structuring Politics: Historical Institutionalism in Comparative Analysis* (Cambridge: Cambridge University Press).

Stoker, G. (1995) 'Introduction' in D. Marsh and G. Stoker (eds), *Theory and Method in Political Science* (Basingstoke: Macmillan).

Stone, A. (1994) 'What is a Supranational Constitution? An Essay in International Relations Theory', *Review of Politics* 56 (3).

Stone Sweet, A. and Sandholtz W. (1997) 'European Integration and Suprantional Governance', *Journal of European Public Policy* 4 (3).

Strange, S. (1983) '*Cave Hic Dragones!* A Critique of Regime Theory, in S. D. Krasner (ed.), *International Regimes* (Ithaca, NY: Cornell University Press).

Strange, S. (1994) *States and Markets*, 2nd edn (London: Pinter).

Strange, S. (1996) *The Retreat of the State* (Cambridge: Cambridge University Press).

Stubb, A. C. J. (1996) 'A Categorization of Differentiated Integration', *Journal of Common Market Studies* 36 (1).

Suhr, M. (1997) 'Robert O. Keohane: A Contemporary Classic', in I. B. Neumann and O. Wæver (eds), *The Future of International Relations: Masters in the Making* (London: Routledge).

Taylor, P. (1968) 'The Functionalist Approach to the Problem of International Order: a Defence', *Political Studies* 16 (3).

Taylor, P. (1975) 'Introduction', in D. Mitrany, *The Functional Theory of Politics* (London: Martin Robertson).

Taylor, P. (1982) 'The European Communities as an Actor in International Society', *Journal of European Integration* 6 (1).

Taylor, P. (1991) 'The European Community and the State – Assumptions, Theories and Propositions', *Review of International Studies* 17 (2).

Taylor, P. (1993) *International Organization in the Modern World: The Regional and the Global Process* (London: Pinter).

Taylor, P. (1994a) 'Functionalism: the Approach of David Mitrany', in A. J. R. Groom and P. Taylor (eds), *Frameworks for International Co-operation* (London: Pinter).

Taylor, P. (1994b) 'Consociationalism and Federalism as Approaches to International Integration', in A. J. R. Groom and P. Taylor (eds), *Frameworks for International Co-operation* (London: Pinter).

Taylor, P. and Groom, A. J. R. (1975) 'Functionalism and International Relations', in A. J. R. Groom, and P. Taylor (eds), *Functionalism: Theory and Practice in International Relations* (London: University of London Press).

Thatcher, M. (1993) *The Downing Street Years* (London: HarperCollins).

Thelen, K. and Steinmo, S. (1992) 'Historical Institutionalism in Comparative Politics', in S. Steinmo, K. Thelen and F. Longstreth (eds), *Structuring Politics: Historical Institutionalism in Comparative Analysis* (Cambridge: Cambridge University Press).

Thompson, K. W. (1980) *Masters of International Thought* (Baton Rouge, LA: Louisiana State University Press).

Tranholm-Mikkelsen, J. (1991) 'Neofunctionalism: Obstinate or Obsolete?', *Millennium: Journal of International Studies* 20 (1).

Tsebelis, G. (1990) *Nested Games: Rational Choice in Comparative Politics* (Berkeley, CA: University of California Press).

Tsoukalis, L. (1997) *The New European Economy Revisited* (Oxford: Oxford University Press).

Underhill, G. R. D. (1994) 'Introduction: Conceptualizing the Changing Global Order', in R. Stubbs and G. R. D. Underhill (eds), *Political Economy and the Changing Global Order* (Basingstoke: Macmillan).

Verdun, A. (1999) 'The Role of the Delors Committee in the Creation of EMU: An Epistemic Community?', *Journal of European Public Policy* 6 (2).

Wæver, O. (1998) 'Insecurity, Security and Asecurity in the West European Non-War Community', in E. Adler and M. Barnett (eds), *Security Communities* (Cambridge: Cambridge University Press).

Wallace, H. (1983) 'Negotiation, Conflict and Compromise: The Elusive Pursuit of Common Policies', in H. Wallace, W. Wallace and C. Webb (eds), *Policy-Making in the European Community*, 2nd edn (Chichester: John Wiley and Sons).

Wallace, H. (1996a) 'Politics and Policy in the European Union: the Challenge of Governance', in H. Wallace and W. Wallace (eds), *Policy-Making in the European Union* (Oxford: Oxford University Press) .

Wallace, H. (1996b) 'The Institutions of the EU: Experience and Experiments' in H. Wallace and W. Wallace (eds), *Policy-Making in the European Union* (Oxford: Oxford University Press).

Wallace, W. (1983) 'Less than a Federation, More than a Regime: the Community as a Political System', in H. Wallace, W. Wallace and C. Webb (eds), *Policy-Making in the European Community* (Chichester: John Wiley and Sons).

Wallace, W. (1990) 'Introduction: The Dynamics of European Integration', in W. Wallace (ed.), *The Dynamics of European Integration* (London: Pinter/RIIA).

Wallace, W. (1994) *Regional Integration: The West European Experience* (Washington, DC: Brookings Institution).

Waltz, K. (1979) *Theory of International Politics* (New York: McGraw Hill).

Warleigh, A. (1998) 'Better the Devil You Know? Synthetic and Confederal Understandings of European Unification', *West European Politics* 21 (3).

Weale, A. and Williams, A. (1992) 'Between Economy and Ecology? The Single Market and the Integration of Environmental Policy', *Environmental Politics* 1 (4).

Weare K. C. (1963) *Federal Government* (Oxford: Oxford University Press).

Webb, C. (1983) 'Theoretical Prospects and Problems', in H. Wallace, W. Wallace, and C. Webb (eds), *Policy-Making in the European Community*, 2nd edn (Chichester: John Wiley and Sons).

Weigall, D. and Stirk, P. (eds) (1992) *The Origins and Development of the European Communty* (Leicester: Leicester University Press).

Wendt, A. (1987) 'The Agent Structure Problem in International Theory', *International Organization* 43 (3).

Wendt, A. (1992) 'Anarchy is What States Make of it: the Social Construction of Power Politics', *International Organization* 46 (2).

Wendt, A. (1994) 'Collective Identity Formation and the International State', *American Political Science Review* 88 (2).

Wendt, A. (1995) 'Constructing International Politics', *International Security* 20 (1).

Wessels, W. (1997) 'An Ever Closer Fusion A Dynamic Macropolitical View on Integration Processes', *Journal of Common Market Studies* 35 (2).

Wheare, K. C. (1963) *Federal Government*, 4th edn (London: Oxford University Press/Royal Institute of International Affairs).

Whitman, R. G. (1997) 'The International Identity of the EU: Instruments as Identity', in A. Landau and R. Whitman (eds), *Rethinking the European Union: Institutions, Interests, Identities* (Basingstoke: Macmillan).

Wight, M. (1966) 'The Balance of Power', in H. Butterfield and M. Wight (eds), *Diplomatic Investigations* (London: Allen and Unwin).

Willetts, P. (1994) 'Transactions, Networks and Systems', in A. J. R. Groom and P. Taylor (eds), *Frameworks for International Co-operation* (London: Pinter) .

Wincott, D. (1995a) 'Political Theory, Law and European Integration', in J. Shaw and G. More (eds), *New Legal Dynamics of European Union* (Oxford: Oxford University Press).

Wincott, D. (1995b) 'Institutional Interaction and European Integration: Towards an Everyday Critique of Liberal Intergovernmentalism', *Journal of Common Market Studies* 33 (4).

Wincott, D. (1996) 'The Court of Justice and the European Policy Process', in J. Richardson (ed.), *European Union: Power and Policy* (London: Routledge).

Wind, M. (1997) 'Rediscovering Institutions: A Reflectivist Critique of Rational Institutionalism', in K. E. Jørgensen (ed.), *Reflective Approaches to European Governance* (Basingstoke: Macmillan).

Wolf, D. and Zangl, B. (1996) 'The European Economic and Monetary Union: "Two-level Games" and the Formation of International Institutions', *European Journal of International Relations* 2 (3).

Wolf, P. (1973) 'International Organization and Attitude Change: a Re-examination of the Functionalist Approach', *International Organization* 27.

Woods, N. (1996) 'The Uses of Theory in the Study of International Relations', in N. Woods (ed.), *Explaining International Relations Since 1945* (Oxford: Oxford University Press).

Woolf, L. (1917) *The Framework of a Lasting Peace* (London: Allen and Unwin).

Woolf, L. (1933) *The Intelligent Man's Way to Prevent War* (London: Gollancz).

Wright, V. (1989) *The Government and Politics of France*, 3rd edn (London: Unwin Hyman).

Wright, V. (1996) 'The National Co-ordination of European Policy-Making: Negotiating the Quagmire' in J. Richardson (ed.) *European Union: Power and Policy-Making* (London: Routledge).

Younger, K. (1959) 'Review of E. B. Haas *The Uniting of Europe*', *International Affairs* 35 (1).

Zacher, M. W. (1991) 'Toward a Theory of International Regimes', in R. L. Rothstein (ed.), *The Evolution of Theory in International Relations: Essays in Honor of William T. R. Fox* (Columbia, SC: University of South Carolina Press).

Index

226

MARISKA

9-14

48-49

73

96-97

128-129

156

185

196-197

198-205